# The Nathan Axelrod Collection

VOLUME 1

# The Nathan Axelrod Collection

VOLUME 1

Moledet Productions · 1927-1934
Carmel Newsreels, Series I · 1935-1948

**Edited by**
Amy Kronish · Edith Falk · Paula Weiman-Kelman

The Center for Preservation of Israeli and Jewish Film
of the Israel Film Archive / Jerusalem Cinematheque
*Lia van Leer, Director*

FLICKS
BOOKS

Rutherford · Madison · Teaneck
Fairleigh Dickinson University Press

**British Library Cataloguing-in-Publication Data**
Nathan Axelrod Collection. - Vol. 1:
Moledet Productions, 1927-34, Carmel
Newsreels, Series 1, 1935-48
1. Kronish, Amy
791.43092
ISBN 0-948911-22-0

**Library of Congress Cataloging-in-Publication Data**
The Nathan Axelrod collection / edited by Amy Kronish, Edith Falk, and
  Paula Weiman-Kelman.
        p.      cm.
  "The Centre for Preservation of Israeli and Jewish Film of the Israel Film
Archive/Jerusalem Cinematheque."
  Contents: Pt. 1. Moledet Productions. 1927-1934, and Carmel newsreels,
series I, 1935-1948.
  Includes index.
  ISBN 0-8386-3575-X (v. 1: alk. paper)
  1. Jews---Palestine---History---20th century---Film catalogs.
2. Palestine---History---1917-1948---Film catalogs.  3. Zionism---
History---Film catalogs.  4. Israel---History---Film catalogs.
5. Newsreels---Catalogs.  6. Centre for Preservation of Israeli and Jewish
Film (Jerusalem)---Catalogs.  I. Axelrod, Nathan, 1905-1987. II. Kronish,
Amy.  III. Falk, Edith.  IV. Weiman-Kelman, Paula.
V. Centre for Preservation of Israeli and Jewish Film (Jerusalem)
VI. Sinematek Yerushalayim.
  DS126.N37  1994
  016.95694'04---dc20                                                93-37190
                                                                         CIP

First published in 1994 by
FLICKS BOOKS
29 Bradford Road
Trowbridge
Wiltshire BA14 9AN   England

Associated University Presses
440 Forsgate Drive
Cranbury
NJ 08512   USA

*in cooperation with* The Center for Preservation of Israeli and Jewish Film
Israel Film Archive / Jerusalem Cinematheque
POB 8561, Jerusalem, Israel 91083
*tel* +972 2 724131 · *fax* +972 2 733076 · *tlx* 26358 CANJR IL

© Israel Film Archive 1993

All rights reserved. No part of this publication may be reproduced, stored in a retrieval system or transmitted in any form or by any means: electronic, electrostatic, magnetic tape, mechanical, photocopying, recording or otherwise, without prior permission in writing from the publishers.

Printed and bound in Great Britain.

# Contents

| | |
|---|---|
| Preface | vii |
| Foreword | viii |
| Introduction | ix |
| How to Use the Catalogue | xii |
| | |
| Moledet Productions · 1927-1934 | 1 |
| Carmel Newsreels, Series I · 1935-1948 | 27 |
| Sample Listings from Additional Carmel Productions | 215 |
| | |
| Subject and Personality Index | 223 |

Dedicated to the memory of Nathan Axelrod ז"ל
*1905-1987*


The Israel Film Archive / Center for Preservation of
Israeli and Jewish Film, the Israel State Archives and
the Axelrod family are particularly grateful to the
**Reginald Ford Foundation** and Madame Germaine Ford
de Maria for their generous support in the
preservation of the Axelrod Collection.

# *Preface*

I remember the first time that I went to meet Nathan Axelrod in the 1960s and I saw his fantastic film collection, mostly nitrate, a time bomb, in the basement of his house. It was clear to me then that this precious collection was deteriorating and required urgent attention.

Many of us who recognised the urgency of the situation actively sought the necessary funds to preserve these treasures. Eventually the collection was purchased by the Israel State Archives with the cooperation of the Ministry of Education for preservation purposes. However, the preservation of the nitrate films in the collection was not begun until 1985, with a major donation from Germaine Ford de Maria, in memory of her husband Reginald Ford, the founder of Cinéac cinemas in France.

The preservation work was completed by the staff of the Center for Preservation of Israeli Film in cooperation and with the assistance of the Service des Archives de Film du Centre National de la Cinématographie, Bois d'Arcy in France.

I wish to thank Germaine Ford de Maria, Dr André Chouraqui, Emmanuel Chouraqui, Dr Moshe Mossek, Ilan de Vries and all the members of the Preservation Center, for their vision, dedication and efforts made on behalf of the preservation of this collection.

And now, after all the years and all the effort, we have the Axelrod collection on safety film, securely in our vaults. And we are very proud to present this first volume of our computerised cataloguing. The collection is saved and is easily accessible to all who are interested. Much appreciation and grateful thanks - especially to the staff of the Israel Film Archive - and to those too numerous to name who have contributed to this wonderful achievement.

**Lia van Leer**

# Foreword

It takes some time to absorb the full flavour of Nathan Axelrod's Palestine. His newsreels from the late 1920s and the 1930s take us back to another time with another tempo. His villages and cities have a different atmosphere; the people look different.

The strongest impression is of the rhythm of life: all Tel Aviv came out when Meir Dizengoff's wife, Ysina, died in 1930. We see the streets taken by masses of mourners - office-holders, scouts, workers, youth movements, the police. Obviously Tel Aviv was then a society much more organic than ours today; everybody knew everybody. The rhythm was slow, time seemed less important than now, the car was absent and everybody walked to important events.

Then there are the leaders of that period. The more we know about them from history books, the deeper the impression on seeing these men on the screen. There is Chaim Weizmann, not the old man we know from the early 1950s, but much younger, sharp, elegant and dignified, his bearing reminiscent of Ronald Storrs' description: "An almost feminine charm combined with a feline deadliness of attack...". Or Nahum Sokolow at a function of the Hebrew University, urbane and amiable, the practised speaker with rounded gestures. And Menachem Ussishkin, the Rock, he is the unsmiling one, his gestures are angular, almost angry, speaking at a commemoration, where Arthur Ruppin and Shaul Tchernichovsky are also participating.

Axelrod's Palestine has its peculiarities but perhaps they belong to the spirit of his time. For instance, there are almost no Arabs in his country. Like many people of his generation (and ours too) he seemed totally absorbed in his Zionist dream. As a former *halutz*, Axelrod had an obvious weakness for *kibbutzim* and settlements in general. However, Tel Aviv was the centre of his country and his work. Jerusalem, strangely enough, is hardly mentioned - the city as such seemed to have no attraction for him.

Nathan Axelrod's newsreels offer us a wonderful and nostalgic trip to our collective past. It is our good fortune that the Israel Film Archive has obtained and preserved this unique material.

**Evyatar Friesel**
Israel State Archivist
December 1993

# Introduction

"The Axelrod film collection is without doubt whatsoever the most comprehensive and important filmic record of the growth of the Jewish National Home in Palestine to be found anywhere in the world and it is of course the collection of a Jewish newsreel filmmaker who lived through all the events depicted in his films... It is difficult to think of a single aspect of the growth of the Jewish National Home over these years of any real importance that is not represented one way or another in this superb collection."
        Taylor Downing, researcher for Thames Television's *Palestine*

\*

Nathan Axelrod, a Russian Jew with a background in film, emigrated to Palestine in 1926. The embryonic Jewish state in which he found himself had no real film industry. Realising the significance of events surrounding him, Axelrod improvised equipment and began filming, eventually editing the material into weekly newsreels. He operated on a shoestring, creating a laboratory/studio in two wooden shacks and mixing his own chemicals. This studio, nicknamed "Eat Your Heart Out, Hollywood!", first served the Moledet company and later became known as Carmel Film.

Axelrod's newsreels differ significantly from those of visiting cameramen working for international newsreel companies. Depicting a world that he loved and was a part of, Axelrod focussed on the establishment of new settlements, draining swamps, irrigating new land, the development of Tel Aviv and the cultural life of the embryonic Jewish state. Every significant aspect of the growth of the Yishuv and the establishment of the State of Israel is represented in his work.

The vast amount of material filmed by Axelrod constitutes a comprehensive documentary archive. In addition, he was the pioneer of dramatic Hebrew language films. In 1931 he scripted and photographed the first locally produced fiction film *Biyemei / Once Upon a Time*, a comedy based on the Purim carnival held each year in Tel Aviv. Feature films continued to be the passion of his career.

The rights to the Axelrod Collection have been acquired by the Israel State Archives which, together with the Reginald Ford Foundation and the Jerusalem Foundation, has signed an agreement for mutual cooperation with the Israel Film Archive in the establishment of a film preservation centre. This centre is responsible for the physical preservation, cataloguing and sale of footage of the films in this collection.

The Axelrod Collection consists of approximately 200 hours of unique visual material. It is divided into four sections:

1. *Moledet Productions · 1927-1934*
Yerushalayim Segal and Axelrod formed Moledet. Segal was the producer

and Axelrod filmed and developed the material. What remains of their fledgling efforts includes innovative commercials for local and imported products, news stories showing important events and cultural life, and experiments for feature films.

2. *Carmel Newsreels: Series I · 1935-1948 / Series II · 1948-1958*
Series I includes weekly newsreels touching on virtually every significant aspect of life in pre-state Israel. The lack of newsreels between the years 1941 and 1945 reflects the difficulties of production during the war years, including lack of film stock and closed screening venues. Series II reflects life in the early years of the state, as well as items on international news.

3. *Additional Carmel Productions*
This collection includes items which were censored by the British authorities. In addition, there are a wide variety of newsreel stories which were not incorporated into newsreels, as well as out-takes from existing newsreels, scenes from dramatic films never completed, and commercial films.

4. *Feature films and their out-takes*
Axelrod was involved in the production and direction of feature films, including the first full-length Hebrew feature film *Oded, Hanoded / Oded, the Wanderer*.

The entire Axelrod Collection has been preserved on 35mm safety film. The dupe positives, dupe negatives and sound are housed in the vaults of the Israel Film Archive for preservation purposes. The Carmel company documentation, including letters, contracts and production notes, has been deposited in the Archive's Research Library. In addition, a videotape copy of most of the Israel Film Archive collection is available to permit easy access for researchers.

A number of newsreels can be seen on film at the Imperial War Museum, London and videotape copies of parts of the collection have been deposited for research purposes at Harvard University, Boston and at Hebrew University, Jerusalem.

In 1990 the Israel Film Archive acquired a computer network including a 386 file server and four work stations, thanks to a donation by the America-Israel Cultural Foundation. In 1991 the archive received a donation of five IBM PS2 computers and a laser printer from IBM Israel, which were added to the network. The network software is the Novell ELS level II Netware. The cataloguing software is ALEPH, a table-driven database system, developed by the Hebrew University of Jerusalem, which was adapted for film cataloguing. The computerisation of the Israel Film Archive collection of more than 17 000 films began.

This volume represents the computerised cataloguing of the entire pre-state Axelrod newsreel collection, including Moledet Productions (1927-1934) and Carmel Newsreels · Series I (1935-1948). In addition, a sample of the cataloguing of other Carmel productions is provided in the appendix.

Film researchers and film-makers, who find that they require more comprehensive indexing than that which is found at the back of this volume, are invited to request a tailored Boolean search.

The preservation and cataloguing of this collection has undergone many stages. The preservation of the nitrate films was funded by the Reginald Ford Foundation and was organised by the staff of the Center for Preservation of Israeli Film, which today has become a formal department of the Israel Film Archive, through the efforts of:

Dr André Chouraqui
Professor Reuven Yaron, State Archivist
Dr Moshe Mossek, Israel State Archives
Yosef Barel, Director of Israel Television, Chairman of the Preservation Center
Shlomo Fachler, Ministry of Finance, member of the board of the Preservation Center
Mayor Teddy Kollek, Ruth Cheshin and Hedva Fogel, Jerusalem Foundation
Ilan de Vries, formerly of the Israel Film Archive

The cataloguing of the Carmel newsreels in this volume is based on initial research prepared by Nathan and Leah Axelrod with the assistance of Yosefa Loshitzky and Ruth Liebskin under the supervision of Ya'akov Gross and Dr Moshe Mossek. This shot-listing has been expanded and corrected with the help of many individuals and institutions who have assisted us in identifying personalities and locations portrayed on the screen. We thank particularly the Central Zionist Archives and the Israeli Documentation Center for the Performing Arts at Tel Aviv University. We welcome any additions or corrections from those familiar with the period.

The following staff assisted us in the painstaking process of viewing, researching, cataloguing and organising the collection:

Shmuel Sermoneta-Gertel
Annette Bellows-Magnus
Cara Saposnik
Amnon Binyamin
Melissa Borenstein-Dor
Tzur Vahab

We are certain that this material can be used to better understand, as well as communicate, the past. Recognising the precious nature of this collection, we are pleased to provide this publication for film researchers and historians.

**Paula Weiman-Kelman**
**Edith Falk**
**Amy Kronish**
*December 1993*

## How to Use the Catalogue

This catalogue contains three main sections:
1    *Moledet Productions* are arranged by cataloguing number (which does not reflect chronological order). Although they were all produced between 1927 and 1934, it has not always been possible to provide specific years for each entry.
2    *Carmel Newsreels* are arranged by original newsreel numbers in chronological order.
3    Appendix of a few examples of *Additional Carmel Productions* arranged by cataloguing number (not chronological order).

The data recorded for each entry contains the following elements: title, date of distribution to the cinemas, short synopsis, length of each part in feet (to determine the length of the part in minutes, divide by 90), shot-listing, Hebrew and English titles off-screen - where there is no English title, the Hebrew title has been translated into English.

The *Subject and Personality Index* at the end of the catalogue is intended as a guide to specific topics, locations and personalities.

Moledet Productions · 1927-1934

■ **MOLEDET [001]** - FUNERAL OF MRS DIZENGOFF · 1930
The funeral procession and burial of Mayor Dizengoff's wife, Tsina Dizengoff, in Tel Aviv, February 23 1930 (509').

TITLE: THE FUNERAL PROCESSION OF MRS. DIZENGOFF, TEL AVIV, 23.2.30.
OPERATOR: NATHAN AXELROD.

כותרת: טקס הלוית המנוחה מרת צ. ח. דיזנגוף אשת ראש עירית תל-אביב ביום ראשון 23.2.30 . צלם: נתן אקסלרוד.

1  Crowd of mourners pass by camera, including uniformed men with Jewish stars, as well as police officers (mid, long).
2  TITLE: THE GOVERNOR OF JAFFA DISTRICT, THE CONSULS AND THE REPRESENTATIVES OF THE ZIONIST EXECUTIVE COME TO PAY THE LAST RESPECTS TO THE DECEASED.

כותרת: ה.מ. מושל מחוז יפו, כ"כ ממשלות חוץ, כ"כ ההנהלה הציונית והועד הלאומי באו לחלוק למנוחה את הכבוד האחרון.

3  Crowd of mourners. People carrying wreaths. Representatives of various countries and religions (long).
4  TITLE: BY "THE HOME OF THE AGED", PROCESSION HALTS AND PRAYERS ARE SAID. כותרת: תפילת "אל מלא רחמים" על יד בנין מושב זקנים.
5  Crowd paused, shot from the front and behind. Groups of scouts in assorted uniforms, assorted ages, boys and girls walk by camera (mid).
6  TITLE: WREATHS OF FLOWERS SENT BY VARIOUS INSTITUTIONS AND ORGANISATIONS, IN WHOM THE DECEASED TOOK AN ACTIVE INTEREST.

כותרת: זרי פרחים לאות הערצה מאת המוסדות ואגודות שונות שהמנוחה תמכה בהם באופן פעיל.

7  TITLE: THE RESIDENTS OF TEL AVIV PAY THEIR LAST RESPECTS.

כותרת: קהל מעריצים

8  Crowds in street shot from above and behind (long).
9  TITLE: THE TOWNSHIP OFFICES CLOSED AND FLAGS LOWERED IN SIGN OF MOURNING.

כותרת: משרדי העיריה נסגרו והדגלים הורדו למחצית התורן לאות אבל.

10  The Tel Aviv Municipality building on Bialik Street, on the corner of Edelson Street. Flags at half-mast (long). Mourners in the courtyard (mid).
11  TITLE: IN THE NAME OF THE CITIZENS OF TEL AVIV, MR ROKEACH [sic] MOURNS FOR THE DEAD.

כותרת: מר רוקח סגן ראש העיר מספיד את המנוחה בשם תושבי תל אביב.

12  Israel Rokah speaking from top of steps of the Municipality building (long).
13  TITLE: IN THE NAME OF ALL THE CONSULS, A REPRESENTATIVE OF THE FRENCH GOVERNMENT EXPRESSES SYMPATHY AND SORROW FOR THE LOSS OF THE MAYOR.

כותרת: בהספד מר נפרד מאת המנוחה בא-כוח ממשלת צרפת בשם כל הקונסולים בא"י.

14  Representative speaking from Municipality building (long). Mourners walk by camera (mid).
15  TITLE IN HEBREW: MAYOR DIZENGOFF ACCOMPANIES, IN THE WAY OF ALL FLESH, HIS WIFE, WHO ACCOMPANIED HIM FAITHFULLY IN ALL OF HIS PUBLIC WORK.

כותרת: ראש עיריית ת"א, מר מ. דיזנגוף (יבדל לחיים) מלוה בדרך כל בשר את רעיתו שהיתה בת לויה נאמנה לו בדרך כל מפעליו הציבוריים.

16  Crowd of mourners pass by camera.
17  TITLE: AT THE CEMETERY. כותרת: בתחנת הגמר לכל חי.

18  Pan of tombstones (long). Coffin lowered to ground. Gravediggers inside grave, brushing in dirt (mid). Wreaths being passed over heads of crowd (long). Handwritten, superimposed on film: THE WAY OF ALL FLESH.
19  TITLE IN HEBREW: MRS. DIZENGOFF, MAY HER SOUL BE LINKED IN THE CHAIN OF LIFE.

כותרת: פ"נ מרת צ.ח. דיזנגוף, תהי נשמתה צרורה בצרור החיים.

20  Grave covered with wreaths and flowers (c.u.).
21  TITLE IN HEBREW: ALL CITIZENS OF ERETZ ISRAEL TAKE PART IN THE MOURNING OF THE MAYOR OF TEL AVIV, WHO LOST THE WIFE OF HIS YOUTH. MAY HE FIND COMFORT IN THE BUILDING OF ISRAEL AND THE FLOWERING OF TEL AVIV.

כותרת: כל תושבי א"י משתתפים באבלו הכבד של ראש עיריית תל אביב במות עליו אשת נעוריו. בבנין הארץ ובפריחתה של עיר טיפוחיו, תל אביב, ימצא נחומים.

■ MOLEDET [002] - EXHIBITION GROUNDS, TEL AVIV · 1928
Exhibition stands at the Central Bus Station, Tel Aviv (41').

HEBREW TITLE: EXHIBITION STANDS (AT THE CENTRAL BUS STATION)

כותרת: תערוכת בתנים (במקום של התחנה המרכזית).

1  Iris shot opens to pan of exhibition, shot from above (long). Gate of exhibition. A couple entering the exhibition, superimposed on the gate.
2  Reverse pan of exhibition buildings with signs in Hebrew and English: JAFFA IRON WORKS. Additional signs unclear.

■ MOLEDET [003] - YEMENITE JEWS
Experiment for an uncompleted dramatic film about Yemenite Jews (76').

1  Unclear shot of grove of eucalyptus trees. Two women and a man sitting in front of old stone house. Young girl with covered head runs down steps.
2  She runs into eucalyptus grove. Fast tracking shot of trees.
3  Frontal shot of girl running between trees and by the banks of a stream.

■ MOLEDET [004] - ADVERTISEMENT FOR CHEMICAL FERTILIZER
Advertisement, with documentary and animated segments, urging farmers to buy Union Fertilizer. Titles use biblical quotations to support Union Fertilizer (461').

1  Opens with a documentary segment showing workers loading sacks onto a truck in front of the factory. The truck drives off as people watch from the pavement.
2  Quotation in Hebrew from The Book of Amos 9:14: "I will restore the fortunes of my people Israel, and they shall rebuild the ruined cities and inhabit them; they shall plant vineyards and drink their wine, and they shall make gardens and eat their fruit".

"ושבתי את שבות עמי ישראל ובנו ערים נשמות וישבו ונטעו כרמים ושתו את יינם ועשו גינות ואכלו את פריהם" (עמוס,ט,יד)

3  Pan of Tel Aviv. Pan of rural village.
4  Cardboard orchard. Hand puts doll of a farmer into orchard.
5  TITLE IN HEBREW: THE WISE FARMER WILL FERTILIZE ON TIME, USING ONLY UNION FERTILIZER.

כותרת: כזמנו יזבל האיכר הנבון וידיק להשתמש רק בזבל אוניון.

6  Animated segment - a farmer doll waters the orchard.
7  Farmer spreading powdered fertilizer around base of tree.

8   TITLE IN HEBREW: MAGNESIUM, PHOSPHATE, NITROGEN ARE ADDED IN ADVANCE, PROMISING A BLESSING OF OIL AND WINE.
    כותרת: זרחן, אשלג, וחנקן, מעורבים בו מראש והוא מבטיח ברכה ביצהר ותירוש.
9   Close-up of bag of fertilizer. Symbol of company: "ENGRAIS COMPLET DISSOUS" written around diamond with the word "UNION", with hands clasped over it.
10  French writing on bag: "AGENCE POUR LA PALESTINE: BRAUDE & SHABTIELI". Close-up of hands sifting powdered fertilizer in bag.
11  TITLE IN HEBREW: UNION FERTILIZER SWEETENS THE FRUIT OF THE TREE AND GIVES A WONDERFUL SMELL.
    כותרת: הזבל איוניון משגיא ומפריח, ממתיק פרי העץ, מרהיב ונותן ריח.
12  Animated sequence: the influence of fertilizer on the tree. Close-up of flowering tree.
13  TITLE IN HEBREW: UNION FERTILIZER PROVIDES WONDERFUL QUALITIES, MAKING EVERY CRATE OF ORANGES A TREASURE.
    כותרת: הזבל איוניון בו תכונה נפלאה, כל תיבת תפוזים אוצר מכילה.
14  An empty orange crate moves through the orchard by itself. Close-up of oranges on tree. Box filling with wrapped oranges.
15  Closed safe, lying on its side. Written on it: PALESTINE ORIENT CO.
16  TITLE IN HEBREW: THOSE WHO SOW WITH TEARS AND FERTILIZE WITH UNION WILL REAP WITH JOY AND BE RICH.
    כותרת: הזורעים בדמעה, ומזבלים ב"איוניון", יקצרו ברנה ויהיו בעל הון.
17  Animated segment: doll of farmer picks up safe in orchard.
18  TITLE IN HEBREW: CARROT, CABBAGE AND MR RADISH EXPECT THEIR SERVING OF UNION.   כותרת: גזר, כרוב ומיסטר צנון מצפים למנת איוניון
19  Animated vegetables reach for fertilizer.
20  TITLE IN HEBREW: AFTER A MEAL OF FERTILIZER, A REFRESHED GARDEN GROWS.   כותרת: לאחר סעודה דשנה, צמחה גינה רעננה.
21  Field of cabbage. Field with open water sprinklers.
22  Ends with Hebrew title, recommending use of Union Fertilizer because it is from a reputable firm, listing of ingredients, address of importers.
    כותרת: פרדסנים, איכרים ובעלי גינות ישתמשו בזבל הכימי המעורב של הפירמה הידועה " איוניון" המכיל את כל החומרים להזנת הצמח חנקן 6%, זרחן 10%, אשלג 8%. שזהו המזון המלא והמתאים לכל סוגי הקרקעות בארץ ישראל. הסוכנים הראשיים לארץ ישראל: מהנדס כ. בראודה ת.ת. שבתי תל אביב, רח' אלנבי.

■ MOLEDET [005] - JUDEAN HILLS
Judean Hills on the outskirts of Jerusalem. Cars driving down the winding road. Seven Sisters (windy stretch of road with seven turns) at Motzah (114').

1   Shots and pans of Judean Hills on the way to Jerusalem.
2   Procession of cars driving down a winding, hilly road. Seven Sisters at Motzah. In the background, a settlement's buildings are seen.

■ MOLEDET [006] - PURIM CARNIVAL · 1928
Newsreel of Purim, Tel Aviv, 1928.

▫ PART A: TITLE: POURIM [sic] 1928, CARNIVAL AT TEL AVIV.
    כותרת: הקרנבל בת"א, פורים תרפ"ח.

1   TITLE: PRODUCED IN THE FIRST PALESTINE STUDIO, MOLEDET, TEL AVIV. HEBREW TITLE: DIRECTOR: YERUSHALAYIM SEGAL.

כותרת: הוצאת המעבדה ע"י הקינו-סטודיה הראשונה בא"י. מולדת - תל-אביב. המנהל: ירושלים סגל.

2   TITLE: OPERATOR: NATHAN AXELROD.   כותרת: צלם: נתן אקסלרוד
3   Mandate Censorship Certificate in English: FILM PURIM CARNIVAL IN TEL-AVIV.
4   TITLE: FIRST PART, TEL AVIV - TOWNSHIP AND GENERAL VIEW.

כותרת: תל אביב, העיריה והעיר...

5   Iris shot of Municipality building.
6   Pan of Tel Aviv rooftops. Tel Aviv street.
7   Calendar page with date in Hebrew and English: February 22 1928.

☐ PART B: PURIM 1928
1   General view of Tel Aviv.
2   Calendar page: 22 February 1928.   דף יומן: א' אדר תרפ"ח.
3   A parade float and children wearing masks.
4   Buildings.
5   Buildings on screen split into three.
6   Buildings superimposed and turning upside-down.
7   A crowd.
8   A float in the shape of a whale.
9   The crowd and men on horseback.

■ **MOLEDET [007] AND [057]** - HECHALUTZ: SCENES FROM AN EXPERIMENTAL FILM · 1927
Scenes from a dramatic film, apparently uncompleted. Scenes include a girl crying, guards on horses, a photographer taking photographs, a man riding a donkey.

☐ PART A (129')
1   Little girl in entrance to house. She walks down the stairs. There appears to be a bandage on her leg (long). She bursts into dramatic tears (c.u.), runs down the stairs and off-screen (long).
2   Armed guards run out of a building, jump onto horses. Guards riding down a dirt road in an orchard, towards camera and then through a field away from camera (long).
3   Photographer, with his head covered by camera cloth, taking a picture and gesticulating with hands. Donkey walks past and stops, evidently interfering with picture. Photographer tries to move it. Puts on monocle.

☐ PART B (34.5')
1   Man in suit, tie and cap riding on donkey towards camera, looks to horizon, stops, shrugs.
2   Man takes out binoculars and looks through them, smiles.

■ **MOLEDET [008] AND [053]** - ADVERTISEMENT FOLKOVITZ & GOLDIN DRY GOODS · 1931
An advertisement for a fabric sale at Folkovitz and Goldin dry goods shop.

☐ PART A (267')
1   TITLE: DRY GOODS FOLKOVITZ AND GOLDIN, TEL AVIV. NAHALAT BENYAMIN 32. CORNER KALISHER. BRANCH: NAHALAT BENYAMIN 9.

כותרת: מונופקוטורה. פלקוביץ את גולדין. תל אביב, נחלת בינימין, פינת קלישר. סניף: נחלת בינימין 9.

2   Exterior of shop. Man standing outside. Policeman in entrance. People walking past. Fade to shop window.
3   TITLE: GREAT CLEARANCE SALE.     כותרת: מכירה כללית גדולה.
4   Pan of shop window, bolts of cloth.
5   TITLE: WE CONTINUE OUR SPECIAL SALE MONDAY, 5TH OF JANUARY 1931.

כותרת: על פי בקשת לקוחתנו הנכבדים שלא הספיקו מסיבות שונות להנות במולואו מההנחות העצומות שנתנו לקהל לרגל חנוכת בית מסחרנו החדש, החלטנו להמשיך את מכירת-החנוכה עד יום 5 לינואר, 1931.

6   View of display windows, people walking by, closer view of window, prices on fabrics.
7   TITLE: ON THE OCCASION OF MOVING OUR STORE TO OUR OWN BUILDING A SPECIAL CONSECRATION SALE WILL COMMENCE ON THE 25TH NOV. UNTIL 15 DEC. 1930
8   Title in Hebrew lists the type of materials to be sold and states that only cash sales are acceptable.
9   TITLE IN HEBREW: A VAST SELECTION OF NEW GOODS JUST RECEIVED; SILK, WOOL, COTTON, FUR, CHOICE FABRICS FOR JACKETS, SUITS, DRESSES, CURTAINS, RUGS AND UPHOLSTERY. CASH SALES ONLY.

כותרת: מבחר גדול של סחורות חדישות שנתקבלו זה עתה, כגון: משי, צמר, כותנה, פרווה, מבחר בדים למעילים, חליפות ושמלות, וילונים, שטיחים, שמיכות מרבדים וציפוי לרהיטים. המכירה רק במזומנים. פלקוביץ את גלדין.

□ PART B (49')
1   People walking in street in front of shop on Rothschild Boulevard.

■ **MOLEDET [009]** - ADVERTISEMENT FOR BELLA BEAUTY PARLOUR
An advertisement for Bella Beauty Parlour in Tel Aviv (153').

1   TITLE: MODERN COSMETIC AND SCIENTIFIC TREATMENT, PRESERVE YOUR YOUTH! THE 'BELLA' BEAUTY PARLOUR.

כותרת: קוסמטיקה מודרנית וטיפול מדעי מעריכים את העלומים. המכון ליופי בלה.

2   Young woman walks upstairs to entrance of beauty parlour, turns around and smiles.
3   Interior of beauty parlour.
4   TITLE: FACE MASSAGE, REMOVING WRINKLES...

כותרת: מסז' בפנים נגד קמטים, טיפול מיוחד בעור: כתמים, שחורים, אבעבועות, סובין, ועוד.

5   Woman giving facial to a woman lying down, using her hands, using electric massager (long, c.u.).
6   TITLE: MANICURE.                                  כותרת: מניקור.
7   Close-up of manicure.
8   TITLE IN HEBREW: MAKE-UP & BEAUTY FOR THE BALL AND DANCE.

כותרת: איפור ויופי בשביל נשפים

9   TITLE IN HEBREW: BEFORE                        כותרת: לפני איפור
10  Before shot of a young girl.
11  TITLE IN HEBREW: AFTER                         כותרת: אחרי איפור
12  After shot of the girl.

13 TITLE IN HEBREW: LATEST NEWS - PARAFFINE BANDAGES FOR REMOVING WRINKLES...

כותרת: חדשות אחרונות - תחבושות פרפין, כצת-מרפא (מיד רדון) משחה מיוחדת להסרת שערות מיותרות ועוד צורכי קוסמטיקה שונים.

14 TITLE: CONSULTATIONS FREE. ROTHSCHILD BOULEVARD. CORNER HERZL STREET (IN THE INSTITUTE OF DR ELIAHU).

ינתן עצות חינם. לפנות למכון ליופי כלה, שדרות רוטשילד 9 פינת הרצל.
(בבית אחד העם, המכון לרנטגן של ד"ר אליהו)

- **MOLEDET [010]** - ADVERTISEMENT FOR CARMEL MIZRACHI HEALTH PRODUCT

An advertisement for an elixir (iron supplement), made by Carmel Mizrachi (194.5').

1 TITLE IN HEBREW: THE POOR INVALID.   כותרת: החולה המסכן.
2 Sick man lying in bed. Nurse caring for him. Table full of medicines.
3 TITLE: THE PROFESSOR IS COMING.   כותרת: הפרופסור בא
4 The doctor arrives. Examines the sick man. Writes a new prescription and leaves.
5 The nurse throws out all the medicines. Long-shot of a car driving down the street, stopping at a shop with sign in Hebrew and English: CARMEL ORIENTAL.
6 TITLE IN HEBREW: EVERYTHING IS VANITY   כותרת: הכל הבל
7 Close-up of a bottle with label in Hebrew: first iron supplement.

כותרת: ברזל חינה ראשון

8 The sick man drinking from a wine glass. Nurse looking at watch. Patient drinking.
9 TITLE IN HEBREW: FROM JUST THE FIRST IRON SUPPLEMENT HE GETS HEALTHIER AND STRONGER.

כותרת: אך ורק "ברזל חינה ראשון" הוא מחלים, ומחזק את השרירים.

10 TITLE IN HEBREW: TWO CUPS BEFORE MEALS AND YOUR LEGS BEGIN DANCING.   כותרת: לפני האוכל שתי כוסות והרגליים מעצמן רוקדות.
11 Patient starts exercising, dancing.
12 TITLE IN HEBREW: HURRAY FOR LIFE   כותרת: הידד,הידד לחיים
13 TITLE IN HEBREW: HINA IRON THE BEST OF ALL

כותרת: ברזל חינה - ראשון ואין שני לו

14 Close-up of three bottles on the medicine table.

- **MOLEDET [011]** - ADVERTISEMENT FOR CARMEL MIZRACHI WINES and LIQUEURS

An advertisement for Carmel Mizrachi wines and liqueurs (127').

1 TITLE: COOPERATIVE SOCIETY OF THE GROWERS OF THE SELLERS [sic] RISHON LE ZIYON AND ZIKHRON YA'AKOV LTD... BRANDIES, LIQUEURS, AND ARAK.

כותרת: אגודת הכורמים הקואופרטיבית של יקבי ראשון לציון וזכרון יעקב

2 Shots of bottles, turning around on the table, to make their labels clear.

- **MOLEDET [012]** - FUNERAL OF MUSA KAZEM AL-HUSSEINI · 1934

Funeral procession of Musa Kazem al-Husseini, President of the Arab Executive, former Mayor of Jerusalem. Includes excellent footage of Arab crowds in the Old City and in the courtyard of the Dome of the Rock (458').

TITLE IN HEBREW, ENGLISH AND ARABIC: FUNERAL OF LATE MUSSA KHASIM PACHA EXECUTIVE

כותרת: הלויתו של נשיא הועד הפועל הערבי מוסא קצים פחה המנוח.

1. Censorship Certificate dated April 10 1934.
2. TITLE IN ENGLISH, HEBREW AND ARABIC: MANY WREATHS HAVE BEEN SENT BY DIFFERENT ORGANISATIONS, THE GOVERNMENTS AND THE CONSULS.

כותרת: זרי פרחים רבים נשלחו מטעם מוסדות שונים, הממשלה והקונסולים.

3. Massive procession of Arabs through East Jerusalem. Pan of rooftops in the Old City.
4. TITLE IN HEBREW, ARABIC AND ENGLISH: ON THE GROUNDS OF THE MOSQUE OF OMAR. כותרת: בחצר מסגד עומר.
5. Large crowd near mosque. Pan including mosque. Assorted shots of crowd, including visibly upset faces of men.
6. Diplomats in shiny top hats walking downstairs.
7. Faces walking slowly past camera (mid).

■ MOLEDET [013] - ZEBULUN VALLEY
Group of visitors inspecting the completion of the draining of the swamps in the Zebulun Valley (495').

1. Men working draining swamp, cars arriving bringing group to inspect project. Group, including men and women, looks at work.
2. Group on wooden bridge, eating in tent, on cement bridge. Pan of field. Man showing narrow drainage ditch.
3. Group listening to assorted speakers. Crowd clapping.

■ MOLEDET [014] - PRODUCTION CREDITS
Production credits of the Moledet Company (12').

1. TITLE: MOLEDET, TEL AVIV. כותרת: מולדת, תל אביב.
2. TITLE IN HEBREW: UNDER THE DIRECTION OF YERUSHALAYIM SEGAL.

צולם ע"י מעבדת "מולדת", תל אביב, בהנהלת ירושלים סגל.

■ MOLEDET [015] and [77] - SHAW COMMISSION OF INQUIRY, TEL AVIV · 1929
Members of Royal Commission of Inquiry at Tel Aviv Municipality building, including Sir Walter Shaw and Mayor Meir Dizengoff.

□ PART A (163')
1. TITLE: VISITE DE LA COMMISSION D'ENQUETE A TEL-AVIV, 8 NOVEMBRE 1929.

כותרת: ביקור ועדת חקירה בעיריית תל-אביב, ביום שישי, 8 לנובמבר 1929.

2. Cars driving up to municipality building.
3. Mayor Meir Dizengoff greets members of the Commission, including Sir Walter Shaw, as they leave their cars.
4. Going upstairs.
5. Pan of municipality square. Photographer.
6. TITLE IN FRENCH, HEBREW AND ENGLISH: SIR WALTER SHAW AND MEMBERS OF COMMISSION. LE CHEF WALTER SHAW ET LES MEMBRES DE LA COMMISSION. כותרת: ראש ועדת החקירה סיר ולטר שאו וחברי הועדה.
7. Dizengoff, Shaw and others walking down steps (mid).
8. Getting into cars. Bialik Street and Edelson Street.
9. Dizengoff waves goodbye.

☐ PART B (8.5')
1   Dizengoff waves goodbye.

■ **MOLEDET [016] AND [086]** - FILM STAR VISITS IN ISRAEL
Fox film star Don José Mojica visits Tel Aviv. Includes shot of the film star on a rooftop in Tel Aviv, with pan of the rooftops of the city (73.5').

☐ PART A (73.5'): TITLE: (handwritten): THE BELOVED FOX FILM STAR, DON JOSE MOJICA, LEAVES THE TEL AVIV TOWNSHIP TO VISIT THE TOWN.

כותרת: כוכב הקולנוע החביב דון חוזה מוזייקה. יוצא לבית עירית ת"א בדרכו לסייר את העיר.

1   Star walks down municipality steps, waves to camera, gets into car.
2   On knees, playing with children, clapping hands. Pan of rooftops.
3   TITLE: THE KIDDIES OF TEL AVIV FOUND IN JOSE MOJICA A VERY SOCIABLE PLAYMATE.

כותרת: ילדי הגנים מצאו בו אוהב נאמן וסובבוהו בשמחה.

4   More children around kneeling star.

☐ PART B (29.5')
1   The film star on a rooftop in Tel Aviv.
2   Mojica waves to the camera. Pan of rooftops.

■ **MOLEDET [017]** - MACCABI SPORTS EVENT · 1929
Opening of Maccabi sports event, Passover 1929, Tel Aviv (377').

TITLE: OLYMPIADE LA MACCABI, TEL AVIV, Pesach, 1929.

כותרת: כינוס מכבי' - הכינוס הארצי של המכבי בא"י, תל-אביב, פסח תרכ"ט.

1   Procession down street crowded with spectators. Motorcycle at head of procession. Men in white uniforms.
2   TITLE: SUR LE TERRAIN DE "MACCABI".

כותרת: התהלוכה ברחוב. על מגרש ה"מכבי".

3   Split-screen: two views of parade, including groups of girls in white, men in white, policemen trying to keep order.
4   Young women throwing, jumping. Young men throwing, jumping.
5   TITLE: LES JUGES.                                  כותרת: השופטים.
6   Pan of judges in white suits.
7   Sir John Chancellor, the High Commissioner, arriving, removes hat to crowd.
8   TITLE: SON EXCELLENCE, LE HAUT COMMISSAIRE.

כותרת: הנציב העליון.

9   Pan of seated crowd, including dignitaries.
10  TITLE IN HEBREW: DIGNITARIES.          כותרת: אורחים נכבדים.
11  TITLE IN HEBREW: PRIZES.                    כותרת: הפרסים.
12  TITLE: MAN ATTEMPTS HIGH-JUMP AND FAILS.

כותרת: קפיצה שלא הצליחה אין הצלמניה מעבירה.

13  Runners on track. Winner (mid). Pan of all participants doing exercises.
14  TITLE: 5000 METRES - LE GAGNANT        כותרת: 5000 מטר - הזוכה
15  TITLE IN HEBREW: MR Y. ALUF, DIRECTOR OF THE OLYMPICS.

כותרת: מר י. אלוף - מפקד בכנס.

16  Synchronised marching. Shots of feet. Assorted shots of crowd.
17  Hebrew title apologises for the fact that Moledet was not able to photograph events at night.

כותרת: הנהלת "מולדת" מצטערת על שאי-אפשר היה לצלם את כל הפרטים.

לרגל חשכת הלילה ומבקשת להבא מאת כל אשר בהם תלוי הדבר להתחשב
עם עובדה זו בכל מקרה שיהיה.

■ **MOLEDET [018]** - HERZL STREET IN TEL AVIV
View of Herzl Street in Tel Aviv (13.5').

1. Tracking shot from vehicle, camera facing forward, down Herzl Street.
2. Pedestrians, including woman pushing baby carriage, man in fez, cyclists, horse and cart.

■ **MOLEDET [019]** - TRADEMARK
Moledet company trademark: Rachel's Tomb with "Moledet" in English and Hebrew (14').

■ **MOLEDET [020]** - PAGODA HOUSE
Nahmani Street in Tel Aviv, with Pagoda House (exterior only) (22.5').

■ **MOLEDET [021]** - EXHIBITION OF ZIONA TAGER · 1929
The Dizengoffs and Yitzhak Katz entering the exhibition of Ziona Tager (27.5').

TITLE: VISITING THE EXHIBITION OF MISS ZIONA TAGER
כותרת: ביקור בתערוכה הציירת ציונה תג׳ר.
1. Well-dressed men and women entering the exhibition, including Tsina Dizengoff, Mayor Meir Dizengoff, Yitzhak Katz and Sue Gottlieb.

■ **MOLEDET [022]** - GYMNASTICS
Gymnastics at Herzliyah Gymnasium. Paramount movie camera filming. Dizengoff speaking at sports rally at Maccabi grounds in Tel Aviv. Flag-raising (195').

TITLE: GENERAL GYMNASTICS AT THE HERZLIYAH COLLEGE AT TEL AVIV
כותרת: התעמלות כללית בגמנסיה הרצליה, בתל-אביב.
1. Assorted views, large group of boys and girls doing exercises. A band. Close-up of faces.
2. TITLE: PARAMOUNT SOUND CAMERA REGISTERS THE VIEW FOR AMERICA.
כותרת: צלמנית שמעונע "פרמונט" רושמת את המחזה בשביל אמריקה.
3. Man with movie camera filming.
4. TITLE: RALLY OF THE SPORTIVE YOUTH OF TEL AVIV ON THE MACCABI GROUND. כותרת: כינוס אגודת הנער הספורטיבי על מגרש המכבי.
5. Crowd scene.
6. TITLE: OPENING SPEECH BY DIZENGOFF OBE, MAYOR OF TEL AVIV.
כותרת: נאום הפתיחה של ראש עיריית ת"א מר מ. דיזנגוף.
7. Dizengoff speaking in midst of crowd.
8. TITLE: FLYING OF THE NATIONAL FLAG. כותרת: הרמת דגל התהלוכה.
9. Flag-raising, procession marching past.

■ **MOLEDET [023]** - PURIM PARADE
Purim parade including large float of three-headed monster, police on horseback, crowds lining the street (24').

■ **MOLEDET [024]** - GUARDS IN ORCHARD
Dramatic sequence in an orchard, marching band and a romantic segment as part of a crowd scene (124').

1. Dramatic sequence of young guards in an orchard.

2  Marching band, with houses in background.
3  Boys running a race.
4  Crowd scene, possibly dramatic sequence, includes young man dressed in white flirting with young woman.

■ **MOLEDET [025]** - GREAT SYNAGOGUE AND BEAUTY QUEEN
Opening of the Great Synagogue in Tel Aviv. A beauty queen from New York visits Tel Aviv (243').

□ PART A: THE GREAT SYNAGOGUE OF TEL AVIV
1  Pan of the Great Synagogue, draped with a national flag. Strings of flags.
2  Pan of crowd outdoors.
3  Interior of sanctuary. Ark, dome.
4  Exterior. Band playing. Dignitaries entering.
5  Pan of men holding Torah scrolls.

□ PART B: BEAUTY QUEEN
1  Beautiful woman looking at camera, gets on train, train pulls out.
2  Young boys make faces at camera.
3  TITLE IN HEBREW AND ENGLISH: MISS SUE GOTTLIEB, WINNER OF THE 'TAG' BEAUTY CONTEST IN NEW YORK VISITING TEL AVIV.

כותרת: העלמה ש. גוטליב - מלכת היופי בנשף "הטאג" בניו יורק מבקרת בתל אביב.

4  Small group of well-dressed men and women looking at the camera. Dizengoff laughing with Sue Gottlieb.

■ **MOLEDET [026]** - CHILDREN IN ORCHARD
Children in orchard at Yakhin. Banana trees. Children running down tracks through an orchard, laughing (57').

■ **MOLEDET [027]** - BUILDING SITE
Activities on construction site (30').

■ **MOLEDET [028]** - OIL REFINERY PIPELINE
First pipeline connecting ships to oil refinery in Haifa (152').

1  Pipe on the beach. Workers on the site.
2  Pan of men, some in suits, some workers, posing for camera. Includes men in fezzes, keffiyehs, work hats, as well as men in uniforms. Evidently workers and management on work site.

■ **MOLEDET [029]** - YAKHIN
Pan of young vineyard (20').

■ **MOLEDET [030]** - ASSIS
Shavuot celebration sponsored by Assis, the fruit juice producers (303').

1  Young men and women in white, dancing around a pole.
2  Children raising baskets, bringing the baskets towards the pole.
3  Large crowd in stadium.
4  TITLE IN HEBREW: "I WOULD LET YOU DRINK OF THE WINE AND OF MY POMEGRANATE JUICE" (The Song of Songs 8:2).

כותרת: "אשקך מיין הרקח מעסיס רימוני" (שיר השירים).

5   TITLE IN HEBREW: ASSIS, THE COMPANY FOR THE FRUITS OF THE LAND OF ISRAEL, PROVIDES CHILDREN WITH COLD WATER IN "JAFFORANGE", THE NATURAL JUICE FROM ORANGES OF THE LAND OF ISRAEL, TO RESTORE THEIR SPIRITS IN A HEATWAVE.
כותרת: החברה לתוצרת הארץ "עסיס" מעניקה לילדים מים קרים ב"יפארונג" המיץ הטבעי מתפוחי זהב א"י, להשיב נפשם משרב.
6   Children drinking juice in paper cups with "Assis" written on them.
7   Pan of crowd. Large group folk dancing in field. Children bringing first fruits.
8   Old man is helped up to the stage.

■ **MOLEDET [031]** - CROWD STROLLING IN TEL AVIV
People strolling in square in Tel Aviv, families, women with parasols (17.5').

■ **MOLEDET [032]** - SHAVUOT
Children in white lined up for a First Fruits Procession on Shavuot (22').

■ **MOLEDET [033]** - PUBLIC PARK
A man reading a newspaper in a public park in Tel Aviv (perhaps Gan Meir) (9').

■ **MOLEDET [034]** - ALLENBY STREET
Massive crowd in Allenby Street, Tel Aviv, shot from above with banners waving (20.5').

■ **MOLEDET [035]** - ALLENBY STREET
Motorcade on Allenby Street, Tel Aviv, including cars, bicycles, motorcycles, crowds lining street. Particularly striking footage (97').

1   Shots of procession of cars. Some with Arabic licence plate numbers.
2   British policeman hopping on a car.
3   Bicycles, motorcycles, crowds lining street.

■ **MOLEDET [036]** - PURIM · 1928
Purim celebrations, including a Yemenite-costumed Queen Esther (80').

1   Queen Esther, full shot on black background. Woman wearing beautiful Yemenite clothes.
2   Large crowd in the park.
3   Crowd, looking at camera (mid).
4   Marching band in uniform. Procession of men.
5   Large crowd by the side of the road.

■ **MOLEDET [037]** - SPORTS ON THE BEACH
Young men doing sports on the beach, including jumping rope, wrestling, boxing (45').

1   Four muscular young men jumping rope, in bathing suits, on roof.
2   Two boxing. Two wrestling on the beach, with the sea in the background.

■ **MOLEDET [038]** - MACCABI MEETING
Hebrew banner for meeting of Maccabi Sports Association (13').

1   Exterior of building.
2   Hebrew sign: WELCOME MACCABI, LONG LIVE HEBREW SPORT.
שלט: ברוכים הבאים, מכבי. יחי הספורט העברי.

## 12   Moledet Productions

■ **MOLEDET [039] - BALLET IN THE PARK**
Ballet inspired by agricultural themes (318').

1. Group of dancers in a public park, palm trees in background.
2. Lead dancer interprets agricultural activities through dance. As she works the land, the group of dancers interprets crops growing.
3. Shot from different angles, the dance continues.

■ **MOLEDET [040] - PURIM PARADE · 1928**
Purim parade in Tel Aviv, shot from above, including float with sign MIKVE ISRAEL, ASSIS (44').

■ **MOLEDET [041] - RAILWAY STATION**
Train pulling into unidentified railway station (146').

1. Tens of people walking by train tracks (long).
2. Crowd (mid). Train enters the station (long).
3. Frontal shot of the train pulling into the station (mid).
4. People disembarking. Crowd receiving the travellers.
5. Sign on billboard: April 1929.
6. Train pulls out from the station. Well-dressed man carrying a walking stick passes in front of camera.

■ **MOLEDET [042], [045], [046] - PURIM · 1928**
Purim parade, rain and shine, in Tel Aviv.

□ PART A (88')
1. Costume parade down street. Crowd by side of street.
2. Horse riders in costume.
3. Floats - one with sign in Hebrew: The Golden Chain of Keren Kayemet LeYisrael (Jewish National Fund). כותרת: שרשרת הזהב של קק"ל.
4. Men on camels.

□ PART B (69')
1. Purim parade down street with shop fronts.
2. Floats.
3. Men on horseback.
4. Costumes.

□ PART C (226')
1. Purim parade down street.
2. Floats, horseback riders, crowd by side of street.
3. One float with Hebrew sign: THE GOLDEN CHAIN OF KEREN KAYEMET LEYISRAEL. שלט: שרשרת הזהב של קק"ל.
4. Decorated cars, wet and windblown, raining.
5. Costumed men and women on horses.

■ **MOLEDET [043] - JEWISH AGENCY BUILDING**
Children entering the Jewish Agency building (73').

1. Children sitting around tables in a yard.
2. A line of children entering a building. Sign on building: Jewish Agency for Palestine, Keren Hayesod. שלט: בנין הסכנות היהודית, קרן היסוד
3. Shots of assorted buildings in Tel Aviv.
4. Chickens in a cage.

■ **MOLEDET [044]** - BRITISH MILITARY PARADE · 1928
British soldiers marching and on horseback through Jerusalem, including the High Commissioner Sir John Chancellor (63').

1   Parade of British soldiers led by marching band and two soldiers leading a goat.
2   Soldiers on horseback escorting Sir John Chancellor's car. Riders and car turn corner to the Jerusalem railway station. The station is decorated with coloured flags.
3   Chancellor gets out of car, reviews troops, King David Hotel in background (unbuilt Khan). Crowd watching.

■ **MOLEDET [045]** - PURIM · 1928
See **MOLEDET [042]**.

■ **MOLEDET [046]** - PURIM · 1928
See **MOLEDET [042]**.

■ **MOLEDET [047]** - FOLK DANCING
Folk dancers performing traditional Yemenite dances. Includes close-up of smiling lead woman. Shot in the Agadati Studio (60').

■ **MOLEDET [048]** - PIPES
Worker painting pipes in an outdoor pipe storage area (36').

■ **MOLEDET [049]** - JEWISH LEGION · November 2 1928
Convoy of trucks of the Jewish Legion on their way to Jerusalem at Seven Sisters turn and on the streets of Jerusalem (73').

1   Series of shots of convoy of trucks full of the Jewish Legion on a hairpin bend of the road to Jerusalem.
2   Shots of the caravan as it enters Jerusalem, frontal shot of cars, through the streets of Jerusalem. Men wave from cars.
3   Arab woman carrying package on her head.
4   Streets of Jerusalem. Uniformed man in front of crowd, stares into camera.

■ **MOLEDET [050]** - JEWISH LEGION · November 11 1928
Members of the Jewish Legion at a memorial ceremony at the military cemetery on Mount Scopus (82').

1   Ceremony in military cemetery on Mount Scopus. Group of men in civilian dress, with medals pinned to their shirts, standing at attention. Man with beard, speaking.
2   Buildings of Mount Scopus in background.
3   Procession through street. Men carrying wreaths. Army marching band in uniform. Soldiers on horseback. Crowd walking.

■ **MOLEDET [051]** - HERZLIYAH GYMNASIUM
Scenes indoors and outdoors at the Herzliyah Gymnasium (133').

1   Teacher lecturing to class. Pan of students at desks.
2   Students fooling around in large group, including a few teachers, in front of the camera.
3   Younger pupils playing ball in courtyard. Teacher stands on table and blows whistle.
4   Pupils exercising in courtyard.

5   Little children walk through courtyard. Mixed group of children in courtyard.
6   Teacher in suit and tie lecturing to class. Pan of students.

■ **MOLEDET [052]** - OPENING OF THE LEVANT FAIR
The opening of the Levant Fair, including dignitaries and British soldiers (42').

1   Dignitaries entering fairgrounds, men in top hats and morning coats. Two men in kilts.
2   Shot of airplane.
3   Crowd gathered. Pan of military orchestra, conducted by man in kilt.

■ **MOLEDET [053]** - ADVERTISEMENT FOLKOVITZ and GOLDIN
See **MOLEDET [008]**.

■ **MOLEDET [054]** - HERZL STREET
Cars with people waving at camera, horse-drawn wagon, pedestrians, cyclists on Herzl Street in Tel Aviv (10.5').

■ **MOLEDET [055]** - ARTISTS EXHIBITION
Exterior of Tel Aviv Museum. Groups of people, possibly artists, on steps in front of museum (19').

1   Museum building, with banner in Hebrew: TEL AVIV MUSEUM, FREE EXHIBITION OF ARTISTS OF ERETZ ISRAEL.

כותרת: מוזאון תל אביב תערוכה חופשית של אמני ארץ ישראל.

■ **MOLEDET [056]** - STREETS OF TEL AVIV
Tree-lined boulevard in Tel Aviv and a main street, both with pedestrians (10.5').

■ **MOLEDET [057]** - HECHALUTZ, EXPERIMENTAL FILM
See **MOLEDET [007]**.

■ **MOLEDET [058/059]** - FUNERAL OF CHAIM ARLOZOROFF
Funeral procession of Chaim Arlozoroff, including crowd shot from street and from above. Assorted shots of coffin being carried. Man reading speech on balcony (160').

■ **MOLEDET [060]** - CARMEL MIZRACHI ADVERTISEMENT
Advertisement for Carmel Mizrachi wines and beverages (104').

1   Real bottles passing through painted archway with sign in Hebrew and French: GRANDES CAVES DE RISHON LE ZION A ZICHRON YA'AKOV.

כותרת: יקבי ראשון-לציון וזכרון יעקב.

■ **MOLEDET [061]** - ADVERTISEMENT FOR CARMEL MIZRACHI
Advertisement for Carmel Mizrachi wines and beverages, showing assorted bottles twisting from side to side (70').

■ **MOLEDET [062]** - THE CHALUTZ, THE FLOWER, THE COW AND THE CHALUTZAH
A comic romance about two pioneering youths. A story of love thwarted by a cow (224').

1   Young man picking wild flowers in field, dressed in white shirt and shorts. Walks in a humorously exaggerated way. A sheep is tied to his waist on a string.

2   He fantasizes giving flowers to a woman who tweaks his ear. In reality, a bug is on his ear, which he wiggles to get the bug off.
3   He walks down the road and over a stream, up to girls hanging clothes on a line.
4   He stands behind a dress and it appears that he is wearing it.
5   Young man finds girlfriend milking cow. The cow eats the flowers before he can give them to her. She laughs. He gives the rest of the flowers to the cow.

■ **MOLEDET [063]** - AGRICULTURAL WORK AT YAKHIN
Irrigation, soil preparation and work in the orchards at Yakhin (333').

1   Engine by wooden hut and wooden tower. Water flowing from pipe into ditch.
2   Man directing flow of water with hoe. Man and woman planting trees.
3   Small tractor ploughing, cultivating.
4   Man laying water pipes in ditch.
5   Water from pipe.
6   Picking oranges.
7   Men raising tower for telephone or electric wires.
8   Man opening gate with sign in Hebrew and English: YAKHIN.   כתובת: יכין
9   Tractor with girl on back drives through.
10  Men placing pipes in ditch.
11  The feet of three men, two barefoot, one in boots (mid).
12  Twisting a pole into the ground. Examining the soil which has been extracted from bottom of pole.
13  Women working in vegetable garden. Watering the vegetables with watering can.

■ **MOLEDET [064]** - PICKING ORANGES, YAKHIN · 1927-34
Picking and packing oranges for export by Yakhin Company (343').

1   Trees in orchard. Pan over tops of trees. Children running down tracks in orchard, towards camera, laughing, holding oranges.
2   Woman follows holding book, reading. Young man passes her.
3   Young woman picking oranges. Older man with white beard picking oranges.
4   Men on tops of ladders picking oranges.
5   Boys sitting around, one reading newspaper attached to a board.
6   Young men pushing cart with baskets on track in orchard.
7   Putting baskets filled with oranges onto cart.
8   Pushing full carts down tracks through orchard.
9   Mounds of oranges in packing house. Sorting oranges.
10  Painting crates with name in English: JAFFCOOP, AMERICAN PACKING.

■ **MOLEDET [065]** - AGRICULTURAL WORK, YAKHIN
Agricultural work by Yakhin Company, including laying pipeline, banana trees and orchard (273').

1   Men walking through fields, twisting long pole (for soil sample) into ground.
2   Laying underground pipeline. Workers cementing pipes.
3   Exterior of building.
4   Bananas on tree. Man walking among banana trees.
5   Gate with sign in Hebrew and English: YAKHIN.   כתובת: יכין
6   Pan of young orchard. Pan of fields. Assorted pan of orchard.

■ **MOLEDET [066]** - AGRICULTURAL WORK, YAKHIN
Agricultural work by Yakhin Company, including horses pulling plough, cultivating and irrigating orchard (107').

1  Man guiding two horses pulling plough.
2  Pan of orchard.
3  Small tractor cultivating an orchard.
4  Turning on water for ditch irrigation in orchard.

■ **MOLEDET [067]** - ADVERTISEMENT FOR LIPTON
Advertisement for Lipton cornflour, custard, tea and imported cigarettes (65').

1  Hand holding can with English label: LIPTONS GENUINE CORNFLOUR.
2  Hand holding can with English: LIPTONS CUSTARD POWDER. Back of can: ENJOY LIPTONS TEA.
3  HEBREW TITLE: MY WIFE WAS RIGHT. LIPTONS CUSTARD IS BETTER THAN ANY OTHER CUSTARD. IT IS NUTRITIOUS. MY FACE IS A WITNESS TO THIS.
4  Can of Lipton cornflour.
5  Spraycan with label: METAL PUTZ! SOLAN.
6  Box with label: SALONICA CIGARETTE COMPANY, CAIRO, PORT-SAID, ALEXANDRIA, SALONIQUE.

כותרת: אכן צדקה אשתי. הקוסטרד של ליפטון טוב הוא מכל קוסטרד אחר. הוא מזין. פני מעידים על כך.

■ **MOLEDET [068]** - ADVERTISEMENT FOR LIPTON TEA
Advertisement for Lipton tea, showing a scene in an Arab coffee house (97').

1  Outdoor café. Two men in western dress drinking tea.
2  Man in fez sits down, claps hands, orders from waiter, lights a cigarette. Waiter serves him tea which he sends back.
3  Waiter with teapot and box of Lipton tea on a tray. It is accepted.
4  Waiter lifts box of tea, showing the contents to the camera.
5  Customer drinks tea happily.

■ **MOLEDET [069]** - BEEHIVES
Farm and barnyard, followed by many beehives in an orchard (37.5').

■ **MOLEDET [070]** - ROWING BOAT NEAR JAFFA
Rowing boat on water near Jaffa (10.5').

■ **MOLEDET [071]** - COFFEEHOUSE
Exterior of coffee house, shot for a Lipton tea advertisement (20.5').

1  Pan of men in outdoor café.
2  Iris shot opens to exterior of European-looking building.
3  Sign: CAFÉ BAR & CINEMA INTERNATIONAL. CE JOANNIDES (sign partially hidden by trees).
4  Sign in Hebrew: CAFÉ.                                    כתובת: קפה

■ **MOLEDET [072]** - BETAR
Assemblage of Betar Youth, including children and young people in dark shirts and striped neckerchiefs (56').

■ **MOLEDET [073]** - OPHIR MOVIE THEATRE
Construction of Ophir movie theatre in Tel Aviv (30.5').

■ **MOLEDET [074]** - TEL AVIV STREETS
Herzl Street and Rothschild Boulevard in Tel Aviv, including the train passing (50').

■ **MOLEDET [075]** - MACCABI'S 25TH ANNIVERSARY
In honour of 25 years of Maccabi sports organisation, there is a large display of young men and women exercising in an outdoor stadium (95').

■ **MOLEDET [076]** - LEVANT FAIR
Scenes in the Levant Fair (94').

1  Group of children near entrance to fairgrounds.
2  Shots of exteriors of booths.
3  Building with sign in English and illegible Hebrew and Arabic: PALESTINE POTASH.
4  Several buildings with illegible signs.
5  Building with sign: Romania.
6  Building with sign: Polski Pawilok.
7  Outdoor café. Tables with umbrellas. Sign: Tnuvah Refreshments.
8  Exterior of exhibit with sign in English: BRITISH THOMSON HOUSTON.

■ **MOLEDET [077]** - DIZENGOFF WAVES FAREWELL
See **MOLEDET [015]**.

■ **MOLEDET [078]** - ARAB RIOT VICTIMS' MEMORIAL
Memorial on the mass grave of victims of riots in Tel Aviv in 1921 (56.5').

1  View of cemetery in Tel Aviv with writing superimposed on picture: THE WAY OF ALL FLESH.
2  Pan of cemetery with Hebrew words superimposed on picture: COMMUNAL GRAVE FOR THE MARTYRS OF 1921.     1921 כתובת: קבר אחים - קדושי
3  Assorted speakers by monument.

■ **MOLEDET [079]** - SHAVUOT CELEBRATIONS
Shavuot celebration, including children dancing in a public park and tables laden with first fruits (100').

1  Children dancing in public park, shot from above.
2  Long tables covered with white cloths and baskets of fruits, chickens.
3  Small children dressed in white, dancing (mid).

■ **MOLEDET [080]** - HORSE RACE
A horse race mainly in long shot, ending with a mid shot of winning riders and their horses (138').

■ **MOLEDET [081]** - THE HEFER VALLEY
Pan of houses and tents in Hefer Valley. Two women and one man washing clothes in metal tubs, smiling (19').

■ **MOLEDET [082]** - MACCABI GAMES
Scenes from the opening of the Maccabi sports games in Tel Aviv in 1928 (214').

1  Young man runs up to jump over pole. Knocks it down.
2  Pan of crowd in outdoor stadium. Young men and women dressed in white, demonstrating exercises and marching in time to music. Band playing.
3  Motorcycles leading parade down street in Tel Aviv.
4  Car full of young men and women dressed in white, with Hebrew sign on front: OUR FUTURE!.     שלט: עתידנו!
5  Men in white suits marching down street. Split-screen with each side showing procession from different angles.

## 18   Moledet Productions

6   Men and women marching down street. Policeman moves crowd to side.
7   Pan of crowd seated in stadium.

■ **MOLEDET [083]** - MACCABI
Scenes from the Maccabi games in 1928 (150').

1   Participants in the Maccabi games, men and women dressed in white marching on the field of an outdoor stadium.
2   Their marching feet (mid).
3   Motorcycles drive by.
4   Men shot-putting. Young women tossing metal ball.
5   Parade on field. Man with camera in foreground.
6   Pan of participants lined up. Pan of trophies on table.
7   Men running a race. Winner panting, being congratulated.
8   Dignitaries walking through crowd.

■ **MOLEDET [084]** - STREET SCENES
A band on Rothschild Boulevard in Tel Aviv. A competition of motorcycle and bicycle acrobatics on Allenby Street. A procession down a crowded street (282').

1   Uniformed band playing outdoors, crowd listening.
2   Upward pan to street, crowds listening.
3   Band marching down Rothschild Boulevard. Small group in Purim costume dancing hora among watching crowd.
4   Motorcycles riding towards camera on Allenby Street.
5   Acrobatics on motorcycles and bicycles.
6   Procession on crowded street including a cart with a sign in Hebrew: "Fechter and Hoffman, established 1911, winner of three gold medallions at the Government Exhibition, Haifa, 1927".

בית חרושת פחטר והופמן תל אביב נוסד ב-1911. קבל 3 מדליות הזהב בתערוכה הממשלתית בחיפה 1927.

7   People climbing into a wagon.

■ **MOLEDET [085]** - SHAVUOT
Shavuot celebrations at the Maccabi stadium (333').

1   Young girls in sailor shirts dancing, forming a human pyramid.
2   Two young girls dancing with tambourines in front of children in costumes.
3   Procession of many children in white, bringing first fruits, in large outdoor stadium.
4   Platform in middle of stadium with large national flag and banners blowing in the wind. Children march to platform (long, mid).
5   Elderly man escorted to platform by young men. Reads from book held close to his face. Escorted back to his seat in the stand.
6   Children passing first fruits to platform (long, mid).

■ **MOLEDET [086]** - FILM STAR VISITS ISRAEL
See **MOLEDET [016]**.

■ **MOLEDET [087]** - BEAUTY QUEEN
Sue Gottlieb, Tag beauty contest winner from New York and entourage, with Dizengoff and entourage. Walking into Tziona Tagar exhibit. Posing for the camera while talking and laughing in the garden (50').

■ **MOLEDET [088]** - OPENING OF GREAT SYNAGOGUE IN TEL AVIV
Opening of Great Synagogue in Tel Aviv, showing large crowd outside (226').

1  Exterior pan of building showing large crowd gathered with national flag.
2  Assorted shots of interior including ark, women's gallery.
3  Exterior of synagogue. Orchestra playing. Dignitaries walking up to synagogue. Man removes top hat.
4  Procession of men carrying Torah scrolls, shot from above.
5  Policemen pushing back thronging crowd, shot from above.
6  Pan of men holding Torah scrolls (mid).
7  Assorted shots of crowd pushing to get into doors, woman wanting to enter their door.

■ **MOLEDET [089]** - PANORAMA OF TEL AVIV
Excellent pan of Tel Aviv from a rooftop, including the Great Synagogue (34.5').

■ **MOLEDET [090]** - HERZL STREET
Herzl Street, near train tracks. Includes pedestrians, shot from moving car (4').

■ **MOLEDET [091]** - TEL AVIV STREETS
Shots of assorted streets in Tel Aviv, including Herzl Street with train barriers opening and a street in the rain shot from a moving vehicle (49.5').

■ **MOLEDET [092]** - COMIC SOCCER EXHIBITION
A comic soccer exhibition in honour of Purim, including a judge in top hat on a donkey, a goalkeeper dressed as a young Hassid, players collapsing exhausted on the field and a potato sack race (45').

■ **MOLEDET [093]** - ADVERTISEMENT FOR KILLARNEY MILK
Advertisement for Killarney milk (128').

1  Picture of an animated cow. Hebrew letters appear on her to spell "Killarney".
2  TITLE IN HEBREW: DRINK ONLY MY MILK. IT IS CLEAN FROM ALL IMPURITIES. I AM HEALTHY AND BEAUTIFUL.

שתו רק את החלב שלי! הוא נקי מכל תערבת זרה! הנני בריאה ויפה!

3  Picture of cow with milk coming from udders.
4  Can of evaporated milk with English letters: KILLARNEY.
5  Pan of building with sign: in Hebrew, English and Arabic: TRADING HOUSE: PALESTINE. SALES ROOM. Pedestrians and cyclists pass by.

מחלקת המכירה.

■ **MOLEDET [094]** - PURIM CELEBRATIONS
Purim celebrations in a kindergarten (174').

1  Children in costumes by table.
2  Chubby little girls in tutus dance around little girl dressed as Queen Esther. Close-up of queen smiling.
3  Pan of more smiling children in costumes. Schoolyard with dancing children and parents watching.
4  Man in top of tree.
5  Two little boys in fake beards, hats, black coats, shake hands.

■ **MOLEDET [095]** - PURIM FROM A ROOFTOP
Pan of parade on Shderot Rothschild and rooftops in Tel Aviv, on Purim. Small group of men in overcoats dancing hora on a rooftop (84.5').

■ **MOLEDET [096]** - BAT'A IN ISRAEL
Advertisement for Bat'a shoe shop in Tel Aviv (112').

1. Propeller plane landing. Name on plane: BAT'A.
2. Man leaves plane. Door blows shut in his face. He reopens door and is greeted by several men.
3. Narrow shop-lined street scene in Tel Aviv.
4. Man entering car at airport.
5. Exterior of shop with sign in Hebrew, English and Arabic: BAT'A.

שלט: באטה

### ■ MOLEDET [097] - PURIM
Purim celebrations in Tel Aviv (155').

1. Pan of comic soccer team in costumes.
2. Little children in costume and parents in procession down crowded street.
3. Men in uniform marching.
4. Cyclists superimposed onto men.
5. Umbrella shop with sign in Hebrew and English: ROSENBERG UMBRELLA FACTORY.
6. Floats, large mask, seen through crowd, policeman on horse down tree-lined street, Yemenite float.
7. Procession shot from above. Sign in Hebrew: Jews from Caucasus.
8. Women in uniform on horseback.

### ■ MOLEDET [098] - AGADATI'S STUDIO
A group of women in traditional oriental dress in Agadati's Studio. Two women perform Yemenite dance while others clap. Women smile, laugh and clown for camera (58.5').

### ■ MOLEDET [099] - GRANDFATHER'S VILLAGE
Yerushalayim Segal's father teaching his grandson Torah, including scenes in the grandfather's village (82').

1. Grandfather Segal with long white beard and grandson, both wearing skullcaps. Reading from a holy book.
2. Close-up of text: Deuteronomy 26 (in Hebrew).
3. Pan of village with houses and trees, dissolves.
4. Banana trees.
5. Boy walking through bushes: shot dissolves into boy playing with water hose.

### ■ MOLEDET [100] - GRAPE HARVEST
Assorted shots of people harvesting grapes and pan of vineyard with hillside in background (68').

### ■ MOLEDET [101] - BASKET OF ORANGES
Little girl, with bow in her hair, playing with oranges in basket. Then eating one (33').

### ■ MOLEDET [102] - SOCCER
Soccer team and game on soccer field (106.5').

1. Feet of soccer players.
2. Pan of smiling faces of soccer team and supporters.
3. Long shot of game on soccer field.

### ■ MOLEDET [103] - HOME MOVIES
Nathan Axelrod and Alexander Penn, with Bella and Sioma, in the yard of the laboratory (37').

■ **MOLEDET [104]** - TEL AVIV STREET SCENES
Assorted street scenes in Tel Aviv (iris shots), including Neve Tzedek, Pagoda House, Kerem Teimanim and an Arab squatting and mixing cement in a bucket, as children watch (45').

■ **MOLEDET [105]** - PRI MAZON, NETANYA
Industrial fruit packing at Pri Mazon in Netanya (118').

1   Long shot of building with sign in English: PRI MAZON.  שלט: פרי מזון.
2   Interior, women sorting piles of fruit.
3   Woman stirring large vat full of fruit.
4   Industrial machinery pouring juice.
5   Women sorting fruit outdoors.
6   Women sorting and packing cucumbers.
7   Close-up of cans.
8   Woman eating cucumber (c.u.).
9   Men and women manufacturing cans.
10  Packing cans.
11  Stacks of cans.

■ **MOLEDET [106]** - DEPUTY COLONIAL MINISTER IN TEL AVIV
Dizengoff and the Deputy Colonial Minister descending the steps of the municipality in Tel Aviv with their entourage, including Israel Rokah, Shoshana Persitz (44.5').

■ **MOLEDET [107]** - ZEBULUN VALLEY TRAIN
The Valley Train and a propeller plane in the Zebulun Valley (59.5').

1   The Valley Train pulls into station.
2   Crowd boarding.
3   Riding in open horse-drawn wagon.
4   Propeller plane with sign in Hebrew, English and Arabic: PALESTINE AIRWAYS LIMITED.
5   The plane circling runway and taking off. Additional small plane on runway with English lettering: SU-ABS.
6   Train pulling into station. Arab in keffiyeh jumps on.

■ **MOLEDET [108]** - ZEBULUN VALLEY SCHOOLCHILDREN
Refinery storage tanks, children leaving school in the Zebulun Valley (54.5').

1   Pan of refinery storage tanks.
2   Exterior of school, children leaving.
3   Children of assorted ages walking down country road.

■ **MOLEDET [109]** - DEPUTY COLONIAL MINISTER IN MOTORCADE IN TEL AVIV
Motorcade on Tel Aviv street, spectators on side of road. Dizengoff sitting in back seat of open car. Arriving at the Municipality. Deputy Colonial Minister and man in safari hat gets out of his car and shakes hands (89').

■ **MOLEDET [110]** - NETANYA
Celebration of the founding of Netanya, including early shots of the tents on the beach (177').

□ PART A: VIEWS OF EARLY NETANYA
1   Tents on beach.
2   Mediterranean Sea. Fields. Cliffs along beach.

## 22  Moledet Productions

□ PART B: CELEBRATION TODAY
1   Two little boys on horseback waving at camera, pan of fields.
2   Crowd scenes with Arabs and Jews sitting around a table, posing for a group portrait.
3   Iris closing shot of tents on beach.
4   Portrait of distinguished-looking bearded man superimposed over a crowd of Arabs and Jews.
5   Pan of the crowd.
6   Open iris shot of group of people standing under welcome banner in Hebrew, decorated with Star of David, and same portrait of bearded man.
7   Group poses for camera, one man gets down on his knee.

■ MOLEDET [111] - FAMILY EATING ORANGES
Edited idyllic family scene around table laden with oranges in outdoor garden (possibly Rothschild Boulevard in Tel Aviv) (33').

1   Family sitting in garden around table (shot from above).
2   Dissolve to shot of family (mid).
3   Dissolve to close-up of oranges on table.
4   Dissolve back to smiling family faces.

■ MOLEDET [112] - LILIENBLUM STREET
Assorted shots of Lilienblum Street in Tel Aviv: mother and child walking down desolate street, buildings, man drives motorcycle through gate (18').

■ MOLEDET [113] - BEAUTY QUEEN DEPARTS BY TRAIN
Sue Gottlieb, Tag beauty queen from New York, departing by train to Egypt (53').

1   Sue Gottlieb smiles at camera (mid).
2   Gottlieb through train window, smiling, with admirers by her side.
3   Train pulls out of station. Passengers wave.
4   Young boys clown around for camera, with departing train in background.

■ MOLEDET [114] - FAMILIES SWIMMING
Group of families diving from a stone wall and swimming in Yarkon River. Fathers holding children in the water. Posing for the camera. Particularly lovely footage (53').

■ MOLEDET [115] - PARADE WITH TORAH SCROLL
Procession of marching band followed by gentlemen in suits carrying a Torah scroll, on the occasion of the opening of Balfouria building in Tel Aviv (24').

1   Marching band in uniform.
2   Marching with Torah scroll under chuppah (canopy) down crowded street.
3   Exterior of building on Allenby Street, at the corner of Ahad Ha'am Street.

■ MOLEDET [116] - ARAB CHILDREN
Crowded street. Group of little Arab boys, each wearing a fez, lined up (26').

■ MOLEDET [117] - CROWD IN WINTER
Tracking shot of crowd in winter clothes, everyone with a hat, lining the street. Faces looking at camera as it passes by (26').

■ MOLEDET [118] - TEL AVIV STREET
Street scene in summer in Tel Aviv (32').

■ **MOLEDET [119], [122], [127], [133], [138]** - CHILDREN ON LINE FOR MOVIE
Crowd of children on street, lining up to see the film *Uncle Tom's Cabin* at the Ophir movie theatre.

□ PART A (9')
1  Crowd of children on the street, lining up to enter the film.

□ PART B (19')
1  Iris shot of poster in Hebrew and English, advertising the film *Uncle Tom's Cabin*.   פוסטר: אוהל הדוד תם.

□ PART C (32.5')
1  Crowds gathering (long, mid). Small children lining the Tel Aviv street.

□ PART D (16.5')
1  Poster in Hebrew and English advertising the film *Uncle Tom's Cabin*.

□ PART E (11')
1  Crowd of children entering the movie theatre, including a baby in a carriage.

■ **MOLEDET [120]** - SHAVUOT
Negative (on video) of Shavuot celebration (13').

■ **MOLEDET [121]** - PURIM
Purim procession including adorable children in costumes (25.5').

■ **MOLEDET [122]** - FILM POSTER
See **MOLEDET [119]**.

■ **MOLEDET [123]** - YAKHIN
Field with towers for electricity or telephone cables. Caterpillar tractor pulling farm implement in field at Yakhin (24').

■ **MOLEDET [124]** - YAKHIN
Man leaving communal shower building; man doing landscaping with revolving water sprinkler, at Yakhin (35').

1  Man walking out of wooden building with towel on his shoulder.
2  Exit of building with sign in Hebrew: MEN.
3  Man hoeing by building. Revolving water sprinkler in foreground.

■ **MOLEDET [125]** - PURIM PARADE · 1931
Purim parade, including large moving float of a castle with costumed guards (mid, 17').

■ **MOLEDET [126]** - ROWING BOAT
Two young men rowing a boat on a river (7').

■ **MOLEDET [127]** - CHILDREN ON LINE
See **MOLEDET [119]**.

■ **MOLEDET [128]** - SCHOOL CALISTHENICS AND BAND
Demonstration of calisthenics, firstly by young men, then by girls. Youth band (89').

1  Young men doing calisthenics, shot from above.

2  Girls doing calisthenics, shot from side and front, many wearing safari hats. White dresses mostly.
3  Youth band, close-up of some instruments.
4  Youngsters criss-cross marching in time to music.

■ **MOLEDET [129]** - GYMNASIA HERZLIYAH
Young people and teachers at Herzliyah Gymnasium. Pan of faces (mid) (59').

■ **MOLEDET [130]** - CHILDREN'S SHAVUOT PERFORMANCE
Little girls offering first fruits in a Shavuot dance in a public park, while parents and other children watch. Man in suit and straw hat directing the dance (97').

■ **MOLEDET [131]** - MORIAH
Two friends greeting each other in front of building with Hebrew sign: MORIAH. Group of unidentified young men and women pose for camera (19').

■ **MOLEDET [132]** - VOLLEYBALL
Young boys playing volleyball over ragged net with teacher watching (132').

■ **MOLEDET [133]** - WAITING ON LINE FOR MOVIE
See **MOLEDET [119]**.

■ **MOLEDET [134]** - CALISTHENICS AT SCHOOL
Outdoor calisthenics, young men, shot from above. Marching in formation, men and women. Interior shot of classroom (See also **MOLEDET [128]**) (47').

■ **MOLEDET [135]** - PEDESTRIANS
People walking on Tel Aviv street by gate, Arab women with heads covered (19.5').

■ **MOLEDET [136]** - HERZLIYAH GYMNASIUM
Group gathered in courtyard of Herzliyah Gymnasium, with Axelrod and older teacher in centre of shot (27').

■ **MOLEDET [137]** - IRRIGATION
Pan of young orchard. Ditch irrigation. Irrigation system is turned on (27').

■ **MOLEDET [138]** - CHILDREN WAITING ON LINE
See **MOLEDET [119]**.

■ **MOLEDET [139]** - GIRLS' CALISTHENICS
Girls doing calisthenics (mid) (see also **MOLEDET [128]**) (7').

Carmel Newsreels, Series I · 1935-1948

■ **CARMEL NEWSREEL I-001** · January 1935
Laying of the cornerstone for the Engineers' Association house (Beit Hamehandes) in Tel Aviv. Preparing the Bat Galim stadium for Maccabia games. A flood at Nahalat Yitzhak. Opening of the Migdalor Cinema in Tel Aviv. The 50th anniversary of the BILU settlement of Gedera.

☐ PART A: LAYING OF CORNERSTONE OF BEIT HAMEHANDES, TEL AVIV (142')
1  Building plans (long, 7).
2  Mayor Meir Dizengoff, Municipal Secretary Yehuda Nedivi and guests approaching the camera (long, 32).
3  High Commissioner Sir Arthur Wauchope sitting with Dizengoff (mid, 46).
4  Wauchope accompanied by Eliahu Epstein (rear view, mid, long, 66).
5  One of the engineers speaks (mid, 82).
6  Wauchope speaks. Pan to the audience, Rabbi Ben Zion Meir Chai Uziel, Dizengoff (mid, 104).
7  The audience applauds (mid, 110).
8  Laying of the cornerstone, spreading cement, Rabbi Uziel spreads cement (mid, 142).

☐ PART B: PREPARING THE MACCABIA (135')
1  Digging (mid, 6).
2  Preparing seats at the stadium (2 shots, long, 25).
3  Large dovecote (mid, 36).
4  Work on the scaffolding (mid, c.u., long, 91).
5  One of the directors of the Maccabia speaks (long, 104).
6  Maccabia directors pass next to the scaffolding (long, 121).
7  Two of the directors (mid, 135).

☐ PART C: FLOODS (51')
1  A hut in the water, a passer-by (long, 9).
2  Rescuing someone from the water (dissolve, long, 25).
3  A child standing in the water, near the huts (dissolve, pan, 37).
4  A bridge in Nahalat Yitzhak, the wadi full of water (long, 51).

☐ PART D: OPENING OF THE MIGDALOR CINEMA IN TEL AVIV (21')
1  The tower lit for the opening (mid, 2).
2  Dissolve to the tower (mid, tilt), downstairs, a sign in Hebrew, "Opening on Saturday Night" (long, 21). כרזה מוארת: מגדלור, הפתיחה במוצאי שבת.

☐ PART E: GEDERA 50TH ANNIVERSARY (151')
1  General view of Gedera (long, 10).
2  One of the huts of the BILU settlers (Leibovitz) (mid, 21).
3  The cemetery (long, 31).
4  Dissolve to Sverdloff's grave (c.u., 39).
5  Overview of the public (long, mid, 75).
6  Menachem Ussishkin, Moshe Smilansky, Meirovich sitting on stage (pan, mid, 87).
7  Ussishkin speaking (mid, 97).
8  Smilansky speaking (mid, 113).
9  Ussishkin speaking (Shaul Tchernichovsky in the audience) (mid, 124).
10 Dr Arthur Ruppin giving a speech (Tchernichovsky in the audience) (mid, 141).
11 The public applauds (mid, 151).

■ **CARMEL NEWSREEL I-002** · March 1935
Yisrael Amikam shows the new Hebrew telegram. The funeral of Zionist leader, Dr S Rosenbaum. Kamzon and the Lithuanian consul meet about the shipment of

films to Lithuania. The anniversary of the Fire Brigade on Rothschild Boulevard in Tel Aviv. The ship *Tel Aviv*, arriving for the first time at Haifa port. A parade of the Maccabi in Jerusalem. Prince Carl Gustav of Sweden visits the country. Visit of Mr Philips of Philips Electronics. A magician on Jaffa Street. Laying of the cornerstone of the Pri Mazon factory in Netanya. Building the Rimon Cinema in Tel Aviv. Preparations for the Adloyada Purim parade. The 10th anniversary of Herzliyah.

□ PART A: AMIKAM AND THE TELEGRAM (29')
1   Yisrael Amikam, who fought for writing telegrams in Hebrew letters, shows the telegram (mid, 21).
2   His wife joins him (mid, 29).

□ PART B: THE FUNERAL OF DR S ROSENBAUM (117')
1   Dr Rosenbaum standing on a balcony, next to a Lithuanian flag (dissolve, long, 11).
2   Rosenbaum (mid, 28).
3   The flag at half-mast (long, 37).
4   A crowd near the house (long, 46).
5   The funeral procession (long, 117).

□ PART C: MEETING WITH THE LITHUANIAN CONSUL (69')
1   The consul meeting with Ya'akov D Kamzon and another person, concerning shipment of films to Lithuania. Looking at magazines (mid, 28).
2   Kamzon saying goodbye to the consul (mid, 45).
3   The three leaving the house (long, 69).

□ PART D: THE FIRE BRIGADE'S ANNIVERSARY (47')
1   The firemen's commander (c.u., 6).
2   Officers shaking hands. Fire engines coming out of the fire brigade building on Rothschild Boulevard (long, 47).

□ PART E: THE SHIP *TEL AVIV* ARRIVING FOR THE FIRST TIME AT HAIFA (324')
1   The lobby and the synagogue of the ship (stills, 38).
2   The owner and his wife (mid, 45).
3   The deck with the Jewish flag (mid, 76).
4   Haifa Port - overview. The entrance to the port (long, 110).
5   The Jewish flag (mid, 120).
6   The name of the ship in Hebrew and English: TEL AVIV (mid, 126).
7   The bridge - the captain and the first officer (mid, 150).
8   The ship seen from the docks (155).
9   Long shot of ships from docks.
10  The dining room (stills, 166).
11  The third officer blowing a whistle (c.u., mid, 174).
12  Dancing hora on the deck (long, 192).
13  A ship comes into the port (long, 198).
14  The shipowner with the Mayor of Haifa, Hassan Bey Shukri (mid, 204).
15  The ship orchestra (long, 215).
16  Sailing boats on the water (long, 221).
17  A sailor flying a Jewish flag on board (long, 256).
18  The decorated ship approaching the quay (long, 260).
19  A ship near the docks (long, 266).
20  Guests boarding the ship (mid, long, 287).
21  Haifa District Commissioner Edward Keith-Roach with Mayor Hassan Shukri and others (long, 294).
22  Keith-Roach, the shipowner, the captain and a woman (mid, 324).

☐ PART F: THE MACCABI PARADE IN JERUSALEM (362')
1. Pan of rows of girls, rows of boys (long, 26).
2. Rows of young Maccabi children (long, 43).
3. One of the heads of the movement distributing something (long, 58).
4. Parade to the stadium (mid, long, 75).
5. Marching (102).
6. Young Maccabi children standing (mid, 116).
7. Flag-raising (long, 154).
8. Calisthenics performed.
9. The public applauds (long, 262).
10. Pan of stadium (301).
11. The Maccabi flag carried by participants (long, 324).
12. Heads of Maccabi and sports people marching in long lines (long, 362).

☐ PART G: THE HEIR TO THE SWEDISH THRONE VISITS THE COUNTRY (67')
1. Cars arriving at the Weizmann home in Rehovot (long, 10).
2. Prince Carl Gustav being received (26).
3. In the courtyard and the house (long, 35).
4. Cars near house (45).
5. Prince Carl Gustav and Weizmann come out of the house.
6. The prince gets into a car, then gets out to photograph Axelrod (long, 67).

☐ PART H: MR PHILIPS VISITS THE COUNTRY (146')
1. Mr Philips, Hayutman and the Dutch consul leave Hayutman's shop in Nahalat Benyamin, they enter a car (long, 85).
2. Near the Dutch consulate. Cars arrive, the men pause briefly for cameras. Philips walks into the courtyard (long, 123).
3. Coming out of the consulate. Philips and his wife wave goodbye (long, 146).

☐ PART I: STREET ART IN JAFFA (211')
1. A crowd of Arabs watching a magician (long, 211).

☐ PART J: LAYING OF THE CORNERSTONE OF THE PRI MAZON FACTORY IN NETANYA (178')
1. Sign in Hebrew: Pri-Mazon  שלט: פרי-מזון
2. Dissolve to camels loaded with bricks.
3. People celebrating (34).
4. The boss and his wife (mid, 44).
5. Mayor of Netanya Ovad Ben-Ami with guests (pan, mid, 72).
6. Speeches (long, 101).
7. Ben-Ami speaking (157).
8. Applause (178).

☐ PART K: CINEMA RIMON BUILDING, TEL AVIV (88')
1. A sign: "Cinema Rimon building" on the building frame (long, 16).

כותרת: בנין קולנוע רמון

2. Men working on the scaffolding (long).
3. Dissolve to a concrete mixer (mid).
4. Pan of building under construction (long, 88).

☐ PART L: PREPARATIONS FOR THE ADLOYADA, PURIM (100')
1. Making huge dolls out of papier-mâché (long, mid, 32).
2. Preparing a model building. German cannons with swastikas. Preparing various decorations (long, 78).
3. The Mugrabi Cinema, decorated with various posters for the Matateh Theatre Purim ball (long, 100).

□ PART M: THE TENTH ANNIVERSARY OF HERZLIYAH (169')
1  Decorated gate with welcome sign (mid, 5).
2  An overview of Herzliyah (long, 9).
3  The centre of festivities, the public gathering (mid, 28).
4  The Mayor gives a speech (mid, 48).
5  A rabbi gives a speech (mid, 69).
6  Horsemen galloping into Herzliyah (long, 90).
7  A representative of the Workers' Council making a speech (mid, 105).
8  Horsemen entering through a decorated gate (long, 144).
9  An overview of the crowd (long, 157).
10 The Mayor making a speech (mid, long, 169).

■ **CARMEL NEWSREEL I-003** · March 1935
According to Axelrod, this newsreel focussed on Purim and was removed, for use in CARMEL NEWSREEL I-075.

■ **CARMEL NEWSREEL I-004** · March 1935
Soccer match between Maccabi and Hapoel. Alexander Ziskind Rabinowitz. The funeral of Rabbi Shlomo Aharonson. A dog show in Tel Aviv.

□ PART A: A SOCCER MATCH BETWEEN MACCABI AND HAPOEL (222')
1  Playing in the stadium between Jaffa and Tel Aviv (long, 79).
2  The public applauds (mid, 102).
3  Public watching, people peeking through fence (long, 144).
4  Playing in the stadium (long, 222).

□ PART B: ALEXANDER ZISKIND RABINOWITZ (11')
1  Rabinowitz (c.u., 11).

□ PART C: RABBI AHARONSON'S FUNERAL (161')
1  The large procession walks down the street (long, 35).
2  Rabbi Ben Zion Meir Chai Uziel passing by.
3  The coffin and the mourners (mid, 64).
4  The crowd near the cemetery. Rabbi Uziel (mid, 101).
5  In the cemetery. Rabbi Avraham Kook eulogizes (long, 108).
6  The crowd (long, 161).

□ PART D: A DOG SHOW IN TEL AVIV (218')
1  A big dog and a small dog (mid, 21).
2  A woman and two dogs (mid, 33).
3  A woman holding a dog (mid, 39).
4  Dogs (mid, 86).
5  The judges (long, 99).
6  Dog training demonstration. A building in background with sign in Hebrew: Maccabi Union (long, 218).     כתוב על הבנין: הסתדרות המכבי.

■ **CARMEL NEWSREEL I-005** · April 1935
Reception for Mr Hill from the Rotary Club, at the Lawrence Coffee Shop, between Jaffa and Tel Aviv. The ship *Roma* arriving with new immigrants at Haifa port.

□ PART A: A RECEPTION FOR MR HILL FROM THE ROTARY CLUB, AT THE LAWRENCE CAFÉ BETWEEN JAFFA AND TEL AVIV (80')
1  The guests at the outdoor café, palm trees behind (long, 29).
2  Mr Hill (c.u., 35).
3  Mr Hill and others (c.u., mid, 55).
4  Pan of posed Rotary members (mid, 80).

□ PART B: THE SHIP *ROMA* ARRIVING AT HAIFA PORT CARRYING NEW IMMIGRANTS (164')
1  New immigrants coming down gangplank (mid, 28).
2  Flags decorating the ship (mid, 43).
3  Immigrants waving from the deck, the public responds from the quay (long, mid, 66).
4  The ship enters the port, trail of black smoke (long, 86).
5  Passengers descending gangplank (long, 99).
6  The ship, the captain, the immigrants (long, mid, 124).
7  Leaving the ship (mid, 131).
8  The ship (long, 139).
9  Haifa from the ship (long, 155).
10 Bringing down luggage and flags (long, 164).

■ CARMEL NEWSREEL I-006 · April-May 1935
The festive opening of the second Maccabia sports events at the stadium in Bat Galim, Haifa.

□ PART A: THE SECOND MACCABIA (358')
1  Going through the gate into the stadium (long, mid, 20).
2  Overview of the stadium with crowds (long, 58).
3  Procession of the Bulgarian delegation with marching band (long, 76).
4  The Yugoslavian delegation (long, 93).
5  Other delegations (long, 135).
6  The Polish delegation (long, 162).
7  A soccer match (long, 170).
8  The delegations at the stadium (mid, 201).
9  Water polo (mid, 215).
10 Massive delegation standing in formation doing gymnastics (mid, 277).
11 Walking in the stadium (mid, long, 295).
12 Swimming and high dive competition (mid, 324).
13 Soccer (long, 352).
14 Flags - Maccabia flag, national flag and British Palestinian flag (mid, 358).

□ PART B: THE SECOND MACCABIA (702')
1  Flags (long, 13).
2  Pan of the soccer players with the umpire (mid, 38).
3  Soccer match (long, 51).
4  Viscount Alfred Mond Melchett in the stands (mid, 57).
5  The match continues, Lord Melchett, pan of the public.
6  The heads of Maccabi arrive with Lord Melchett (mid, 134).
7  Parade of the delegations in the stadium (mid, 57).
8  The Danzig delegation (long, 176).
9  The South African delegation.
10 The Turkish delegation (long, 199).
11 Overview of the delegations (long, 211).
12 The French delegation (long, 216).
13 The Greek delegation (long, 247).
14 The Egyptian delegation (long, 255).
15 Lord Melchett speaks (long, mid, 280).
16 The delegations, Lord Melchett speaking, the public (long, 306).
17 The delegations passing next to the stage (long, 386).
18 Jellpeth making a speech (long, 393).
19 Gymnastics (mid, 399).
20 The British delegation and Lord Melchett saluting (mid, 428).
21 A crowd around the Bat Galim swimming pool (long, 442).
22 Diving, the public, the judges showing scores (mid, long, 525).

23  Gymnastics (mid, long, 571).
24  The funeral of a sportsman who died during the Maccabia, procession of fellow sportsmen (mid, 660).
25  The public at the stadium (long, 673).
26  The German delegation (long, 685).
27  Feet marching (mid, 702).

■ **CARMEL NEWSREEL I-007** · May 1935
The celebration of the 10th anniversary of the Hebrew University, at the amphitheatre on Mount Scopus.

□ PART A: CELEBRATION OF THE TENTH ANNIVERSARY OF THE HEBREW UNIVERSITY AT THE AMPHITHEATRE ON MOUNT SCOPUS (170')
1  The guests (pan, long, 11).
2  Dr Judah Magnes and others on the stage, the public (mid, long, 34).
3  The orchestra with conductor Carl Salomon, the public (long, 54).
4  Salomon (mid, 60).
5  Dr Weizmann giving a speech (mid, 77).
6  Orchestra and public (long, 83).
7  Nahum Sokolow giving a speech (long, mid, 125).
8  Menachem Ussishkin in the public, Sokolow still talking, the public applauds and sings the Hatikvah (long, mid, 170).

■ **CARMEL NEWSREEL I-008** · May-June 1935
The Hapoel sports events.

□ PART A: THE HAPOEL MEETING (542')
1  Flags on stage (mid, 12).
2  Marching to the stadium. Cameraman at side (long, 30).
3  Hapoel leader, Ya'akov Berger, giving directions (mid, 40).
4  The Magen David Adom team leading procession onto the stadium (long, 57).
5  A leader making a speech (mid, 65).
6  The delegates listening (mid, 75).
7  Delegations (Beit Alpha, Gvat, etc.) entering the stadium (mid, long, 184).
8  The Hapoel Orchestra (mid, 198).
9  Marching in the stadium (long, 228).
10  Women performing calisthenics (mid, 251).
11  Lord Melchett extends greetings (mid, 270).
12  Marching in the stadium (long, 302).
13  Horse riders come in. Behind them, the procession continues (mid, long, backwards, 376).
14  Running (backwards, mid, 388).
15  Throwing the javelin (backwards, long, 394).
16  Jumping (backwards, long, 419).
17  Calisthenics on the field (long, 425).
18  Shot-put, running (backwards, long, 450).
19  Running, shot-put, javelin throwing, gymnastics, dodge ball match (mid, long, 521).
20  Soccer teams passing by (long, 542).

□ PART B: THE HAPOEL MEETING (421')
1  Orchestra passing by, flag parade (mid, 24).
2  Calisthenics (long, 55).
3  Entering the stadium (mid, long, 147).
4  High-jump (backwards, mid, 154).
5  A teacher demonstrates an exercise, rows of people follow in calisthenics (long, mid, 212).

6  Long-jump, high-jump (long, 239).
7  Running, relay race (long, 325).
8  The winners; javelin throw, shot-put, high-jump (long, mid, 383).
9  Rowing competition on the Yarkon River with horses grazing on the banks (long, 421).

■ **CARMEL NEWSREEL I-009** · June-July 1935
The festivities in honour of Maimonides at his tomb in Tiberias. Laying the cornerstone of Kfar Maccabi at Haifa Bay, overlooking the Zebulun Valley.

☐ PART A: MAIMONIDES FESTIVITIES IN TIBERIAS (492')
1  The tomb of Maimonides in Tiberias, people praying (c.u., long, 15).
2  TITLE IN HEBREW: SOKOLOW (OF BLESSED MEMORY) AT MAIMONIDES' TOMB (c.u., 21). (He had visited the site and then died before the title was written.)
3  Nahum Sokolow arriving, sitting next to the tomb.
4  The site of the ceremony, the decorated and engraved entrance gate (mid, long, 55).
5  Other decorations (mid, 82).
6  The crowd on the square (long, 117).
7  Orchestra and parade, view of the Sea of Galilee (mid, long, 162).
8  The decorated gate lit up, the parade continues (mid, 200).
9  Menachem Ussishkin and Rabbi Ben Zion Meir Chai Uziel arrive (mid, 208).
10  The square once again (long, 244).
11  The Arab Mayor makes a speech, preceded by a woman speaking (mid, 244).
12  The public with background shot of gate and the Sea of Galilee (long, 27).
13  The Mayor talking (mid, 286).
14  Speeches, Sokolow on the stage (mid, 337).
15  A man in the crowd speaking.
16  The crowd near the tomb (long, 475).
17  The crowd on the square (mid, 487).
18  Sokolow speaks (mid, 492).

☐ PART B: LAYING THE CORNERSTONE OF KFAR MACCABI AT HAIFA BAY (90')
1  Members of Young Maccabi and guests climbing up the hill (long, 35).
2  Menachem Ussishkin and the heads of Maccabi. Ussishkin makes a speech. Two of the Maccabi people make a speech (mid, 62).
3  Overview of the Zebulun Valley (mid, 79).
4  Ussishkin makes a speech (mid, 90).

■ **CARMEL NEWSREEL I-010** · June-July 1935
An exhibition in honour of Chaim Nahman Bialik, one year after his death. Parade of British soldiers in honour of King George's Jubilee. Opening of King George Street in Tel Aviv.

☐ PART A: BIALIK EXHIBITION (ONE YEAR AFTER HIS DEATH) (447')
1  An exhibition hall, Bialik's statue (long, 48).
2  Iris shot of bust of Bialik's head (dissolve to a poster) (c.u., 78).
3  The cemetery, tilt to the tombstones (Nordau, Achad Ha'am, Bialik) (long, 109).
4  Writers carrying wreath to Bialik's grave (Barash).
5  Alexander Ziskind Rabinowitz talking (mid, 156).
6  Rabinowitz laying wreath, saying kaddish. Many tombstones in background (mid, 200).
7  Leaving the cemetery.
8  People passing by the grave on their way out (long, c.u., 237).

9   Entering the Bialik exhibition (long, 271).    שלט: תערוכת ביאליק
10  Exhibition of manuscripts (mid, 284).
11  Three posters in Hebrew:
    "Strengthen our culture, create a culture fund"
    "Hebrew culture creates the healthy instincts of the nation"
    "A culture fund, an eternal memorial for the nation's genius" (The Bialik Fund).

שלט: "בצרו את תרבותנו הקימו קרן לתרבות.", "התרבות העברית יוצרת את האינסטינקטים הבריאים של האומה.", "קרן התרבות זכרון נצח לגאון האומה."

12  Publishing companies which printed Bialik's books, by country, posters, press clippings (long, 372).
13  Bialik's beginnings (long, 396).
14  Manya, his wife (mid, 405).
15  Sitting at tables (long, 440).
16  Flag at half-mast (mid, 447).

□ PART B: KING GEORGE V JUBILEE (149')
1  Parade of soldiers wearing safari hats and uniforms (long, 60).
2  Parade of armoured vehicles (long, 96).
3  Soldiers on trucks, tanks behind them (long, 120).
4  Parade (long, 149).

□ PART C: OPENING OF KING GEORGE STREET (161')
1  Police officials, Eliahu Epstein in the background (mid, 47).
2  Decorating the gate and placing the ribbons (mid, 24).
3  Crowds on the roofs, the balconies and in the street.
4  The sign: King George V (c.u., 130).
5  The decorated gate. Axelrod's brother-in-law filming (long, 148).
6  British police orchestra and officers sitting at tables (mid, long, 98).
7  Planes fly over in formation (long, 121).
8  Mayor Meir Dizengoff comes out of the car and is received by officers, parade continues (long, 140).
9  Dizengoff waves to crowd. Cutting of the ribbons (long, 161).

■ **CARMEL NEWSREEL I-011** · Summer 1935
The inauguration of Kfar Summets. Demolition of the old Betar Club in Tel Aviv. Completion of the new Histadrut building, Brenner House in Tel Aviv, named in memory of Y C Brenner. Reburial of Rabbi Herzog. Rothschild Boulevard in Tel Aviv.

□ PART A: THE INAUGURATION OF KFAR SUMMETS (73')
1  Kfar Summets - barracks, guests (long, 36).
2  Eliahu Epstein and guests from South Africa. Moshe Shertock (Sharett) (mid, 73).

□ PART B: DEMOLITION OF THE OLD BETAR CLUB IN TEL AVIV (92')
1  Men working with picks at demolition of old inn (khan) (long, 70).
2  Plans of the new club (mid, 92).

□ PART C: COMPLETION OF BRENNER HOUSE IN TEL AVIV (59')

כתובת: בית ברנר

1  Work done on the electrical system (long, 35).
2  The Brenner House. Scaffolds on the new Brenner House (long, 59).

## Carmel Newsreels: Series 1

☐ PART D: REBURIAL OF RABBI HERZOG (46')
1 The Great Synagogue.
2 The funeral procession coming out.
3 Rabbi Ben Zion Meir Chai Uziel speaking (long, 46).

☐ PART E: THE "PARLIAMENT" ON ROTHSCHILD BOULEVARD (93')
1 People walking on Rothschild Boulevard.
2 Feet.
3 Men reading newspapers *Davar, Ha'aretz, Doar Hayom, Haboker, Hayarden*.
"דבר", "הארץ", "דואר היום", "הבוקר", "הירדן".
4 Men urinating, shot from behind.
5 A group of people talking.
6 Two religious men talking (93).

■ **CARMEL NEWSREEL I-012** · Lag Ba'omer 1935
Lag Ba'omer festivities in Meiron. Arabs from the Kadouri school at Tulkarm on a visit to the Mikveh Israel school. Sports day of all the schools in Jerusalem.

☐ PART A: LAG BA'OMER FESTIVITIES IN MEIRON (358')
1 The road from Safed to Meiron (long, 17).
2 Safed (long, 38).
3 Shimon Bar Yohai's Tomb. The crowd gathering (long, 76).
4 A procession arriving at Meiron by car and by foot (long, 105).
5 A look at the crowd through the gate (mid, long, 126).
6 A procession of people dancing with a Sephardic Torah scroll at the gate. Dancing on the square (mid, long, 210).
7 Dancing (long, mid, 234).
8 A woman and her family (mid, 242).
9 Overview of the dancers. A man on the shoulders of another (long, 290).
10 Mount Meiron, the camping area, the area in front of the tomb, people dancing (long, 346).
11 The entrance to Shimon Bar Yohai's cave (mid, long, 354).
12 Arabs watching from roofs (long, 358).

☐ PART B: KADOURI AGRICULTURAL SCHOOL STUDENTS ON A VISIT TO MIKVEH ISRAEL (120')
1 The Arab students from Tulkarm, going through the gate (long, 23).
2 The students going through the fields, other boys working in fields (mid, long, 74).
3 Explanations about the crops (mid, 91).
4 The avenue (long, 105).
5 The students coming down the avenue (long, 120).

☐ PART C: A SPORTS DAY OF ALL THE SCHOOLS IN JERUSALEM (201')
1 A parade of the schoolchildren (long, 55).
2 Overview of the stadium, long-jump (long, 79).
3 Jewish and Arab teachers (long, 97).
4 The spectators (long, 118).
5 Arab children watching (long, 135).
6 The dignitaries (long, 156).
7 Running (long, 176).
8 Long-jumps (long, 201).

■ **CARMEL NEWSREEL I-013** · Summer 1935
Building of Beilinson Hospital. 10th anniversary of *Davar* newspaper.

□ PART A: BUILDING OF A KUPAT HOLIM HOSPITAL (THE BEILINSON HOSPITAL) (120')
1   Mixing plaster (c.u., 15).
2   Working on the scaffolds, building a brick wall (mid, 58).
3   Building work (long, 120).

□ PART B: THE 10TH ANNIVERSARY OF THE *DAVAR* NEWSPAPER (MAY 31ST) (94')    כותרת על עיתון: דבר: עיתון פועלי ארץ ישראל
1   *Davar* headlines (c.u.).
2   Dan Pines, Yitzhak Yatsiv and another member of the staff (mid).
3   Berl Katznelson (mid).
4   Newspaper sellers coming out on Allenby Street (long).
5   Three oval framed shots of men at desks.
6   Men at clerk's desk.
7   Switchboard.
8   Shots of newspaper workers (94).

■ **CARMEL NEWSREEL I-014** · Summer 1935
Soccer game of Maccabi Avshalom playing against Greece. Inauguration of the King George V Park in Ramat Gan.

□ PART A: MACCABI AVSHALOM AGAINST GREECE (182')
1   Flags blowing, playing soccer (long, 80).
2   The flags, the spectators (mid, long, 96).
3   Both teams (mid, long, 153).
4   Soccer (long, 125).
5   Children watching through a hole in the fence (mid, 160).
6   The public at the gate (mid, 166).
7   A child passing under the fence. Soccer scenes. Boys watching game from top of tree. Pan of soccer teams with coaches (mid, 182).

□ PART B: INAUGURATION OF THE KING GEORGE V PARK IN RAMAT GAN (253')
1   Hanging the sign. Dignitaries (mid, 31).
2   The sign in Hebrew, Arabic and English: KING GEORGE V PARK (mid, 39).

שלט: גן מלך גורג'
3   Children entering the park, receiving bags. Kindergarten and schoolchildren entering the park (mid, long, 199).
4   A man in a top hat (mid, 215).
5   View of park, British flag and Jewish flag near the entrance (long, 233).
6   The view (long, 253).

■ **CARMEL NEWSREEL I-015** · June 1935
The celebration of Shavuot at the Tel Aviv stadium.

□ PART A: SHAVUOT 1935 IN TEL AVIV (63')
1   A page from the Bible (mid, 25).
2   A page from a calendar, June 7th (mid, 32).
3   A procession bringing fruit at the Tel Aviv stadium (long, 49).
4   A play, showing the walls of Jerusalem (mid, 63).

■ **CARMEL NEWSREEL I-016** · June 1935
The funeral of prominent Zionist leader, Shmaryahu Levin. Visit of High Commissioner Wauchope in Netanya. Laying of the cornerstone of the Habimah House in Tel Aviv (the ceremony was held a few days late due to the death of Shmaryahu Levin who was on the Honorary Board of Habimah).

□ PART A: SHMARYAHU LEVIN'S FUNERAL (72')
1   The public (long, 16).
2   The funeral procession (mid, 26).
3   The funeral continues (long, 72).

□ PART B: HIGH COMMISSIONER WAUCHOPE VISITS NETANYA (256')
1   Sir Arthur Wauchope planting a tree (mid, 24).
2   Driving on Herzl Street (long, 60).
3   Walking to the site (long, 82).
4   Wauchope and Ben-Ami walking, with crowd following (mid, 99).
5   Arriving at the planting site (long, 108).
6   Wauchope and Ben-Ami standing (mid, 115).
7   Ribbon cutting and the public applauds (long, 149).
8   The path between the hills and the sea.
9   The municipality building (long, 171).
10  Wauchope coming out of his car, greets crowd (mid, 181).
11  A banner across the road with Hebrew and English: "Welcome". People milling underneath (mid, long, 193).
12  Wauchope and Ben-Ami going through the crowd (mid, long, 205).
13  Speech, Wauchope standing by (mid, 217).
14  Wauchope making a speech (mid, 227).
15  Wauchope and his retinue coming out of the municipality building, which is bedecked in British and Jewish flags (long, 256).

□ PART C: LAYING OF THE CORNERSTONE OF THE HABIMAH THEATRE IN TEL AVIV (156')
1   Wauchope making a speech, Hanna Rovina standing by (mid, 9).
2   The cornerstone (c.u., 15).
3   Signing the charter: Wauchope, Mayor Dizengoff. Margot Klauzner standing in the back (mid, 24).
4   The orchestra (mid, 35).
5   Rovina, Wauchope and Moshe Shertok (Sharett). Wauchope sitting down between Dizengoff and Rovina. Margot Klauzner in the public.
6   Dizengoff and Wauchope sign the charter (mid, 138).
7   The charter (mid, 87).
8   Rovina reading (mid, 124).
9   The charter (c.u., 144).
10  Shertok puts the charter in its case (mid, 156).

■ **CARMEL NEWSREEL I-017** · June-July 1935
Hapoel sports events on the Tel Aviv beach. Chess game - one plays against thirty. The Maccabi team with the trophy which was won in Beirut. Fire at the Ideal factory. Mayor Meir Dizengoff and Menachem Ussishkin going abroad.

□ PART A: HAPOEL MEMBERS AT THE TEL AVIV BEACH (170')
1   Large group of people in bathing suits. The leader orders the group to stand at attention (c.u., 3).
2   The group stands at attention (pan, long, 29).
3   Children running together (long, 48).
4   Women running (mid, 54).
5   Volleyball match (long, 88).
6   Long-jump and saw-horse vault (long, 115).
7   High-jump (mid, 135).
8   Shot-put (c.u., mid, 153).
9   Naked baby and his mother in the water (mid, 170).

□ PART B: CHESS GAME - ONE AGAINST THIRTY (67')
1   The tables of the players, one player walking from table to table (long, 224).
2   One player (c.u., 32). Dissolve to a chess board.
3   Playing chess (c.u., 67).

□ PART C: MACCABI WITH THE CUP THEY WON IN BEIRUT (74')
1   The team running into the stadium (mid, 10).
2   The team with the cup (on it, a ball and a cap) (pan, mid, 42).
3   The cup on a table (tilt down, c.u., 63).
4   The engraving on the table (c.u., 74).

□ PART D: AFTER THE FIRE AT THE IDEAL FACTORY (82')
1   Pan of the ruins of the factory (mid, 59).
2   The smoking ruins of the factory (long, 82).

□ PART E: DIZENGOFF AND USSISHKIN GOING ABROAD (117')
1   Menachem Ussishkin and his wife embarking (mid, 16).
2   Ussishkin and his wife on the deck (mid, 27).
3   Ussishkin and Meir Dizengoff talking (mid, 37).
4   Pan of the crowd on board and the musicians playing the anthem (mid, 58).
5   People standing on the deck and watching, the sea (mid, 82).
6   Ussishkin and Dizengoff on board (pan, mid, 107).
7   The ship smokestack blowing steam, siren (mid, 117).

■ **CARMEL NEWSREEL I-018** · July 1935
Soccer match of Maccabi Hapoel. High Commissioner Wauchope visits Mikveh Israel. Riding motorbikes in the Jordan Valley and in the Galilee.

□ PART A: SOCCER - MACCABI HAPOEL (89')
1   The match (long, 11).
2   Two of the players take command of the ball (long, 19).
3   The match, the public (long, 89).

□ PART B: HIGH COMMISSIONER WAUCHOPE VISITS MIKVEH ISRAEL (121')
1   Sir Arthur Wauchope and his entourage receive explanations about Mikveh Israel (mid, 68).
2   Wauchope and his entourage standing (mid, 81).
3   Tour of the chicken coop. Ribbon waiting to be cut.
4   Entourage walking through grounds. Wauchope enters his car (long, 88).
5   Receiving explanations next to the buildings (mid, 106).
6   Passing near the camera (mid, 121).

□ PART C: RIDING MOTORBIKES IN THE JORDAN VALLEY AND THE GALILEE (932')
1   The bikes leave Tel Aviv, near the Municipality.
2   The bikes on the road (dolly, mid, 53).
3   The bikes (c.u., 75).
4   Overview of the bikes on the mountain road (long, 100).
5   The countryside around Tulkarm-Nablus (long, 146).
6   The bikes in motion (mid, 161).
7   The bikes climbing mountains (mid, long, 240).
8   The bikes, Lea Axelrod filming. Close-up of bike, motor, revving an engine (long, 263).
9   The monastery on Mount Tabor, the group with a monk (mid, 279).
10  The view from Mount Tabor, a hike to the top (long, 304).
11  The bikes going down Mount Tabor (long, 352).
12  The bikers travelling at night (long, 405).

13  The bikes on the mountain road (long, 471).
14  The bikes (mid, 495).
15  Travelling in the mountains (filmed from a car, long, 546).
16  Travelling in the mountains (long, 555).
17  A road in the Galilee, two donkeys and a horse (long, 560).
18  Filming the bikes from a car (dolly, long, 615).
19  The bikes in the mountains (701).
20  Arab villages in the Galilee (long, 742).
21  The mountains of the Galilee (long, 777).
22  The road itself (dolly, long, 813).
23  The Jordan Valley, the bikes climbing (long, 840).
24  The map of the country, with the route of the trip mapped out (long, 932).

■ **CARMEL NEWSREEL I-019** · July 1935
Laying sewer pipes in the sea at Jaffa. Ceremony of the cornerstone laying for the new building of the General Zionist Club in Tel Aviv. A visit to the religious scouts camp near Rehovot, including unique footage of teenagers praying.

□ PART A: BUILDING THE SEWERS IN JAFFA (399')
1  Laying sewer pipes in the sea in Jaffa (long, mid, 82).
2  Elevator with columns (mid, 110).
3  A workman pulling a rope (c.u., 115).
4  A column going into the water (mid, 134).
5  The concrete column sliding into the water (c.u.). A hand working the pump (mid, 155).
6  Winding up the rope as a weight is descending (mid, long, 179).
7  The weight hits the column (mid, 190).
8  The dock, the works and the sea (long, 213).
9  The dock, with Jaffa in background (240).
10  Pulling on chains to lower the pipe into the sea (mid, 372).
11  Shots of men through the pipe. Waves, Jaffa seen from the sea, waves flowing over the pipe (392).
12  Placing concrete columns in the sea (long, 399).

□ PART B: LAYING THE CORNERSTONE OF THE GENERAL ZIONIST CLUB IN TEL AVIV (87')
1  Crowd gathering (long, 18).
2  Pan of small group standing. The third on the right is the paediatrician, Dr Dov Gurevitz (mid, 33).
3  Speech (mid, 43).
4  The crowd, the scaffolding (long, 63).
5  Two elderly men pour concrete on the cornerstone and greet each other (87).

□ PART C: THE RELIGIOUS SCOUTS AT THEIR CAMP NEAR REHOVOT (288')
1  Grove of trees near Rehovot, dissolve to a guard passing by the tents (long, 43).
2  Pan of children sleeping in a tent (long, 58).
3  The guard looks at his watch, the bugle is blown (mid, 90).
4  The children leaving the tents (mid, long, 105).
5  Washing and brushing teeth (long, 130).
6  Sitting in a circle and praying, wearing prayer shawls and phylacteries (long, 140).
7  Religious scouts praying, close-up of cantor. Girls praying separately (long, 155).
8  Standing in prayer (225).
9  Boys and girls cooking (long, 230).
10  Bringing food and serving it (mid, long, 244).

11  Children eating (mid, long, 258).
12  A man blowing a whistle and a young man beating a drum (mid, 276).
13  The flag is raised. The scouts stand at attention (long, 288).

■ **CARMEL NEWSREEL I-020** · Summer 1935
Laying the cornerstone of the Max Fein Vocational School. Building the Tel Ephraim neighbourhood in Pardess Katz. Swimming competition of Maccabi in Tel Aviv. A storm over the Mediterranean Sea.

□ PART A: LAYING THE CORNERSTONE OF THE MAX FEIN VOCATIONAL SCHOOL (111')
1  The seated crowd (long, 17).
2  Table of honour. Speech. Rabbi Ben Zion Meir Chai Uziel, on the side (mid, 44).
3  Guests and students (long, 61).
4  High Commissioner, Sir Arthur Wauchope, gives a speech (mid).
5  Israel Marminsky (Executive Secretary of the Histadrut) speaking (mid).
6  Wauchope signing a document (c.u., mid).
7  A crowd (long, 111).

□ PART B: BUILDING THE TEL EPHRAIM NEIGHBOURHOOD IN PARDESS KATZ (93')
1  An orchard (long, 3).
2  The first house (long, 17).
3  A street with small houses. Construction work (long, 56).
4  An overview of the orchard (long, 63).
5  A steam roller driving onto a road (mid, long, 76).
6  An overview of the orchard (long, 80).
7  Stonework for the road, working on the road (93).

□ PART C: MACCABI AT THE TEL AVIV SWIMMING POOL (200')
1  Water polo game (long, 38).
2  Large group of boys jump into water and swim towards the camera.
3  Swimming competition, Australian crawl (long, 87).
4  Girls diving into pool. Swimming competition, breast-stroke (mid, long, 131).
5  Five boys diving into the pool (175).
6  Divers seen beneath the water (mid, 200).

□ PART D: STORMY SEA (65')
1  An overview of the stormy sea (long, 11).
2  Black flag, bathing dangerous (c.u., 19).
3  An overview of the sea in the direction of Jaffa (long, 43).
4  An overview of the waves, with boats rocking back and forth (long, 65).

■ **CARMEL NEWSREEL I-021** · Summer 1935
Opening of the room in memory of Theodor Herzl at the Jewish Agency building in Jerusalem. A holiday for the worker and his family. Elections for the 19th Zionist Congress in Lucerne. The first anniversary of the death of Chaim Nahman Bialik. Young Judea summer camp.

□ PART A: OPENING OF THE HERZL ROOM AT THE JEWISH AGENCY BUILDING IN JERUSALEM (177')
1  Rabbi Meir Berlin (Bar Ilan) giving a speech, the crowd listening (mid-long, 40).
2  The entrance to the Jewish National Fund - Jewish Agency building, with a banner: IF YOU WILL IT, IT IS NO DREAM (mid, 52).

כתובת: אם תרצו אין זו אגדה.

3  Pan of VIPs on balcony with view of city behind them. Crowd listening.
4  The Herzl Room, dissolve with portraits of Herzl's family (mid, 177).

☐ PART B: HOLIDAY FOR THE WORKER (56')
1  Speeches (mid, 29).
2  A crowd raising a flag (long, 42).
3  Young child working with a spade and adults join in (mid, long, 56).

☐ PART C: ELECTIONS TO THE 19TH ZIONIST CONGRESS (162')
1  Poster - Israel Workers Party - on a taxi (mid, 77).

שלט: רשימת פועלי ארץ ישראל

2  General Zionists party poster hanging on a house. Posters on "walking" billboards (mid, 96).
3  "Away with the profiteering, choose list A" (c.u., 105).

כרזה: הלאה הספסרות, בחר א'.

4  Poster about List B (c.u., 111).
5  Poster of List C, the Hebrew State Party (Grossman) (c.u., 118).
6  List F, Torah V'Avodah, Hapoel Hamizrachi (c.u., 126).
7  List G, The General Zionists (c.u., 131).
8  Menachem Ussishkin's List (c.u., 137).
9  A building with a poster. The building of the polls (long, 145).
10 Distributing leaflets near the polling station (mid, 162).

☐ PART D: ONE YEAR ANNIVERSARY OF BIALIK'S DEATH (163')
1  Pan on home of Bialik (long, 34).
2  Scouts' parade (long, 82).
3  Scouts departing and writers entering (long, 120).
4  Scouts line the entrance to the cemetery. They get pushed out of the way as the official procession arrives.
5  Young people follow camera at entrance to Bialik home.
6  A crowd at the cemetery (long, 134).
7  Near the grave (mid, long).
8  Writers, amongst them Alexander Ziskind Rabinowitz (bearded), at the cemetery (mid). Crowd (long, 163).

☐ PART E: SUMMERCAMP OF THE YOUNG JUDEA IN TEL AVIV (382')
1  The beach. Children entering the water (Mayor Rokah in the background) (long, 47).
2  Children exercising (mid, long, 74).
3  Children playing in the sand (c.u., mid, long, 123).
4  Serving food (mid, long, 132).
5  Sitting at the table and eating (mid, long, 203).
6  Pan across indoor dining room with windows open to the view.
7  Games, embroidery (c.u., mid, 257).
8  Playing ping-pong (mid, 268).
9  Basket weaving. Woodwork (mid, 309).
10 Rest, napping (mid, long, 382).

■ **CARMEL NEWSREEL I-022** · Summer 1935
Summer camp for schoolchildren in Tel Aviv. Scouts' camp in Ben Shemen, including re-enactment of "capture the flag" game.

☐ PART A: SUMMER CAMPS FOR SCHOOLCHILDREN IN TEL AVIV (185')
1  Masses of children running on the beach (long, 45).
2  Close-up of dozens of adorable faces of children passing by in pairs. Background (mid, long, 87).

42    Carmel Newsreels: Series 1

3   Many children jumping in front of the camera (long, 100).
4   Children playing in the water (mid, long, 107).
5   A little girl (mid, 114).
6   Children jumping in front of the camera under shower head. Children crowd around an outdoor shower (mid, 122).
7   Pan of all the people on the beach and in the water (long, 156).
8   Children on buses wave as buses pull away (long, 185).

□ PART B: SCOUTS' CAMP IN BEN SHEMEN (505')
1   A pan of the scouts' camp with tents (long, 27).
2   The scouts sneak into camp and then run into the woods.
3   Evening assembly. Playing "capture the flag". Lowering the flag. Children sleeping in tents.
4   Dramatised segment: playing "capture the flag".
5   Rival scouts sneaking into the camp and talking and leaving the camp. A scout guarding the flag, rival scouts sneaking behind.
6   A blanket is thrown on the guard's head. A child steals the flag and runs away. The guard blows his whistle (mid, long, 360).
7   The chief asks the scouts to save the flag. Masses of children run (378).
8   The children fight to take the flag back from their rivals and win (long, 430).
9   Bugle and assembly. All the scouts run from assembly (long, 468).
10  The children come back victorious, with boy holding flag carried on another's shoulder (long, 505).

■ **CARMEL NEWSREEL I-023** · August 1935
Labour youth council. Street scenes of the city of Jaffa. The aftermath of a fire in Nahalat Yitzhak. A religious school in the Yemenite neighbourhood of Kerem HaTeimanim in Tel Aviv. Digging for water at Kibbutz Na'an.

□ PART A: HANOAR HA'OVED YOUTH MOVEMENT IN KIBBUTZ NA'AN (101')
1   A group walking in the Na'an paths (long, 43).
2   The interior of a building (long, 52).
3   Iris shot opens on large meeting of young people listening to a lecture (c.u., long, 98).
4   Children seated at desks (long, 101).

□ PART B: WHAT'S HAPPENING IN JAFFA (99')
1   Pan of a street in Jaffa, with assorted types of people (Jerusalem Avenue) (mid, 8).
2   A samovar. Preparing coffee. Cutting shwarma (c.u., 21).
3   A cafeteria (mid, 27).
4   An Arab selling drinks on the pavement (mid, 35).
5   The entrance to the Governor's office. A cart selling petrol passing by (long, 63).
6   Scribes near the governor's offices (Arabs wearing fezzes).
7   Overview of a street with peddlers (long, 82).
8   A coach station (long, 82).
9   "Tamarhindi" (drink sold from an urn on a peddler's back) peddler (mid, 99).

□ PART C: NAHALAT YITZHAK AFTER A FIRE (61')
1   Pan on the remains of the fire. A policeman. Sprinkling water (long, 48).
2   Activating a fire engine. A crowd watching (mid, 61).

□ PART D: YEMENITE JEWISH NEIGHBOURHOOD IN TEL AVIV (75')
1   General view of neighbourhood, Kerem HaTeimanim (long, 20).
2   Exterior of religious school (pan, mid, c.u., 54).
3   Little children studying religious text.

4   Close-up of child rocking back and forth as he studies.
5   Interior of school. Assorted shots of students learning (mid, 75).

□ PART E: FINDING WATER IN KIBBUTZ NA'AN (116')
1   Working near a well. Drilling (mid, c.u., 74).
2   Connecting the pump.
3   General view of the orchards of Na'an (long, 116).

■ **CARMEL NEWSREEL I-024** · August 1935
Opening of Old Age Home in Tel Aviv. Procession for Saudi Arabian Crown Prince in Jerusalem, including wonderful views of crowds at Jerusalem railway station and the surrounding streets. Gathering of Young Maccabi youth movement in Zichron Ya'akov. Caricatures of the delegates to the 19th Zionist Congress in Lucerne. Elections for the founding congress of the New Zionist Organization in Tel Aviv, including street scenes of Tel Aviv.

□ PART A: OPENING OF OLD AGE HOME IN TEL AVIV (246')
1   Exterior on Allenby Street (long, 10).
2   Party in the courtyard. Elderly woman (mid, c.u., 37).
3   Guests enter building. Elderly people sit down (pan, mid, 77).
4   Elderly entering the home. The home from the street (long, 129).
5   Elderly toasting, seated separately at tables (pan, c.u., long, 246). Man carrying large challah, toothless woman laughing.

□ PART B: RECEPTION FOR SAUDI ARABIAN CROWN PRINCE FAISAL (188')
1   Meeting place in Jerusalem. Massive crowds waiting (pan, long, 49).
2   British army marching band, with King David Hotel in background, followed by marching soldiers outside railway station (long, 81).
3   Massive crowd of Arabs, with procession of cars and men on horses (long, 91).
4   Arab crowd, street. Policeman directing traffic. Convoy passing (long, 188).

□ PART C: GATHERING OF YOUNG MACCABI AT ZICHRON YA'AKOV (265')
1   General view of Maccabi Hatzair encampment (long, c.u., 29).
2   Line-up. Flag-raising. Bugle (mid, 79).
3   Marching in camp (mid, 120).
4   Sitting by tables, singing and clapping. Playing accordion (mid, 142).
5   Dancing hora. Accordion, horn and mandolin (mid, c.u., 180). Tents in background.
6   Eating, bringing cups out of kitchen (mid, 242).
7   Dancing hora with musical accompaniment (mid, 265).

□ PART D: 19TH ZIONIST CONGRESS IN LUCERNE (28')
1   Caricatures of delegates to the congress (28).

□ PART E: ELECTIONS FOR THE FOUNDING CONGRESS OF THE NEW ZIONIST ORGANIZATION (144')
1   Sign on front of car in Hebrew: "Today, Elections for the Founding Congress of the New Zionist Organization. Go to vote". Sign on back of car: "Fulfill your obligation. Go and vote".

שלט: על מכונית: יהודי לאומן. היום, הבחירות לקונגרס היסוד ההסתדרות הציונית החדשה. לך לקלפי.

2   Flag on building. Placards on wall. Wonderful street scene in Tel Aviv with sleeveless workmen on first floor roof, crowds in the streets. Paper flyers flying through the air. Mid-shots of people on street looking at the camera.
3   Older man in uniform holding large flag. Ballot box.

4   Cross-section of population, waiting in long line to vote. Old man with beard, woman with large white scarf, man in fez, man in tie and hat, men in berets.
5   Men in caps, vests, safari hats. People with bicycles, children. Atmospheric sequence (144).

■ **CARMEL NEWSREEL I-025** · August 1935
Muslim celebration of Nebi Rubin Feast in Jaffa. Inauguration of the new Histadrut building in Tel Aviv, named in memory of Yosef Chaim Brenner.

▫ PART A: GATHERING FOR THE NEBI-RUBIN FEAST IN JAFFA (142')
1   General view of a street in Jaffa (long, 13).
2   Crowd gathers for the feast. Festive procession. Pan of the crowd, the houses and the mosque (long, mid, 69).
3   Dancing and singing (c.u., 83).
4   Procession passes among the crowd (long, 100).
5   Dancing and shaking hands among the crowd (c.u., 127).
6   Crowd celebrating in the street (long, 142).

▫ PART B: INAUGURATION OF BRENNER HOUSE IN TEL AVIV (218')
1   Building in construction, sign in Hebrew: BRENNER HOUSE (mid, 21).

שלט: בית ברנר

2   Completed building, people on the porch.
3   Cleaning the pavement (long, 45).
4   Deputy Mayor speaking. Leader of Tel Aviv Workers' Committee speaking (mid, 69).
5   Standing on the porch, workers' (red) flag in middle (mid, 75).
6   Plastering the outer walls (mid, 87).
7   Man speaking (mid, 99).
8   Cleaning around the building. More plastering (long, mid, 118).
9   The building and the porch (long, 132).
10  Pan of the sign in Hebrew: THE HISTADRUT.
11  Alexander Ziskind Rabinowitz and his wife, standing by the sign (mid, 142).
12  Crowd enters building. Sign on the building (mid, 183).
13  Sign in Hebrew: HISTADRUT - Y C BRENNER. Crowd on the porch.

שלט: הסתדרות - י.ח. ברנר

14  Sign in Hebrew: Inauguration of Brenner House (long, mid, 218).

שלט: פתיחת בית ע"ש י.ח. ברנר

■ **CARMEL NEWSREEL I-026** · August 1935
Tearing down shacks in the Maccabi neighbourhood. Sewage construction on Trumpeldor Street in Tel Aviv. Sights of Jerusalem. Traffic in Tel Aviv.

▫ PART A: TEARING DOWN SHACKS IN THE MACCABI NEIGHBOURHOOD (212')
1   Pan of partially destroyed shacks. British policeman by the ruins (pan, mid, 75).
2   A couple of inhabitants. Pan of their possessions (mid, 98).
3   Inhabitants among the ruins (pan, c.u., 143).
4   A baby in a crib. His mother next to him. Inhabitants' possessions (mid, c.u., 212).

▫ PART B: SEWAGE CONSTRUCTION IN TRUMPELDOR STREET IN TEL AVIV (117')
1   Digging trenches (mid, 12).
2   Pouring cement, laying pipes (mid, 60).
3   General views of the construction (long, 117).

## PART C: SIGHTS OF JERUSALEM (153')
1. Pan of the Jewish Agency building (long, 9).
2. Jeshurun Synagogue under construction (long, 12).
3. Streets of Jerusalem, dissolve to the YMCA tower, dissolve to Ben Yehuda Street, Zion Square, Jaffa Road (43).
4. YMCA entrance (long, 55).
5. Pan of a square in Jerusalem. Tilt, people in the street (mid, 76).
6. Man dumping dirt out of wheelbarrow (mid, 82).
7. Modern building (long, 96).
8. People coming out of the Old City (mid, 105).
9. Cement mixer by Jeshurun Synagogue, pouring cement (long, mid, 139).
10. King David Hotel (mid, 147).
11. Jewish Agency - Keren Kayemet Building (long, 153).

## PART D: TRAFFIC IN TEL AVIV (122')
1. A street in Tel Aviv, buses, cars, people (long, 28).
2. News-stand on the pavement, people passing (mid, 38).
3. Buses and bicycles on the road. People waiting for the bus (mid, 64).
4. On the pavement, waiting for the bus, getting on the bus (mid, 92).
5. Buses and cars on the street (long, 103).
6. By Magen David Adom Square, policeman directs traffic, buses and wagons pass (122).

# CARMEL NEWSREEL I-027 · August 1935
Funeral of Rabbi Avraham Kook, including footage of the Old City of Jerusalem. Relay race for the Elimelech Kuperstein Trophy. Concluding ceremonies at the Hapoel Children's Summer Camp in Tel Aviv. Sports in the Hapoel Camp in Ben Shemen.

## PART A: FUNERAL OF RABBI KOOK (384')
1. Poster announcing death of Rabbi Avraham Kook, with his picture. Additional mourning notices (mid, 17).  שלט: נפלה עטרת ראשונו
2. Massive crowds mourning in the streets of Jerusalem (long, 35).
3. Crowded balconies and roofs (long, 45).
4. Crowds of people, near the Old City Walls (long, 64).
5. Pan of streets of Jerusalem, empty of people. Near the Rabbinate. A crowd near Rabbi Kook's house in the Old City (long, mid, 153).
6. Talmud Torah and Yeshivah students (mid, 167).
7. Massive crowds in the funeral procession. Crowded roofs and balconies. Sitting on tiled roofs (264).
8. Pan of the street, crowds, passing in the alleys of the Old City, and going down to the Mount of Olives. Clear shot of the Mount (297).
9. Pan of buildings in the Old City, crowds.
10. Diplomats. Shiny top-hats among crowd at the funeral. One of the cameras on the Old City Wall, filming the event. Funeral crowd (long, 384).

## PART B: RELAY RACE FOR THE ELIMELECH KUPERSTEIN TROPHY (79')
1. Crowd. Runners lining up (mid, 25).
2. Race begins through the city streets. The winner (mid, 79).

## PART C: FAREWELL CEREMONIES AT THE END OF HAPOEL CHILDREN'S SUMMER CAMP IN TEL AVIV (173')
1. Children on the shore and in the sea, playing (54).
2. Exercising. Small children marching with the flag. Leaving the camp (long, 173).

□ PART D: SPORTS IN THE HAPOEL CAMP IN BEN SHEMEN (280')
1   General view of fields of Ben Shemen (long, 25).
2   Someone lying down, having his blood pressure taken. Digging for construction (49).
3   Men lined up, at attention and at ease. Young men and women exercising (long, 110).
4   Volleyball game. Men without shirts learning to high-jump. Women long-jumping (long, 192).
5   Javelin throw. Pole vault. Human pyramid (mid, 258).
6   Dancing hora around the flag (long, 280).

■ **CARMEL NEWSREEL I-028** · Summer 1935
Hapoel motorcyclists leaving Tel Aviv. Three hundred new immigrants from Yemen arriving at the port of Tel Aviv. Hapoel excursion to the Dead Sea. Extraordinary footage of the rocky crags and fresh water streams of Nahal Zarkon, Nahal Arnon and Nahal Yabuk. The Hassidic Rabbi Admor of Gur arrives in Palestine.

□ PART A: HAPOEL'S MOTORCYCLISTS LEAVING FOR THE JORDAN RIVER (34')
1   Starting the motorcycles. Leaving from Tel Aviv (long, 34).

□ PART B: THREE HUNDRED NEW IMMIGRANTS FROM YEMEN ARRIVING AT THE PORT OF TEL AVIV (47')
1   Yemenite Jew arranging his baggage (9).
2   Yemenite family standing and sitting (long, 23).
3   Loading baggage on a truck (long, 47).

□ PART C: HAPOEL EXCURSION TO THE DEAD SEA (322')
1   Sunrise on the Dead Sea. Pan of Dead Sea, with boats in water. Line-up of Hapoel groups. Getting on boats at Kalya (long, 66).
2   Sitting in boats, foam of wake in background. Faces of young men and women singing (mid, 110).
3   Dancing a hora. Pan of Nahal. Hiking in Nahal. Bathing in the fresh water streams. Tilt upwards to the hills (long, 189).
4   Arriving at Nahal Yabuk. Pan of scenery. Swimming in the stream (mid, long, 259).
5   In the hills at Nahal Arnon. Young people playing and diving in the stream (long, 322).

□ PART D: THE GREAT RABBI ADMOR OF GUR, ARRIVES IN ISRAEL (45')
1   The Hassidim waiting by the entrance. A policeman on guard (long, 21).
2   Greeting the rabbi. Pushing the policeman (mid, 40).
3   Photo of a painting of the rabbi (mid, 45).

■ **CARMEL NEWSREEL I-029** · September 1935
The 75th birthday of Y H Rabinitzky. Laying the foundation stone for the synagogue in Avihail in Emek Hefer. The Tel Aviv Volunteer Fire Brigade demonstrates fire-fighting equipment and techniques.

□ PART A: ON THE OCCASION OF THE 75TH BIRTHDAY OF Y H RABINITZKY (25')
1   Rabinitzky sitting behind a table covered with plants and flowers, reading a book. Dissolve to close-up of his face (25).

□ PART B: LAYING OF FOUNDATION STONE FOR THE SYNAGOGUE IN AVIHAIL IN THE VALLEY OF HEFER (137')
1   General view of the small houses of Avihail (long, 57).
2   Architectural drawing of the proposed synagogue (mid, 65).

3   By the gate with the sign in Hebrew: Avihail Synagogue (long, 73).
    שלט: בנין הכנסת אביחיל
4   Representative speaking (mid, 89).
5   Man holding Torah scroll on dais.
6   Stage and crowd. Rabbi speaks (long, c.u.).
7   By the cornerstone (mid, long, 117).
8   Dancing hora with the Torah (long, 137).

□ PART C: TENTH ANNIVERSARY OF THE TEL AVIV VOLUNTEER FIRE DEPARTMENT (281')
1   Fire Department marching band, followed by members of the Fire Department (long, 33).
2   Line-up in front of the fire station.
3   Officers of the Fire Department, in uniform (long, 66).
4   A lit-up Star of David and the symbol of the Fire Department on a building on Rothschild Boulevard (mid, 79).
5   Fire engine leaving fire station, driving down the street.
6   Water tanker.
7   Firemen climbing up a ladder. Pan of firemen (mid, long, 146).
8   Commander gives an order (c.u., mid, 154).
9   Spraying water on the buildings (long, 190).
10  Bringing people down the ladder (long, 205).
11  Attaching the hoses (mid, long, 221).
12  Using the water hoses.
13  Raising the ladder (281).

■ **CARMEL NEWSREEL I-030** · September 1935
New immigrants on their way to Israel on the ship *Tel Aviv*. Mayor Meir Dizengoff returning to Israel with Golda Meir on the ship *Excelsior*. Tzvi Lieberman bringing farmers to Israel on the ship *Polonia*. Carmel Film extends New Year's greetings.

□ PART A: NEW IMMIGRANTS ON THEIR WAY TO ISRAEL ON THE SHIP *TEL AVIV* (137')
1   The ship at Crete, dissolve to shoreline (long, 13).
2   Children playing on the deck, in a sand box. The orchestra, the adults playing a board game.
3   Children playing on the floor (mid, long, 66).
4   Pan of shore at Crete (long, 78).
5   Dancing hora, whirlpools in the waves.
6   Girl on a swing. Sailor pushing her (mid, long).
7   General view of the sea, fishing boats (long).
8   Dancing hora, crew members join in.
9   Ship captain with binoculars.
10  Lined up at the clinic (137).

□ PART B: DIZENGOFF RETURNING TO ISRAEL ON THE SHIP *EXCELSIOR* (45')
1   The ship in Jaffa port. Small boats around it (long, 13).
2   Dizengoff, Golda Myerson (Meir) and another young woman, on a boat to shore (mid, 20).
3   Line of cars waiting at the port (long, 39).
4   Sunset (45).

□ PART C: TZVI LIEBERMAN, BRINGING FARMERS TO ISRAEL, ABOARD THE *POLONIA* (69')
1   Boats loaded down with goods, in Jaffa port (mid, 29).
2   Crowd waiting at entrance to port.

48    Carmel Newsreels: Series 1

3    A British policeman hits an Arab shoeshine boy, throwing him out of the port (long, 37).
4    The *Polonia* surrounded by small vessels (mid, 49).
5    Passengers disembarking via the small boats (mid, 69).

□ PART D: CARMEL FILM EXTENDS NEW YEAR'S GREETINGS (78')
1    TITLE IN HEBREW: The administration of Carmel Film, together with the management of the theatre, wishing you a happy and successful new year with a flowering of immigration.

כתובת: הנהלת יומני כרמל יחד עם הנהלת קולנוע זה מברכות את הקהל
בשנה טובה ומוצלחת ופריחת העליה.

2    Adorable children act out the changing year. The old year departs and the new year arrives (78).

■ CARMEL NEWSREEL I-031 · September 1935
The funeral of Yitzhak Leib Goldberg. Art exhibition of Maneh Katz. Laying of foundation stone for elementary school in Afula.

□ PART A: THE FUNERAL OF Y L GOLDBERG (143')
1    Announcement of mourning for Yitzhak Leib Goldberg (c.u., 10).
2    Flag at half-mast (mid, 18).
3    Large crowd gathered in courtyard to hear eulogy (shot from above, long, 30).
4    Carrying the coffin, loading it onto vehicle (mid, 94).
5    Funeral procession through street (143).

□ PART B: MANEH KATZ EXHIBITION IN TEL AVIV (119')
1    Close-up of Maneh Katz smiling (5).
2    Maneh Katz, with his pictures in the background (mid, 13).
3    Series of close-ups of paintings. Close-up of painting of old man and girl. Line of paintings on the wall. People looking at the paintings (119).

□ PART C: LAYING OF FOUNDATION STONE FOR SCHOOL IN AFULA (157')
1    General view of Afula. Camera pans (55).
2    Children going to school (mid, 69).
3    Pan of three men who participated in ceremony. Crowd applauding. Man speaking to crowd. Another speaker. Applauding (112).
4    Two more speakers. Crowd (157).

■ CARMEL NEWSREEL I-032 · October 1935
Students of the Zebulun Naval High School greeting the ship *Bat Galim*. The funeral of Dr Sela (Blubstein) in Tel Aviv. Celebrating the inauguration of the Levant Fair. The completion of a water plant from the Yarkon River to Givat Hashlosha.

□ PART A: STUDENTS OF THE ZEBULUN NAVAL HIGH SCHOOL GREETING THE SHIP *BAT GALIM* (80')
1    Small sailing boats on water. Young boys in sailor shirts rowing (mid, 20).
2    Boats in the water (long, 29).
3    Boy on boat signalling with flags (mid, 33).
4    Assorted shots of boats on water, tilt to mouth of the Yarkon River (long, 57).
5    Officer of Zebulun School shaking hands with men from the *Bat Galim* ship. All dressed in formal naval uniforms (mid, 80).

□ PART B: THE FUNERAL OF DR SELA (BLUBSTEIN) IN TEL AVIV (20')
1    Funeral procession down street (long, 20).

□ PART C: CELEBRATING THE INAUGURATION OF THE LEVANT FAIR (59')
1. Statue of flying camel, symbol of the Levant Fair, at top of pole (long, 12).
2. Long set tables, filled with people eating in the Café Galina (pan from above, then from side, long, mid, 51).
3. Crowd clapping (59).

□ PART D: COMPLETION OF WATER PLANT FROM YARKON RIVER TO GIVAT HASHLOSHA (231')
1. General view of the source of the Yarkon River in Rosh Ha'ayin (long, 11).
2. The pipe for the pump, in the Yarkon. The inside of the pumping station (mid, 40).
3. Pipe leading to aqueduct. Water flowing through aqueduct. Assorted views of aqueduct (111).
4. Water flowing from the aqueduct into field where man hoes it into trenches (mid, 128).
5. Pan of aqueduct (mid, 143).
6. Pan of field with aqueduct in distance. Trenches filled with water (mid, 188).
7. Water flowing through trench into field (mid, 219).
8. Pan of field with plants (long, 231).

■ **CARMEL NEWSREEL I-033** · October 1935
Sports competition of the police in Jerusalem. Young Maccabi camp on Seven Mills on the Yarkon River. Ceremony at a Rishon Lezion school which is transferring the Jerusalem flag to another school (the school which collected the most money through Jewish National Fund blue boxes would receive the Jerusalem flag for one year).

□ PART A: SPORTS COMPETITION OF THE POLICE IN JERUSALEM (537')
1. Two views of men running races. Pan of crowd including men and women in European clothing and men in fezzes (mid, long, 26).
2. Pan of uniformed band (mid, 31).
3. British and Palestine police greet British Cabinet Secretary as he leaves car with women. They stand at attention as the band plays British anthem. Pan past sportsmen at attention to British flag blowing in the wind (63).
4. Riding competition (long, 96).
5. Race of Palestine police. Several wearing hats (klafkim). The winners (long, mid, 119).
6. Men racing, jumping over hurdles. Men high-jumping. Man in suit next to uniformed policeman noting down results (long, mid, 154).
7. Horseback riding. High-jumping (long, 181).
8. Horses jumping over hurdles (long, 225).
9. Pan of crowd (long, 240).
10. Sportsmen in white trousers and sleeveless shirts march past crowd. Exhibition of calisthenics, jumping over a wooden exercise horse (long, 319).
11. Exercise evacuating wounded, who are wearing keffiyehs and galabiyehs (long, 357).
12. Horse jumping hurdles (recorded in reverse, long, 378).
13. Table with trophies. Distribution of prizes. Pan of prizewinners (mid, long, 455).
14. Members of Abdullah's legion marching to get prizes (mid, 465).
15. More distribution of prizes (mid, 473).
16. Police demonstrating charge with bayonets (long, 489).
17. Tug of war (mid, 520).
18. Repeat of footage of horse jumping hurdles (backwards, long, 537).

□ PART B: YOUNG MACCABI CAMP ON SEVEN MILLS ON THE YARKON RIVER (74')

1 Young boys in bathing suits doing exercises in front of tents in the woods (mid, 16).
2 Swimming in the Seven Mills waterfall. Jumping from stone wall into Yarkon River (long, 53).
3 Boys in loincloths/bathing suits doing Indian dance near tent in woods (mid, 74).

☐ PART C: RISHON LEZION SCHOOL SAYING FAREWELL TO JERUSALEM FLAG (155')
1 General view of the children in the schoolyard with the Jerusalem flag (long, 28).
2 Dignitaries on the staircase, above the children. Pan of children applauding.
3 Procession of dignitaries with flag, walking down path lined with children (long, 125).
4 The dignitaries and the children on a main street in Rishon Lezion (155).

☐ PART D: THE JERUSALEM FLAG RECEIVED BY A SCHOOL IN JERUSALEM
1 Pan of children with flags in the courtyard of the Jewish Agency building in Jerusalem.
2 Assorted speakers (mid, 45).
3 Children marching with flags, including the national flag.
4 Large group of children reciting with hand motions (mid, 115).
5 Children marching.
6 Shapiro, the organiser of the celebration, signals to the children with the Jerusalem flag to come forward. One boy with skullcap (169).
7 Menachem Ussishkin and other dignitaries walk past the children.
8 Passing the flag from one group to another. Procession with Jerusalem flag.
9 Close-up of the flag (231).
10 Spectators on roof (long, 237).
11 Pan of dignitaries, Ussishkin etc., and children with flag marching before them (260).

■ **CARMEL NEWSREEL I-034** · October 1935
Camp of the Young Labour movement. Religious Scouts flag-raising and prayer. Betar Youth visiting the grave of Sarah Aaronsohn. Hapoel motorcycle races.

☐ PART A: CAMP OF THE YOUNG LABOUR MOVEMENT ON THE CARMEL (82')
1 Children walking to the wooden gate of the camp. Dissolve to an exhibition of children's drawings (mid, 35).
2 Pan of youth lined up listening to someone speaking (mid, 55).
3 Dancing hora (mid, 60).
4 Bandaging hands.
5 Cooking in a large vat. Slicing bread (82).

☐ PART B: RELIGIOUS SCOUTS FLAG-RAISING AND PRAYER (103')
1 Rabbi Ben Zion Meir Chai Uziel with scouts' leader (long, 2).
2 Flag-raising. Scouts standing at attention, boys and girls separate (long, 24).
3 The national flag (mid, 28).
4 Scouts listen as rabbi speaks (mid, 49).
5 Scouts pass the flag through the crowd. Assorted shots of scouts praying (including overhead pan, mid, long, 103).

☐ PART C: TITLE: COMMEMORATION FOR SARAH ARONSON [sic] AT ZICHRON YA'AKOV (146')

כותרת: עלית הנוער הבית"רי על קברה של שרה אהרנסון ז"ל בזכרון-יעקוב

1 The symbol of Betar with a photograph of Sarah Aaronsohn (mid, 22).

2 Procession of children, with Betar Youth carrying wreath. Blowing trumpet (long, 38).
3 Betar Youth in uniform, marching. Tilt from grave to youth holding flag (mid, 104).
4 Speaker on podium (mid, 116).
5 Crowd milling (mid, 131).
6 Holding the flag and singing (mid, 146).

□ PART D: MOTORCYCLE MEET OF HAPOEL (163')

כותרת: תרגילי אופנוע של הפועל

1 Men on motorcycles on outdoor soccer field.
2 Motorcycle race including obstacle course. Scrambling under blanket, bobbing for apples (mid, 163).

■ **CARMEL NEWSREEL I-035** · October 1935
Water festival, Simchat Beit Hashoeva, in a new settlement Ein Iron. The funeral of Rabbi Yekhezkiel Robinson in Petah Tikva. Deganya in preparation for its 25th anniversary celebrations. The Polish ship *Kosciuszko* arriving in Israel.

□ PART A: WATER FESTIVAL IN A NEW SETTLEMENT EIN IRON (133')
1 Pan of settlement (long, 44).
2 Side of the reservoir with a sign in Hebrew: And You Shall Draw Water With Joy.   כתובת: ושאבתם מים בששון.
3 A red flag with words in Hebrew: Workers Council Karkur.

כתובת: מועצת פועלי כרכור.

4 The national flag. The flags blowing in the wind (mid, long, 59).
5 Arabs and Jews congregated for celebration in front of water-tank (pan, long, 81).
6 Pan of photographs in an outdoor exhibit, including Herzl (mid, 81).
7 Speaker. Crowd outside. Sprinzak speaking and crowd listening (long, mid, 119).
8 Opening taps, water pouring out of the reservoir (long, 133).

□ PART B: THE FUNERAL OF RABBI YEKHEZKIAL ROBINSON IN PETAH TIKVA (63')
1 Funeral procession. Body wrapped, carried on stretcher (long, 56).
2 Crowd listening to funeral oration (mid, long, 32).
3 Crowd and funeral procession (mid, 63).

□ PART C: DEGANYA IN PREPARATION FOR ITS 25TH ANNIVERSARY CELEBRATIONS (89')
1 Dissolves of various sites in kibbutz (long, 56).
2 Cemetery, tombstones including the murdered Barsky and A D Gordon (c.u., 75).
3 General view of cemetery (long, 84).
4 Close-up of tombstone (89).

□ PART D: THE POLISH SHIP *KOSCIUSZKO* ARRIVING IN ISRAEL (223')
1 Hull of ship with name: *KOSCIUSZKO* (mid).
2 General view of ship. Polish flag (long, mid, 28).
3 Sailors checking papers of passengers on boat. Sailor at wheel, steering.
4 Passengers on deck chairs. Sailor greeting man in suit.
5 Smokestacks on boat. Pan of port. Raising the national flag on board.
6 Checking papers. Passengers disembarking onto small boats.
7 Small boat full of luggage. Unloading crates from ship. National flag (223').

## Carmel Newsreels: Series 1

■ **CARMEL NEWSREEL I-036** · Winter 1935
Romanian pilots visiting Israel. Tel Aviv on rainy days. Schoolchildren at a performance of the new Palestine film *Land of Promise* at Migdalor Cinema. Hayovel village built by B'nei Binyamin. Construction of a new village on the lands of the Jewish National Fund, built according to the terrace system.

☐ PART A: ROMANIAN PILOTS VISITING ISRAEL (124')
1   Underground pool of water in Ramla.
2   Small plane landing. Romanian pilots get off plane (23). Reception for the pilots with the Romanian consul at the Tel Aviv Municipality (mid, 40).
3   Municipal building on Bialik Street (long, 45).
4   Aerial photograph with wing blocking camera (mid, 51).
5   Aerial shots of Tel Aviv (long, 124).

☐ PART B: TEL AVIV ON RAINY DAYS (80')
1   Street covered in water. Truck passes. Horse and cart with bread wagon (long, 27).
2   Houses with water. Walking in puddles inside (long, 50).
3   Digging ditches to drain water (long, 57).
4   Puddles (long, 80).

☐ PART C: SCHOOLCHILDREN IN LINE AT MIGDALOR MOVIE THEATRE FOR SCREENING OF *LAND OF PROMISE* (23')
1   Tilt from film poster to crowd (long, 23).

☐ PART D: HAYOVEL VILLAGE BUILT BY B'NEI BINYAMIN (58')
1   Pan of houses in Yovel village (long).
2   Working in the vegetable garden. Woman picking tomatoes (long, mid, 58).

☐ PART E: VILLAGE ON JEWISH NATIONAL FUND LAND BUILT ACCORDING TO THE TERRACE SYSTEM (66')
1   General view of houses at time of settlement (long, 28).
2   Finishing work on the water pool (long, 45).
3   Houses. Preparing soil for building (long, 66).

■ **CARMEL NEWSREEL I-037** · November 1935
Soccer game between Hapoel and Maccabi teams. Armistice Day at the military cemetery in Jerusalem. First day of the academic year at Hebrew University. Inauguration of the Z D Levontin Library in Rishon Lezion.

☐ PART A: SOCCER GAME BETWEEN HAPOEL AND MACCABI TEAMS (126')
1   Soccer match, shadows on the field (long, 68).
2   Crowd of spectators behind fence. Game (long, 126).

☐ PART B: ARMISTICE DAY AT THE MILITARY CEMETERIES IN JERUSALEM (232')
1   Crowd gathering by the military cemetery on Mount Scopus (long, 44).
2   Pan of cemetery.
3   Statue of large cross.
4   Crowd gathering (long, 78).
5   The Jewish Legion marches past camera (long, 90).
6   Palestine police marching (long, 123). View of city behind them.
7   British military band marching, British soldiers (long, 175).
8   Invited guests followed by young students (long, 205).
9   Jewish Legion passing (mid, long, 219).
10  Police laying wreath (mid, 232).

□ PART C: FIRST DAY OF ACADEMIC YEAR AT THE HEBREW UNIVERSITY IN JERUSALEM (80')
1    Pan of the university on Mount Scopus (long, 9).
2    Students gathering (long, 26).
3    General view of the other side of the university. Courtyard. Dissolve to other side of courtyard (long, 80).

□ PART D: INAUGURATION OF Z D LEVONTIN LIBRARY IN RISHON LEZION (114')
1    The library. Guests entering (long, 23).
2    Interior of library. People taking books (long, 68).
3    Guests leaving library - among them Rabbi Uziel and Meirovitch from Bilu (long, 114).

■ **CARMEL NEWSREEL I-038** · November 1935
Completing construction of the radio station in Ramallah. Ceremony in Zichron Ya'akov marking the anniversary of Baron de Rothschild's death. High Commissioner Sir Arthur Wauchope visiting Jaffa Port. A fire in Nahalat Yitzhak. The inauguration of a laboratory for raising insects useful for agriculture.

□ PART A: COMPLETING CONSTRUCTION OF THE RADIO STATION IN RAMALLAH (372')
1    Base of antennae tower. Pan of site in Ramallah where the station is built. Upward pan of antennae (long, 43).
2    Director of the station with Mr Hayutman, Philips agent (mid, long, 58).
3    Working on putting together equipment. Dissolve to assorted technical projects (149).
4    Exterior of building. Hayutman and the director (mid, 176).
5    Technician scaling the antennae tower (236).
6    Sending boxes up tower. Men running, pulling rope to raise boxes (long, 283).
7    The area shot from above (long, 335).
8    Hayutman and director. The rope being rolled on the spool (long, mid, 372).

□ PART B: ONE YEAR ANNIVERSARY OF BARON DE ROTHSCHILD'S DEATH (37')
1    General view of street in Zichron Ya'akov. Pan of crowd.
2    Sign in Hebrew: To the father of the Yishuv, Baron de Rothschild.

שלט: "אבי הישוב", הברון בנימין דה רוטשילד

3    Speaker (mid, long, 37).

□ PART C: HIGH COMMISSIONER SIR ARTHUR WAUCHOPE VISITING JAFFA PORT (84')
1    The High Commissioner getting on a ship (long, 19).
2    Customs officials by the dock. Pan of dock from a moving boat (long, 32).
3    The commissioner getting on the boat, filmed from the sea (long, 51).
4    The commissioner on the boat (long, 84).

□ PART D: THE FIRE IN NAHLAT YITZCHAK (71')
1    People gathered near the site of the fire (long, 13).
2    Fire-fighters putting out the fire (long, 52).
3    People by the site (long, 71).

□ PART E: INAUGURATION OF A LABORATORY FOR RAISING INSECTS USEFUL FOR AGRICULTURE (126')
1    People outside laboratory (long, 8).
2    Interior shot of test tubes and jars filled with insects. Woman opens closet and

works with a petrie dish (mid, 46).
3   People outside the laboratory.
4   A hand places insects on plants. Plants with diseases (mid, 101).
5   Mould on oranges being scraped off (long, 119).
6   Close-up of insect (126).

■ **CARMEL NEWSREEL I-039** · November 1935
Examinations for plumber certification. Construction of a pumping station in Rosh Ha'ayin for bringing water to Jerusalem. Citrus sorting and packing. Loading oranges onto ship in Jaffa Port.

◻ PART A: PLUMBERS' EXAMINATIONS (95')
1   Welding and other plumbing operations performed under supervision (32).
2   Plumbers stand in line to hand in projects (pan, mid, 67).
3   Municipal inspectors (pan, mid, 95).

◻ PART B: CONSTRUCTION OF ROSH HA'AYIN PUMPING STATION TO PROVIDE WATER TO JERUSALEM (144')
1   Construction (long, 21).
2   Digging a ditch and piling earth on the embankment (long, 117).
3   Construction near Antipatros, Arabs and Jews (long, 77).
4   Earthworks (long, 117).
5   Laying pipes (long, 144).

◻ PART C: CITRUS SEASON IN REHOVOT (275')
1   Warehouse containing packing materials (45).
2   Taking a break in the orchard - mainly Yemenite Jews (mid, 77).
3   Woman sorting oranges (mid).
4   Machine sorting oranges according to size (mid, 132).
5   Warehouse and packing (mid, 211),
6   Arab workers loading crates onto boat in Jaffa Port (mid, 239).
7   Boat leaves port heading for ship (mid, 264).
8   Loading crates onto ship (mid, 275).

■ **CARMEL NEWSREEL I-040** · November 1935
Flooding in Tel Aviv and the Galilee - rescuing survivors, searching through debris, wading through water.

◻ PART A: FLOODS IN PALESTINE (missing, 153')
1   Tel Aviv streets filled with water. Cyclists going through the water and people walking on the side of the road. A motorcycle half underwater. Wagons and cars in the water (long, 54).
2   Salvaging possessions. Firemen carrying survivors (long, 102).
3   People standing near flooded houses (long, 126).
4   People crossing on improvised bridges made out of tin and wooden planks. Flooded houses (long, 153).

◻ PART B: AFTERMATH OF FLOODING IN THE GALILEE
1   Destroyed homes and debris swept by the flood water (long, 29).
2   Arabs searching for their belongings among the debris (long, 53).

■ **CARMEL NEWSREEL I-041** · November 1935
Opening of Assuta Hospital in Tel Aviv. Tel Aviv municipal elections - placards/posters. Inauguration of King George V Jubilee Forest.

◻ PART A: OPENING OF ASSUTA HOSPITAL IN TEL AVIV (302')
1   Assuta Hospital and surrounding fields (pan and dissolve, long, 52).

2  Hospital corridor and nurse (long, 67).
3  Opening ceremony - speeches, people seated at tables and eating (mid, 102).
4  Hospital director welcomes Chief Rabbi Ben Zion Meir Chai Uziel. Guests tour the wards (mid, 123).
5  Operating room, equipment and various other rooms (mid, 183).
6  Guests tour wards (mid, 197).
7  X-ray machine and modern kitchen (mid, 168).
8  Hospital nursery (mid, 302).

□ PART B: TEL AVIV MUNICIPAL ELECTIONS (118')
1  People near notice-board and close-up of election posters (mid, 39).
2  Distributing leaflets; cyclists carrying placards; posters on cars and buildings (mid, 97).
3  Cars with placards (long, 118).

□ PART C: TITLE: INAUGURATION OF KING GEORGE V JUBILEE FOREST (105')

כותרת: חגיגת נטיעה של יער המלך גורג'

1  Gate on hilltop from which British and Jewish flags are flying (mid, long, 18).
2  Crowd, including Rabbi Meir Berlin (Bar Ilan) (mid, 48).
3  Crowd near sign (long, 62).
4  Chaim Weizmann and entourage arriving at planting site (mid, 74).
5  Menachem Ussishkin planting a tree (mid, c.u., 89).
6  Sign on gate in English and Hebrew: King George V Jubilee Forest - "And when you enter the land you shall plant" (mid, long, 105).

כותרת: וכי תבואו אל הארץ ונטעתם. (ויקרא י"ט, כ"ז)

■ CARMEL NEWSREEL I-042 · December 1935
Children celebrating Chanukah in Givatayim. Shaul Tchernichovsky's 60th birthday. A shop display competition in honour of "Bitzaron Aid Society Week". Yehoshua Hankin's 70th birthday.

□ PART A: CHANUKAH CELEBRATIONS IN BOROCHOV SECTION OF GIVATAYIM (271')
1  Iris shot of Borochov section of Givatayim. Children marching with flags. Dissolve into another street and children marching there (long, 52).
2  Close-up of children (mid, 79).
3  Children marching downhill to empty field (later site of amphitheatre) (long, 114).
4  Children dancing in a circle. Children in the centre are singing (mid, long, 162).
5  Children in menorah formation performing gymnastics (long, 179).
6  Chanukah theme games (mid, long, 218).
7  Close-up of children passing (c.u., mid, 237).
8  Overview - crowd on the hilltop watching children performing (long, 271).

□ PART B: SHAUL TCHERNICHOVSKY'S 60TH BIRTHDAY (21')
1  Shaul Tchernichovsky sitting at his desk (mid, 13).
2  Tchernichovsky carrying his briefcase (long, 21).

□ PART C: BITZARON AID SOCIETY WEEK - SHOP DISPLAY COMPETITION (165')
1  Streets and shop windows (long, 26).
2  Close-up of shop windows (dissolve from window to window) (mid, 58).
3  Close-up of shop window. Dissolve to other windows (mid, 124).
4  More shop windows (mid, 165).

□ PART D: CELEBRATION IN HONOUR OF YEHOSHUA HANKIN'S 70TH BIRTHDAY (109')
1. Portrait of Theodor Herzl in the Jewish Agency hall (tilt down). Guests at celebration (pan, mid, 31).
2. Yehoshua Hankin sitting and listening to a speech (mid, 38).
3. The audience clapping (long, 55).
4. Arthur Ruppin speaking (mid, 66).
5. Menahem Ussishkin speaking (mid, 77).
6. Moshe Shertok (Sharett) speaking (mid, 84).
7. Audience clapping (long, 109).

■ CARMEL NEWSREEL I-043 · December 1935
Fashion show at Rimon Cinema in Tel Aviv. A soccer match. Dedication of Magen David Adom building in Tel Aviv. *Ha'aretz* daily newspaper celebrates its 5000th issue.

□ PART A: FASHION SHOW AT RIMON CINEMA (178')

כותרת: תצוגה אופנה בקולנוע "רימון"

1. Models walking across the stage (long, 92).
2. Close-up of models (mid, 124).
3. Models on split-screen (long and c.u., 178).

□ PART B: SOCCER MATCH BETWEEN TRICOLOUR AND MACCABI TEL AVIV (152')
1. The team comes out carrying a flag (long, 19).
2. The team runs onto the pitch (long, 38).
3. The team poses for the camera (mid, long, 53).
4. Various shots of the game (long, 77).
5. The crowd streams onto the pitch (long, 124).
6. Various shots of the crowd watching the match (long, 152).

□ PART C: DEDICATION OF NEW MAGEN DAVID ADOM BUILDING IN TEL AVIV (39')
1. The building decorated with flags (tilt up, mid, 27).
2. Festive gathering in hall, marking the occasion (front and back, mid, 39).

□ PART D: *HA'ARETZ* DAILY NEWSPAPER CELEBRATES ITS 5000TH ISSUE (58')
1. Members of the newspaper editorial board, seated (mid). Management door with names on it: Aharon Cohen, Zalman Shavlov (mid, 20).
2. Cohen and Shavlov sitting opposite each other (mid, 46).
3. Three men seated - Yishayahu Klinov (one of the editors of *Ha'aretz*) in the centre (mid, 58).

■ CARMEL NEWSREEL I-044 · December 1935
The presentation ceremony of the Bialik Awards (speakers include: Professor Klausner, David Ben Gurion). Train wreck in Hadera. Opening of Eretz Israel-France Association Library in Tel Aviv. Full lunar eclipse. Laying of cornerstone for Dvir Bialik publishing house in Ramat Gan (speakers include: Ben Gurion, Shaul Tchernichovsky, Mayor Meir Dizengoff, Chief Rabbi Ben Zion Meir Chai Uziel, Yitzhak Ben Zvi).

□ PART A: BIALIK AWARDS CEREMONY IN JERUSALEM (149')
1. Guests sitting at tables (pan), shot of speaker and pan of guests - Shaul Tchernichovsky, Arthur Ruppin, Menachem Ussishkin, Granot (mid, long, 52).
2. Sammy Grunman speaking, Tchernichovsky seated next to him (mid, 62).
3. Shaul Tchernichovsky (mid, 72).

4  Professor Klausner speaking (mid, 108).
5  Audience clapping (mid, 129).
6  David Ben Gurion speaking (mid, c.u., 149).

□ PART B: TRAIN CRASH IN HADERA (71')
1  Wrecked railroad carriage near the tracks. Overturned engine. Various shots of overturned carriages (pan, mid, 71).

□ PART C: OPENING OF ERETZ ISRAEL-FRANCE ASSOCIATION LIBRARY IN TEL AVIV (50')
1  Opening ceremony - speakers and audience clapping (mid, 50).

□ PART D: LUNAR ECLIPSE (138')
1  The moon during the entire eclipse (entirely covered) (long, 96).
2  The moon gradually reappears (long, 138).

□ PART E: CORNERSTONE LAYING FOR DVIR-BIALIK PUBLISHING HOUSE IN RAMAT GAN (154')

שלט: דביר-ביאליק

1  Gate and sign (long, 7)
2  Guests arriving (mid, 14).
3  Chief Rabbi Uziel arriving (mid, 25).
4  The crowd around the dais and a speaker (long, 49).
5  Two people sitting (one possibly C N Bialik's widow). Another speaker and crowd. Yitzhak Ben Zvi speaking (mid, long, 81).
6  Chief Rabbi Uziel speaking and crowd applauding (mid, 106).
7  The crowd. Shaul Tchernichovsky (mid, 110).
8  Tchernichovsky speaking (mid, 118).
9  The crowd applauding (long, 127).
10 Meir Dizengoff speaking and the crowd applauding (mid, long, 154).

■ **CARMEL NEWSREEL I-045** · Winter 1935
Opening of Mikveh Israel archaeological exhibition. Exhibition of Made-in-Palestine textiles. Children visit the Tel Aviv Zoo. Reception for Rabbi Moshe Avigdor Amiel upon his arrival in Palestine.

□ PART A: OPENING OF ARCHAEOLOGICAL EXHIBITION AT MIKVEH ISRAEL (166')
1  Guests near entrance (long, 15).
2  Christian clergy in long white robes arriving (long, 23).
3  Guests approaching exhibition along tree-lined avenue. British High Commissioner Sir Arthur Wauchope, accompanied by Eliahu Kraus, the director of Mikveh Israel and his archaeologist daughter. All enter the exhibition hall (long, 63).
4  The exhibition and a close-up of a vase (dissolve, long, 105).
5  Various exhibits (long, 126).
6  A single exhibit (c.u., mid, 132).
7  A number of exhibits arranged in a row and a single exhibit (c.u., mid, 144).
8  The dig site (long, 158).
9  The exhibition's organiser - daughter of Mikveh Israel director (mid, long, 166).

□ PART B: EXHIBITION IN TEL AVIV OF TEXTILES MANUFACTURED IN PALESTINE, AT BRENNER HOUSE (34')
1  Textiles - clothing, upholstery, carpets (long, 34).

□ PART C: SCHOOLCHILDREN VISIT THE TEL AVIV ZOO (219')
1  The children arrive at the zoo (long, 10).

2   The children look at a porcupine (mid, long, 37).
3   The children watch the porcupine feed (mid, long, 55).
4   The zoo's director tells the children about the lioness (mid, long, 78).
5   Baby deer (mid, long, 97).
6   Deer eating from someone's hand as children look on (mid, long).
7   A vulture. Vulture feeding (mid, 162).
8   Children looking at birds. A stork (long, 184).
9   Birds (mid, 219).

□ PART D: RECEPTION FOR RABBI AMIEL UPON HIS ARRIVAL IN PALESTINE (148')
1   Banner: "Welcome Moshe Avigdor Amiel" (mid, 8).

שלט: ברוך הבא משה אבינדור עמיאל

2   Crowd in the street (long, 16).
3   Rabbi Amiel greets people as he makes his way through the crowd (c.u., mid, 28).
4   Hassidim running to meet the Rabbi. Rabbi Amiel entering the arrival hall (long, 59).
5   A beadle, dressed in Turkish fashion and carrying a staff, clears a path for the rabbi through the crowd (mid, long, 83).
6   The entourage fills waiting buses (long, 102).
7   Near a house decorated with a "Welcome" banner, crowd applauds as rabbi and entourage arrive and enter the house (long, 148).

■ **CARMEL NEWSREEL I-046** · Winter 1935
Memorial service for Ahad Ha'am. Press conference on opening of Levant Fair. Completion of Kupat Holim (sick fund) building. Boxing matches between Hapoel and Maccabi sports clubs.

□ PART A: GRAVESIDE MEMORIAL SERVICE FOR AHAD HA'AM (145')
1   Bouquet of flowers on the grave (tilt up). People at the graveside (long, 28).
2   Pan of crowd from cantor (long, 46).
3   Crowd (long, 60).
4   Ahad Ha'am's house on Ahad Ha'am Street in Tel Aviv (long, 84).
5   Ahad Ha'am's study - books, desk, various objects on the desk (115).
6   A page written in his hand (long, mid, 123).
7   Ahad Ha'am's phylacteries and prayer shawl (c.u., mid, 134).
8   A large portrait of Ahad Ha'am (mid, 145).

□ PART B: PRESS CONFERENCE ON OPENING OF LEVANT FAIR (138')
1   At Café Galina at the exhibition (pan, long, 20).
2   Dais and guests at tables (long, 61).
3   Speakers (mid, long, 87).
4   Journalists writing. The first speaker continues (122).
5   Kaplan speaking (mid, long, 138).

□ PART C: COMPLETION OF NATIONAL SICK FUND (KUPAT HOLIM) BUILDING (50')
1   The almost completed building (long, 50).

□ PART D: BOXING MATCHES BETWEEN HAPOEL AND MACCABI SPORTS CLUBS (253')
1   All the boxers standing in the ring, passing and pairing off (long, 30).
2   The first, second, third, fourth and fifth matches (long, 193).
3   The sixth match (long, 253).

## CARMEL NEWSREEL I-047 · Winter 1935-36
Mourning the death of King George V - dignitaries and crowd at Government House in Jerusalem. Triplets born. Soccer match between Maccabi and Hapoel. Henrietta Szold arrives in Israel.

□ PART A: MOURNING THE DEATH OF KING GEORGE V IN PALESTINE (172')
1   The Jewish flag at half-mast. The crowd at Government House in Jerusalem. Pan to mounted police and an open car followed by mounted police and the crowd (mid, long, 65).
2   A number of men slowly leave a church and get into a car standing in front of Government House and drive away, followed by mounted police (mid, 172).

□ PART B: TRAFFIC ACCIDENT NEAR MOTZA (22')
1   The road and overturned truck (carrying bricks) (long, c.u., 22).

□ PART C: TRIPLETS BORN (27')
1   The triplets (mid, 27).

□ PART D: SOCCER MATCH BETWEEN MACCABI AND HAPOEL (120')
1   The crowd at the ticket counters (pan, mid, 17).
2   Both teams run onto the field - first Hapoel, then Maccabi (mid, 46).
3   The game (mid, long, 78).
4   The crowd behind the fence (mid, 88).
5   The game (long, 94).
6   VIPs watching the game from under an awning and the crowd cheering (mid, 106).
7   The game (long, 120).

□ PART E: HENRIETTA SZOLD ARRIVES IN PALESTINE (108')
1   A ship nears Jaffa Port. Henrietta Szold on a boat arrives at the dock (long, 33).
2   The boat (pan, mid, 37).
3   Henrietta Szold coming ashore (mid, 44).
4   Children presenting her with flowers (mid, 94).
5   Szold driven away in a car (mid, 108).

## CARMEL NEWSREEL I-048 · Winter 1935-36
Distribution of saplings to children on Tu B'shvat in Tel Aviv. "Co-operative Council" convention in Zichron Ya'akov, showing the town and wine cellars. Made-in-Palestine exhibition at the Technion in Haifa. Athletics competition in Tel Aviv.

□ PART A: DISTRIBUTION OF SAPLINGS TO CHILDREN ON TU B'SHVAT IN TEL AVIV (155')
1   "Welcome" sign in Hebrew at entrance. Children leaving the plant nursery near Jabotinsky Street in Tel Aviv, with saplings (mid, 39).
2   Kindergarten children walking (mid, 46).
3   Distributing saplings to the children (mid, 77).
4   A girl receiving a sapling (c.u., 89).
5   Distribution of saplings, close-ups of happy children (c.u., long, 112).
6   The children leaving, carrying saplings (mid, 155).

□ PART B: "CO-OPERATIVE COUNCIL" CONVENTION IN ZICHRON YA'AKOV (227')
1   A banner: "Co-operative Council" (mid, 8).   שלט: מרכז הקואופרציה
2   Zichron Ya'akov and the banner (long, 15).

3   The wine cellar at Zichron Ya'akov (long, 24).
4   The building in which the convention is being held (tilt up to the flag). A street in Zichron Ya'akov. Men getting off a bus (long, mid, 78).
5   Entering the building (mid, 118).
6   Zichron Ya'akov (long, 130).
7   The hall and audience (mid, 144).
8   The journalists' table. The journalists taking notes on the speeches (mid, 154).
9   A number of speakers (mid, 181).
10  Pan of board members to the speakers; the audience applauding (mid, 227).

☐ PART C: MADE-IN-PALESTINE EXHIBITION AT THE TECHNION IN HAIFA (104')
1   Furniture exhibit (dissolve); logos and textiles (pan).
2   Shots of various products: Hillel Pharmaceuticals, Shemen Cosmetics (mid, 104).

☐ PART D: ATHLETICS COMPETITION AT MACCABI STADIUM IN TEL AVIV (350')
1   A number of athletes and various shots of both teams (mid, long, 31).
2   The team captains exchange flags (long, 50).
3   Women's race - the finish (long, 67).
4   The high-jump (men and women) (mid, 91).
5   Hurdle race - spectators applauding (long, 134).
6   Men's shot-put (mid, 154).
7   Women's shot-put. Officials measuring distance (mid, 22).
8   Team captains (c.u., 234).
9   Women's long-jump (mid, 267).
10  Javelin-throw (mid, 285).
11  The winners are congratulated (mid, 295).
12  Pole-vault (mid, long, 326).
13  Backwards shot of pole-vault (long, 350).

■ **CARMEL NEWSREEL I-049** · Winter 1935/36
Tree-planting celebration held by orthodox Jews in Bayit Vegan. A stormy Mediterranean Sea. German immigrant youth harvesting (with sickles) at Deganya. Children stage a Tu B'shvat play.

☐ PART A: CELEBRATIONS AT BAYIT VEGAN (138')
1   Gate and banner in Hebrew: "Planting Celebrations in Bayit Vegan - Welcome". British and Jewish flags on the gate. Banner in Hebrew: "And the Study of Torah Above All" (mid, long, 23).

שלט: חג הנטיעות בבית-וגן ברוכים הבאים. שלט: "ותלמוד תורה כנגד הכל"

2   A crowd of orthodox Jews (mid, 33).
3   A band; pan of the crowd; speakers (mid, 94).
4   Planting a tree (mid, 105).
5   Men dancing hora (mid, 119).
6   The band and a flag (mid, 138).

☐ PART B: A STORMY MEDITERRANEAN SEA (63')
1   Boats on a stormy sea - Jaffa Port (mid, 44).
2   Waves washing over the wharf and steps (mid, 63).

☐ PART C: GERMAN IMMIGRANT YOUTH HARVESTING AT DEGANYA (30')
1   Iris shot of Deganya. General view of Deganya (long, 25).
2   Harvesting with sickles in unison (mid, 30).

## PART D: TU B'SHVAT (367')
1. People celebrating on roof of building and in the courtyard in front of it.
2. Children dancing in groups of threes. A play about the watering of trees (long, 36).
3. The children approach. Their counsellors are carrying watering cans. The children approach with their teachers (long, 80).
4. The children (in costume) water the "trees" and dance (long, 192).
5. The children dance up a hill (long, 246).
6. The children pass saplings from hand to hand, dancing and singing up the hill. A shot of a flag.
7. Sign in Hebrew: And the Land Cannot be Sold (Leviticus 25:23).

שלט: והארץ לא תמכר לצמיתות

8. The children participating in the play continue to perform (367).

## ■ CARMEL NEWSREEL I-050 · April 1936
The Levant Fair - opening ceremony, pavilions, guests.

### PART A: THE LEVANT FAIR (281')
1. Flags at the exhibition (mid, 8).
2. British High Commissioner Sir Arthur Wauchope speaking (mid, 16).
3. Wauchope, Tel Aviv Mayor Dizengoff and entourage leaving a pavilion (long, 25).
4. A large crowd at the opening (long, 33).
5. Wauchope speaking (mid, 41).
6. Wauchope and other dignitaries in top-hats are escorted through fair.
7. General view of the exhibition, raising of Levant flag (mid, 48).
8. Fair directors and dignitaries stand while anthems are played (long, 236).
9. The Polish pavilion (exterior) (long, 185).
10. The British pavilion (exterior) (long, 173).
11. The Belgian pavilion (exterior) (long, 179).
12. Walking at the exhibition, while band plays in foreground (long, 145).
13. A large crowd at the opening (long, 162).
14. Flags superimposed (long, 58).
15. Mayor Meir Dizengoff, the High Commissioner and entourage walking at the exhibition. The High Commissioner shakes hands, continues walking among the pavilions (mid, long, 105).
16. The Romanian pavilion (exterior) (long, 168).
17. Great Britain pavilion.
18. The Dutch pavilion (exterior) (long, 189).
19. The Norwegian pavilion (exterior) (long, 192).
20. A street at the exhibition (long, 197).
21. The Made-in-Palestine pavilion (exterior) (long, 202).
22. A British military band playing near the entrance to the exhibition and a crowd standing behind the band (long, 224).
23. General view - the crowd stands when the band begins to play (long, 230).
24. The exhibition flag, portraying a flying camel, is raised (mid, long, 281).

### PART B: THE LEVANT FAIR (14')
1. Meir Dizengoff speaking with Dr Chaim Weizmann (long, 19).
2. The fair directorate and dignitaries standing while anthems are played - the High Commissioner, Meir Dizengoff, Kaplan and Weizmann (long, 14).

### PART C: THE LEVANT FAIR (236')
1. Flags at the exhibition (mid, 9).
2. British High Commissioner Sir Arthur Wauchope speaking (mid, 15).
3. Meir Dizengoff, the High Commissioner and entourage leaving a building. A

large crowd at the opening (long, 34).
4 Sir Arthur Wauchope speaking (mid, 41).
5 The High Commissioner and his entourage pass by various pavilions (mid, long, 71).
6 General view of the exhibition and raising of the exhibition flag. The crowd stands at attention (long, 153).
7 A military band (long, 169).
8 Pavilions (long, 183).
9 The opening. The crowd gathering as the High Commissioner arrives (long, 109).
10 General view - the exhibition seen from above (long, 203).
11 Dizengoff and guests enter the fair (long, 236).

■ **CARMEL NEWSREEL I-051 - I-059**
These numbers were accidentally omitted when the newsreels were originally numbered.

■ **CARMEL NEWSREEL I-060** · April 1936
Introduction of Hebrew sound film work at the studios of Carmel Film. Scenes from two dramatic films:
- *Oded the Wanderer* (Chaim Halachmi, 1933), the first feature film produced in Palestine, whose plot involves a lost boy's wanderings, is an excuse to show local scenery;
- *Once Upon A Time* (Chaim Halachmi, 1932), a short Purim comedy.
A Polish airplane lands in Tel Aviv. Mayor Meir Dizengoff speaks on British Empire Day.

❑ PART A: THE INTRODUCTION OF SOUND NEWSREELS (140')
1 Akiva Vardimon of Carmel Film speaking (mid, 140).

❑ PART B: MEIR DIZENGOFF CONGRATULATES CARMEL FILM (ON THE INTRODUCTION OF SOUND) (69')
1 Dizengoff speaking (mid, 69).

❑ PART C: WORK AT CARMEL FILM (92')
1 Aaron Bloch filming with a sound camera and Nathan Axelrod, wearing headphones, supervising (mid, long, 15).
2 The editing room. At editing tables. Nathan Axelrod cutting film. Near Axelrod is Yehoshua Edri making notes and behind them, Yehudit Bloch is splicing (mid, long, 34).
3 Moshe Wechsler sitting near sound equipment with a laboratory worker from Afula (46).
4 The same laboratory worker, with a boy named Moshe Tawil (who played the supporting role in *Oded the Wanderer*, developing film, hanging in strips on wooden racks (long, mid, 62).
5 The laboratory worker from Afula with Yehoshua Edri in the print room (mid, long, 79).
6 Aaron Bloch rolling wet film on a drying wheel (mid, long, 92).

❑ PART D: A PURIM CARNIVAL (115')
1 A street in Tel Aviv (long, 10).
2 A crowd jumping in front of the camera to have their pictures taken (long, 24).
3 Motorcycles (long, 42).
4 A crowd trying to pass in front of the camera. One man pushes the crowd back in an attempt to be seen by the camera. Maccabi marches by, followed by workers and children. The crowd making faces at the camera. Youth march by (long, 115).

□ PART E: MENACHEM USSISHKIN CONGRATULATES CARMEL FILM (ON THE INTRODUCTION OF SOUND) (197')
1  Ussishkin speaking - refers to the significance of Hebrew-speaking newsreels for the diaspora (mid, long, 197).

□ PART F: A POLISH AIRPLANE LANDS IN TEL AVIV (116')
1  A Polish airplane lands between Tel Aviv and where the municipality building stands today. There is a crowd (long, 17).
2  Meir Dizengoff speaking. Superimposition of title: M. DIZENGOFF WELCOMES THE POLISH AIRMAN. Behind him stands Shimon Sammet (mid, long, 36).

כותרת: דיזינגף נועם

3  The Polish consul speaking (in Polish) (mid, long, 116).

□ PART G: NATHAN AXELROD SPEAKING ON THE INTRODUCTION OF SOUND (35')
1  Nathan Axelrod speaking (mid, long, 35).

□ PART H: SCENE FROM *ODED THE WANDERER* (91')
1  Shimon Pazner, playing Oded, lying among the rocks, waking up (mid, c.u., 58).
2  Close-up of his friend, played by Moshe Tawil. Dissolve to the third boy (Klinger). They shake hands and go with Tova (mid, 91).

□ PART I: A SCENE FROM *ONCE UPON A TIME* (10')
1  A scene from *Once Upon A Time* (long, 10).

□ PART J: MEIR DIZENGOFF SPEAKING ON BRITISH EMPIRE DAY (107')
1  Dizengoff speaking. Next to him is Municipal Secretary Yehuda Nadivi (mid, long).
2  Pan of audience - women wearing hats (long).
3  Dizengoff speaking (mid, long, 107).

□ PART K: BRACHA ZEFIRA AND NAHUM NERDI PERFORM THE SONG *HA'AVODAH* (145')
1  Nahum Nerdi at the piano plays the introduction to *Mi Yatzilenu Mira'av* ("WHO WILL SAVE US FROM HUNGER") (mid, long, 23).
2  Bracha Zefira (145).

■ **CARMEL NEWSREEL I-061** · November 14 1936
Opening of Beilinson Hospital. Airplane landing at the new airfield in Lod. The Palestine Royal Commission (Peel Commission) arrives. Armistice Day at the British military cemetery at Mount Scopus in Jerusalem, including British soldiers, Palestine Police and Jewish Legion Veterans.

□ PART A: OPENING OF BEILINSON HOSPITAL (313')
1  High Commissioner Sir Arthur Wauchope speaking English. The crowd (mid, long, 98).
2  Pan of the completed building. Dissolve to parts of the buildings (long, 144).
3  General view of a large crowd gathering (long, 153).
4  The High Commissioner gets out of his car and is received by Moses Beilinson (long, 178).
5  The High Commissioner and his entourage walk through the crowd (long, 109).
6  Beilinson speaking near the table of dignitaries (mid, long, 221).
7  The crowd listening (long, 230).
8  People standing in front of building, nurses on balconies (long, 238).

9   The Deputy Mayor (from the Mapai party) speaking (mid, long, 246).
10  General Secretary of the Histadrut, Israel Marminsky, speaking (mid, long, 313).

□ PART B: AT THE NEW AIRFIELD IN LOD (109')
1   An airplane passes overhead and lands on the runway (long, 48).
2   People getting out of the airplane (mid, long, 56).
3   The runway (long, 76).
4   Two men talking near the airplane. Near them are the pilot, the manager of the field and a man from the Shell company (mid, long, 91).
5   The pilot gets into the plane and takes off (long, 109).

□ PART C: MEMBERS OF THE PALESTINE ROYAL COMMISSION ARRIVE (24')
1   The Peel Commission arrives in Palestine (long, 13).
2   Members of the commission enter the commission's offices (long, 24). Sign: PALESTINE ROYAL COMMISSION (in Hebrew and Arabic).

שלט: משרד הועדה המלכותית לפלשתינה (א"י)

□ PART D: ARMISTICE DAY CEREMONIES AT THE BRITISH WAR CEMETERY ON MOUNT SCOPUS, JERUSALEM (225')
1   British police lead the procession, followed by "Highlanders" (long, 23).
2   British soldiers followed by "Highlanders" carrying rifles (mid, long, 52).
3   Palestine Police and Jewish Legion veterans wearing medals (mid, long, 81).
4   Jewish Legion veterans pass near the graves, carrying the brigade flag (long, 99).
5   The High Commissioner gets out of his car. He is saluted by the soldiers who stand at attention while the anthem is played (long, 137).
6   Pan of the crowd and tombstones (long, 158).
7   Clergy followed by marching soldiers (long, 177).
8   General view of the ceremony (long, 214).
9   Wreaths - including a wreath inscribed in Hebrew and English: "Va'ad-Leumi Jewish Community of Palestine" (mid, 225).

■ **CARMEL NEWSREEL I-062** · November 20 1936
Funeral of Moses Beilinson. High Commissioner Wauchope testifies before the Peel Commission. Elections in Rishon Lezion. The barn at Nahalal. Yosef Goland sings *Tel Aviv*. The Palestine Philharmonic Orchestra rehearses with William Steinberg. Naomi Lief in a Bedouin dance.

□ PART A: BEILINSON'S FUNERAL (96')
1   The funeral procession leaves the Histadrut building (long, 27).
2   The procession through the streets of Tel Aviv - filmed from above (long, 64).
3   Employees of the *Davar* daily newspaper pass by carrying a black banner. David Remez can be seen in the crowd (long, 96).

□ PART B: THE HIGH COMMISSIONER GOES TO TESTIFY BEFORE THE PEEL COMMISSION (11')
1   A plaque on a building: "Palestine Royal Commission" (6).

שלט: משרד הועדה המלכותית לפלשתינה א"י

2   The High Commissioner entering the building (mid, 11).

□ PART C: MUNICIPAL ELECTIONS IN RISHON LEZION (29')
1   Voters entering a polling station. Party representatives near the entrance handing out leaflets. Police maintaining order (long, 9).
2   Posters: "Vote for the Workers Party"; a farmers' party poster (mid, 22).
3   Handing out leaflets near a polling station (long, 29).

□ PART D: THE BARN AT NAHALAL (10')
1   The barn at Nahalal (long, 10).

□ PART E: YOSEF GOLAND IN THE SONG *TEL AVIV* (73')
1   A policeman directing traffic. The policeman remains in the background (long, 8).
2   Yosef Goland dressed as a policeman (mid, 48).
3   Goland superimposed on a background of Tel Aviv (mid, long, 73).

□ PART F: THE ORCHESTRA GOING TO REHEARSE WITH STEINBERG (46')
1   Conductor William Steinberg (mid, long, 9).
2   Members of the orchestra enter a building on their way to rehearsal, carrying their instruments (long, 46).

□ PART G: NAOMI LIEF IN A BEDOUIN DANCE (75')
1   An interpretive Bedouin dance (75).

■ **CARMEL NEWSREEL I-063** · November 1936
Dr Chaim Weizmann visits Tel Aviv Port, the first Jewish port in 2000 years, which is opened to replace the striking Jaffa Port. Flooding in Tel Aviv. The Meir Dizengoff Art Museum (Tel Aviv Museum). A caravan of camels carrying sand for construction across the Yarkon River.

□ PART A: DR CHAIM WEIZMANN VISITS TEL AVIV PORT (36')
1   Weizmann visits Tel Aviv Port (mid, long, 36).

□ PART B: THE FIRST RAIN OF THE YEAR IN TEL AVIV (103')
1   Flooding near the bridge in Nahalat Yitzhak. Shadows of people on the water (long, 6).
2   Wagons and cars in the water (long, 22).
3   People bailing water out of their homes with buckets (mid, 38).
4   A motorcycle stuck in water above its wheels.
5   A flooded street.
6   Cars stuck in water.
7   People floating on rafts (long, 103).

□ PART C: THE TEL AVIV MUSEUM (141')
1   A bust of Weizmann (c.u., mid, 1).
2   A bust of Dizengoff (c.u., mid, 2).
3   A bust of Weizmann (c.u., mid, 10).
4   A bust of Dizengoff. The shutter closes (c.u., mid, 22).
5   TITLE: THE MEIR DIZENGOFF ART MUSEUM, TEL-AVIV
    כותרת: מוזיאון ע"ש דיזנגוף בתל-אביב
6   A different bust of Dizengoff. Dissolve to exhibit hall (pan). Various paintings (pan of five paintings, c.u., mid, long, 141).

□ PART D: CAMELS (110')
1   A camel chewing on the beach (mid, 10).
2   Men loading sand into crates strapped to camels (long, 25).
3   A caravan of camels crossing the Yarkon River (long, 54).
4   Loading sand, a caravan passing and loading sand again. Close-up of camels crossing the river (91).
5   A caravan of camels carrying building-sand across the Yarkon (long, 110).

■ **CARMEL NEWSREEL I-064** · December 4 1936
Reception at Tel Aviv Municipality for Maccabi athletes returning from competition

in the United States. Building a glider. M Fliederbaum plays "The Ba'al Shem Tov" on the violin.

☐ PART A: RECEPTION FOR RETURNING MACCABI ATHLETES AT THE TEL AVIV MUNICIPALITY (304')
1   Maccabi members arrive at the Tel Aviv Municipality and present Israel Rokah with an American flag. Rokah speaking (mid, long, 84).
2   Rokah welcomes the Maccabi delegation (c.u., 252).
3   The head of the Maccabi delegation speaking (c.u., 304).

☐ PART B: TITLE: MOTORLESS PLANES (25')
1   Building a glider (c.u., mid, 25).    כותרת: דאונים

☐ PART C: M FLIEDERBAUM PLAYS *THE BA'AL SHEM TOV* (195')
1   Violinist Fliederbaum plays *The Ba'al Shem Tov* (mid, 92).
2   The violin and fingers (c.u., 143).
3   Continues to play (mid, 195).

■ **CARMEL NEWSREEL I-065** · December 11 1936
Members of the Peel Commission visit Rehovot and depart from Lod Airport. A Wizo exhibition of products made-in-Israel. A skit from the Matateh Theatre, *Matzav Meyuchad*.

☐ PART A: THE PALESTINE ROYAL COMMISSION VISITS REHOVOT (65')
1   Members of the Peel Commission standing and talking in an orchard (long, 35).
2   A convoy of cars comes to stop (long, 54). The Peel Commission at Lod airport - leaving the country (long, 65).

☐ PART B: A MADE-IN-PALESTINE EXHIBITION SPONSORED BY WIZO (192')
1   The exhibition hall and the banner of the insurance companies which organised the exhibition. The exhibition (pan, long, 24).
2   Exhibits: Shemen, Okava, Broka. A table with cakes. The Palestine General Insurance Company - children's policy "C". Sova, Elite, Assis (192).

☐ PART C: A SKIT FROM THE MATATEH (BROOM) THEATRE'S *MATZAV MEYUCHAD* ("A SPECIAL SITUATION") (173')
1   Neighbours shouting to each other from their windows (one of the actors is Shmuel Rodansky) (long, 65).
2   Neighbours playing cards through their windows on opposite sides of the street (one bets two shillings and the other decides that it is time to eat) (long, 119).
3   A couple, sitting on a wooden board spanning the street, sing a song (long, 173).

■ **CARMEL NEWSREEL I-066** · December 18 1936
Construction at the Tel Aviv exhibition grounds, the Histadrut pavilion there and the after-effects of the fire. Building a bridge over Wadi Musrara. Laying the cornerstone of a synagogue in Tel Aviv's Hatikvah neighbourhood. Naomi Lief and Yosef Goland sing a Yemenite song (*Yom Hashabbat*).

☐ PART A: FIRE AT THE EXHIBITION GROUNDS (85')
1   Construction site. A burnt car.
2   The Histadrut pavilion before the fire (long, 85).

□ PART B: BUILDING A BRIDGE OVER WADI MUSRARA (65')
1  The narrow old bridge. One bus waiting while another crosses the bridge in the opposite direction (long, 27).
2  Building the new bridge (65).

□ PART C: LAYING THE CORNERSTONE OF THE SECOND SYNAGOGUE IN THE TEL AVIV "HATIKVAH" NEIGHBOURHOOD (112')
1  A street in the Hatikvah neighbourhood in Tel Aviv. People coming to the celebration. A "Welcome" banner and a crowd gathering (92).

שלט: ברוכים הבאים בשם ה'

2  A band playing. The crowd (long, 112).

□ PART D: WOMAN HAULING STONES (16')
1  A woman hauling wagons filled with stones (long, 16).

□ PART E: NAOMI LIEF AND YOSEF GOLAND SINGING *YOM HASHABBAT* ("THE SABBATH DAY") (254')
1  Yosef Goland and Naomi Lief in Yemenite dress singing *Yom Hashabbat* (The Sabbath) (mid, 61).
2  Naomi Lief begins to dance and Goland joins in (long, 145).
3  Goland (c.u., mid, 160).
4  Naomi Lief (c.u., mid, 180).
5  Goland and Lief (mid, 241).
6  Goland and Lief in street clothes (mid, 254).

■ **CARMEL NEWSREEL I-067** · December 27 1936
High Commissioner Sir Arthur Wauchope visits Tel Aviv Port. Arturo Toscanini arrives in Palestine. Celebrating completion of Tel Aviv Port. Exporting citrus fruit.

□ PART A: BRITISH HIGH COMMISSIONER SIR ARTHUR WAUCHOPE VISITS TEL AVIV PORT (70')
1  General view of the port (pan, long, 17).
2  The High Commissioner with port directors and Mayor Israel Rokah (mid, 35).
3  The port. Unloading sacks from a boat (long, mid, 54).
4  The High Commissioner talking to a group of men (mid, 60).
5  The High Commissioner and entourage walking along the dock (mid, 70).

□ PART B: TOSCANINI ARRIVES IN PALESTINE (24')
1  His plane lands at Lod (long, 13).
2  Toscanini passes with his back to the camera (mid, 24).

□ PART C: CELEBRATING THE COMPLETION OF TEL AVIV PORT (39')
1  Pan of the guests in large hall (long, 21).
2  Bank manager Arthur Ruppin speaking (mid, 25).
3  A table and close-up of guests (mid, 33).
4  A different table (mid, 39).

□ PART D: CITRUS SEASON (32')
1  Lifting crates from the dock to load onto a boat (mid, 8).
2  Loading the crates onto the boat (mid, 12).
3  The boat approaching a ship (long, 32).

■ **CARMEL NEWSREEL I-068** · January 1 1937
Sending a crate of oranges to King George VI - children waving goodbye to the boat carrying the oranges. Avraham Shlonsky speaking on 15th anniversary of his literary career. A fierce storm in Palestine - flooding, rough sea, wind damage.

☐ PART A: SENDING A CRATE OF ORANGES TO KING GEORGE VI (49')
1  A boat leaving the dock (mid, 16).
2  Children waving to the boat (mid, 24).
3  The boat approaching a ship (long, 49).

☐ PART B: AVRAHAM SHLONSKY ON THE 15TH ANNIVERSARY OF HIS LITERARY CAREER (102')
1  Shlonsky speaking (mid, 102).

☐ PART C: YOUTH PREPARING TO SETTLE IN TEL HAI

☐ PART D: A FIERCE STORM IN PALESTINE (141')
1  Waves hitting the shore. Waves and debris wash over the wharf. Pan of moored boats tossed by the waves (long, 45).
2  Flooded road and trees standing in water (mid, 51).
3  Destroyed shacks and bent trees blowing in the wind (mid, 81).
4  A broken tree leaning on power lines (mid, 86).
5  Broken trees (mid, 107).
6  Damage, people passing, overturned tables, flooded shacks, an overturned notice-board (mid, 141).

■ **CARMEL NEWSREEL I-069** · January 8 1937
Celebration of the 35th anniversary of the Jewish National Fund. Speakers are: Avraham Kamini, National Chairman of the Jewish National Fund; Leib Yaffe, Chairman of the Keren Hayesod; and Berl Katznelson.

☐ PART A: CELEBRATING THE 35TH ANNIVERSARY OF THE JEWISH NATIONAL FUND (197')
1  TITLE IN HEBREW: THE JEWISH NATIONAL FUND AT 35.

כותרת: קרן הקימת למלאת 35 שנים לה.

2  TITLE IN HEBREW: MR KAMINI, THE NATIONAL CHAIRMAN OF THE JEWISH NATIONAL FUND OPENS THE CONGRESS (mid, 22).

כותרת: מר קמיני - יו"ר הקרן הקימת הארצית פותח את הכנס

3  Avraham Kamini speaking (mid, 90).
4  TITLE IN HEBREW: LEIB YAFFE'S SPEECH! (mid, 95).

כותרת: נאומו של לייב יפה

5  Keren Hayesod chairman Leib Yaffe speaking (mid, 160).
6  TITLE IN HEBREW: BERL KATZNELSON EXPOUNDS AS FOLLOWS: (mid, 167).

כותרת: ברל כנצלסון - נושא דבריו לאמור

7  Berl Katznelson speaking (mid, 197).

■ **CARMEL NEWSREEL I-070** · January 15 1937
Tenth anniversary of the death of Ahad Ha'am. High Commissioner Sir Arthur Wauchope visits the Yizhar factory. Keren Hayesod gathering. Soccer match between Hapoel and a team from Vienna. The Viennese team visits an orchard. Rabbi Yitzhak Herzog arrives in Palestine.

☐ PART A: TENTH ANNIVERSARY OF THE DEATH OF AHAD HA'AM (54')
1  Still photograph of Ahad Ha'am (mid, 4).
2  His tombstone (long, 8).
3  People arriving at the cemetery, standing near his grave. General view of the cemetery (long, 42).
4  Close-up of a speaker and laying a wreath (mid, 54).

## PART B: THE HIGH COMMISSIONER VISITS THE YIZHAR FACTORY (106')
1  The High Commissioner's Rolls Royce arrives at the factory and he is met by the plant's directors (long, 13).
2  The factory's owner explaining something to the High Commisssioner (mid, long, 19).
3  The laboratory and other parts of the factory (long, 51).
4  The exterior of the factory (long, 69).
5  The High Commissioner being taken around the plant (106).

## PART C: KEREN HAYESOD'S "NATIONAL TAX" MONTH GATHERING (138')
1  The dais; the audience; Keren Hayesod director Leib Yaffe speaking (mid, 20).
2  The audience applauding (long, 42).
3  The dais (long, 50).
4  Leib Yaffe speaking (mid, 138).

## PART D: SOCCER MATCH BETWEEN HAPOEL AND A TEAM FROM VIENNA (98')
1  Crowd at the gate (long, 13).
2  The visiting team comes onto the field (long, 23).
3  The team captains shake hands (mid, 32).
4  The game (long, 51).
5  The spectators (long, 66).
6  The game (long, 98).

## PART E: THE SOCCER TEAM FROM VIENNA VISITS AN ORCHARD AND IS GIVEN A CRATE OF ORANGES (51')
1  The team and hosts standing near orange crates, playing around, tossing oranges to each other (long, 21).
2  Filing a crate, sealing it and presenting it to the team (mid, long, 40).
3  Team members walking with sacks of oranges on their shoulders (long, 51).

## PART F: RABBI YITZHAK HERZOG ARRIVES IN PALESTINE (171')
1  TITLE IN HEBREW: WELCOME RABBI! THE GREAT RABBI YITZHAK HERZOG, NEW CHIEF RABBI OF PALESTINE ARRIVES (mid, 11).

כותרת: ברוך הבא רבינו ! הרב הגדול יצחק הרצוג רבה הראשי החדש של ארץ ישראל.

2  A crowd gathering at Haifa port (Haifa) (long, 22).
3  Rabbis and Yishuv leaders (mid, 29).
4  A boat carrying Rabbi Herzog reaches the dock (long, 37).
5  The crowd behind a barrier (mid, 41).
6  Rabbi Herzog leaves the boat and climbs up the stairs, and is met by leaders of the Yishuv (mid, 50).
7  Close-up of Rabbi Herzog surrounded by people (mid, 60).
8  The rabbi's followers begin to leave Haifa port. Herzog leaves the port - shakes hands - is preceded by a beadle in Turkish dress, carrying a staff. Haifa District Commissioner Edward Keith-Roach (mid, 77).
9  A banner in Hebrew: "Welcome in the Name of God". The crowd cheering. Rabbi Herzog (mid, 11).

שלט: ברוך הבא בשם ה' לכבוד מורינו ורבינו הרב הראשי לארץ ישראל.

10  Rabbi and Mrs Herzog sitting in a train (mid, 120).
11  People running along a platform at the station. A crowd on the platform (long, 137).
12  Rabbi Herzog at the window of train carriage. A crowd on the platform carrying umbrellas (mid, long, 159).
13  Rabbi Ben Zion Meir Chai Uziel awaiting Rabbi Herzog (mid, 165).
14  A crowd at Tel Aviv railway station (mid, 171).

■ **CARMEL NEWSREEL I-071** · January 22 1937
The anniversary of the *Ha'aretz* daily newspaper. The Ravitz Choir singing. Shaul Tchernichovsky speaking in the studio in honour of Hebrew Language Week. Danya Levine and her dance troupe.

☐ PART A: NEWSPAPER MONTAGE (47')
1 The 5000th issue of the *Ha'aretz* daily (mid).
2 An issue of the *Davar* daily.
3 Various newspapers (mid).
4 A printing press in action (mid, 47).

☐ PART B: MR RAVITZ AND HIS CHOIR (114')
1 The all-male choir (children and adults) (long, 144).
2 Close-up of the choir (mid, 64).
3 General view of the Ravitz Choir (long, 114).

☐ PART C: SHAUL TCHERNICHOVSKY SPEAKING (69')
1 Shaul Tchernichovsky speaking in the Carmel studio, in honour of Hebrew Language Week (mid, 69).

☐ PART D: DANYA LEVINE AND HER TROUPE DANCE *MASSADA* (339')
1 Dancers on a black background.
2 Danya Levine and dancers perform (mid, 339).

■ **CARMEL NEWSREEL I-072** · January 29 1937
Rabbi Yitzhak Herzog visits Tel Aviv. Yitzhak Ben Tzvi speaks on Naturalisation Month.

☐ PART A: RABBI YITZHAK HERZOG VISITS TEL AVIV (55')
1 Tables set for reception (mid, long, 7).
2 The crowd waiting outside (long, 16).
3 Alexander Ziskind Rabinowitz arrives (mid, 20).
4 Rabbi Herzog arrives (long, mid, 34).
5 A speech in his honour and pan of the audience (long, 55).

☐ PART B: YITZHAK BEN TZVI AND DAVID WERNER SENATOR SPEAK ON NATURALISATION MONTH (250')
1 Ben Tzvi speaks, referring to problems of foreign residents in Palestine and their obligations to the Jewish national institutions (mid, long, 17).
2 Another speaker addresses the same topic.
3 D W Senator of Hebrew University speaks (mid, long, 250).

■ **CARMEL NEWSREEL I-073** · February 6 1937
Children celebrating Tu B'shvat - processions, singing, dancing.

☐ PART A: GERMAN IMMIGRANT YOUTH ARRIVE AT HAIFA PORT

☐ PART B: CHILDREN'S TU B'SHVAT PLAY 1937 (170')

☐ PART C: TU B'SHVAT, 1937 (65')
1 Children with watering cans walk in procession (long, 16).
2 Scouts marching - some carrying shovels.
3 Scouts marching with bugles and drums.
4 Scouts go on stage and play bugles and drums.
5 Children reciting, dancing, marching (65).

### ■ CARMEL NEWSREEL I-074 · February 6 1937
Celebration of Tu B'shvat and of laying the cornerstone for a school in Kiryat Avodah (Holon). Construction of Beit Hadar in Tel Aviv.

□ PART A: TWO CELEBRATIONS AT KIRYAT AVODAH IN HOLON (TU B'SHVAT AND LAYING OF A CORNERSTONE FOR A SCHOOL) (90')
1   A crowd gathers (long, 10).
2   Children dressed up for Tu B'shvat (mid, long, 23).
3   Tauber speaking (mid, 26).
4   General view of the site. The crowd (long, 54).
5   Cornerstone of the Kiryat Avodah school (mid, 67).
6   General view of the dunes at Kiryat Avodah (long, 90).

□ PART B: CONSTRUCTION OF HADASSAH HOUSE IN JERUSALEM (17')
1   General view of the site. Preparations for construction. Digging foundations (long, 17).

□ PART C: CONSTRUCTION OF HADAR HOUSE IN TEL AVIV (213')
1   Construction work. Working with girders. A crane lifting construction materials (long, 64).
2   Construction work - including welding (long, 213).

### ■ CARMEL NEWSREEL I-075 · February 21 1937
Purim celebrations in Tel Aviv (1933-37), including dancing, parades, decorations and floats. Mayor Meir Dizengoff on horseback.

□ PART A: TEL AVIV PURIM CELEBRATIONS 1933 (1041')
1   Houses and streets of Tel Aviv (long, 19).
2   Building floats for the Adloyada parade (mid, long, 47).
3   Decorated buildings - the Mugrabi Cinema decorated with posters announcing the Matateh Theatre's Purim ball (long, 61).
4   Building floats. Decorating the streets (152).
5   Opening the Purim megillah scroll. Close-up of the megillah. A Purim noisemaker. The official poster for the 1933 Purim celebrations (mid, 194).
6   Adults and children celebrating - taking part in the parade and presentations, dancing, singing. The parade floats. Distributing flags to children (mid, c.u., 538). Close-up of adorable children in costumes.
7   Newspapers of the day, reporting world crises (headlines referring to the Nazis) and posters announcing Purim plays, the Agadati ball, etc. (mid, 555).
8   Turning pages of a calendar, counting off the days of celebration from March 3 1933 to March 12 1933.
9   TITLE IN HEBREW: PURIM 1933. FIREMEN'S BAND MARCHES BY AT THE HEAD OF THE PARADE, AS WELL AS MEN ON HORSES (long, 590).
כותרת: פורים תרצ"ג
10  Children in Herbert Samuel Square. Balconies and rooftops crammed with spectators. Men riding horses (long, 978).
11  TITLE IN HEBREW (on a background of fireworks): SEE YOU ON PURIM, 1934 (mid, 1041). כותרת: להתראות בפורים תרצ"ד

□ PART B: TEL AVIV PURIM CELEBRATIONS 1935 (968')
1   Poster on a notice-board, announcing Purim celebrations and the second Maccabia games (mid, long, 44).
2   Decorations on the Ohel Theatre and other buildings. Dancing in the streets at Magen David Adom Square. Firemen's band marches by (long, 135).
3   Dizengoff rides by on a horse (mid, 137).
4   Parade floats - shots from 1934. Dancing in the streets. A children's play on

the seashore (not part of the Purim celebrations). Dancing and singing (long, 264).
5  Scenes from the 1934 Purim parade. A crowd near the Mugrabi Cinema. Dizengoff's car passes. Floats - including a mock Nazi tank painted with swastikas, carrying a large effigy of Hitler (long, 330).
6  A policeman directing traffic. Decorations. The parade. The crowd. The 1935 parade (long, 533).
7  The parade, tourists, camels. Floats advertising local products (Lodzia, Assis, Elite, Shemen). A float advertising a baby-carriage manufacturer with the slogan "Be fruitful and multiply and fill the earth". Distributing handbills.

פרסומת: "פרו ורבו ומלאו את הארץ"

8  Cows in the parade. The Jewish National Fund float (long, 968).

□ PART C: TEL AVIV PURIM CELEBRATIONS (ADLOYADA) (461')
1  The Adloyada parade. Spectators on balconies and rooftops. The crowd at Herbert Samuel Square. A band playing (long, 311).
2  Decorations on buildings moving on the screen. A band and people dancing (mid, 35).
3  Tel Aviv streets at night, decorated with lights. People dancing, dissolve to laughing faces. A giant blindfolded female figure with something in each hand (as if weighing one against the other).
4  A band, moving decorations and upside-down "dancing" houses (461).

□ PART D: TEL AVIV PURIM CELEBRATIONS (102')
1  Meir Dizengoff riding a horse in the Adloyada parade. Streets filled with people. A crocodile float (long, 43).
2  The Lieber chocolate company float. Dancing at Magen David Adom Square - decorated for the holiday. Dizengoff on horseback among the crowd (mid, c.u., 102).

■ **CARMEL NEWSREEL I-076** · February 28 1937
Youth visit the grave of Yosef Trumpeldor at Tel Hai. Construction of a bridge on the Yarkon River. South Yehuda region schoolchildren meet in Rehovot. Press conference at the construction site of the Habimah Theatre.

□ PART A: HANOAR HA'OVED YOUTH VISIT THE GRAVE OF YOSEF TRUMPELDOR (96')
1  On the way to Tel Hai (by bus) (mid, 8).
2  Walking to the grave (long, 33).
3  Standing on a roof in the Tel Hai courtyard (mid, 37).
4  Walking to the grave (long, 58).
5  At the grave - the lion monument (mid, long, 96).

□ PART B: CONSTRUCTION OF A BRIDGE OVER THE YARKON RIVER (HERZLIYAH ROAD) (116')
1  A wood and iron structure (mid, 17).
2  Pouring concrete, the architects on hand (long, 51).
3  Various shots of the bridge (mid, 69).
4  The bridge and the river - from below (long, 84).
5  Engineers and contractors talking (mid, 95).
6  The bridge (long, 105).
7  Drinking a toast (mid, 116).

□ PART C: SCHOOLCHILDREN FROM THE SOUTH YEHUDA REGION GATHER IN REHOVOT (111')
1  The children on parade (long, 45).

2   The children marching in a clearing near the school (long, mid, 78).
3   The children exercise together in the schoolyard (long, 111).

◻ PART D: PRESS CONFERENCE AT THE HABIMAH THEATRE (258')
1   Guests arriving (long, 12).
2   The dais, a long table with food, man eating a banana (pan, mid, 34).
3   Someone explaining the construction plan on site (long, 51).
4   General view of the building (first floor) under construction (long, 124).
5   Guests eating and drinking (mid, 135).
6   Habimah official speaking (mid, 230).
7   Someone speaking (mid).
8   View of Tel Aviv, the buildings and people (258).

■ **CARMEL NEWSREEL I-077** · March 7 1937
Old Safed. Flying glider-planes on the beach. Firemen extinguishing a fire in Tel Aviv's Montefiore neighbourhood. A ball and handicrafts fair for the Amal vocational school in Tel Aviv. The writer Z Anochi reading *Bar Abba* aloud.

◻ PART A: THE OLD CITY OF SAFED (20')
1   Alleyways, Arabs and Jews (20).

◻ PART B: GLIDER-FLYING (130')
1   A truck followed by a motorcycle brings the gliders to the beach. The gliders are unloaded and assembled (mid, 54).
2   Gliders in flight (long, 93).
3   Launching the glider by pulling it with a rope, along a hilltop. The glider lifts off and glides down towards the sea (mid, long, 130).

◻ PART C: A FIRE IN TEL AVIV'S MONTEFIORE NEIGHBOURHOOD (35')
1   Firemen putting out the fire (long, 35).

◻ PART D: AMAL VOCATIONAL SCHOOL BALL IN TEL AVIV (63')
1   Guests sitting at tables and a woman speaking (long, 18).
2   Making a wicker chair. Selling handicrafts (mid, 49).
3   Dancing a waltz (long, 63).

◻ PART E: Z ANOCHI READS *BAR ABBA* (227')
1   The writer Z Anochi reading aloud from the play *Bar Abba* (227).

■ **CARMEL NEWSREEL I-078** · March 14 1937
A diamond wedding anniversary at an old age home. A fancy ball honouring locally produced products at San Remo Casino. Mrs Yosefa Shocken singing a love song.

◻ PART A: A DIAMOND WEDDING ANNIVERSARY AT AN OLD-AGE HOME (111')
1   The couple passes by as everyone applauds (mid, 32).
2   The couple sitting among the guests (mid, c.u., 48).
3   Drinking a toast (mid, long, 64).
4   Dancing around the couple (long, 111).

◻ PART B: MADE-IN-PALESTINE BALL AT THE SAN REMO CASINO IN TEL AVIV (14')
1   Dancing at the ball. Women dancing in dresses on which the names of companies are printed (Okava, Elite, Atara Coffee) and a woman wearing a crown on which the word "chocolate" (in Hebrew) is visible (mid, 14).

◻ PART C: YOSEFA SHOCKEN SINGING A LOVE SONG (199')
1   Shocken appears among the trees in a wadi (Wadi Musrara - Ayalon) and

begins to sing (long, 37).
2  Shocken singing in the studio (mid, 199).

■ **CARMEL NEWSREEL I-079** · March 21 1937
Growing and packing flowers at a nursery in Ramat Gan. Building the settlement of Ein Hakoreh. A fire at the settlement pavilion at the Tel Aviv exhibition grounds. Matateh Theatre skit *Oh Toscanini*.

☐ PART A: FLOWERS AT BRYER'S NURSERY (115')
1  Flowers on bushes (long, 29).
2  Individual flowers (c.u., 60).
3  The nursery (long, 80).
4  A woman working in the flower fields and a woman walking among the flowers (mid, 83).
5  Preparing packing crates (long, 104).
6  Packing flowers (mid, long, 115). TITLE IN HEBREW: BRYER FLOWERS, RAMAT GAN, 52 BIALIK STREET. INDEPENDENT NURSERIES IN BNEI ZION AND KFAR SABA.

כתובת: פרחים בריר, רמת גן רחוב ביאליק 52. משתילות עצמיות בכני ציון

ובכפר סבא

☐ PART B: BUILDING THE SETTLEMENT OF EIN HAKOREH (13')
1  Working on the security fence (long, 13).

☐ PART C: A FIRE AT THE SETTLEMENT PAVILION AT THE TEL AVIV EXHIBITION GROUNDS (83')
1  The settlement pavilion during the 1936 exhibition (long, 29).
2  The same pavilion after the fire. Searching among the debris (83).

☐ PART D: THE MATATEH THEATRE'S *OH TOSCANINI* (503')
1  Two cantors - one Ashkenazi and the other Sephardi (played by Landau and Shmuel Rodansky) - come before a rabbi and complain that people want to hear nothing but Toscanini and that the public is possessed by a dybbuk (an evil spirit) (mid, 196).
2  A woman enters, wailing, with her daughter. She complains to the rabbi that her daughter is possessed by the Toscanini dybbuk. The rabbi says a miracle is needed to exorcise an entire community (mid, 337).
3  Another actor enters bringing a black cantor from America, whom he says is the miracle they need. All present ask the black man (who says he comes from a long line of cantors going back to Abyssinia) to prove he is a cantor (long, 387).
4  The black cantor (an imitation of Al Jolson) sings a Hassidic melody and all join in singing and dancing. "Heed not that I am black and that the sun has darkened me" (Song of Songs), "I am a Jew and my melodies are Jewish" (503).

מילות השיר: " אל תראוני שאני שחרחורת ששזפתני השמש" , אני יהודי

ונגינותי יהודיות.

■ **CARMEL NEWSREEL I-080** · March 28 1937
Yosef Aaronowitz's funeral. Colonel John Henry Patterson (former commander of the Jewish Legion) visits the construction site of Metzudat Ze'ev (named for Ze'ev Jabotinsky).

☐ PART A: FUNERAL OF YOSEF AARONOWITZ (127')
1  The funeral procession (63).
2  The funeral procession passes through the square in front of the municipality building (long, 127).

□ PART B: COLONEL PATTERSON VISITS THE CONSTRUCTION SITE OF METZUDAT ZE'EV IN TEL AVIV (150')
1   Patterson and entourage arrive at the construction site (long, 27).
2   Patterson (mid, long, 36).
3   The building under construction. Colonel Patterson receiving explanations from the builders. The building (89).
4   Colonel Patterson speaking (mid, 150).

■ CARMEL NEWSREEL I-081 · April 6 1937
Opening of the new Hadar Hacarmel road in Haifa. Public relations tour of Hillel Pharmaceuticals. Athletics competition in Rehovot. The quarry in Migdal Tzedek. The first flight of the Poland-Palestine air route.

□ PART A: OPENING THE HADAR HACARMEL ROAD IN HAIFA (87')
1   Guests arriving (long, 14).
2   Haifa District Commissioner Edward Keith-Roach arrives and is greeted by dignitaries. Haifa Mayor Hassan Shoukri arrives and they pose for a photograph (long, 34).
3   Keith-Roach speaking (mid, long, 45).
4   The crowd. The Mayor speaking (mid, long, 61).
5   Cutting the film (long, 74).
6   The road. A carriage passing (long, 87).

□ PART B: PUBLIC RELATIONS TOUR OF THE HILLEL PHARMACEUTICALS COMPANY (101')
1   General view of the factory. Guests arriving at the gate (long, 19).
2   Guests in an auditorium listening to the factory manager. The factory manager speaking (long, mid, 36).
3   Work at the factory. The laboratory (mid, 80).
4   The manager speaking (mid, 83).
5   The guests leaving the factory (long, 101).

□ PART C: ATHLETICS COMPETITION IN REHOVOT (76')
1   The schoolyard. The winner being carried on shoulders. The shot-put. The high-jump (a girl). The marathon (long, 50).
2   Soccer (long, 76).

□ PART D: THE MIGDAL TZEDEK QUARRY (116')
1   General view of Migdal Tzedek (long, 27).
2   Working the quarry (long, 55).
3   A machine making gravel. Machine parts. Working on the gravel-making machine (long, 103).
4   Wagons filled with gravel (116).

□ PART E: THE ARRIVAL OF THE FIRST FLIGHT OF THE POLAND-PALESTINE AIR ROUTE (137')
1   An airplane arrives at Lod Airport (long, 30).
2   Passengers disembark (long, 57).
3   Pan of the aircraft (long, 76).
4   Objects scattered on the ground (mid, long, 84).
5   Passengers board the airplane (long, 106).
6   Passengers seated in the airplane (long, 114).
7   The airplane is started and takes off (long, 137).

■ CARMEL NEWSREEL I-082 · April 12 1937
High Commissioner Sir Arthur Wauchope visits Petah Tikva. Laying a cornerstone for the Hapoel Hamizrachi building in Bnei Brak, with speeches by Rabbi Ben Zion

**76** *Carmel Newsreels: Series 1*

Meir Chai Uziel and Rabbi Moshe Avigdor Amiel. Building the settlement of Beit Yosef. Memorial service for the heroes of Petah Tikva (killed on the road to Rosh Ha'ayin). A road accident on the road to Petah Tikva - an overturned bus.

□ PART A: THE HIGH COMMISSIONER VISITS PETAH TIKVA (195')
1   Iris shot: general view of Petah Tikva and various shots of the city (95).
2   A crowd gathers in the central square (long, 106).
3   High Commissioner Sir Arthur Wauchope arrives and ascends the municipality building stairs accompanied by Mayor Shlomo Stampfer (long, 141).
4   The Mayor speaking. Wauchope speaking (long, 153).
5   The High Commissioner and the Mayor descending the municipality building steps (long, 178).
6   Wauchope and the Mayor are greeted by the crowd (long, 195).

□ PART B: LAYING A CORNERSTONE FOR THE HAPOEL HAMIZRACHI BUILDING IN BNEI BRAK (74')
1   Decorated gate and banner in Hebrew: "Welcome in the Name of God" (long, 8).   שלט: ברוכים הבאים בשם ה'
2   A crowd gathering. Rabbi Amiel and Rabbi Uziel (28).
3   The dais. Rabbi Amiel speaking (long, 60).
4   Rabbi Uziel speaking (mid, long, 67).
5   General view of the site (long, 74).

□ PART C: BUILDING THE SETTLEMENT OF BEIT YOSEF (50')
1   On the way to the Tower and Stockade settlement site (long, 11).
2   Singing on the way to the site. Raising the tower (long. 50).
3   Women preparing sandwiches (long, 24).
4   Men walking in the fields, where other men are harvesting.
5   Trucks drive by on a road, trucks loaded with people.
6   Pan across a large group arriving at the new settlement.
7   Women preparing sandwiches and peeling eggs.
8   Avraham Herzfeld singing with the others (long, 34).
9   Arab guests sit with the group - eating and drinking (long, 50).

□ PART D: MEMORIAL CEREMONY FOR THE HEROES OF PETAH TIKVA (71')
1   A large crowd standing near the municipality building (long, 9).
2   Mayor Stampfer speaking (mid, 16).
3   The monument to those killed in Petah Tikva - erected on the spot where they fell (on the road to Rosh Ha'ayin) (mid, 26).
4   A crowd standing around the monument (long, 46).
5   Mounted security guards in the streets of Petah Tikva (long, 71).

□ PART E: A ROAD ACCIDENT NEAR PETAH TIKVA (18')
1   Moving the overturned bus (long, mid, 18).

■ **CARMEL NEWSREEL I-083** · April 19 1937
Harvesting and packing potatoes for Tnuva. After the fire in Nahalat Binyamin. Improving the Carmel Market in Tel Aviv. English boy scouts visit Tel Aviv. Mrs Wolodka sings a lullaby, with the sunset and the sea.

□ PART A: HARVEST-TIME (107')
1   General view of the field (dissolve, long, 19).
2   Women working in the field (mid).
3   The fields (long, 28).
4   Washing the produce (mid, 48).
5   Picking potatoes, putting them in crates, sealing and stacking the crates (mid, 95).

6  Crates marked in English: New potatoes-Tnuva-grown in Palestine.
7  Vegetables at the market (mid, long, 107).

□ PART B: AFTER THE FIRE IN TEL AVIV'S NAHALAT BINYAMIN NEIGHBOURHOOD (24')
1  Nahalat Binyamin after the fire (long, 24).

□ PART C: IMPROVEMENTS IN THE MARKETS OF TEL AVIV (108')
1  Arab vendors at a marketplace (mid, long, 42).
2  Fruit, vegetable and other stands, all displaying the Made-in-Palestine seal (long, mid, 86).
3  Close-up of apples with flies on them (102).
4  The market (108).

□ PART D: ENGLISH BOY SCOUTS IN TEL AVIV (191')
1  The scouts marching, carrying scouting equipment (mid, 9).
2  Pitching a tent (mid, 37).
3  Setting up flagpoles for the British and Jewish flags (long, 48).
4  Joint roll-call. The Jewish flag is raised. The scouts perform straight-arm salutes (mid, long, 99).
5  General view of the Tel Aviv suburb where the scouts' camp is located (long, 104).
6  A boy scout being awarded a merit badge (mid, 118).
7  The English scouts get off their bus and enter the Tel Aviv municipality building (mid, 118).
8  Tel Aviv Mayor Israel Rokah speaking, followed by one of the English guests (mid, 152).
9  The scouts leave the building and fall into formation outside (mid, 168).
10  The scouts walking along railroad tracks near the seashore (long, 191).

□ PART E: MRS WOLODKA SINGING A LULLABY (195')
1  Wolodka singing near a cradle (long, 99).
2  Wolodka standing near the cradle (mid, 195).

□ PART F: MRS WOLODKA SINGING A LULLABY (75')
1  Sunset over the sea (c.u.).
2  Reeds in the water (long).
3  A baby in the cradle (c.u.).
4  Clouds (long).
5  The sun reflecting on the water (long).
6  Trees and sky (through a red filter). Cactus and sky (long, 75).

■ **CARMEL NEWSREEL I-084** · April 26 1937
A children's Lag Ba'omer parade and exhibition in Petah Tikva. Tel Aviv scouts celebrate Lag Ba'omer around a bonfire. Scenes from the play *The Emperor Jones*.

□ PART A: LAG BA'OMER PARADE IN PETAH TIKVA (124')
1  Children marching through the streets of Petah Tikva (long, 39).
2  Mayor Shlomo Stampfer of Petah Tikva speaking (mid, 45).
3  Semaphore demonstration on the field (long, 56).
4  The parade (long, mid, 86).
5  Marching to the soccer field (long, 98).
6  Many children participating in a semaphore demonstration (mid, long, 124).

□ PART B: TEL AVIV SCOUTS' LAG BA'OMER BONFIRE (92')
1  Scouts (boys and girls) preparing the bonfire (mid, long, 26).
2  Sitting around the fire (long, 32).

3   The fire (mid, 50).
4   Silhouette of someone playing the violin in front of the fire (mid, 59).
5   Dancing around the fire (silhouette) (mid, 92).

□ PART C: *THE EMPEROR JONES* ON STAGE (82')
1   Jones sitting in front of a tent delivering a monologue (long, 82).

□ PART D: *THE EMPEROR JONES* ON STAGE (400')
1   Jones' head - tired and dreaming (c.u., 5).
2   Black rebel leader's head with painted face (c.u., 13).
3   Caesar Jones running in the woods. He stops, leans against a tree and sits down (long, 56).
4   Caesar Jones mocks himself (mid, 138).
5   Close-up of Jones, upon which scenes from the days that he was a slave are superimposed (c.u., 171).
6   Jones' head (c.u., 236).
7   Slavery scenes - also superimposed on Jones' head (mid, long, 297).
8   Jones being sold (mid, 324).
9   Dancer Gertrude Kraus and her troupe dance as Jones prays (long, 400).

■ **CARMEL NEWSREEL I-085** · May 2 1937
May Day celebrations in a stadium in Tel Aviv. Laying a cornerstone for a building of Mizrahi Pioneer Women in Tel Aviv. Musician Shultz is honoured by the Polish consul. Poverty in Jerusalem is shown in honour of Social Welfare Week. Lag Ba'omer procession with Torah scrolls in Meiron.

□ PART A: MAY DAY IN TEL AVIV (270')
1   Marching to the Maccabia stadium near the Yarkon River (long, 40).
2   The crowd (long, 57).
3   The crowd in the stands. Everyone sits down after the anthem is sung (long, 79).
4   The dais, decorated with a banner and a flag. Pan of those on the field (long, 110).
5   The crowd applauds (long, 129).
6   The parade, carrying flags, marches by the dais (mid, long, 173).
7   The crowd applauds (long, 182).
8   On the dais are Histadrut leaders, including David Remez and Ya'akov Zerubavel (mid, 192).
9   Passing before the dais (long, 217).
10  Athletes (Hapoel sports club) go by (mid, 238).
11  The dais with banner. Someone speaking (mid, 253).

שלט: אחד במאי - חג העבודה הבין לאומי

12  The crowd in the stands (long).
13  The youth groups march in. People with flags leading huge crowd across the field (270).

□ PART B: LAYING A CORNERSTONE FOR THE MIZRACHI PIONEER WOMEN'S BUILDING IN TEL AVIV (75')
1   A "Welcome" banner. The crowd (mid, 13).

שלט: ברוכים הבאים בית צעירות מזרחי ע"י הסתדרות נשים מזרחי

2   A crowd of women (mid, 19).
3   Rabbi Moshe Avigdor Amiel and Rabbi Ben Zion Meir Chai Uziel speak (respectively) and take their seats (mid, 29).
4   Two more speakers and the crowd listening (mid, 50).
5   Rabbi Uziel speaking (long, 64).
6   Guests seated at tables (long, 75).

☐ PART C: MUSICIAN SHULTZ HONOURED (57')
1   Shultz arrives at the Polish consulate, guests (including a woman in peasant dress) (long, 19).
2   The consul pins a medal on Shultz's lapel and shakes his hand (mid, 46).
3   Shultz wearing his medal and the crowd applauding (mid, 57).

☐ PART D: SOCIAL WELFARE WEEK IN JERUSALEM (102')
1   A social worker sorting cards (long, 10).
2   Poor neighbourhoods in Jerusalem (long, 28).
3   Shots of poor children and elderly men and women (mid, 70).
4   Children sitting around a table (mid, 79).
5   A girl working on a loom and children playing in a social welfare institution (mid, 102).

☐ PART E: LAG BA'OMER IN MEIRON (47')
1   A procession with Torah scrolls, from Safed to Meiron. Men wearing fez hats and keffiyehs also in the crowd (mid, 47).

■ **CARMEL NEWSREEL I-086** · May 9 1937
Children perform gymnastics at Shalva High School in Tel Aviv. Celebrations in Jerusalem, Netanya, Haifa and Tel Aviv in honour of the coronation of King George VI.

☐ PART A: LAG BA'OMER CELEBRATION AT SHALVA HIGH SCHOOL IN TEL AVIV (256')
1   Children on parade (mid, long, 16).
2   Children's play. Gymnastics display. Children watching from the rooftop. The children performing gymnastics and dancing (mid, long, 125).
3   Gymnastics - jumping over a vaulting-horse, a tug-of-war and playing leap-frog (long, 167).
4   A first aid drill (long, 187).
5   A sack-race, a fake boxing match - the crowd applauds and the winner raises his arm (long, 256).

☐ PART B: JERUSALEM CELEBRATES THE CORONATION OF KING GEORGE VI AT THE ARMY BASE IN TALPIOT (90')
1   Dignitaries arriving - including army officers (mid, long, 29).
2   High Commissioner Sir Arthur Wauchope speaking.
3   Soldiers marching - including "Highlanders" (long, 70).
4   Cavalry, wearing keffiyehs (possibly of the Arab Legion) (long, 90).

☐ PART C: NETANYA CELEBRATES THE CORONATION OF KING GEORGE VI (139')
1   Firemen blowing trumpets to announce the coronation (mid, 8).
2   General view of Netanya with decorated streets (long, 24).
3   Decorations - City Hall - a crowd gathering (mid, long, 55).
4   Schoolchildren perform gymnastics (long, 97).
5   Jewish Legion veterans (mid, 78).
6   Soldiers marching and a band (long, 97).
7   The crowd (long, 106).
8   Ovad Ben-Ami speaking and the crowd listening (pan, mid, long, 131).
9   Decorations and the Jewish flag (long, 139).

☐ PART D: HAIFA CELEBRATES THE CORONATION OF KING GEORGE VI (175')
1   The royal seal and three flags (mid, 7).
2   The streets decorated with flags and crowns (long, 51).
3   Infantry and cavalry on parade (long, 90).

4   Dignitaries - including Haifa Mayor Hassan Bey Shukri (mid, 115).
5   Haifa District Commissioner Edward Keith-Roach getting out of a car (mid).
6   The District Commissioner reviews the parade (mid, long, 144).
7   Soldiers on parade. The flag is raised and the District Commissioner salutes (long, 175).

□ PART E: TEL AVIV CELEBRATES THE CORONATION OF KING GEORGE VI (291')
1   A crowd gathering (mid, 9).
2   Jewish Legion veterans arrive, wearing their medals (mid, 39).
3   Boy scouts on parade (long, 45).
4   Guests arrive at Meir Park and sit at tables. Rabbis Amiel and Uziel can be seen seated at one of the tables (long, mid, 86).
5   Mayor Israel Rokah speaks. Yehuda Nadivi also appears. Waiters moving among the tables. The guests applaud (mid, 102).
6   Tel Aviv lit up at night, including the municipality building decorated with lights in the shape of a crown (long, 291).

■ **CARMEL NEWSREEL I-087** · May 16 1937
Shavuot celebrations at Shalva High School in Tel Aviv, in Hadera and Netanya. Celebrating the anniversary of the opening of Tel Aviv Port.

□ PART A: TITLE: PALESTINE "SCHAVUOTH" FESTIVALS (379')
1   TITLE IN ENGLISH AND HEBREW: "PALESTINE SCHAWUOTH [sic] FESTIVALS". FIRST FRUIT CELEBRATIONS AT SHALVA HIGH SCHOOL IN TEL AVIV. DIRECTED BY TEHILLA RESSLER. MUSIC BY H. LADENDORF (mid, 14).

כותרת: חגיגת הבכורים בגימנסיה "שלווה" בתל-אביב". במוי: תהלה רסלר.
מוסיקה: ח. לדנדורף.

2   The children's play. The children present the "first fruits" (long, mid, 100).
3   The play (about the harvest and The Book of Ruth) (mid, long, 309).
4   The audience and the children carrying banners. The children dance on stage. The audience (long, 379).

□ PART B: SHAVUOT CELEBRATIONS IN HADERA (47')
1   Schoolchildren bring the "first fruits" (long, 26).
2   Dancing (long, 47).

□ PART C: INTRODUCTION TO SHAVUOT CELEBRATIONS (23')
1   A band and children marching in the streets.
2   A sign in Hebrew: "He who works his land shall eat his fill of bread" (long, 23).

פלקט: עובד אדמתו ישבע לחם.

□ PART D: SHAVUOT CELEBRATIONS IN NETANYA (94')
1   Children carrying the "first fruits" walking on a background map of Palestine - the music is the song *Salenu Al Ktefenu* ("OUR BASKETS ON OUR SHOULDERS") (23).
2   A baby in a baby-carriage - both baby and carriage decorated with flowers. A child on a bicycle (mid, 29).
3   The crowd sits (long, 40).
4   Mayor Ben-Ami speaking (mid, 48).
5   A choir. A school procession and presenting of first fruits (mid, long, 94).

□ PART E: ANNIVERSARY OF THE OPENING OF TEL AVIV PORT (133')
1   Banner in Hebrew: "Long Live Tel Aviv Port". Pan of the crowd (long, 20).

כתובת: יחי נמל תל-אביב.

2  Athletic competitions near the docks - diving, walking on a narrow plank over the water (long, 45).
3  General view of the port and moored boats (long, 55).
4  The port (long, 64).
5  The dock (long, 73).
6  A boat (long, 82).
7  The crowd. A boat (long, 128).
8  Swimming marathon (long, 133).

■ **CARMEL NEWSREEL I-088** · May 23 1937
Kindergarten children bring Shavuot "first fruits". First anniversary of Shmaryahu Levin's death. High Commissioner Sir Arthur Wauchope participates in a tree-planting ceremony at Kfar Shmaryahu. The "Gilali" quartet sings *Oh Shoes*. Construction.

□ PART A: TEL AVIV KINDERGARTEN CHILDREN BRING SHAVUOT "FIRST FRUITS" (76')
1  Kindergarten children carrying "first fruits" (long, 21).
2  The children, told about the custom of bringing the first fruits to Jerusalem, present their "first fruits" (long, mid, 68).
3  A pile of "first fruits" (mid, 76).

□ PART B: UNVEILING A TOMBSTONE ON THE GRAVE OF SHMARYAHU LEVIN (ON THE FIRST ANNIVERSARY OF HIS DEATH) (61')
1  The tombstone (mid, 8).
2  A wreath is laid on the grave. Prayers are recited (mid, 35).
3  Alexander Ziskind Rabinowitz recites the prayer for the dead (mid, 44).
4  A cantor recites psalms (mid, 61).

□ PART C: PLANTING TREES IN KFAR SHMARYAHU (196')
1  General view of Kfar Shmaryahu - houses, fields (long, 28).
2  Building houses (mid, 42).
3  People arriving at the celebration site (mid, long, 57).
4  Two people talking (mid, 64).
5  High Commissioner Wauchope and other dignitaries arriving (long, 96).
6  The guests sitting at tables and eating (long, 124).
7  High Commissioner Wauchope speaking (long, 131).
8  Another speaker (mid, 139).
9  The High Commissioner holding a portrait of Shmaryahu Levin (mid, 151).
10  Going to plant trees (long, 166).
11  Sir Arthur Wauchope and others planting trees (long, 166).
12  Wauchope departs (mid, 196).

□ PART D: MOSHE WILENSKI'S "GILALI" QUARTET (175')
1  The quartet sings *Oh Shoes* (mid, 69).
2  A wheelbarrow at the singers' feet and tilt up to their faces (mid, 175).

□ PART E: TITLE: NEW BUILDING ON THE RUINS OF THE PAST (126')

כותרת: על חורבות העבר - בנין ויצירה.

1  Manufacturing bricks (mid).
2  Digging foundations. A crane lifts bricks up to the roof (mid).
3  Laying bricks (mid).
4  Bending girders. A lift on scaffolding (mid, long, 126).

■ **CARMEL NEWSREEL I-089** · May 30 1937
A painting of Jerusalem by Ludwig Blum is displayed at the Tel Aviv Museum.

Internationally famous Yiddish film star and director Maurice Schwartz visits Carmel Film Studio during the production of *Over the Ruins*. A school for the blind in Jerusalem - prayers, handicrafts, study, recreation, music.

▫ PART A: A PAINTING OF JERUSALEM AT THE TEL AVIV MUSEUM (57')
1   An exhibition hall at the museum and the painting hanging on the wall (mid, 9).
2   Pan of the painting from the Dome of the Rock over the entire city (c.u., 30).
3   Tilt up and down of the painting (c.u., 57).

▫ PART B: MAURICE SCHWARTZ VISITS CARMEL FILM (91')
1   Alfred Wolf brings Maurice Schwartz in to the studio during the production of *Over the Ruins* - view of the actors and children. Schwartz shakes hands with Nathan Axelrod and with Danya Levine (long, 28).
2   Maurice Schwartz holds Nathan Axelrod's eldest son, Moshe, in his arms and speaks.
3   Schwartz, standing alone, speaks in Hebrew of his joy at being in Palestine (mid, 91).

▫ PART C: SCHOOL FOR THE BLIND IN JERUSALEM (188')
1   Prayers at the school for the blind.
2   Blind children playing with toys with the assistance of their teacher. The teacher gives a girl a doll. The girl holding the doll (mid, 46).
3   Two children with the teacher at the piano (mid, 54).
4   Handicrafts - weaving (long, mid, 99).
5   Eating (long, 113).
6   Reading Braille (long, 125).
7   Playing chess (mid, 132).
8   Studying in Braille in a classroom (long, 137).
9   A teacher reads aloud from a book in Braille. A student band plays tunes - including "Hatikva" (later the anthem of the Jewish state) (mid, 188).

■ **CARMEL NEWSREEL I-090** · June 7 1937
Athletics exhibition at graduation from Hapoel sports club leadership training course.

▫ PART A: HAPOEL LEADERSHIP COURSE GRADUATION (144')
1   General view of the site (long, 6).
2   Marching exercises (long, 21).
3   The band (mid, 28).
4   Marching (mid, 37).
5   Athletic exhibition in groups and pairs (long, mid, 83).
6   The crowd (mid, 89).
7   Athletic exhibition and running an obstacle course (mid, 144).

■ **CARMEL NEWSREEL I-091** · June 14 1937
The Palestine Maritime League meets aboard the ship *HAR ZION*, en route to Cyprus.

▫ PART A: MEETING OF THE MARITIME LEAGUE (EN ROUTE TO CYPRUS) (171')
1   On the deck of the *HAR ZION* (mid, 12).
2   Tel Aviv Port and boats (long, 16).
3   On deck - the band playing and people listening to the music (long, 45).
4   Abba Choushi speaking and the audience (mid, 64).
5   Abba Choushi speaking (c.u., 86).
6   People listening to the speaker (pan, mid, 97).
7   Journalists, including Klinov of *Ha'aretz* (mid, 105).

8  The writing hand of a journalist (mid, 109).
9  David Remez speaking (c.u., 130).
10 One of the Maritime League officials speaking (c.u., 158).
11 General view of the crowd in the room (long, 167).
12 The exterior of the ship (long, 171).

■ **CARMEL NEWSREEL I-092** · June 21 1937
Presentation of the "Jerusalem flag" at a school in Hadera. Laying a cornerstone for a shopping centre in Netanya. Beit Hinuch pupils visit Neveh Haim. Laying a cornerstone for the settlement of Hulda.

□ PART A: PRESENTATION OF THE "JERUSALEM FLAG" IN HADERA (151')
1  Schoolchildren, with wreaths on their heads, marching with palm branches and a flag on a pole - in the Hadera schoolyard (mid, long, 64).
2  The crowd (mid, 76).
3  A speaker (mid, 86).
4  Children jumping for joy. The crowd in the schoolyard (mid, 97).
5  Presenting the flag. A speaker (mid, long, 151).

□ PART B: LAYING A CORNERSTONE FOR A SHOPPING CENTRE IN NETANYA (77')
1  The municipality building and people gathering (long, 10).
2  People listening to a speech (mid, 23).
3  Laying the cornerstone (mid, 40).
4  People seated in a hall. A speaker (mid, 56).
5  A festive meal and speakers, man pouring draught (long, 77).

□ PART C: BEIT HINUCH PUPILS VISIT NEVEH HAIM (188')
1  General view of Neveh Haim (pan, long, 26).
2  Pupils of the Beit Hinuch school arrive carrying flags (long, 49).
3  General view of the area (pan, long, 79).
4  Street in Neveh Haim. Gardens. Interior of the synagogue (mid, long, 100).
5  Adults and children in various shaded spots (mid, 141).
6  Adults and children eating and drinking (mid, 154).
7  The children playing in parks in Neveh Haim (long, 165).
8  A teacher tells the children a story (mid, 181). Close-up of little girl as they all sit under the trees.
9  Houses in Neveh Haim (pan, long, 188).

□ PART D: LAYING A CORNERSTONE FOR NEW SETTLEMENT OF HULDA (119')
1  General view of the site (long, 21).
2  A three-figured statue (mid, 33).
3  The crowd walking towards the site (long, 66).
4  A banner in Hebrew on the gate: "We shall go up by the light of our faith" (long, 75).   כתובת על השער: באור אמונתנו נעלה.
5  Two elderly men in oriental dress (mid, 81).
6  A young man speaking and the crowd listening to him (pan, mid, 95).
7  A speaker. Men signing a paper (mid, 100).
8  Laying the cornerstone (tilt up) (mid, 119).

■ **CARMEL NEWSREEL I-093** · June 28 1937
Opening of Bialik House and ceremony in memory of Chaim Nahman Bialik. Hapoel boat returns from Cyprus: its six sailors are welcomed. Building a new neighbourhood on the banks of the Yarkon River. Maccabi youth on parade. Harvest celebrations at Kibbutz Mizrah, in the Jezreel Valley, including beautiful footage of the settlement.

□ PART A: OPENING OF BIALIK HOUSE AND MEMORIAL SERVICE FOR CHAIM NACHMAN BIALIK (96')
1   A bust of Bialik from afar. Dissolve to close-up of the bust (mid,14).
2   Garden and entrance to the house (no. 22) (tilt up to the house) (long, 33).

כתובת: בית ח.נ. ביאליק

3   People entering the house (mid, 45).
4   People standing in the garden (mid, 52).
5   People leaving the house (long, 64).
6   Memorial service near Bialik's grave at cemetery on Trumpeldor Street. Pan of large crowd at graveside, with many monuments in background (long, 96).

□ PART B: HAPOEL BOAT - *THE TRUMPELDOR* - RETURNS FROM CYPRUS (65')
1   The sailing boat entering Tel Aviv Port (long, 36).
2   The sailors welcomed at the dock (mid, 58).
3   The six sailors, wearing Greek sailors' hats (pan, mid, 65).

□ PART C: BUILDING A NEW NEIGHBOURHOOD ON THE BANKS OF THE YARKON RIVER (137')
1   General view of the site (pan, long, 14).
2   A tractor preparing the land and levelling the site (mid, 51).
3   Workers filling carts with earth, pushing them along tracks, emptying them and returning (long, mid, 137).

□ PART D: MACCABI ON PARADE IN HONOUR OF MR GRADINGER (44')
1   Pan of Maccabi youth in formation (long, 13).
2   Children walking with bicycles (mid, 21).
3   Raising the flag (on a pole affixed to a basketball hoop) (mid, 44).

□ PART E: TITLE: KIBUZ [sic] MIZRAH CELEBRATES THE HARVEST FEAST (211')

כותרת: חג הקציר בקבוץ מזרע (בעמק יזרעל)

1   TITLE: HARVEST FESTIVAL IN THE KEREN HAYESOD SETTLEMENT MIZRAH
2   Pan of Kibbutz Mizrah with water tower in background (long, 49).
3   Sacks of grain (pan, long, 64).
4   A silo with a banner in Hebrew: "And the storehouses shall be filled with grain" (biblical). A banner in Hebrew on a house: "And you shall live in peace on your land" (biblical) (mid, 80).

כתובת על מגדל תבואה: ומלאו הגרנות בר. כתובת על בית: וחיו על אדמתכם לבטח.

5   A gate decorated with hay (mid, 89).
6   The procession passing through the fields (pan and c.u.), some on horseback. A sign in Hebrew: "Thus we began". Followed by a horse-drawn plough and young people carrying scythes and pitchforks.
7   Sign in Hebrew: "Thus we continued". Followed by tractors and farm machinery decorated with flowers (mid, long, 155).

פלקט: ככה התחלנו, ככה המשכנו

8   A truck carrying children. The procession reaches a courtyard.
9   A gate with a banner in Hebrew: "And the time of threshing will reach the time of gathering the fruit of the vine" (biblical) - "Strength and Courage in the Dwelling of the Socialist Worker of the Soil" (long, 194).

כתובות על השער: און ועוז במשכנות עובד האדמה הסוציאליסטי - והשיג לכם דיישאת בציר וכו'.

10  A speaker (dissolve to decorations) (mid, 211).

■ **CARMEL NEWSREEL I-094** · July 4 1937
Election of delegates to the 20th Zionist Congress, which will take place in Zürich. Maurice Schwartz leaves Palestine by airplane. Technical exhibition at the Montefiore School in Tel Aviv. Building Kibbutz Tirat Tzvi, in the Beit Shean Valley.

☐ PART A: ELECTING DELEGATES TO THE 20TH ZIONIST CONGRESS (55')
1   Zionist Shekel certificate made out to Nathan Axelrod aged 32, of Montefiore neighbourhood, Tel Aviv. Dissolve to election posters. Dissolve to people on their way to the polls (mid, long, 14).
2   Dropping ballots into the box at the Beit Hamoreh polling station (mid, 20).
3   Exterior of Beit Hamoreh and people waiting in line to vote (long, mid, 42).
4   At the ballot boxes (mid, 55).

☐ PART B: MAURICE SCHWARTZ LEAVES PALESTINE (49')
1   A plane on the ground. Painted on the side of the plane (in Polish): POLSKIE LINJE LOTNICZE "LOT". People getting on the plane (mid, long, 23).
2   Maurice Schwartz saying goodbye to friends and going aboard the plane (mid).
3   The plane's propellers begin to turn (mid, 49).

☐ PART C: TECHNICAL EXHIBITION AT MONTEFIORE SCHOOL (170')
1   A group of people enter the school (mid, 12).
2   A sign in Hebrew: "Radio Department" (tilt up). Dissolve to various radio models. Pan of children working on the radio sets (some split-screen shots) (mid, 101).   שלט: מחלקת הרדיו
3   A sign in Hebrew: "Electronics and Mechanics Department" (tilt up). Dissolve to various motors. Working motors (mid, 151).
   שלט: מחלקת החשמל ומכניקה
4   A sign in Hebrew: "Construction Department" (tilt up) (mid, 164).
   שלט: מחלקת הבנין
5   A sign in Hebrew: "Aviation Department" (mid, 170).   שלט: מחלקת האוירה

☐ PART D: BUILDING KIBBUTZ TIRAT TZVI (42')
1   General view of the site during construction (long, 22).
2   Building the kibbutz (incomplete) (long, 42).

■ **CARMEL NEWSREEL I-095** · July 11 1937
Hanoar Ha'oved youth movement camp at Nahlat Yehuda. Construction of the Dubek cigarette factory in Bnei Brak. Hapoel Tel Aviv sports club holds a training course in boating on the Yarkon River.

☐ PART A: HANOAR HA'OVED YOUTH MOVEMENT CAMP IN NAHLAT YEHUDA (94')
1   Marching with buglers (long, 20).
2   Raising the flag. All stand at attention (long, 45).
3   The movement's leader (David) speaking and the children listening (long, 57).
4   The tent camp and David with the children (91).
5   The flag (long, 94).

☐ PART B: CONSTRUCTION IN BNEI BRAK (THE DUBEK CIGARETTE FACTORY) (73')
1   Iris shot of Bnei Brak (long, 31).
2   Final stages of construction at the Dubek cigarette factory (long, 63). Men pouring cement.   שלט: דובק בע"מ
3   The building near completion (long, 73).

## 86  Carmel Newsreels: Series 1

□ PART C: HAPOEL TEL AVIV HOLDS A COURSE IN BOATING (143')
1  Marching - most in bathing-suits (long, 16).
2  A pennant is presented and the flag raised with Yarkon River in background (long, 43).
3  Roll-call at the dock (long, 61).
4  Director of Hasneh Insurance company speaking and the crowd listening (78).
5  Cutting the ribbons which are holding the boats. Letting the boats down into the water (long, mid, 95).
6  Sailing boats leaving the dock (long, 112).
7  Rowing. Pan of people on the wharf. Flags arranged in nautical fashion (long, 143).

■ **CARMEL NEWSREEL I-096** · July 18 1937
Pioneer Women's House in Tel Aviv, including scenes of sewing, ironing, handicrafts and reading. Views of Jerusalem - boys with sidelocks, David's Tower, Jaffa Gate and ramparts. Members of gliders club attend camp in the Jezreel Valley. Reception held in Petah Tikva for Maccabi athletes returning from abroad.

□ PART A: TITLE: BETH HAHALUZOTH TEL AVIV (134')

כותרת: בית החלוצות בתל-אביב

1  The exterior of the building (long, 25).
2  A woman sitting in the lobby is joined by another woman and together they enter the lecture hall.
3  The sewing and ironing room (long, 93).
4  Women weaving chairs and small tables. The same chairs and tables on display in a shop window (long, 120).
5  Women reading at tables (long, 134).

□ PART B: TITLE: NEW BUILDINGS AT JERUSALEM (30')

כותרת: שאלו שלום ירושלים ישליו אוהביך - ירושלים העתיקה והחדשה

1  Boys with sidelocks (long, 18).
2  David's Tower (long, 21).
3  A horse-drawn carriage with an Arab driver, passing by Jaffa Gate (long, 30).

□ PART C: GLIDER CAMP IN THE JEZREEL VALLEY (98')
1  Members of the club standing next to the gliders (long, 23).
2  Working on the gliders (there are cigarette advertisements painted on the sides of the gliders) (long, 47).
3  Men carrying a glider on their shoulders (long, 66).
4  Standing in a field (long, 83).
5  A young man seated in a glider receiving instructions from a man standing next to the craft. Walking up a hill. More instructions given to the man sitting in the glider (mid, long, 98).

□ PART D: RECEPTION FOR MACCABI PETAH TIKVA ATHLETES RETURNING FROM ABROAD (50')
1  Reception for the team - the Petah Tikva crowd cheering (long, 10).
2  Mayor Shlomo Stampfer and A Shapiro. A young man standing next to them is speaking (mid, long, 17).
3  The crowd (long).
4  A member of the team (in uniform) speaks and presents a pennant, given to the team while abroad, to Stampfer (long, 50).

■ **CARMEL NEWSREEL I-097** · July 25 1937
Laying a cornerstone for a school in Kfar Malal, named in memory of Yosef Aaronovitch. Inspection of wine-making at Rishon Lezion. High Commissioner Sir

Arthur Wauchope visiting Zichron Ya'akov. Building the new settlement of Kfar Menachem.

☐ PART A: TITLE: LAYING THE CORNERSTONE TO THE SCHOOL IN THE NAME OF JOSEPH AARONOVITCH (88')

כותרת: הנחת אבן הפינה לביה"ס ע"ש י. אהרונוביץ בכפר מל"ל

1  A decorated entrance gate, with the village of Kfar Malal in the background (long).
2  The crowd near the construction site (long, 21).
3  The crowd and the flag of Kfar Malal (long, 13).
4  Children walking to the site in formation (long, 48).
5  A choir singing (mid, long, 60).
6  A speaker. Children listening to the speaker. Another speaker (79).
7  Laying the cornerstone (mid, 88).

☐ PART B: TITLE: VINTAGE AT RISHON LEZION (72')

כותרת: הבציר בראשון לציון

1  Rabbis arrive at the wine-cellar for inspection (29).
2  Pouring grapes into a vat. A rabbi holding a bunch of grapes (mid, long, 47).
3  The rabbis on their way to supervise the winemaking. Sitting at set tables (72).

☐ PART C: TITLE: VINTAGE AT ZICHRON YA'AKOV (106')

כותרת: הבציר בזכרון יעקב

1  Iris shot of Zichron Ya'akov (long, 17).
2  A children's tent-camp. A counsellor blowing a whistle, the children waking up, leaving the tents, lining up for roll-call and scattering.
3  Children eating (10).
4  British High Commissioner Sir Arthur Wauchope visiting (long, 92).
5  Someone reading a speech. Sitting down to eat. The High Commissioner speaking with someone (106).

☐ PART D: TITLE: THE COLONY MENACHEM (174')

כותרת: העליה לכפר מנחם

1  Preparing the convoy of trucks and horses for the journey (long, 29).
2  The barren site which will be the new settlement of Kfar Menachem (long, 47).
3  The trucks arrive, are unloaded and the settlers begin building their camp. Arab neighbours come to watch (90).
4  Building the fence. Putting up shacks. Setting up the camp (163).
5  Moving a shack. Putting up a tower (long, 174).

■ **CARMEL NEWSREEL I-098** · August 2 1937
Laying a cornerstone for the BILU school in Tel Aviv. A press conference of Hasneh Insurance Co. at a rest home in Zichron Ya'akov. Betar Youth on parade. The High Commissioner visits Tel Aviv Port. Children on the beach listen to a little girl named Ruti recite verse about swimming.

☐ PART A: TITLE: LAYING THE CORNERSTONE OF THE MUNICIPAL SCHOOL AT TEL AVIV (68')   כותרת: אבן הפינה לבית הספר ביל"ו בת"א

1  Assembling at the site on Rothschild Street. Drinks are served to dignitaries (long, 51).
2  Mayor Israel Rokah speaking (mid, long, 57).
3  David Zvi Pincas speaking (long, 68).

## 88   Carmel Newsreels: Series 1

□ PART B: TITLE: BANQUET GIVEN TO JOURNALISTS BY "HASNEH" AT ZICHRON YA'AKOV (120')

כותרת: מסיבת עתונאים מטעם "הסנה" כבית ההבראה "חיים מחודשים" בזכרון יעקב

1 Iris shot of the "Haim Mehudashim" (Renewed Life) rest home in Zichron Ya'akov (13).
2 Iris shot of people walking in tree-lined grounds of rest home and talking. A nurse speaker. The director of the Haifa branch of Hasneh speaking (mid, 51).
3 Sitting on lounge chairs outside.
4 General view of the grounds.
5 Playing tennis.
6 Three children (one in a bathing-suit) playing with a ball.
7 A couple strolling along a tree-lined path (long, 120).

□ PART C: TITLE: LIGHT ATHLETICS OF JUNIORS (101')

כותרת: תרגילי משטר ביום "בית"ר-הצעירה" בתל-אביב

1 General view of the parade grounds (long, 17).
2 Betar Youth (boys and girls) on parade. Marching with the flag. Various marching formations (long, 101).

□ PART D: TITLE: VISIT OF THE HIGH COMMISSIONER [TO TEL AVIV PORT] (112')   כותרת: לבקורו של הנציב העליון בנמל תל-אביב

1 High Commissioner Wauchope getting out of his car, meeting with port managers, viewing the port blueprints.
2 Walking along the dock.
3 Speaking with the port managers. Visiting port structures.
4 Getting into his car (112).

□ PART E: RUTI RECITING ON THE BEACH (183')
1 Ruti (a little girl) telling group of children how she was taught to swim (long, 4).
2 The beach and bathers (long, 24).
3 Children in the water, coming out of the water, sitting down to listen to Ruti (46).
4 Ruti telling how her father taught her to swim (59).
5 A drawing of a girl swimming and a frightening man next to her (65).
6 Ruti speaking to the children (c.u., mid, 89).
7 The children listening to Ruti's story. The sea (102).
8 A drawing of a boy among the waves (108).
9 Ruti describing how to swim (127).
10 A drawing of a fish in water, moving its tail, mouth and eye (c.u., 147).
11 Ruti continues to recite (in verse) (183).

■ **CARMEL NEWSREEL I-099** · August 9 1937
Delegates on board a ship, on their way to the 20th Zionist Congress in Zürich. Firemen putting out a fire in Tel Aviv. Inauguration of the domestic air service, Palestine Airways Limited, with roundtrip flight from Tel Aviv to Haifa. Retrospective of the first 99 Carmel newsreels: the second Maccabia; Nahum Sokolow at Maimonides' tomb; bringing Shavuot "first fruits" at the Maccabia Stadium; Betar Youth parade; Rabbi A Y Kook at Rabbi Schneerson's funeral. M Shulsinger sings *Wine Cellars* at the Rishon Lezion winery.

□ PART A: CONGRESS DELEGATES ON THEIR WAY TO ZÜRICH (60')
1 Congress delegates together on deck. Avraham Herzfeld sitting on deck and singing (pan, long, mid, 36).
2 People on deck, including writer Sammy Gronemann and Moshe Halevy (mid, 60).

☐ PART B: TITLE: FIRE AT THE TRADING HOUSE OF OCHSHORN, TEL AVIV (41')
כותרת: שריפה גדולה בתל אביב
1   Firemen putting out the fire (ladders, hoses) (long, 41).

☐ PART C: TITLE: FIRST PALESTINE AIRLINE (327')
כותרת: השירות האוירי המקומי הראשון בארץ
1   An air crew standing next to a plane marked "Palestine Airways Limited" (long, 23).
2   The pilot starts the plane and gives the "thumbs-up" sign. The propeller begins to turn (mid, 40).
3   Aerial shots of Tel Aviv from North Tel Aviv to the sands south of the city.
4   The plane coming in for landing (long, 187).
5   Landing in Haifa (from inside the plane) (long, 202).
6   The plane lands (long, 215).
7   Getting out of the plane. Greeted by Haifa District Commissioner Edward Keith-Roach (mid, long, 239).
8   The District Commissioner shakes the pilot's hand. A crowd near the plane (mid, long, 255).
9   Haifa airfield.
10  The plane returns to Tel Aviv where the crew is greeted by Tel Aviv dignitaries, including Mayor Israel Rokah (long, 319).
11  Sitting at tables (long, 327).

☐ PART D: TITLE: RETROSPECT OF THE *CARMEL WEEKLY* UP TO THE 100 ISSUE (168')     כותרת: סיכום "יומן כרמל ה-100"
1   Tilt up to a fountain and buildings (long, 21).
2   A gathering (long, 29).
3   TITLE: THE SECOND MACCABIA (32)     כותרת: המכביה השניה
4   Parade at the stadium. The crowd, including Lord Melchett. A soccer match. Diving competition. A gymnastics exhibition (long, 63).
5   TITLE IN HEBREW: THE LATE NAHUM SOKOLOW AT MAIMONIDES' TOMB (68).     כותרת: נחום סוקולוב ז"ל על קבר הרמב"ם
6   Sokolow arriving at the tomb. Sokolow speaking (mid, 80).
7   TITLE (partial): ASSEMBLEMENT [OF HAPOEL]
8   Hapoel athletes on parade. Gymnastics exhibition (long, 97).
כותרת: כינוס "הפועל"
9   TITLE: [FIRST] FRUIT
10  Bringing the "first fruit" at the Maccabia stadium near the Yarkon River (long, 118).
11  TITLE: CARNIVAL AT TEL AVIV     כותרת: עדלידע
12  TITLE: REASSEMBLEMENT OF BETAR AT TEL AVIV (long, 128)
כותרת: כנוס הבית"ר בת"א
13  Betar Youth on parade (long, 146).
14  TITLE: THE RABBI KOOK IN HIS LIFE (154)     כותרת: הרב קוק ז"ל
15  Rabbi Kook speaking at the funeral of Rabbi Schneerson (mid, 168).

☐ PART E: TITLE: *WINE CELLARS* SONG BY COMPOSITOR ZEIRA (459')
HEBREW TITLE: DRINK, MY DARLING. COMPOSITION: M. ZEIRA. WORDS: ZEV BAR-DEMION. SUNG BY: M. SHULSINGER. WITH M. BUCKSBAUM (HEBREW THEATRE). ACCOMPANIMENT: M. WILENSKY.
כותרת: שתה יקירי, מוסיקה: מ. זעירא מלים: זאב בר-דמיון ע"י הזמר מ. שולזינגר בהשתתפות מ. בוקסבוים (תיאטרון עברי) לווי: מ. וילנסקי
1   Wine barrels in Rishon Lezion (tilt up) (mid, 41).
2   Shulsinger puts his head under a spigot and drinks directly from the barrel.

Filling a glass, he stumbles around as if drunk and then begins to sing (mid, 101).
3   Shulsinger singing (mid, c.u., 210).
4   General view of a vineyard, sprinklers and young people picking grapes (long, 243).
5   Shulsinger in the wine cellar, sitting and singing (mid, 263).
6   Singing - split-screen: Shulsinger and the image of Noah (305).
7   Noah (c.u., 308).
8   Split-screen Shulsinger and Noah (316).
9   Shulsinger drinking wine. Dissolve to his nose smelling the wine (mid, 345).
10  Another character in biblical dress (perhaps Lot) drinking wine (long, c.u., 391).
11  Shulsinger continues to sing (long, 409).
12  The biblical character continues to sing and Shulsinger follows suit. Shulsinger falls asleep on a barrel and spills his glass (459).

■ **CARMEL NEWSREEL I-100** · August 16 1937
Opening of the Zebulun Sailing Club in Tel Aviv. Cantor Gershon Sirota visits Palestine. Constructing a bridge over Wadi Musrara. Harvesting, packing and selling ethrogim (citrons) and lulavim (palm branches) for the holiday of Succot.

□ PART A: TITLE: OPENING CEREMONY OF THE TEL AVIV YACHT CLUB (97')
כותרת: הנפת הדגל של מועדון השייטים בתל אביב
1   Members of the club seated while Tauber, the club chairman, speaks (mid, 25).
2   Flags (long, 39).
3   Starting a boat race. Boats sailing on the Yarkon River (mid, long, 97).

□ PART B: TITLE: CANTOR SIROTA ARRIVED IN PALESTINE (97')
כותרת: קבלת פנים לחזן גרשון סירוטה
1   General view of the area (pan, long, 32).
2   Cantor Sirota being welcomed (mid, 56).
3   Sirota sitting at the head of a table at a reception in his honour (mid, 73).
4   Pan of guests at the reception (long, 80).
5   Sirota walking with entourage (long, 97).

□ PART C: TITLE: WORK CARRIED ON NEAR THE MUSRARA BRIDGE (114')
כותרת: לפני גמירת גשר מוצררה החדש
1   The Petah Tikva road before the bridge (long, 30).
2   Constructing the bridge. Sawing wood, pulling wagons, working on pipes (114).

□ PART D: TITLE: THE ETHROG SEASON IN PALESTINE (131')
כותרת: עונת האתרוגים החלה
1   Picking ethrogim (citrons), wrapping them in flax and packing them in crates (long, 50).
2   Picking an ethrog (c.u., 61).
3   Picking lulavim (palm branches) and binding them (mid, 102).
4   As the holiday of Succot approaches, shops are selling ethrogim and lulavim with signs advertising (mid, 131).

■ **CARMEL NEWSREEL I-101** · August 23 1937
First flight from Paris to the airfield at Lod. High Commissioner Sir Arthur Wauchope visiting Hadassah Hospital construction site, Mount Scopus. The 20th Zionist Congress in Zürich. 40th anniversary of the 1st Zionist Congress in Basel.

## Carmel Newsreels: Series 1 91

□ PART A: TITLE: RECEPTION FOR FRENCH PILOTS AT THE LYDDA AERODROME (113')

כותרת: קבלת פנים לטייסים צרפתיים בשדה התעופה בלוד (9).

1 French pilots Mlle Nichola and M Schumacher disembarking from plane (mid, 36).
2 Pilots receiving flowers and greetings (mid, 57).
3 Pilot talking to camera. Hebrew, with French accent (mid, 101).
4 Plane about to take off (113).

□ PART B: TITLE: H.E. THE HIGH COMMISSIONER VISITING HADASSAH HOSPITAL, JERUSALEM (49')

כותרת: ביקורו של ה. מ. הנציב העליון בבנין המרכז הרפואי של הדסה (הר הצופים, ירושלים) (7).

1 High Commissioner Wauchope arrives with his entourage at the construction site of the new medical centre Hadassah Hospital, Mount Scopus, Jerusalem.
2 Construction workers working on building (long, 49).

□ PART C: THE 20TH ZIONIST CONGRESS IN ZÜRICH (35')
1 Delegates by the Congress building in Zürich (long, 13).
2 Pan of the Zürich State Theatre, where the Congress is being held.
3 Banner in Hebrew: Zionist Congress (mid, 35).

□ PART D: TITLE: 40TH ANNIVERSARY OF THE FIRST ZIONIST CONGRESS AT BASEL (182')     כותרת: יובל ה-40 לקונגרס הציוני הראשון בבזל (11).

1 Train station in Zürich. By the departing train. Sign on train in Hebrew and German: Special train to Basel, in honour of the 40th anniversary of the Zionist Congress (mid, 27).
2 Scenery from the train on the way to Basel (long, 58).
3 Scenery in Basel (long, 73).
4 Delegates entering building (mid, 81).
5 Exterior of Congress building (Casino) (long, 111).
6 Delegates including Aharon Zisling and David Remez enter building (mid, 125).
7 Menachem Ussishkin (c.u., 133).
8 Dr Nahum Goldman among the crowds entering the building. Goldman talking to someone in the crowd (mid).
9 Pan of street in Basel to location of Congress building with large banner in Hebrew: ZIONIST CONGRESS (long, 182).     שלט: הקונגרס הציוני

■ CARMEL NEWSREEL I-102 · August 30 1937
Launching of the boat *Ofek* by the Zebulun Sailing Club. The unveiling of the Haganah Memorial at Kibbutz Huldah. Ceremony of bringing Torah scrolls to the new Shivat Zion Synagogue in Tel Aviv. The Hapoel harmonica band performing.

□ PART A: TITLE: NEW ZEVULUN SAILING BOAT (79')

כותרת: חנוכת ספינת "אופק" בשבוע של "זבולון" תל אביב (12).

1 Crowd assembled on the banks of the Yarkon River (long, 31).
2 Young boys in sailor suits, members of Zebulun, lined up for ceremony (long, 54).
3 Club President speaking (mid, 70).
4 Large sailing boat, *Ofek*, decorated with flags on the Yarkon River (long, 79).

□ PART B: TITLE IN HEBREW: HAGANAH MEMORIAL AT HULDAH (125')

כותרת: הסרת הלוט מעל מצבת ההגנה בחולדה (11).

1 Monument covered in black cloth. Jewish Settlement Police (ghaffirs) standing by monument. Pan of crowd (mid, long, 41).

2  Unveiling monument (mid, 58).
3  Crowd standing at attention (long, 71).
4  Close-up of Yitzhak Ben Tzvi speaking (79).
5  Pan of crowd and podium. Woman speaking (long, 112).
6  Monument with honour guard of ghaffirs (long, 125).

□ PART C: TITLE: INAUGURATION OF SHIVAT ZION SYNAGOGUE (140')

כותרת: חנוכת בית הכנסת "שיבת ציון" בתל אביב

1  Guests entering the synagogue, shot from roof of building (long, 21).
2  Chief Ashkenazi Rabbi Moshe Avigdor Amiel and his entourage bringing the Torah scrolls from the old building to the new. Long procession down street crowded with spectators on sides. Torah scrolls under canopy (long, 108).
3  General view of exterior of synagogue (long, 129).
4  Interior of building (long, 140).

□ PART D: THE HAPOEL HARMONICA BAND (174')
1  Young boys with blue shirts (workers' shirts) with white strings, playing drums. Girls playing accordions.
2  Harmonicas join in. Orchestra and conductor (long, 102).
3  Drums and cymbals (mid, long, 114).
4  Two girls playing accordions (mid, long, 123).
5  General view of orchestra (long, 174).

■ **CARMEL NEWSREEL I-103** · September 6 1937
Swimming competition between Maccabi Haifa and Greece at the Bat Galim stadium in Haifa. The Betar School ship *Sarah A* arriving in Haifa and touring Tel Aviv. Young immigrants from Germany on the boat en route to Palestine.

□ PART A: TITLE: COUNTRY MATCH BETWEEN MACCABI HAIFA AND THE GREEK SELECTED TEAM (179')

כותרת: התחרות בין ארצות יוון - א"י בשחיה וכדור מים בחיפה (13).

1  General view of the swimming pool and the competitors in the water (long, 29).
2  Pan of swimmers near the pool and the crowd (long, 39).
3  Greek swimmers enter the water; afterwards, Israeli swimmers (long, 55).
4  The crowd, which includes 4000 spectators. The swimmers. Crowd stands for British, Greek and Hebrew national anthems (long, 79).
5  The pool, the swimmers swimming the crawl (long, 144).
6  Water polo (long, 179).

□ PART B: TITLE: THE SAILING VESSEL *SARAH A* ARRIVING AT HAIFA (202')

כותרת: אונית הלימודים של בית"ר "שרה א'" הניעה לחיפה.

1  The boat, named for Sarah Aaronsohn, approaches Haifa port (long, 19).
2  Crowd waiting (long, 29).
3  The boat nears the port. The port and health authorities board (long, 45).
4  Meeting the French captain and his assistant Yechiel Halperin (mid, long, 48).
5  Visitors boarding the boat. Betar students with the visitors on the boat (long, 83).
6  The student sailors and officers marching to the cemetery (long, 117).
7  Standing in the cemetery at the grave of Max Nordau.
8  HEBREW TITLE: THE STUDENT SAILORS AND THE OFFICERS FROM THE *SARAH A* VISIT IN THE TEL AVIV MUNICIPALITY AND IN THE OLD CEMETERY (158).

שלט: הקצינים והמלחים של "שרה א" מבקרים בעיריית תל אביב ובבית הקברות הישן

9  Group enters the Tel Aviv Municipality (long, 180).
10 Mayor Israel Rokah speaking to group in the Mayor's office. Pan of group (long, 202).

□ PART C: TITLE: THE GERMAN YOUTH ALIYAH (103')

כותרת: עלית הנוער העברי מגרמניה (9).

1  Smokestack of a ship with smoke coming out (long, 15).
2  Clear footage of dancing hora on deck of ship (36).
3  Youth sitting in a circle, on the ship, having a serious discussion. Close-ups of faces of the new immigrants (79).
4  Swimming in the pool of the ship (long, 103).

■ CARMEL NEWSREEL I-104 · September 13 1937
Meir Dizengoff visiting refugee children in Jaffa, filmed in 1936. Unveiling of the tombstone on the grave of Dizengoff. Unloading imported cars in the port of Tel Aviv. Laying the foundation stone for Kiryat Amal, a new neighbourhood near Haifa. Funeral of murder victim Eliyahu Weiss in Haifa. Recreation car competitions at Haifa.

□ PART A: DIZENGOFF VISITING REFUGEE CHILDREN FROM RIOTS IN JAFFA, 1936 (141')
1  Dizengoff comes to the refugee camp (long, 6).
2  Children playing in the water on the beach. Adorable shots of naked small children. Dizengoff walks among them, children surround him (long, 34).
3  Dizengoff distributing small gifts to the children (long, 56).
4  Dizengoff speaking (long, 141).

□ PART B: TITLE: FRAGMENTS OF DIZENGOFF'S LIFE. COMMEMORATION OF MR DIZENGOFF'S ANNIVERSARY (83')

כותרת: יום השנה לפטירתו של דיזנגוף. גלוי המצבה של מאיר דיזנגוף, וצינה ז"ל (16).

1  Crowd gathering in cemetery (long, 30).
2  Sephardi Chief Rabbi Ben Zion Meir Chai Uziel, Ashkenazi Chief Rabbi Moshe Avigdor Amiel and Mayor Israel Rokah by the memorial (long, 37).
3  The cantor chants *El Maleh Rahamim* (long, 50).
4  Crowd around grave. Leaving the cemetery (long, 72).
5  Honour guard of scouts by the memorial (long, 83).

□ PART C: TITLE: UNLOADING THE FIRST AUTO AT THE TEL AVIV PORT (78')

כותרת: פריקה של אוטומובילים בנמל תל אביב (12).

1  Crowd around car, drinking from bottles, pushing to get into photographs with the new car. Pushing the car (long, 30).
2  Sign on car in Hebrew: Ford, the first car brought through Tel Aviv harbour (mid, long, 36).
3  People standing near the car to get their pictures taken (long, 46).
4  The car driving through the streets of Tel Aviv (long, 78).

□ PART D: TITLE: LAYING THE CORNERSTONE AT KIRYAT AMAL (117')

כותרת: קרית עמל מפעל חדש של מרכז השכון ע"י חיפה (12).

1  An empty hill next to what is today Tivon (long, 32).
2  Gates with a welcome sign in Hebrew (long, 40).
3  People with flags on a decorated stage (long, 48).
4  Laying cornerstone, various individuals take turns pouring concrete (long, 71).
5  General view of crowd listening (mid, long, 95).
6  Possibly the director of the Haifa branch of Hasneh speaks to the crowd (mid, long, 111).

## 94    Carmel Newsreels: Series 1

7   The flag of Kiryat Amal blowing in the wind (mid, 117).

☐ PART E: TITLE: WEISS'S FUNERAL AT HAIFA (113')

כותרת: לוית הנרצח אליהו ויס בחיפה.

1   Very large crowd panned from above. Men carrying black coffin. Loading onto car.
2   Funeral procession down street jammed with people (long, 113).

☐ PART F: CAR COMPETITIONS IN HAIFA (201')
1   General view of site (long, 13).
2   Small orchestra playing (mid, 19).
3   Competition, carrying an egg around a car, car driving through a course of bottles. Short car race. Eating yoghurt in the car. Motorcycle driving around bottles (long, mid, 170).
4   The judges (long, 177).
5   The winning car (mid, 201).

■ **CARMEL NEWSREEL I-105** · September 20 1937
Hashomer gathering in Netanya. Completing the Tel Aviv-Haifa highway. The Deputy High Commissioner visits the Okava factory. Lilli Sandberg performs an acrobatic dance.

☐ PART A: HASHOMER GATHERING IN NETANYA (100')
1   A speaker on a balcony decorated with flags and a picture of Theodor Herzl. People crowded on the roof and other balconies of the building.
2   The crowd standing below the balcony. A Hashomer flag.
3   Marching.
4   Speaking from the balcony. Next to the speaker is a man in uniform with various medals and ribbons (including a cross-shaped decoration).
5   The crowd below the balcony. The building decorated with flags (100).

☐ PART B: TITLE: FINISHING OF THE HIGH-ROAD HAIFA - TEL AVIV (92')

כותרת: חגיגת גמירת כביש החדש חיפה - תל-אביב

1   Working on the road (long, 10).
2   Dignitaries come to see progress on the road (long, 25).
3   Work on the road (long, 53).
4   A finished section of road. Haifa District Commissioner Edward Keith-Roach cuts a ribbon.
5   People getting on a bus and into cars and waiting in line to use the new road (long, 83).
6   Paving the road (mid, 92).

☐ PART C: TITLE: THE SUBSTITUTE OF THE HIGH-COMMISSIONER IS VISITING THE OKAVA-FACTORY IN RISHON LEZION (102')

כותרת: ביקור מ"מ הנציב העליון בביה"ר אוקבה בראשון לציון

1   General view of the Okava factory (long, 20).
2   The Deputy High Commissioner getting out of his car and walking towards the factory with the factory directors (long, 49).
3   Inside the factory - watching the production process (mid, 87).
4   The Deputy High Commissioner (long, 102).

☐ PART D: TITLE: LILLI SANDBERG IN HER ACROBATIC-GROTESK [sic] DANCES (171')     כותרת: לילי סנדברג בקטעים מריקודיה האקרובטיים-גרוטסקיים
1   The dancer holds up a copy of *Ha'aretz* daily newspaper.
2   The dancer, wearing masks on the front and back of her head, performs

various acrobatic moves (mid, long, 111).
3   Acrobatics in another costume (long, 171).

■ **CARMEL NEWSREEL I-106** · September 27 1937
Opening of the Haifa-Tel Aviv highway. Completion of the "Massada" Hebrew-language encyclopedia. Aviation day in Petah Tikva, including aerial shots of Petah Tikva and the citrus groves. Poet H Leivik visits Palestine. Boy scouts' summer camp.

☐ PART A: TITLE: OPENING OF THE NEW HAIFA - TEL-AVIV HIGHWAY (165')

כותרת: פתיחת הכביש החדש

1   Dignitaries arriving (long, 36).
2   Shaking hands (long, 61).
3   District Commissioner Edward Keith-Roach arrives in his car (long, 88).
4   Serving cold drinks (long, 100).
5   The set tables, a speaker (mid, 116).
6   The District Commissioner speaking (mid, 126).
7   The set tables and guests. Speakers (long, 165).

☐ PART B: TITLE: FESTIVAL AFTER FINISHING OF THE GENERAL HEBREW ENCYCLOPEDIA MASSADA (76')

כותרת: סיום האנציקלופדיה העברית הכללית מסדה

1   The encyclopedia (dissolve, mid, 26).
2   The party celebrating the completion of the encyclopedia (pan, mid, 54).
3   Shaul Tchernichovsky speaking (mid, 60).
4   Professor Yosef Klausner speaking (mid, 67).
5   Another speaker (mid, 76).

☐ PART C: TITLE: FLYING DAY AT PETAH-TIKVA (187')

כותרת: יום התעופה בפ"ת

1   A crowd at a field near Petah Tikva (mid, 16).
2   Getting into a Palestine Airways Ltd plane. The plane taking off (mid, 35).
3   Petah Tikva's citrus groves, from the air (long, 63).
4   The plane - exterior and interior. Aerial shots of Petah Tikva (mid, long, 100).
5   The pilot through the window and the plane in the air.
6   A turning propeller (c.u., long, 111).
7   Petah Tikva from the air (long, 151).
8   A large crowd (mid, 156).
9   Petah Tikva citrus groves from the air.
10  The plane landing (long, 187).

☐ PART D: TITLE: THE POET LEIVIK IN PALESTINE (56')

כותרת: המשורר לייוויק בארץ

1   The Yiddish poet H Leivik arrives with entourage (on the street where the Tel Aviv Opera now stands) (long, 19).
2   The poet standing next to Histadrut leader Jacob Zerubavel (mid, 24).
3   Leivik speaking at a reception (pan, mid, 56).

☐ PART E: YOUTH SCOUT CAMP (189')    כותרת: מחיי הצופים במחנה

1   A eucalyptus grove - shot from a moving vehicle (long, 30).
2   Boys lying in hammocks strung between the trees and getting out of the hammocks (long, 76).
3   The boys, dressed as American Indians, wearing loincloths and feathers, climb down from the trees and gather around one (supposed to be the leader). They take part in a swearing-in ceremony with hatchets (mid, 189).

## Carmel Newsreels: Series 1

■ **CARMEL NEWSREEL I-107** · September-October 1937
A soccer match between Maccabi and Hapoel. Max Fein Vocational School in Tel Aviv. Horse races at Lod. Zebulun sports club boat races and ceremonies in Haifa. Rina Nikova's dance studio performs *The Shepherd*.

□ PART A: SOCCER MATCH BETWEEN MACCABI AND HAPOEL IN TEL AVIV (106')
1   Hapoel comes onto the field (mid, 11).
2   The teams standing opposite each other, exchange pennants and return to their places (mid, long, 50).
3   The game, billboard advertising ALIYAH cigarettes seen in the background (long, 106).

□ PART B: TITLE: PROFESSIONAL SCHOOL ON THE NAME OF MAX FEIN, TEL-AVIV (105')　　　　　　　　　　כותרת: ביה"ס המקצועי ע"ש מקס פיין
1   The school (exterior). Dissolve to a classroom and students at desks (long, 21).
2   Children in a classroom. A student and a teacher standing near a blackboard (mid, 59).
3   A lesson (long, 68).
4   Work with various machines, including lathes, in a workshop (105).

□ PART C: TITLE: HORSE RACES AT LYDDA (173')　　כותרת:מרוץ סוסים בלוד
1   The crowd at the track, including many Arabs (pan, mid, long, 39).
2   Jockeys and horses preparing for the race, the start of the race (mid, 65).
3   The crowd near the track (pan, long, 88).
4   The race (long, 113).
5   The crowd, the race, the crowd (mid, 121).
6   Pan of a well-dressed group standing around a speaker (mid, 173).

□ PART D: TITLE: ZEBULUN REVIEW AT HAIFA (128')

　　　　　　　　　　　　　　　　　　　　כותרת: מיפקד זבולון בחיפה
1   Zebulun members at roll-call (long, 22).
2   Their commander speaking (mid, 28).
3   The members and another speaker (mid, 49).
4   Getting into the boats (long, 67).
5   The crowd watching (mid, 72).
6   The boats sailing (long, 116).
7   Awarding prizes (long, 128).

□ PART E: RINA NIKOVA'S DANCE STUDIO PERFORMS "THE SHEPHERD" (163')
1   Dancers in Bedouin costume (163).

■ **CARMEL NEWSREEL I-108** · October 11 1937
Kindergarten children visit the zoo in Tel Aviv. Train derailed near Rosh Ha'ayin, by Arabs protesting the Peel Commission's Partition Plan. Actor Ze'ev Berlinsky, in Yemenite costume, tells a Yemenite story about the Messiah.

□ PART A: TITLE: KINDERGARTEN PUPILS VISITING ZOOLOGICAL GARDENS AT TEL-AVIV (273')　　　　　　כותרת: ביקור גני ילדים בגן החיות בתל אביב
1   A lioness and cubs (mid, 29).
2   Children watching (mid, long, 36).
3   A trainer playing with the lion cubs (long, 61).
4   Monkeys playing in a cage. Children amused by the monkeys (long, 110).
5   Children behind a fence. The children watching deer (long, 141).

6  White mice and the children watching the mice (long, 173).
7  An aquarium (mid, long, 191).
8  Children near cages with birds (long, 106).
9  Parrots, children and nestlings (273).

□ PART B: TITLE: AFTER THE RAILWAY DISASTER NEAR RAS-EL-EIN (122')
כותרת: אחרי התנגשות ברכבת על יד ראש העין
1  The engine, wheels, carriages (48).
2  A crane lifting carriages (87).
3  A group of soldiers guarding the site (mid, 94).
4  An overturned engine (mid, long, 113).
5  Pan of the train wreck (long, 122).

□ PART C: ZE'EV BERLINSKY TELLS A YEMENITE STORY ABOUT THE MESSIAH (124')
1  Ze'ev Berlinsky in street clothes. Dissolve to Berlinsky in Yemenite costume.
2  He relates that the Messiah will be Sephardi and his donkey Ashkenazi. He, Berlinsky, a Yemenite, will stand behind the donkey and yell "jia, jia" to make it move.
3  Dissolve to Berlinsky in street clothes (mid, 124').

■ **CARMEL NEWSREEL I-109** · October 18 1937
Export of citrus fruit from Tel Aviv port. Preparing the stadium for the third Maccabia. Zebulun sports club welcomes Mrs Diamond. Rina Nikova's dance studio performs an oriental dance - *The Cuckoo*.

□ PART A: TITLE: BEGINNING OF THE CITRUS TRANSPORT SEASON (182')
כותרת: עונת משלוח ההדרים בנמל תל-אביב החלה
1  Workers carrying crates at the port (mid, long).
2  Picking fruit (mid, c.u.).
3  Carrying crates of fruit in the citrus grove (mid).
4  Wrapping the fruit (long).
5  Carrying the crates to a boat (mid, long, 112).
6  Arranging the crates in the boat (long, 138).
7  Boats loaded with citrus fruit leaving Tel Aviv Port (long, 153).
8  A crane lifting the crates from a boat onto a ship (long, 182).

□ PART B: TITLE: PREPARATION WORKS TO THE THIRD MACCABIADE [sic] (55')
כותרת: לקראת המכביה השלישית
1  Preparing the stadium (levelling ground with hoes and shovels) (mid, 55).

□ PART C: TITLE: MRS DIAMOND VISITING THE SPORT CLUB ZEBULUN AT TEL AVIV (109')
כותרת: החגיגה הימית של זבולון בתל אביב
1  Zebulun members standing along the banks of the Yarkon River (long, 24).
2  Raising the flag (mid, long, 43).
3  Mrs Diamond speaking. Club members listening.
4  Zebulun rowing boats on the Yarkon River (long, 97).
5  Closing ceremony (long, 109).

□ PART D: TITLE: ORIENTAL DANCE BY RINA NIKOVA'S STUDIO (372)
כותרת: ריקוד מזרחי ע"י הסטודיו של רינה ניקובה - קבל פרס בתחרות המחול בתל-אביב
1  Dancers in oriental costume dance and sing an oriental song (long, 96).
2  The dancers gather around a well (long, 172).

3   The dancers come forth one by one, singing and dancing, one carrying a drum (long, 372).

■ **CARMEL NEWSREEL I-110** · October 25 1937
Flooding in Tel Aviv. Views from the Galilee: Rosh Pina, Tel Hai, the Hula Valley, Kfar Gil'adi. Spreading pesticide in the fight against malaria in the Hefer Valley. A mandolin orchestra and a singer.

□ PART A: TITLE: FIRST RAINFALL IN TEL-AVIV (88')   כותרת: גשמים בעיתם
1   Wadi Musrara swollen with flood-waters. Flooded streets. People floating on rafts. A truck struggling to get through the water (long, 88).

□ PART B: TITLE: VIEWS FROM THE GALILEE (119')
כותרת: "הגלילה" מוסיקה: עמנואל פונג'וב
1   Iris shot of the lion monument in Tel Hai (long, 22).
2   Pan of Tel Hai (long, 35).
3   An aqueduct leading to Kfar Giladi (long, 47).
4   Hachshara (agricultural training) youth working in a garden (long, 69).
5   Tel Hai (long, 80).
6   View of the Hula Valley from Rosh Pina. Trees in Rosh Pina (long, 100).
7   TITLE IN HEBREW: AYELET HASHACHAR (103).
8   Chicks (119).

□ PART C: TITLE: FIGHT AGAINST MALARIA IN EMEK CHEFER (195')
כותרת: מלחמה נגד מלריה בעמק חפר
1   Tents in the Hefer Valley (pan, long).
2   Young men and women washing clothes (long).
3   Pan of the Hefer Valley, including Kibbutz Ma'abarot (long).
4   The Alexander River (long).
5   Pan from the banks of the river to Kibbutz Ma'abarot (long).
6   Shovelling pesticide (in powder form) (long).
7   Putting on waterproof clothing. Filling tins with pesticide powder (mid).
8   Walking to the river, getting into a boat and rowing away (long).
9   A man wearing a gas mask spreading pesticide by hand along the banks of the river (long).
10  Removing the waterproof clothing (long).
11  Removing plants from the river with long poles (long, 181).
12  Spreading pesticide by hand from the boat (mid, 195).

□ PART D: TITLE: CONCERT OF MANDOLINE [sic] ORCHESTRA (235')
כותרת: תזמורת המיתרים ע"י ועדת התרבות של ההסתדרות. המנצח: יואל ואלכה, זמרה: אלי קורץ
1   TITLE IN HEBREW: THE STRING ORCHESTRA OF THE HISTADRUT'S CULTURAL COMMITTEE. CONDUCTOR: YOEL VALBA. SINGER: ELI KURTZ.
2   The orchestra (long, 57).
3   Pan of the musicians (111).
4   A female singer, sings a song about a rose (mid, 167).
5   The orchestra (long, 235).

■ **CARMEL NEWSREEL I-111** · November 1 1937
Unveiling of tombstone for Moses Beilinson. Completion of the Funds building on Herzl Street in Haifa. Armistice Day ceremony in Ramleh.

☐ PART A: TITLE: UNVEILING BEILINSON'S MONUMENT (53')
כותרת: יום השנה למותו של מ. ביילינסון ז"ל
1   The tombstone (long, 17).
2   The crowd (long, 29).
3   Alexander Ziskind Rabinowitz praying near the grave (long, 36).
4   The crowd (long, 47).
5   Leaving the cemetery (long, 53).

☐ PART B: TITLE: COMPLETING THE CONSTRUCTION OF THE FUNDS BUILDING AT HAIFA (85')     כותרת: גמר בנין בית הקרנות בחיפה
1   Herzl Street in Haifa - various shots of the new building (long, 85).

☐ PART C: ARMISTICE DAY IN RAMLEH (278')
1   Arrival - officials, dignitaries, army officers (long, 47).
2   Walking to the ceremony - clergy, followed by diplomats and dignitaries (long, 89).
3   A large stone cross (tilt up) and pan of the crowd (97).
4   The cemetery and the ceremony (pan, long, 145).
5   A military band (long, 153).
6   Soldiers and bugles (long, 167).
7   Soldiers leaving in formation (long, 183).
8   Dignitaries leaving (long, 206).
9   Laying a wreath (long, 237).
10  British police (long, 278).

■ **CARMEL NEWSREEL I-112** · November 8 1937
The funeral procession of Rosa Cohen. Renovation work at the port of Tel Aviv. The Shulamit theatre group re-enacts a visit from Israel to Yemen.

☐ PART A: TITLE IN HEBREW: ROSA COHEN'S FUNERAL IN TEL AVIV (79')
כותרת: לוויית רוזה כהן בת"א
1   The honour guard near the casket (long, 22).
2   The funeral procession leaving (long, 79).

☐ PART B: TITLE IN HEBREW: RENOVATION WORK IN THE PORT OF TEL AVIV (221')     כותרת: עבודות שיפור בנמל ת"א
1   Pan of boats at the Tel Aviv shore (long, 22).
2   Renovation work. A bulldozer digging (long, 87).
3   Measuring and directing the building of concrete columns in the sea (long, 106).
4   A diver preparing for underwater work. He is lowered into the water (mid, long, 168).
5   Air is pumped to the diver through a pump. A pressure meter (twice, 190).
6   Taking the diver out of the water and helping him out of wet suit (221).

☐ PART C: TITLE IN HEBREW: *A VISITOR FROM ISRAEL IN YEMEN* PERFORMED BY THE EASTERN THEATRICAL GROUP 'SHULAMIT' OF ISRAEL (346')
כותרת: אורח מא"י בתימן ע"י להקה תיאטרונית מזרחית א"י "שולמית"
1   Sitting and singing Yemenite songs. Drinking coffee. The guest carrying a huka is carried to a place of honour.
2   Sitting close. The guest is asked to tell about what is happening in Israel (mid, long, 183).
3   Everyone begins to sing (long, 194).
4   Someone gets up, the area is cleared and a dance begins to the rhythm of the song (mid, 285).

5   Close-ups of those seated on the floor who are encouraging the dancers. Women clap their hands. The dance comes to an end (c.u., 346).

■ **CARMEL NEWSREEL I-113** · November 15 1937
Children at the Ziv school in Tel Litwinsky. Jewish National Fund handicrafts exhibition in an immigrant camp in Tel Aviv. Song contest awards ceremony.

☐ PART A: TITLE: ONE DAY AMONG THE PUPILS OF THE ZIV SCHOOL (155')
כותרת: מחיי הילדים בחברת הילדים "זיו" בתל-ליטווינסקי
1   Children waking up in the morning. One child hits another with a pillow, a third does a headstand; two small children jump on their beds as an older child comes to help them dress.
2   Children help unload milk cans from dairy truck (mid, 88).
3   The exterior of the school (long, 119).
4   A child climbs a meteorological tower, checks the instruments and makes notes (mid, 137).
5   Children making meteorological tables on a blackboard (mid, 148). Exercising (long, 155).

☐ PART B: TITLE: HANDICRAFTS EXHIBITION (152') TITLE IN HEBREW: JEWISH NATIONAL FUND HANDICRAFTS EXHIBITION IN IMMIGRANT CAMPS IN TEL AVIV.   כותרת: תערוכה לעבודות יד של הקק"ל במחנות העולים בת"א
1   Immigrant housing (long, 13).
2   Presenting their work - models, a Chanukah menorah, paintings (mid, 34).
3   Working on a model of a house (mid, 42).
4   The exhibits including a micrographic map of Palestine (mid, 112).
5   Pan of the hall and visitors (long, 152).
6   TITLE: EXHIBITION OF IMMIGRANT HAND WORKS IN TEL AVIV.
כותרת: תערוכת עבודות הפליטים בתל אביב

☐ PART C: TITLE: PRIZE DISTRIBUTION IN NATIONAL HEBREW SONGS COMPETITION (45')   כותרת: חלוקת הפרסים בהתחרות הזמרה בתל-אביב
1   Tel Aviv Mayor Israel Rokah awards prizes. Moshe Wallin, organiser of the event, stands in back. The winners stand with their trophies (mid, 45).

■ **CARMEL NEWSREEL I-114** · November 22 1937
Children in Tel Aviv celebrate Chanukah. The Chief Justice arrives at Tel Aviv District Court. The High Commissioner visits Tel Aviv Port. A pier is installed at Tel Aviv Port. British soldiers arrive in Palestine. Borochov schoolchildren on parade.

☐ PART A: TITLE: SCHOOLCHILDREN CELEBRATING THE HANUKKA LIGHTS FESTIVAL (88')   כותרת: בתי הספר חוגגים את חג האורים
1   High school students gathering, holding unlit torches (long, mid, 34).
2   Girls standing on stage and holding torches, recite their parts (mid, 43).
3   A speaker (Rabbi Uziel is visible in the background). The children listening and waving their torches. Chanukah candles are lit (mid, 65).
4   A procession of children holding burning torches at night (long, 79).
5   A large Chanukah menorah on a water tower on Balfour Street. A menorah and a Star of David, lit up at night (88).

☐ PART B: TITLE: CHIEF JUSTICE AT TEL-AVIV DISTRICT COURT (56')
כותרת: זקן השופטים בבית המשפט בת"א
1   A crowd waiting outside the court house. A detachment of police (under the

command of Tel Aviv Police Chief Major Schiff) standing at attention (long, 26).
2 Judges standing outside the court house.
3 The Chief Justice arrives by car and is received by the judges.
4 The judges enter the courthouse (mid, 56).

□ PART C: TITLE: H.E. THE HIGH COMMISSIONER VISITING THE TEL AVIV HARBOUR (43') כותרת: לשובו של הנציב העליון - ה.מ. מסייר את נמל ת"א.
1 High Commissioner Wauchope gets out of his car and is received (mid, 32).
2 Wauchope walking along the wharf (mid, 43).

□ PART D: TITLE: IRON PONTOON OF LOCAL MAKE AT TEL-AVIV HARBOUR (94') כותרת: דוברת ברזל מתוצרת הארץ בנמל ת"א
1 Lowering an iron pier into the water with a crane (mid, 94).

□ PART E: TITLE: RECENT ARRIVAL OF SOLDIERS IN TEL AVIV (81') כותרת: חיילים חדשים מגיעים לת"א
1 British soldiers arriving in trucks and marching with a band at the exhibition grounds (long, mid, 81).

□ PART F: TITLE: REVIEW OF SCHOOLCHILDREN AT BOROCHOV QUARTER (155') כותרת: מפקד ילדי בית הספר בשכונת בורוכוב
1 Children marching (mid, long, 39).
2 Exercises (mid, long, 125).
3 The children marching in menorah formation (long, 151).
4 A menorah on the school roof (mid, 155).

■ **CARMEL NEWSREEL I-115** · November 29 1937
Hapoel celebrates the 17th anniversary of the Histadrut in Tel Aviv. High Commissioner Sir Arthur Wauchope attends a memorial service in Nazareth, for the assassinated District Commissioner from the Galilee, Lewis Y Andrews. Children from the Borochov neighbourhood in Tel Aviv present a Chanukah play.

□ PART A: TITLE: SPORTIVE FESTIVAL OF HAPOEL AT TEL-AVIV (218') כותרת: 17 שנות קיום הסתדרות העובדים מפקד "הפועל" בתל-אביב
1 Marching with flags (mid, 42).
2 The crowd and marching (mid, 82).
3 Hapoel directors (mid, 90).
4 The crowd and young women marching (long, 112).
5 General view of the stadium and the parade (long, 159).
6 A speaker (mid, 173).
7 Marching with flags in the stadium (long, 201).
9 A procession of motorcycles in the stadium (long, 218).

□ PART B: THE HIGH COMMISSIONER ATTENDS A MEMORIAL CEREMONY FOR LEWIS Y ANDREWS IN NAZARETH (86')
1 TITLE: THE HIGH COMMISSIONER VISITS IN NAZARETH
כותרת: ה.מ. הנציב העליון באזכרת אנדריוס בנצרת
2 A church in Nazareth (tilt up, mid, 27).
3 High Commissioner Wauchope and entourage walking in an alleyway (long, 43).
4 Leaving the church.
5 The High Commissioner gets into his car and the crowd disperses (long, 86).

□ PART C: TITLE: CHANUKKA FESTIVALS IN BOROCHOV SCHOOL (374')
כותרת: חגיגת חנוכה בבי"ס של בורוכוב
1   The children put on a play about the Chanukah story - Greeks and Jews; Hannah and her seven sons; Mathityahu the Priest (374).

■ **CARMEL NEWSREEL I-116** · December 6 1937
Opening of a room in memory of Theodor Herzl. British Mandate Treasurer W Johnson visits the Izhar oil factory. Poet Avigdor Hame'iri celebrates his 25th literary anniversary. Mekoroth Water Company installing an irrigation system in the Jezreel Valley.

□ PART A: OPENING OF HERZL'S ROOM IN JERUSALEM (103')
1   Pan of the library in Herzl's room (long, 19).
2   A desk (mid, 30).
3   Various writings (c.u., 45).
4   Medals (c.u., 54).
5   The hat Herzl wore on his trip to the East (c.u., 72).
6   A Torah ark (mid, 82).
7   Writings (c.u., 89).
8   A Jewish National Fund certificate from the Golden Book (c.u., 98).
9   A Jewish National Fund collection box (c.u., 103).

□ PART B: TITLE: MR W JOHNSON TREASURER OF PALESTINE VISITING THE IZHAR FACTORY (128')
כותרת: ביקור מנהל האוצר מר ג'ונסון בבית חרושת יצהר
1   Mr Johnson arrives at the factory (long, 17).
2   Seeds are poured into a vat. Various procedures and machines are explained to Mr Johnson (mid, 98).
3   Mr Johnson leaves the factory (long, 128).

□ PART C: TITLE: THE 25TH LITERARY ANNIVERSARY OF THE POET AVIGDOR HAMEIRI (96')
כותרת: לחצי יובלו הספרותי של המשורר אבינדור המאירי. המשורר
בשיחתו עם בא-כח הנער
1   Avigdor Hame'iri speaking to a child, explains how a person's worth is gauged by his contribution to society (mid, 96).

□ PART D: TITLE: IRRIGATION SYSTEM OF THE KISHON VALLEY THE MEKOROTH WATER CO. WORKS (179')
כותרת: הוי כל צמא לכו למים. השקאת עמק יזרעאל המערבי ע"י חברת
מקורות
1   General view of the Jezreel Valley (pan, long, 55).
2   Scattered pipes and the drilling site (mid, 80).
3   Welding pipes (c.u., 101).
4   Drilling (mid).
5   Lowering pipes into trenches (long, 179).

■ **CARMEL NEWSREEL I-117** · December 13 1937
First national home-owners meeting. Riflery competition in Haifa (at the Bat Galim swimming pool). The two Brothers Zion and Mordechai Tuvya perform a tap-dance routine.

□ PART A: TITLE: FIRST NATIONAL MEETING OF THE HOUSE-OWNERS IN PALESTINE (159')
כותרת: הועידה הארצית הראשונה של בעלי הבתים בארץ ישראל

1 Rabbi Ben Zion Meir Chai Uziel and Rabbi Moshe Avigdor Amiel arrive (mid, 28).
2 The dais with a banner in Hebrew: "The First National Meeting of the Homeowners of Eretz Israel. Tevet 15-16, 1937". A speaker. The audience (mid, 52).

שלט: הועידה הארצית הראשונה של בעלי הבתים בארץ-ישראל ט"ו-ט"ז טבת, תרצ"ח 1937

3 A speaker. The audience (mid, 52).
4 Mayor Israel Rokah speaking. The audience (mid, 72).
5 Another speaker (mid, 84).
6 A worker, walking in a field where parcels of land are marked off, begins to dig (long, 98).
7 Buildings in Tel Aviv (dissolve from building to building) (mid, 139).
8 General view of Tel Aviv (long, 159).

□ PART B: TITLE: SHOOTING COMPETITION WITH HUNTING-GUNS IN HAIFA (127')   כותרת: התחרות בקליעה למטרה מרובי ציד בחיפה
1 Participants and spectators arrive (long, 21).
2 A participant shooting while someone takes his picture (mid, 33).
3 Shooting, standing in a line (mid, 50).
4 Pan of spectators and judges (mid, 62).
5 The judges at their table (mid, 68).
6 The targets (long, 73).
7 Women shooting (mid, 93).
8 Skeet-shooting (long, 127).

□ PART C: BROTHERS ZION AND MORDECHAI TUVYA TAP-DANCING (168')
1 Children playing leap-frog.
2 One boy takes out a harmonica and the brothers begin to tap-dance, as the other boys look on (long, 76).
3 The brothers compete with each other, dancing on a crate (long, 168).

■ **CARMEL NEWSREEL I-118** · December 20 1937
Immigrants arrive on the *SS POLONIA*. A reception held on board the ship for Yishuv leaders and the press. Construction of the government hospital (later, Rambam Hospital) and immigrants' buildings in Haifa. Treating crippled children in Jerusalem.

□ PART A: TITLE: JOURNALISTS BANQUET ON BOARD SS POLONIA (197')

כותרת: ביקור באי-כח מוסדות ציבוריים באניה "פולוניה" לקראת חדוש קו הנסיעות

1 The *SS POLONIA* at sea. Various shots of the ship and the immigrants on its decks on their way to Palestine (long, 51).
2 The ship docks in Haifa (long, 75).
3 The ship's officers raise a Jewish flag as the crew stands at attention (long, 111).
4 A reception in the officer's dining hall for officers and guests.
5 A speaker (long, 146).
6 The decks. Unloading timber. Loading crates of oranges (long, 197).

□ PART B: TITLE: NEW BUILDINGS IN HAIFA GOVERNMENT HOSPITAL (83')

כותרת: בנין בית החולים הממשלתי בחיפה

1 The hospital near completion. Scaffolding.
2 Pan of the building (long, 83).

☐ PART C: TITLE: THE NEW IMMIGRATION BUILDING IN HAIFA (48')

כותרת: בנין בית בעולים בחיפה

1  Pan of construction.
2  Various shots of the building (long, 48).

☐ PART D: TITLE: ACTIVITIES OF THE SOCIETY FOR CRIPPLED CHILDREN IN JERUSALEM (201')     כותרת: העזרה לילדים נכים בירושלים

1  Doctors receiving reports on the children (mid, 29).
2  Crippled children in the hospital (mid, 46).
3  Doctors administer various treatments to the children - electricity, bandages, exercise (mid, 137).
4  The children knitting and sewing - one child takes another's measurements. The children in a classroom (mid, 186).
5  The children dancing (long, 201).

■ CARMEL NEWSREEL I-119 · December 27 1937
Laying a cornerstone for Maccabi House in Kiryat Motzkin and constructing municipal schools in Tel Aviv. Strongman Shimon Rudi pulls a car with his teeth. Jewish Agency meeting on behalf of Keren Hayesod.

☐ PART A: TITLE: LAYING CORNERSTONE OF MACCABI HOUSE AT KIRIATH MOTZKIN NEAR HAIFA (116')

כותרת: הנחת אבן הפינה לבית מכבי בקרית מוצקין ע"י חיפה

1  Maccabi members march to the site of the ceremony (long, 51).
2  Pan of the crowd and speakers (long, 70).
3  The crowd being held back. Reading the dedication scroll. Signing the scroll. The crowd (long, 116).

☐ PART B: TITLE: EXTENSION OF NET OF MUNICIPAL SCHOOLS AT TEL-AVIV (94')     כותרת: הרחבת רשת בתי-הספר העירוניים בתל-אביב

1  Construction of new schools (pan, long, 94).

☐ PART C: FEAT OF STRONGMAN SHIMON RUDI IN THE STREETS OF TEL AVIV (13')
1  Shimon Rudi pulls a car with a chain held between his teeth (long, 13).

☐ PART D: JEWISH AGENCY MEETING ON BEHALF OF KEREN HAYESOD (193')
1  The audience (long, 18).
2  The dais: Eliezer Kaplan on the side, Yitzhak Gruenbaum in the centre (mid, 37).
3  Various shots of speakers: the director of Keren Hayesod Tel Aviv, Eliezer Kaplan and Moshe Shertok (Sharett) (c.u., mid, 193).

■ CARMEL NEWSREEL I-120 · January 3 1938
Tel Aviv Port on a stormy winter day. Tree-lined streets in Tel Aviv.

☐ PART A: TITLE: TEL AVIV HARBOUR IN A WINTER DAY (122')

כותרת: נמל תל-אביב ביום חורף

1  The port. Boats leaving and entering through high waves (long, 122).

☐ PART B: TITLE IN HEBREW: TREES AND GREENERY FOR THE IMPROVEMENT OF TEL AVIV (71')     כותרת: עצים וירק לשיפור תל אביב

1  A row of trees and benches. A woman knitting. Greenery near the Habimah Theatre (mid, c.u., 31).

2   Children running along a tree-lined avenue. A park (dissolve, 48).
3   A tree-lined street (71).

☐ PART C: TITLE IN HEBREW: A *MITZVA DANCE* - DANYA LEVINE AND HER STUDIO (210')
1   The dance (long, 210).

■ **CARMEL NEWSREEL I-121** · January 10 1938
Kindergarten children celebrate Tu B'shvat. Inauguration of the Beit Hamehandes (Engineers' House) in Tel Aviv. The students' ball at the Technion in Haifa. A Labour Youth harmonica band accompanied by an accordion.

☐ PART A: TITLE IN HEBREW: TU B'SHVAT AT A KINDERGARTEN IN TEL AVIV (118')   כותרת: חגיגות ט"ו בשבט לילדי הגן הדוגמאי בתל-אביב
1   The kindergarten is decorated and tables are arranged outside. Children come out of the kindergarten (long, 23).
2   The children carrying saplings and singing in a choir (mid, 73).
3   Children digging in the soil.
4   The children sitting around the tables outside and eating (mid, long, 108).
5   A child watering a tree (mid, 118).

☐ PART B: TITLE: INAUGURATION OF THE ENGINEERS' BUILDING AT TEL AVIV (117')   כותרת: פתיחת בית המהנדס בתל-אביב
1   The dais - including High Commissioner Sir Arthur Wauchope and Rabbi Ben Zion Meir Chai Uziel. A speaker (pan, long, 44).
2   The audience applauding (long, 53).
3   Dignitaries pouring concrete (long, 78).
4   The engineers' building on Dizengoff Street.
5   People entering and leaving the building (long, 117).

☐ PART C: TITLE: THE STUDENTS BALL AT THE JEWISH POLITECHNICUM [sic] IN HAIFA (125')   כותרת: הנשף המסורתי של הסטודנטים בטכניון העברי בחיפה
1   Watching a dance performance on stage (long, 57).
2   Technion students dancing (long, 71).
3   The hall and decorations (mid).
4   Students dancing (long, 94).
5   Coffee in an adjacent room. More dancing (125).

☐ PART D: TITLE: BRASS BAND CONCERT (146'). TITLE IN HEBREW: HARMONICA BAND OF WORKING YOUTH OF ERETZ ISRAEL. CONDUCTED BY TZVI BERDICHEVSKY.
כותרת: תזמורת המפוחיות של הנוער הארץ-ישראלי העובד, בניצוחו של צבי ברדיצ'בסקי
1   Various shots of the band and the conductor (long, mid, 146).

■ **CARMEL NEWSREEL I-122** · January 17 1938
A forest in Kiryat Anavim. Alexander Ziskind Rabinowitz's 84th birthday. A soccer match between Palestine and Greece. An Offenbach operetta performed in Hebrew.

☐ PART A: FOREST IN KIRYAT ANAVIM (65')
1   General view of Kiryat Anavim and the surrounding hills, terracing and tree-planting (pan, long, 65).

☐ PART B: TITLE: THE POET A. Z. RABINOVICHT [sic] 84TH ANNIVERSARY (42')
כותרת: כה לחי! הסופר הישיש ר׳ אלכסנדר זיסקינד רבינוביץ (אז"ר) בן 84 שנים
1   Rabinowitz leaving his house and walking towards the camera.
2   Speaking in front of the camera in the studio (long, 42).

☐ PART C: A SOCCER MATCH BETWEEN PALESTINE AND GREECE (112')
1   The Greek players come onto the field (long, 16).
2   Pan of the two teams posing for a photograph. Standing at attention while the anthems are played (long, mid, 32).
3   Exchanging pennants (mid, long, 46).
4   The game. The crowd cheering. The referees. A goal (long, 112).

☐ PART D: TITLE: OPENING OF THE CAMERA-OPERA SEASON (245')
כותרת: אמנות זעירה
1   TITLE IN HEBREW: THE ERETZ ISRAEL CAMERI-OPERA, DIRECTED BY BENO FRANKEL. *LE MARIAGE AUX LANTERNES* BY OFFENBACH.
כותרת: קמר-אופרה ארץ ישראלית בהנהלת בנו פרנקל. קטע מתוך "אירוסים לאור פנסים" מאת אופנבך
2   The performance (sung in Hebrew) (long, mid, 245).

■ **CARMEL NEWSREEL I-123** · January 24 1938
Dr Chaim Weizmann addresses the General Zionist Association in Tel Aviv. High Commissioner Sir Arthur Wauchope visits the "Pri-Peri" juice factory near Rehovot. Hanna Maierzuk (Meron) sings *Serochei Naalaim* ("Shoelaces").

☐ PART A: TITLE: MEETING OF THE GENERAL ZIONIST ASSOCIATION IN TEL AVIV (93')
כותרת: ד"ר חיים וייצמן באסיפת התאחדות הציונים הכלליים בתל-אביב
1   A woman speaking in English (long, 57).
2   Weizmann speaking (long, 93).

☐ PART B: TITLE: H. E. THE HIGH COMMISSIONER VISITING THE CITRUS JUICE FACTORY "PRI-PERI" NEAR REHOVOT (193')
כותרת: ביקור פרידה של ה.מ. הנציב העליון בביח"ר למיצי הדר "פרי-פרי" ע"י רחובות
1   Stacking crates of fruit (long, mid).
2   The High Commissioner enters the factory and observes the production process (long, 26).
3   The fruit is taken on a conveyor belt, cut and squeezed. Workers sorting fruit (mid, 117).
4   The High Commissioner looks on as the juices are mixed. The exterior of the factory. Barrels (mid, 169).
5   A pile of rinds for mulch (long, 185),
6   The High Commissioner leaves (mid, 193).

☐ PART C: TITLE: *SEROCHEI NAALAIM* (SHOELACES) SONG BY HANNA MAIERZAK [sic] (200')
כותרת: חנה מאירצ׳ק בשיר הילד העצוב "שרוכי נעליים"
1   Children peddling in the street - shoelaces, newspapers (mid, 41).
2   Hanna Maierzuk (Meron) calls out her wares (shoelaces), walks towards a house and sits down on the steps - singing the first verse (mid, 126).
3   Maierzuk approaches a passer-by, runs through the street and sings the second verse (long, 200).

■ **CARMEL NEWSREEL I-124** · January 31 1938
Jerusalem council elections. A Maccabi athletics competition in Rehovot. Opening Zina Dizengoff Square in Tel Aviv to the public. Scenes from the Ohel Theatre's *The Forest*.

☐ PART A: TITLE: ELECTIONS TO THE JERUSALEM COMMUNITY COUNCIL (58')

כותרת: הבחירות לקהילת ירושלים

1   Crowd near a polling station (long, 9).
2   Posters and handbills (long, 44).
3   At the polling station (long, 58).

☐ PART B: TITLE: SPORT EXERCISES BY THE MACCABI IN REHOVOT (99')

כותרת: התחרויות באתלטיקה קלה ברחובות

1   A crowd near the track (long, 14).
2   Women at the starting line - begin to run (long, 51).
3   Men's race (long, 57).
4   Shot-put, high-jump and pole-vault (long, 99).

☐ PART C: TITLE: OPENING THE ZINA DIZENGOFF SQUARE IN TEL AVIV (101')

כותרת: ככר צינה דיזנגוף ת"א פתוח לרשות הקהל

1   The finished square (pan, long, 46).
2   Buildings - seen through the square (tilt up from the fountain) (long, 69).
3   Various shots of the fountain at night (long, 101).

☐ PART D: SCENES FROM *THE FOREST* BY HA'OHEL THEATRE (362')
1   Chopping down trees and singing (long, 37).
2   Two friends meet; the actor holding the balalaika is Meir Margalit (long, 96).
3   Chopping down trees and singing (long, 104). An actress tells actor Yehuda Gabai how the landlord has been tormenting her (mid, long, 167).
4   The wandering actor approaches the landlord dressed as an officer, and meets the landlord's wife (mid, long, 225).
5   The actor and a maidservant (mid).
6   Gabai and his beloved daughter (mid, long, 295).
7   Dancing (long, 362).

■ **CARMEL NEWSREEL I-125** · February 7 1938
Launching a new boat at Tel Aviv port. The Palestine Orchestra returns from Egypt. Lithuanian Independence Day celebrated in Tel Aviv. Floods.

☐ PART A: TITLE: LAUNCHING A NEW MOTOR-BOAT IN TEL AVIV PORT (96')

כותרת: הורדת סירה חדשה בנמל ת"א

1   The name of the boat, painted on its side, is uncovered. The boat is lowered with ropes into the water (mid, long, 33).
2   The boat is launched. The crowd (long, 96).

☐ PART B: TITLE: THE PALESTINE ORCHESTRA RETURNING FROM EGYPT (76')

כותרת: התזמורת הארצישראלית חוזרת מסיבובה במצרים

1   The train at the station in Tel Aviv. The orchestra's baggage is taken off the train. The passengers begin to disembark from the train (long, 36).
2   The orchestra is greeted. The musicians, carrying their instruments, get on a bus (long, 76).

☐ PART C: TITLE: FESTIVAL OF LETTONIA [sic] INDEPENDENCE DAY IN TEL AVIV (55')

כותרת: חג העצמאות של ליטא בת"א

1   A photograph of the Lithuanian president. Sitting at set tables at the

1   A photograph of the Lithuanian president. Sitting at set tables at the Lithuanian embassy. Speeches (c.u., 46).
2   Rabbis, including Rabbi Uziel, sitting together at a table (long, 55).

☐ PART D: TITLE: THE LAST RAINS IN PALESTINE (92')

כותרת: הגשמים האחרונים בארץ

1   Trees surrounded by water (mid, 56).
2   An overflowing wadi (long, 23).
3   Firemen pull a donkey harnessed to a wagon, from the water (mid, 56).
4   A man pulled from the water beats his arms to warm up. Police near the wadi. A donkey is pulled up the banks of the wadi. The wagon remains in the water (long, 92).

■ **CARMEL NEWSREEL I-126** · February 14 1938
The opening of Tel Aviv port to passenger traffic.

☐ PART A: OPENING TEL AVIV PORT TO PASSENGER TRAFFIC (184')
1   The port (long, 7).
2   Waving flags (long, 11).
3   Menachem Ussishkin speaking (mid, long, 77).
4   The crowd (long, 86).
5   Moshe Shertok (Sharett) speaking (mid, long, 150).
6   Lights at the port, city hall and in the streets (long, 184)

■ **CARMEL NEWSREEL I-127** · February 21 1938
Laying a cornerstone for Andrews Hospital in Netanya, in memory of Lewis Y Andrews, the late District Commissioner for the Galilee who was assassinated by Arab nationalists. Paper collection and recycling in Tel Aviv. Outgoing High Commissioner Sir Arthur Wauchope pays final visits to Hadera and Pardes Hanna.

☐ PART A: TITLE: INAUGURATION OF ANDREWS HOSPITAL IN NETANYA (180')

כותרת" הנחת אבן הפינה לבית החולים ע"ש ל. אנדריוס בנתניה

1   High Commissioner Wauchope arrives. The crowd. Mayor Oved Ben-Ami speaks (33).
2   A woman speaking (long, 44).
3   The High Commissioner speaking (long, 52).
4   Laying the cornerstone (long, 81).
5   Walking down the hill - Wauchope and Ben-Ami (long, 96).
6   Ben-Ami speaking (mid, long, 124).
7   Standing at attention while the anthems are played (*God Save the King* and *Hatikva*) - visible are Wauchope, Ben-Ami and Moshe Sharett (mid, long, 180).

☐ PART B: JEWISH NATIONAL FUND PAPER RECYCLING PLANT IN TEL AVIV (257')
1   Children collecting waste paper (long, 25).
2   A housewife empties rubbish in a rubbish can and paper in a wooden collection bin (long, 41).
3   Workers collecting the waste paper bins and emptying them into a truck (mid, 82).
4   Arranging the waste paper at the recycling plant (long, 111).
5   A machine shreds the paper (122).
7   Shredded paper is put in a vat and then compressed (mid, long, 178).
8   Packages of paper are loaded for shipment (mid, long, 195).
9   The paper is loaded on boats at Tel Aviv Port (mid, long, 210).
10  TITLE: PAPER COLLECTION IN TEL AVIV

כותרת: ניר אשפות לתועלת מפעל הניר של הקרן הקיימת לישראל בת"א

## Carmel Newsreels: Series 1

11 Children eating sandwiches and making a pile of the paper wrappings (mid, long, 251).
12 Schoolchildren (long, 257).

□ PART C: TITLE: LEAVE-TAKING OF H. E. THE HIGH COMMISSIONER AT HADERA (153')     כותרת: ביקור הפרידה של ה.מ. הנציב העליון בחדרה
1 The crowd lines both sides of the road (long, 18).
2 The High Commissioner gets out of his car and the crowd cheers. The High Commissioner tips his hat to the crowd. It is raining and the crowd is holding umbrellas (long, 49).
3 The High Commissioner says farewell to various people (long, 68).
4 The crowd - holding umbrellas - receives the High Commissioner as he comes out of a building. Wauchope stops to talk to people (long, 100).
5 TITLE: LEAVE-TAKING OF H.E. THE HIGH COMMISSIONER AT PARDES-HANNA     כותרת: ביקור הפרידה של ה.מ. הנציב העליון בפרדס חנה
6 The High Commissioner and the crowd in Pardes Hanna (long, 124).
7 The High Commissioner planting a tree (long, mid, 153).

■ **CARMEL NEWSREEL I-128** · February 28 1938
Arrival of the new High Commissioner Sir Harold MacMichael. An exhibition of paintings by Matosofsky. The Jewish Hunters Association plants a forest in honour of its chairman, Dr Walter Moses. Archaeological exhibits at the Rockefeller Museum in Jerusalem.

□ PART A: TITLE: ARRIVAL OF THE NEW HIGH COMMISSIONER H.E. SIR HAROLD MACMICHAEL (116')
כותרת: הוד מעלתו הנציב העליון החדש הגיע לארץ
1 Haifa decorated with flags (long, 22).
2 A crowd waiting behind a fence (mid, 31).
3 Dignitaries arrive to greet the new High Commissioner (long, 45).
4 The battleship carrying the High Commissioner coming into port (long, 63).
5 The High Commissioner walking through a portal preceded by a "Highlander" (long, 90).
6 A crowd near a train platform. The train pulling out (long, 116).

□ PART B: AN EXHIBITION OF THE WORKS OF PAINTER MATOSOVSKY (73')
1 Mayor Israel Rokah speaking. The artist, the paintings and the crowd (mid, 24).
2 Dissolve to the paintings (mid, 49).
3 Rokah and the artist shake hands (mid, 61).
4 The artist speaking. Standing next to him is Dr Shaul Tchernichovsky (long, 73).

□ PART C: TITLE: INAUGURATION OF FOREST PLANTATION IN THE NAME OF DR MOSES, CHAIRMAN OF THE JEWISH HUNTERS ASSOCIATION (114')
כותרת: נטיעת חורשה ע"י אגודת הצידים העברים בא"י ע"ש ד"ר מוזס
1 Sign in Hebrew: Dr Moses Forest - Planted by the Jewish Hunters Association of Palestine (mid, 18).
2 Pan of Association members listening to a speech (long, 51).
3 The head of the Hunters Association speaking. To his right is Dr Walter Moses (mid, 62).
4 The hunters applaud, plant saplings in a row and fire shots in the air (long, 114).

□ PART D: TITLE: ROCKEFELLER MUSEUM AT JERUSALEM (363')
כותרת: בית הנכאות ע"ש רוקפלר בירושלים
1  Pan of the building. Dissolve to a pool seen through a wrought-iron gate and another shot of the museum (long, 47).
2  Restoring ancient pottery (mid, long, 81).
3  A clay pot is brought to the exhibit room and placed on a shelf (mid, long, 148).
4  A mummy (mid, 158).
5  Various exhibits - including a sword and a burial urn (mid, 311).
6  Ossuaries - including one with a Hebrew inscription (mid, 340).
7  Tilt from exhibits to ceiling (long, 363).

■ **CARMEL NEWSREEL I-129** · March 6 1938
Putting out a fire at a lumberyard in Rehovot and police searching for clues. Children's parade on Tel Hai Day in Pardes Hanna. Hapoel walking race in Tel Aviv. Construction of the new neighbourhood of Tel Shalom in Pardes Hanna.

□ PART A: TITLE: FIRE IN TIMBER STORE - REHOVOT (134')
כותרת: שרפה במחסן העצים ברחובות
1  Firemen arrive with their equipment (mid, 12).
2  Putting out the fire (pan, mid, long, 77).
3  A Bedouin tracker and police looking for clues (long, 134).

□ PART B: TITLE: RALLY OF SHOMRON CHILDREN ON TEL HAI DAY AT PARDESS-HANNA (172')    כותרת: כנוס ילדי השומרון ביום תל-חי בפרדס חנה
1  General view of Pardes Hanna (pan, long, 25).
2  Dissolve to a school and to another building (long, 41).
3  Children listening to a speaker (long, 51).
4  Children marching (mid, 130).
5  The children do calisthenics together (long, 172).

□ PART C: TITLE: WALKING MATCH OF "HAPOEL" AT TEL-AVIV (118')
כותרת: התחרות בהליכה של "הפועל" בתל-אביב
1  The participants ready to begin (long, 20).
2  The race begins. The winner crosses the finishing-line and is awarded the prize (long, 105).
3  The winner is carried away on shoulders (mid, 118).

□ PART D: TEL SHALOM - A NEW NEIGHBOURHOOD IN PARDES HANNA (43')
1  General view of Pardes Hanna (pan) and beginning construction on the new neighbourhood (long, 21).
2  Building the first houses (mid, 43).

■ **CARMEL NEWSREEL I-130** · March 13 1938
Children's Purim celebrations in Ahuza in Haifa and in Rishon Lezion. Meeting of the Committee for Travelling Exhibitions. Yosef Goland sings *Hora Hadasha*.

□ PART A: TITLE: PURIM FESTIVAL OF THE KINDERGARTEN AT RISHON LEZION (178')    כותרת: חגיגת-פורים של גן-הילדים בראשון-לציון
1  Children in costume coming out of the kindergarten (mid, 50).
2  The garden where the celebration is taking place. A band (long, 72).
3  A child presents a tree-planting certificate (mid, 91).
4  The children receiving packets of Purim delicacies. Setting tables (mid, 113).
5  Decorations.
6  The children eating (mid, long, 155).

7 Teachers and children sitting at a table and looking at a school photograph (mid, 167).
8 Various shots of the party (long, 178).

☐ PART B: TITLE: MEETING OF THE COMMITTEE OF TRAVELLING EXHIBITIONS (74')  כותרת: ישיבת הועד לארגון תערוכת א"י נודדת
1 The dais (pan, mid, 20).
2 Mayor Israel Rokah speaking (mid, 42).
3 Journalists taking notes (mid, 52).
4 Another speaker (mid, 74).

☐ PART C: TITLE: PURIM FESTIVAL AT AHUZA HAIFA (152')
כותרת: תהלוכת פורים באחוזה-חיפה
1 Pan of crowd holding banners (long, 23).
2 Babies and mothers holding a banner (mid, 37).
3 Babies in carriages decorated with flowers (mid, 56).
4 Kindergarten children in costume. A band (mid, 115).
5 General view of Ahuza and the parade (long, 125).
6 A decorated car and decorated camels (mid, 152).

☐ PART D: YOSEF GOLAND SINGS ZEIRA'S *HORA HADASHA* (183')
1 TITLE IN HEBREW: BACK FROM HIS EUROPEAN TOUR, YOSEF GOLAND SINGS *HORA HADASHA* (NEW HORA) BY ZEIRA. WORDS BY ORLAND. PIANO: SARAH GOLAND (9).
כותרת: אחרי שובו מסבובו בארצות אירופה הזמר יוסף גולנד בהורה חדשה של זעירא. מלים: אורלנד. ע"י הפסנתר: שרה גולנד
2 Yosef Goland sings (mid, 183).

■ **CARMEL NEWSREEL I-131** · March 20 1938
Dedication of Allenby Park in Haifa. High school track and field day in Petah Tikva. Journalists visit a Tel Aviv stadium and are shown preparations for the Maccabia. A butterfly exhibition in Tel Aviv. Hapoel relay race in Tel Aviv.

☐ PART A: TITLE: INAUGURATION OF THE PUBLIC GARDEN ON THE NAME OF LORD ALLENBY AT HAIFA (140')
כותרת: פתיחת הגן הציבורי על הכרמל ע"ש הלורד אלנבי בחיפה
1 General view of Haifa (pan, long, 27).
2 District Commissioner Sir Edward Keith-Roach and Mayor Shukri arrive (long, 58).
3 A woman (possibly Mrs Allenby). Mayor Shukri speaking (mid, 74).
4 Guests walking along the road; in the park (long, 140).

☐ PART B: TITLE: SCHOOL SPORT IN PETAH TIKVA (96')
כותרת: יום הספורט המסורתי של תלמידי ביה"ס למסחר כת"א, על מגרש המכבי כפ"ת
1 Raising the flag. Pan of the children on the field (long, 36).
2 The long-jump (long, 59).
3 Races and the high-jump (long, 96).

☐ PART C: TITLE: PREPARATIONS FOR THE "MACCABIA" (88')
כותרת: ביקור עתונאים באצטדיון ה"מכבי" בתל-אביב
1 Improvements underway in the stadium (long, mid, 66).
2 Journalists being taken around and shots of renovations (long, mid, 88).

## Carmel Newsreels: Series 1

☐ **PART D: TITLE: BUTTERFLIES EXHIBITION IN TEL-AVIV (118')**

כותרת: תערוכת הפרפרים בת"א

1. The exhibition hall and children looking at the butterflies (long, 32).
2. A girl looking at the butterflies (mid, 63).
3. Butterflies (c.u., 112).
4. The hall (long, 118).

☐ **PART E: TITLE: SPORTS BY HAPOEL (151')**

כותרת: מרוץ השליחים של "הפועל" בת"א

1. Four participants, wearing backpacks, crawling on their stomachs (mid, long, 60).
2. Relay race - walking and carrying other members of the team (mid, 90).
3. Carrying a member of the team on a stretcher. On bicycles. The crowd and participants (long, 151).

■ **CARMEL NEWSREEL I-132** · March 27 1938

The arrival of the *SS POLONIA* and the *SS EGYPT* passenger ships at Tel Aviv port. The passengers being ferried to shore on boats. The High Commissioner Sir Arthur Wauchope and Tel Aviv Mayor Israel Rokah go aboard. Customs and passport control. A crowd meeting the ship.

☐ **PART A: TITLE: FIRST ARRIVAL - *SS EGYPT* AND *SS POLONIA* AT TEL-AVIV PORT (489')**

כותרת: שהחיינו וקימנו... הורדת נוסעיים הראשונים בנמל ת"א

1. Waiting behind the port gates. A policeman is allowing those with passes to enter the port (long, 21).
2. British and Jewish Agency passport control (long, 35).
3. Various shots of passengers leaving the ship, boarding boats, on their way to shore, docking and leaving the boats. Children are helped ashore (long, 139).
4. TITLE: THEY ARE MET AND TAKEN ASHORE IN THE "TOZERET HA-ARETZ" (MADE-IN-ISRAEL) LIGHTER, *ALIYA*.

כותרת ביידיש: און דאן קומען כסדר שיפן און די עליה שטיינגט... די שיפל "עליה" דערמונטערט.

5. Boats en route from the ship to shore (long, 163).
6. Those holding permits enter the port to meet the arriving passengers (long, 180).
7. A ship and boats ferrying passengers ashore (223).
8. A group of journalists (long, 235).
9. The ship from afar and people on the docks (long, 248).
10. The High Commissioner, Sir Arthur Wauchope, Tel Aviv Mayor Israel Rokah, other dignitaries and customs officials getting into boats. The dignitaries and officials reach the ship and go aboard (long, 307).
11. Boats with passengers from the ship, docking. A boat en route to shore (long, 327).
12. Policemen at the gate. There is a crowd behind them.
13. The *SS POLONIA*, decorated with flags (mid, long, 422).
14. Immigrants in a boat wave to those on shore, arrive at the dock and are helped ashore (long, 410).
15. In the arrivals hall (long, 419).
16. An orthodox priest (mid, long, 422).
17. Baggage is cleared at customs and loaded on a car (mid, 471).
18. The ship from afar and passengers on a boat (long, 489).

■ **CARMEL NEWSREEL I-133** · April 3 1938

High Commissioner Sir Harold MacMichael's first visit to Tel Aviv. Hashomer (watchman's organisation) horse race in Petah Tikva. Journalists at the Kremener

"Vulcan" factory in Haifa are shown how bath-tubs are made. Maccabi sports meet in Tel Aviv.

□ PART A: TITLE: THE HIGH COMMISSIONER IN TEL AVIV (74')

כותרת: הביקור הראשון של ה.מ. הנציב העליון החדש בת"א

1  A crowd. The High Commissioner gets out of his car and is welcomed by municipal officials (long, 40).
2  The High Commissioner descending the municipality building steps, accompanied by Mayor Israel Rokah, Dov Hoz and other officials (long, 74).

□ PART B: TITLE: HORSE RACE OF THE WATCHMEN AT PETAH TIKVA (76')

כותרת: כנוס השומרים בפתח תקוה

1  A gate flying the Jewish and British flags and a pan of the crowd (long, 26).
2  A man on horseback, followed by a band (long, 26).
3  Members galloping on horseback (long, 76).

□ PART C: TITLE: JOURNALISTS VISIT AT THE KREMENER FACTORY AT HAIFA (167')     כותרת: ביקור עתונאים כבית"ר "וולקן" בחיפה
1  The exterior of the factory (long, 9).
2  Journalists arrive at the factory, are shown moulds used in the production of bath-tubs (long, 26).
3  The journalists look on as finished bath-tubs are lowered on ropes (long, 54).
4  Journalists watch bath-tubs being coated with enamel and put into a kiln (long, 86).
5  A press forming bath-tubs. Other steps in the manufacturing process (long, 160).
6  The journalists leave the factory (long, 167).

□ PART D: TITLE: SPORT-MEETING OF THE MACCABI IN TEL AVIV (314')

כותרת: פתיחת כנוס "המכבי" בתל-אביב

1  Various shots of Maccabi members marching with flags, banners and a band (92).
2  Decorated stands and spectators (long, 117).
3  Various shots of the crowd and parade (long, 242).
4  The dais. Maccabi officials stand at attention and at ease as they are saluted with lowered flags (long, 280).
5  Speeches and shots of the crowd (long, 314).

■ **CARMEL NEWSREEL I-134** · April 10 1938
Closing ceremony of the national Maccabia athletics competition in Tel Aviv. Laying a cornerstone for a vocational school for girls in Tel Aviv. Inauguration of Hanesi'im Public Park in Ramat Gan. Ben Gurion launches a new Hapoel boat and Hapoel boat races on the Yarkon River.

□ PART A: TITLE: SPORT MEETING OF THE MACCABI IN TEL AVIV (49')

כותרת: נעילת המכביה הארצית בתל-אביב

1  Calisthenics (mid, long, 42).
2  The crowd (long, 49).

□ PART B: TITLE: FOUNDATION OF THE NEW WOMAN WORKERS HOUSE IN TEL AVIV (96')      כותרת: אבן פינה לבי"ס מקצועי ולמעון צעירות בתל-אביב
1  Close-up of the dedication scroll. The scroll is lowered, revealing the dais (long, 35).
2  A woman reads the dedication scroll, followed by a speaker (mid, long, 50).

3   The guests take their seats. Another speaker (mid, 71).
4   Filling the cornerstone with cement (mid, long, 86).
5   A toast (mid, long, 96).

☐ PART C: TITLE: INAUGURATION OF A PUBLIC GARDEN AT RAMAT GAN (178')
כותרת: חנוכת "גן הנשיאים" ברמת-גן
1   A crowd at the new park (long, 34).
2   Mayor Avraham Krinitzi and a British official (mid, long, 37).
3   A woman removes the cloth covering the new sign: The Hanesi'im Park (long, 112).
4   Guests and various shots of the park: a playground, a fountain (mid, 178).

☐ PART D: TITLE: HAPOEL YACHT SPORT ON THE YARKON RIVER
1   TITLE IN HEBREW: DEDICATION OF THE HAPOEL ROWBOAT IN MEMORY OF YA'AKOV BERGER (123')
כותרת: חנכת הסירה של הפועל ע"ש יעקב ברנגר ז"ל
2   David Ben Gurion and Hapoel officials (mid, long, 36).
3   Rowing race on the Yarkon River (long, 60).
4   Hapoel Yam roll-call (long, 77).
5   Ben Gurion cuts the ribbon holding the boat. Hapoel members get into the boat and push off (115).
6   A rowing race on the Yarkon (long, 123).

■ CARMEL NEWSREEL I-135 · April 17 1938
Hapoel walking race in Haifa. Laying a cornerstone for the Mizrahi religious agricultural school at Kfar HaRoeh. Ambulances, which arrive from Paris, are delivered as a gift to Magen David Adom, Tel Aviv. Yiddish actor Avraham Morevsky arrives in Palestine. Laying a cornerstone for an orphanage in Ramat Gan.

☐ PART A: TITLE: WALKING-MATCH OF "HAPOEL" IN HAIFA (109')
כותרת: התחרות הליכה של "הפועל" בחיפה
1   Athletes and spectators wait at the track in Hadar Hacarmel. The athletes are each given a knapsack (33).
2   The race begins. Young men walking with knapsacks on their backs (69).
3   Young women walking (long, 78).
4   The crowd near the starting-line. Young men and women walking (109).

☐ PART B: TITLE: THE NEW "MISRAHI" [sic] AGRICULTURAL YESHIVA NEAR HADERA
1   TITLE IN HEBREW: FOUNDATION STONE LAYING FOR A RELIGIOUS AGRICULTURE SCHOOL OF MIZRACHI IN HEFER VALLEY (137').
כותרת: הנחת אבן-הפינה לישיבה החקלאית של ה"מזרחי" בעמק חפר
2   A crowd near a gate bearing a "welcome" banner (long, 30).
3   Men wearing keffiyehs eating at a table (long, 39).
4   A speech (long, 63).
5   Rabbi Yitzhak Halevi Herzog speaking. Other guests (mid, long, 84).
6   Depositing the dedication scroll in a cement drum and pouring cement over it (long, mid, 103).
7   Afternoon prayers (long, 116).
8   Drinking a toast and dancing (long, 137).

☐ PART C: TITLE: DELIVERY OF TWO AMBULANCES TO THE "MAGEN DAVID ADOM" (91')
כותרת: אמבולנסים חדשים למגן-דוד-אדום ת"א
1   The ambulances (long, 19).

2   A plaque in Hebrew: This Ambulance is the Gift of the Committee for Magen David Adom in Paris (c.u., 25).
3   The interior of one of the ambulances (mid, 42).
4   An audience and the chairman of Magen David Adom speaking. Another speaker (mid, 79).
5   Three ambulances (long, 91).

□ PART D: TITLE IN HEBREW: ACTOR MOREVSKY VISITS PALESTINE (55')
1   Yiddish actor Avraham Morevsky arrives at Tel Aviv port (mid, 25).
2   Morevsky shakes hands with a number of people and leaves the port (mid, 55).

□ PART E: TITLE: LAYING OF THE FOUNDATION-STONE OF THE ORPHAN-ASYLUM IN RAMAT-GAN (110')   כותרת: הנחת אבן הפינה לבית היתומים בר"ג
1   Children, a gate bearing a sign, guests (long, 25).
2   Speeches. Rabbi Ben Zion Meir Chai Uziel sitting on the dais. Rabbi Uziel speaking. Pan of the crowd (72).
3   The orphans (long, 95).
4   Laying the cornerstone - Rabbi Uziel participates (long, 110).

■ **CARMEL NEWSREEL I-136** · April 24 1938
An entire newsreel devoted to the development of the fishing industry. Fish breeding in the Sachneh River. Breeding carp in ponds. Fishermen on the Mediterranean Sea near Haifa, on Lake Hula at Kibbutz Hulata and on the Sea of Galilee.

TITLE: DEVELOPMENT OF FISHERY IN PALESTINE (1029')
TITLE IN HEBREW: MARITIME DEPT., JEWISH AGENCY.
כותרת: היומן מוקדש לחידוש הדיג העברי - מפעולות מחלקת הים של הסוכנות היהודית
TITLE IN HEBREW: ARRANGEMENT BY MOSHE WILENSKY, THE GILALI QUARTET SINGING *THE FISHERMAN'S SONG*. WORDS BY LEAH GOLDBERG, MUSIC BY MOSHE WILENSKY.
כותרת: המוסיקה עובדה ע"י משה וילנסקי בהשתתפות הרביעיה גיללי, שיר הדייגים - מלים לאה גולדברג, מנגינה משה וילנסקי

□ PART A: FISH-BREEDING IN THE SAKNEH [sic] RIVER
1   The Sachneh River under rushes and algae (long, 41).
2   The river after having been cleaned up (Tel Amal, today Nir David, is in the background) (long, 53).
3   The dam on the Sachneh. Jewish Agency officials and journalists walking along the dam - including Bar Kochva-Mayerowitz, Dr Widra and others (mid, 86).
4   A fish-breeding expert from Yugoslavia presents one of the "new immigrants" from Yugoslavia - a giant carp (mid, 112).
5   (Filmed 8 months later) The river near the dam (long, 133).
6   Tel Amal members spread a net across the river (mid, long, 156).
7   Fish in the water (long, 173).

□ PART B: TITLE: BREEDING OF CARPS IN THE POOLS OF JEWISH FARMS IN PALESTINE   כותרת: עם חדש הדג העברי גדול קרפיונים במשקים
1   General view of the Beit Shean Valley, Sachneh surrounded by rushes.
2   Digging a ditch with shovels, a drill and a steam-shovel. The ditch filled with water.
3   Fish-ponds.

4   Fish in a net in the water. Fishermen standing around the net - one holds up a large fish.
5   Hatchlings in a net in the water. Someone runs his hands through the hatchlings and picks up a handful of them.
6   Rowing on one of the ponds.
7   A rowing boat on a lake. A settlement in the background.
8   A close-up of the boat, which is loaded with sacks.
9   The man in the boat opens a sack and pours the contents (powder) into the water.
10  Fish near the water's surface.
11  Two men in front of microscopes - one is dissecting a fish, the other is placing a sample on a microscope slide.
12  A group of men wading into the water with a net. Two others are near the shore feeding out the net.
13  Pulling in the net with the catch.
14  Transferring fish from small nets to a metal drum. Emptying the drum into a wooden cart hitched to a donkey.
15  The cart is taken to a plant. Fish and water pouring into storage tanks. The exterior of the plant and a truck.

□ PART C: FISHING
1   Sunset over the Mediterranean Sea (long).
2   Fisherman leaving Haifa Port (mid, long).
3   The fishing boat at sea. A sailing boat (long).
4   A wheel spinning - lowering the net into the water (c.u.).
5   Pulling in the net and sorting the catch (long).
6   A dog eating a fish on the deck (mid).
7   Lake Hula and Kibbutz Hulata (long).
8   Kibbutz members walking along a dock to their fishing boats (long).
9   Rowing on Lake Hula, lowering a net and beating the water with an oar in order to drive fish into the net (long, c.u.).
10  The boat. Pulling in the net and removing the fish from it (long, c.u., long).
11  Kibbutz Ein Gev and the Sea of Galilee (long).
12  Fishermen carrying their gear and getting into their boats (mid).
13  Rowing on the lake, the sunset with the Arbel in the background. Lowering nets (mid, long). An oar and beating the water with an oar (c.u., mid).
14  The water seen through rushes and the moonlight reflecting off the water's surface (mid).
15  Fish in a net (mid).
16  The boat on the lake, rowing, removing fish from a net and folding nets (long, mid, c.u.).
17  Tiberias seen from the Sea of Galilee (long).
18  An oar in the water (c.u.).
19  Sunrise, fishermen returning to shore and women helping to unload the boats - women take the nets and men take the fish (long, mid).
20  Young women hanging out nets at Ein Gev (mid).
21  A fisherman rowing and another handling the nets. Fishermen returning home. Women hanging out nets. Shots of Haifa from a fishing boat (long, mid, 1029).

■ **CARMEL NEWSREEL I-137** · May 1 1938
Tel Aviv schoolchildren assemble for a sports day. Mapai, the Land of Israel Workers' Party, convention in Rehovot. The Matateh Theatre's satirical piece entitled: *Land of Milk and Honey and Oil*. A fire in the Tel Aviv neighbourhood of Abu-Hedra.

☐ PART A: TITLE: ASSEMBLING OF THE SCHOOLPUPILS IN TEL AVIV (131')
כותרת: הכנוס הספורטיבי של בתי הספר בתל-אביב
1  Boys playing dodge ball (pan, long, 35).
2  Girls playing dodge ball (long, 48).
3  Children at assembly (long, 75).
4  A relay race and the crowd, including Zvi Neshri (long, 103).
5  The judges' podium (long, 116).
6  Schoolchildren's procession (long, 131).

☐ PART B: TITLE: ASSEMBLING OF THE LABOUR-PARTY OF PALESTINE IN REHOVOT (63')
1  HEBREW TITLE: CONVENTION OF THE LAND OF ISRAEL WORKERS' PARTY, IN REHOVOT.  כותרת: ועידת מפלגת פועלי א"י ברחובות
2  A banner in Hebrew: The Fourth Convention of the Land of Israel Workers' Party (long, 20). שלט: הכינוס הרביעי של פועלי ארץ-ישראל
3  The exterior of the building hosting the convention. Delegates leaving the building (long, 63).

☐ PART C: FROM THE MATATEH THEATRE GROUP'S PLAY - *LAND OF MILK AND HONEY AND OIL* (599')
1  Announcement in Hebrew: "Citizens! Fulfill your duty to the Civil Headquarters". And another announcement: "Friend! Join in for Mishan".
כרזה: אזרח מלא חובתך ל"מפדה האזרחי". כרזה שניה: חבר! הט שכם ל"משען"
2  Four landowners share one glass of tea (the actors starting from the left: Abale, Moshe Hurgal, Yosef Oxenberg and Zalman Leviush) and each holds a spoon (55).
3  Mrs M Schneider (mid, 64).
4  They sing about the prosperity they used to have.
5  The shoemaker (played by London) approaches and they all coax a young man who is digging (mid, 271).
6  One of the actors plays a capitalist who gives money for oil digging (mid, 283).
7  Another actor and Mrs Schneider (mid, 303).
8  The shoemaker's wife says: "Quiet! It's not nice when wives interfere in their husbands' business, after all you have a war for oil."
9  They all make digging gestures and urge the man who is digging (long, 342).
10  The shoemaker's wife says: "Give us oil and oil."
11  Close-up of the ground and a hoe digging in the soil, when suddenly a gush of oil bursts out (382).
12  Coaxing the man digging (long, 395).
13  Taking down the "Mafda" sign (mid, long, 405).
14  Dancing.
15  Dancing in the street and singing the *Prosperity Song* (long, 471).
16  They continue to dance and one of the men inquires about purchasing some land (long, 533).
17  The dancing continues and two Yemenite men and two women join in as they all sing the *Prosperity Song* (long, 599).

☐ PART D: TITLE: FIRE IN TEL AVIV (225')
כותרת: השרפה הגדולה בשכונת אבו-חדרה בתל-אביב
1  Ruins.
2  *Davar* daily newspaper headline (in Hebrew): Day of Bloodshed in Jaffa.
כותרת: יום הדמים ביפו

118   *Carmel Newsreels: Series 1*

3   A fireman with a hose.
4   Smouldering ruins.
5   Firemen and hoses.
6   A man searching through the debris.
7   A policeman guarding goods saved from the fire.
8   Smoking ruins (225).

■ **CARMEL NEWSREEL I-138** · May 8 1938
Inauguration of the Judge Louis Brandeis School in Herzliyah with Mrs Brandeis attending ceremony. Chicken coop, dairy and rest home at Kibbutz Givat Brenner. Performance of the orchestra of the Ahad Ha'am School for boys, in honour of school health week.

□ PART A: TITLE: INAUGURATION OF THE SCHOOL IN THE NAME OF JUDGE BRANDEIS (103')   כותרת: פתיחת בית הספר ע"ש לואי ברנדייס בהרצליה
1   A teacher walking with children (mid, long, 21).
2   Children standing in the schoolyard (long, 37).
3   Mrs Brandeis arrives (mid, long, 44).
4   Menachem Ussishkin speaking (long, 55).
5   A crowd standing in front of the school (long, 71).
6   A sign in Hebrew on the school building: Brandeis School. A woman speaking and a flag (103).

□ PART B: TITLE: DEVELOPMENT OF THE KIBBUZ [sic] GIVATH BRENNER (274')

כותרת: התפתחותה של "גבעת ברנר"
1   Chickens (30).
2   A woman collecting eggs in the chicken coop and making notations (mid, long, 59).
3   Weighing and grading the eggs (mid, long, 84).
4   Cows and a man leaving the cowshed with a pail of milk (mid, long, 106).
5   Separating the milk and the cream at the kibbutz dairy (151).
6   TITLE IN HEBREW: VEGETARIAN REST HOME (157).

כותרת: הבית הצמחוני "הבראה"
7   Various shots of the rest home and garden (long, 189).
8   A woman waking up and getting out of bed (mid, long, 223).
9   Trees waving in the breeze and a woman writing in a room (mid, long, 220).
10  The dinner bell. Guests gather in the dining hall (mid, long, 230).
11  A woman writing and going outside (mid, long, 230).
12  Sitting at a table and eating (long, 225).
13  A woman outdoors (long, 263).
14  The exterior of the rest home (long, 274).

□ PART C: HEALTH WEEK AT THE AHAD HA'AM SCHOOL FOR BOYS (141')
1   Various shots of the school orchestra playing.
2   Pan of the orchestra - violins, sections.
3   The conductor turns around and takes a bow (long, 141).

■ **CARMEL NEWSREEL I-139** · May 13 1938
A dog show at the Mount Carmel Hotel in Haifa. Preparing land for the construction of Kiryat Yam outside Haifa in the Zebulun Valley. Animals at the Tel Aviv Zoo. Shavuot celebrations - children bringing "first fruits".

□ PART A: TITLE: DOG SHOW ON THE MOUNT CARMEL (140')

כותרת: תערוכת כלבים בחיפה
1   The entrance to the Mount Carmel Hotel (long, 16).

2   The dogs and their owners enter the exhibition hall (mid, long, 27).
3   The exhibition hall. The dogs being led around the judges' table (long, 61).
4   Close-up of first dog. Two other dogs being led before the judges (94).
5   Various shots of the dogs and their owners (long, 112).
6   Dogs jumping hurdles (140).

☐ PART B: TITLE: KIRYATH YAM BAYSIDE LAND CORPORATION START NEW SUBURB IN HAIFA BAY (142')

כותרת: "קרית-ים" התחלת בנין שכונה חדשה ע"י חברת גב ים לקרקעות בעמק זבולון

1   Pan of a map of the construction site (long, 26).
2   Pan of the sand dunes at the Kiryat Yam construction site (long, 55).
3   Tractors levelling off the area (long, c.u., 117).
4   Wagons loaded with sand (mid, 132).
5   Building a road (long, 142).

☐ PART C: TITLE: BIOLOGIC [sic] INSTITUTE IN TEL-AVIV (180')

כותרת: פינה בגן החיות ע"י המכון הביאולוגי בתל-אביב

1   Alligators feeding on fish (mid, long, 45).
2   Tortoises feeding (mid, 77).
3   Various shots of ibex (mid, 180).

☐ PART D: TITLE: PALESTINE "SCHAWUOTH" [sic] FESTIVALS
TITLE IN HEBREW: *HALLELUJAH*, BRINGING THE FIRST FRUITS. MUSIC BY EMMANUEL PUGCHOV (316').

כותרת: "הללויה" הבאת בכורים. מוסיקה: עמנואל פונג'צ"ב

1   Children in a stadium, acting out the bringing of the first fruits (shot in 1933) (long, 95).
2   Children in a stadium, bringing the "first fruits" (mid, long, 171).
3   "Priests" (dressed in bedsheets) receiving the "first fruits" (long, 184).
4   A child (Moshe Axelrod) in biblical costume and flowers bearing a basket of "first fruits", superimposed on a Jewish National Fund collection box. A second child superimposed on the collection box (c.u., 214).
5   Receiving "first fruits" (1933) (long, 247).
6   Children walking with sheaves of wheat. Huge procession in large stadium shot from above.
7   Children wearing wreaths of flowers in a Shavuot play (long, 316).

■ **CARMEL NEWSREEL I-140** · May 20 1938
A flower exhibition in Tel Aviv. Children in Tel Aviv celebrate Shavuot - bringing first fruits.

☐ PART A: TITLE: FLOWERS EXHIBITION AT TEL-AVIV (131')

כותרת: תערוכת פרחים וצמחי בית כת"א

1   General view of the exhibition (long, 33).
2   Various shots of flowers (c.u., 67).
3   Cactus plants (c.u., 91).
4   Various flowers (c.u., mid, 131).

☐ PART B: "FIRST FRUITS" CELEBRATION AT SHALVA HIGH SCHOOL IN TEL AVIV (152')
1   Children and parents seated (long, 6).
2   The children's Shavuot play, bringing the "first fruits" (long, 152).

□ PART C: TITLE: FRUIT OFFERING FESTIVITIES BY THE SCHOOL PUPILS IN TEL AVIV (165')   כותרת: תלמידי בית חינוך בצפון ת"א מביאים בכורים מפרי עמלם
1  Children bringing their first fruits in a procession on the streets of Tel Aviv, including wagons and donkeys (long, 49).
2  The children sitting in the wagons (long, 59).
3  Guests arriving. A tower bearing a banner in Hebrew: "Every Tower is a New Foothold and Every Foothold a Spark of Hope for the Redemption of Israel". Children on the tower (long, 93).

כתובת על המגדל: כל מגדל נקודה חדשה כל נקודה חדשה זיק תקווה לגאולת ישראל

4  Children harvesting in the field as a crowd looks on (long, 139).
5  Pan of the crowd with the tower at the centre (long, 149).
6  Bringing the first fruits (c.u., 165).

■ **CARMEL NEWSREEL I-141** · May 27 1938
Habimah Theatre troupe returns from abroad. The syndicate for maritime industry completes its first export order to be shipped to Cyprus. The Hebrew Soldiers Organization's marksmanship competition (called the Festival of the Hunters' Association, in order to avoid British Mandate censorship). A Torah scroll, donated by Hapoel Hamizrachi, is presented to the synagogue aboard the ocean-liner *HAR ZION*.

□ PART A: TITLE: "HABIMA" HAS RETURNED (63')

כותרת: לשובכם של חברי "הבימה"

1  A banner in Hebrew on a building: Welcome Back "Habima" (long, 21).
2  Habimah actors getting out of a boat and coming ashore - including Menachem Gensin, Ari Kutai, Hanna Rovina and painter Reuven Ruben.
3  Walking towards the camera (mid, 63).

□ PART B: TITLE: CASSON DESPATCH FROM TEL-AVIV PORT (140')

כותרת: להתפתחות התעשיה - יצירת ברכת ברזל ענקית

1  Various shots of work on a large open iron tank - including welding (mid, 75).
2  The tank (tilt up) (long, 86).
3  Work on the tank (mid, 91).
4  People waiting on the dock for the tank to be lowered into the water (long, 119).
5  The tank being lowered into the water. Handwritten on its side, in Hebrew: "Syndicate for maritime industry, produced by 'Ichud' and lowered into the sea by 'Kav' crane" (long, 140).

כתובת בגיר בצד המיכל: סינדיקט לעבודות ים, הוצא לפועל ע"י "אחוד", ההורדה לים ע"י "קב" מנוף.

□ PART C: TITLE: THE FESTIVAL OF THE HUNTERS' ASSOCIATION AT HAIFA (183')   כותרת: הכנוס הספורטיבי של אגודת הציידים כהר הכרמל היפה.
1  The hunters arrive (long, 42).
2  Spectators (long, 51).
3  The Association chairman speaking (mid, 57).
4  Children's marksmanship competition (mid, 71).
5  Women's competition (long, 92).
6  Men's competition (long, 105).
7  The targets (long, 115).
8  Writing down the scores and men firing at the targets (long).
9  The firing-range and Jewish and British flags (long, 183).

□ PART D: TITLE: INAUGURATION OF THE SYNAGOGUE (ON THE *HAR ZION* OCEAN-LINER) (155') כותרת: הכנסת ספר תורה לאוניה העברית הר-ציון
1   Dancing on the dock with a Torah scroll (long, 39).
2   The Torah scroll is taken on board a boat (long, 49).
3   Singing (mid, 60).
4   The boat approaches the *HAR ZION* (long, 73).
5   Taking the Torah scroll on board the *HAR ZION* (mid, 80).
6   Praying on deck. The Torah scroll is presented to the ship's captain. More dancing (mid, long, 146).
7   The ship's mast decorated with flags (long, 155).

■ **CARMEL NEWSREEL I-142** · June 4 1938
Opening of the new central post office on Jaffa Road in Jerusalem. Public relations dinner in honour of the Rabbi Kook Institute. *Ha'aretz* daily newspaper celebrates its 20th year. A children's home in Even Yehuda, established by Devorah Kahanovich.

□ PART A: TITLE: OPENING CEREMONIES AT THE NEW CENTRAL POST OFFICE IN JERUSALEM (119') כותרת: חנכת בנין הדאר החדש בירושלים
1   General view of the building (long, 22).
2   A crowd outside the building; dignitaries, including Arabs, rabbis, orthodox priests; police. The following are present: Menachem Ussishkin, Rabbi Herzog (long, 39).
3   High Commissioner Sir Harold MacMichael arrives and enters the building.
4   The crowd lining both sides of the street in front of the building.
5   The High Commissioner leaves the building and gets into his car (mid, 119).

□ PART B: TITLE: FESTIVAL IN FAVOUR OF THE RAW [sic] KOOK INSTITUTE IN TEL-AVIV (67') כותרת: מסבה ל"מוסד הרב קוק" בתל-אביב
1   The audience listening to a rabbi speaking (long, 33).
2   Books published by Mossad Harav Kook (Rabbi Kook Institute) (mid, 46).
3   Rabbi Yehuda Maimon speaking. The audience and waiters walking between the tables (mid, 67).

□ PART C: TITLE: 1918-1938 20TH ANNIVERSARY OF *HA'ARETZ* DAILY NEWSPAPER (91') כותרת: עתון הארץ חוגג את מלאת 20 שנות קיומו 1918-1938
1   Iris shot of the *Ha'aretz* building (long, 13).
2   Iris shot of the first newspaper in the Hebrew language (mid, 28).
3   The paper in a different format - *Hadshot Ha'aretz*, with the name of the paper printed in English as well *Palestine News* (mid, 36).
4   A further change in format - *Ha'aretz*, with obituaries for Yosef Trumpeldor (mid, 42).
5   Obituaries for Lord Balfour (mid, 47).
6   An issue of *Ha'aretz* - an advertisement for the works of Shaul Tchernichovsky and Chaim Nachman Bialik (mid, 53).
7   The *Ha'aretz* building, corner Nahlat Binyamin and Allenby Street in Tel Aviv (long, 91).

□ PART D: TITLE: FESTIVAL IN THE CHILDREN'S HOME AT EWEN [sic] YEHUDA (181') כותרת: המעון העממי לילדים באבן-יהודה
1   A general view of Even Yehuda - the village and orchards (long, 50).
2   A crowd arrives and looks through a fence at the children inside the children's home, originally established in 1937 in Ramat Gan (long, 98).
3   The children working in the garden, taking care of a donkey, a cow and

chickens (washing, watering and feeding) (long, 159).
4   Guests sitting at a table and listening to a speaker (mid, 170).
5   A woman speaking (mid, long, 181).

■ **CARMEL NEWSREEL I-143** · July 1 1938
A Wizo children's home in Tel Aviv. The opening of the Jewish Hunters' Association Netanya branch. School sports day in the Afula region. Ada Schack sings a song about the grape harvest.

☐ PART A: TITLE: THE "WIZO" INSTITUTIONS (165')

כותרת: סיור במוסדות "קרן הילד" בתל-אביב

1   A group of women posing near babies in cribs (mid, 20).
2   Young children eating at a table and a nurse helping them. A baby in a crib (mid, c.u., 46).
3   Children in the garden with their nurses (long, 64).
4   Distributing clothing to the children. The children dancing in a circle. A baby in a crib. A sign in Hebrew on the façade of the building: "Tel Aviv Municipality - Municipal Home for Children" (long, 140).
5   Various shots of boys and girls (mid, 165).

☐ PART B: TITLE: OPENING OF THE HUNTERS' ASSOCIATION BRANCH AT NATHANYA [sic] (118')

כותרת: פתיחת הסניף של אגודת הצידים העברים בנתניה

1   Various speakers (mid, 30).
2   Members raise their rifles and fire in the air (mid, 55).
3   The Jewish Hunters Association flag (c.u., 60).
4   Skeet-shooting (mid, 91).
5   Marksmanship competition in a lying position (mid, 100).
6   Marksmanship competition in a standing position. Judges inspecting the targets through binoculars (mid, 112).
7   Two men lying down on the firing range - one aiming and the other looking through binoculars (118).

☐ PART C: TITLE: SPORT FESTIVAL OF THE SCHOOLS IN AFULAH (132')

כותרת: הכנוס הספורטיבי של בתי הספר בגוש עפולה

1   A banner in Hebrew on the gate: "The Second Athletic ..." and a Jewish flag (mid, 20).
2   A barrel race (long, 40).
3   Two blindfolded boys play tag (long, 75).
4   Marching and group exercises (long, 132).

☐ PART D: TITLE: HARVEST SONG BY HEDE SCHACK (45')
1   TITLE IN HEBREW: SONG BY ADA SCHACK, ACCOMPANIMENT BY GRETA SCHACK, MUSIC BY YARIV EZRACHI.

כותרת: לקראת עונת הקציר שיר ענבים מאת עדה שאק - ליווי: גרטה שאק

מנגינה: יריב אזרחי

2   Grape harvest (long, 19).
3   A woman harvesting grapes, with the town of Zichron Ya'akov in the background. Ada Schack raises a cluster of grapes and sings (long, 45).

■ **CARMEL NEWSREEL I-144** · July 8 1938
A collection of Hebrew newspapers and historical headlines. Marine life at the Tel Aviv Zoo. Wrestler Ben Sherman performs feats of strength. Aryeh Megido sings *Leila Peleh* (*Wondrous Night*).

☐ PART A: ZALMAN PAVSNER'S NEWSPAPER COLLECTION (168')
1  Pavsner sorting his collection (mid, 10).
2  A stack of newspapers (long, 17).
3  Various newspapers: *Hayenu, Halvanon, Havazeleth, Ha'ariel, Les Portes de Sion, Yehuda Veyerushalayim, Hazvi* (c.u., mid, 85).
4  A telegram sent to *Hazvi* by Emile Zola, as it appeared in the paper with a Hebrew translation and a headline (in Hebrew): "Emile Zola sentenced to a year in prison and a fine of 3000 francs" (c.u., mid, 97).
5  *Olam Katan* children's newspaper (c.u., mid, 107).
6  *Hashkafa* headline: "A Telegram Has Arrived Announcing the Burial of Dr Herzl Today. Sephardic leaders have decided to conduct public eulogies of the great man" (c.u., mid, 117).
7  Headline (in *Hazvi*): "The True Revolution ..." (c.u., mid, 130).
8  *Haor* headline: "The Western (Wailing) Wall Affair - Fiction and Fact" (c.u., mid, 141).
9  A newspaper entitled *War News* (c.u., mid, 156).
10 *Doar Hayom* (Daily Mail) headline: "Our Writ of Liberty" (c.u., mid, 168).

☐ PART B: PALESTINE MARINE FLORA AND FAUNA AT THE BIOLOGICAL INSTITUTE ON YEHUDA HALEVI STREET IN TEL AVIV (97')
1  A sea anemone and fish (mid, 32).
2  A sea crab (mid, 44).
3  A crab in a borrowed shell (mid, 49).
4  Fish of various types near the shell in which the crab is hiding (mid, 83).
5  A marine flower which closes when touched and reopens when the danger has passed (mid, 97).

☐ PART C: TITLE: THE ATHLETE SHERMAN IN HIS EXERCISES (57')
כותרת: בן שרמן המתאבק העולמי בתרגיליו לקראת הופעותיו בארץ
1  Ben Sherman places a rope around his neck and "hangs himself" (33).
2  Sherman hoists himself up by his neck with a man on his back (mid, long, 46).
3  Sherman forms a "bridge", with a man sitting on his stomach (mid, long, 57).

☐ PART D: TITLE: A SONG BY A. MEGIDO (146')
1  TITLE IN HEBREW: ARYEH MEGIDO SINGING *WONDROUS NIGHT*. MUSICAL ADAPTATION BY M. WILENSKY. PIANO: BERTHA VAZA.
כותרת: אריה מגידו בשיר לילה פלא. עבוד המוסיקה: מ. וילנסקי. ע"י
הפסנתר: ברטה וזה
2  Megido awaiting instructions from Nathan Axelrod. Megido singing (there are two flies buzzing around his suit throughout the song) (mid, 146).

■ CARMEL NEWSREEL I-145 · July 15 1938
Palestine marble exhibition in Tel Aviv. Opening of a teachers seminary for women in Tel Aviv. Biblical plants at the Mikveh Israel Agricultural School. Three dances performed by Lola Fliederbaum's dance studio.

☐ PART A: TITLE: EXHIBITION OF PALESTINE MARBLE IN TEL AVIV (105')
כותרת: תערוכת השיש הא"י בתל-אביב
1  The exhibition hall and visitors looking at marble exhibits (long, 28).
2  A holy ark of marble (to house Torah scrolls) (mid, 38).
3  A marble table. Visitors (mid, long, 58).
4  Various types of unpolished marble (c.u., 77).
5  Various marble desk accessories (mid, 85).
6  A marble Chanukah menorah (candelabra) (c.u., 92).
7  A marble gravestone (mid, 100).

8   A holy ark (mid, 105).

☐ PART B: TITLE: OPENING OF THE WOMEN TEACHERS SEMINARY IN TEL AVIV (86')    כותרת: חנכת הבית של בית המדרש למורות וגננות בתל-אביב
1   Students (dressed alike) and teachers march with banners to the seminary building and enter (long, 86).

☐ PART C: TITLE: BIBLICAL PLANTS IN THE AGRICULTURAL SCHOOL AT MIKVEH-YISRAEL (213')
כותרת:צמחי תנ"ך בגני בית-הספר החקלאי במקוה-ישראל
1   Palm trees (mid, long, 17).
2   Dissolve to a cluster of dates on a tree (mid, 26).
3   Olive trees, caper plants, fig and pomegranate trees, and other trees and flowers (mid, 213).

☐ PART D: TITLE: A DANCE BY LOLA FLIEDERBAUM-STUDIO, PIANO: BERTHA VAZA (278')
1   TITLE IN HEBREW: DANCES: MARIONETTE DANCE, POLKA. MUSIC: B. SCHULTZ. PIANO: BERTHA VAZA.
כותרת: מרקודי הסטודיה של לולה פלידרבאום. 1) מיניאטורות 2 "פולקה"
מוסיקה: ב. שולץ. ע"י הפסנתר: ברטה וזה
2   The marionette dance (with two dancers) (143).
3   A polka (211).
4   A third dance (278).

■ **CARMEL NEWSREEL I-146** · July 22 1938
The establishment of the settlement of Hanita by volunteers and Jewish Settlement Police (ghaffirs).

☐ PART A: BUILDING THE SETTLEMENT OF HANITA
1   Signalling the group's arrival, using mirrors (c.u.).
2   A road.
3   Signalling with flags (mid).
4   Arriving in trucks (long).
5   A company of ghaffirs (Jewish Settlement Police) arrives (long).
6   The site on which the settlement was to be founded and the surrounding hills (long).
7   The ghaffirs fall in for the climb to the settlement site (long).
8   Volunteers unload donkeys brought by truck (mid).
9   The ghaffirs fall in and begin the climb. Followed by the volunteers (two of whom were killed that night) (long, mid).
10  Taking equipment and carrying it up to the settlement site - volunteers, ghaffirs, donkeys. *Davar* newspaper editor Yatziv carrying wooden beams. Taking a rest (long, mid).
11  Preparing the site - clearing underbrush, laying pipes (long).
12  Volunteers and ghaffirs taking a rest (mid).
13  Ghaffirs climbing up the hill with dogs (long).
14  Clearing the underbrush. Avraham Herzfeld working (mid).
15  Banging fence-posts into the ground. Putting up tents (mid).
16  A rabbi carrying a Torah scroll under a canopy. Dancing around the rabbi and the scroll.
17  Moshe Shertok (Sharett) and Yitzhak Ben Zvi (mid).
18  Sitting on the ground and eating - Jews and Arabs (mid).
19  Building a shack (mid, long).
20  Herzfeld singing. Pan of others sitting around and singing - including Ezrahi (of

the Jewish National Fund) and Moshe Shertok (long, mid).
21  Building the fence (mid).
22  Everything has been completed. Sitting down to eat at a table (long).
23  Two weeks later: a car enters the settlement (long).
24  Work on the fence (long).
25  Signalling with mirrors and a flag that the outpost has been established (mid).
26  Tents and the settlement from the distance. A ghaffir standing guard, with the settlement in the distance (mid, long).

■ **CARMEL NEWSREEL I-147** · July 29 1938
Building the settlement of Ma'aleh Hahamisha. Singer A Mindlin sings *The Song of the Five* (about the five Jews who were killed at the site, for whom Kibbutz Ma'aleh Hahamisha was named).

□ PART A: TITLE IN HEBREW: A NEW SETTLEMENT ESTABLISHED IN THE JUDEAN HILLS - MA'ALEH HAHAMISHA (465')

כותרת: בהרי יהודה הוקם ישוב חדש "מעלה החמשה"

SECOND TITLE IN HEBREW: *THE SONG OF THE FIVE* - SUNG BY A. MINDLIN. WORDS: S. SHALOM, MUSIC: M. ZEIRA, AT THE PIANO: BERTHA VAZA. *SONG OF THE CONQUERING YOUTH* - SUNG BY THE GILALI QUARTET. WORDS: A. HARUSI, MUSIC: M. WILENSKY.

כותרת שניה: שיר החמישה מושר ע"י א. מינדלין מלים: ע. שלום מוסיקה: מ. זעירא ע"י הפסנתר: ברטה וזה. שיר הנוער הכובש מושר ע"י הרביעיה גללי מלים: ע. הרוסי מוסיקה: מ. וילנסקי

1  Mindlin sings *The Song of the Five* (mid, 109).
2  Planting the Forest of the Five. A close-up of a stone marking the spot where the five fell (mid, 133).
3  Photographs of the five (mid, 133).
4  The graves of the five (mid, 153).
5  The stone at the spot where they fell (mid, 159).
6  The hills surrounding Ma'aleh Hahamisha. Planting trees (mid, 177).
7  Mindlin singing (mid).
8  Iris shot of Ma'aleh Hahamisha (long).
9  Passing roof tiles from hand to hand and building a roof (long).
10  Digging a trench (mid).
11  Installing a searchlight on the outer fence (long).
12  Gravel for filling the fence. Working on a roof (long).
13  Standing guard at the fence (long).
14  Signalling to Jerusalem with flags (long).
15  Clearing the site of stones (long).
16  Carrying a barbed wire gate (long).
17  Reading the dedication scroll. Close-up of the scroll. The scroll is placed in a bottle, which is then sealed and placed in the cement foundation.
18  Avraham Herzfeld speaking (c.u., long).
19  Other speakers (mid).
20  Working with gravel, carrying it to the outer fence (long).
21  The completed outpost (long, 465).

■ **CARMEL NEWSREEL I-148** · August 6 1938
Funeral of Ramat Hakovesh martyrs. Maurice Schwartz arrives at Lod Airport. The Tel Aviv beach in summer. Snakes at the Tel Aviv Zoo.

□ PART A: FUNERAL OF RAMAT HAKOVESH MARTYRS (48')
1  Large crowd in Ramat Hakovesh and funeral procession begins (long, mid, 28).
2  The coffins are placed in graves and covered with earth (mid).
3  Various shots of the funeral procession (48).

□ PART B: TITLE: MAURICE SCHWARTZ IN PALESTINE (71')
כותרת: מוריס שוורץ בארץ
1. Lod airport and a plane arriving (long, 19).
2. Schwartz is met, shakes hands and leaves the airport (mid, 52).
3. People coming to meet Schwartz (mid, 71).

□ PART C: TITLE: THE TEL AVIV BEACH IN SUMMER (114')
כותרת: לעונת הרחיצה - על שפת הים בתל-אביב
1. People at the beach (long, 42).
2. A corn vendor and the crowd on the beach. Men exercising (mid, 95).
3. A dog and a boy in the water.
4. Men performing stunts on the beach (mid, 114).

□ PART D: TITLE: SNAKES IN THE BIOLOGIC [sic] INSTITUTE AT TEL AVIV (110')  כותרת: נחשים מקומיים בגן-החיות ע"י המכון הביולוגי בת"א
1. Snakes of various types (long, 40).
2. Someone displays the teeth and venom structure of a snake. A snake approaching a mouse (mid, 66).
3. A black snake (long, 76).
4. The mouse runs away. The snake catches it, wraps itself around the mouse and swallows it (long, 110).

■ **CARMEL NEWSREEL I-149** · August 13 1938
Hanoar Ha'oved youth movement members at Kibbutz Alonim, at Sheikh Abrek (Beit Shearim), working and guarding the land.

□ PART A: TITLE: DEVELOPMENT OF THE KIBBUTZ "ALLONIM" (825')
1. TITLE IN HEBREW: HANOAR HAOVED GROUP ALONIM ON THE LAND OF SHEIKH ABREK LIVING A LIFE OF LABOUR AND GUARDING THE LAND.
כותרת: על אדמת שיך אבריק קבוצת הנוער העובד "אלונים" כחיים בעבודה ובשמירה
2. TITLE IN HEBREW: ACCOMPANIED BY THE BAND AND CHOIR OF THE BOROCHOV NEIGHBOURHOOD BRANCH OF HANOAR HAOVED.
כותרת: לווי ע"י תזמורת ומקהלה של חברי הנוער העובד בסניף שכונת בורוכוב
3. A photograph of Alexander Zeid (mid).
4. Pan of Camp Givat Zeid and the camp from a distance (long).
5. A clock showing the hour 04:30 (c.u.).
6. A stable. Someone leading horses out of the stable (long).
7. A yard filled with cows. A girl feeding a calf. Boys milking goats. A girl goes through the dining room into the kitchen (mid).
8. Feeding chickens. Milking goats. Letting the goats out to pasture (long, c.u.).
9. Returning from night-watch to the ruins of Tab'un (long).
10. General view of the ruins of Tab'un (mid, long).
11. Sounding a gong to call everyone to the dining hall. Someone waking up. Everyone leaving their tents, going to wash and entering the dining hall (mid, long).
12. Two girls talking, others reading. Riding to work on a wagon. Threshing grain with a donkey. Gathering the hay and making into bundles (mid).
13. Digging a trench for pipes (long).
14. A smithy (mid).
15. Shoemaking (mid, long).
16. Returning from the field with a hay-laden wagon (long).
17. Goats at pasture in the hills (mid, long).

18 A goatherd feeding a goat. Male goats fighting. A close-up of the goatherd. The goats scatter and the goatherd sends his dog to round up the herd (mid, c.u., long).
19 Returning from work in a wagon - some of the men are armed (mid).
20 Showering (mid).
21 Walking arm-in-arm through Zeid Woods (mid, long).
22 Visiting Zeid's grave. Wreaths on the graves in the cemetery (mid, long).
23 A general view of Tivon - a few houses and shacks (long).
24 A girl swinging in a hammock. Sitting together - playing various musical instruments (mid, long).
25 Sitting together at sunset (long, 761).
26 Receiving arms and going out on guard duty (long).
27 The watch-tower (mid, long).
28 Ghaffirs (Jewish Settlement Police) taking up positions in the trenches around the ruins of Tab'un.
29 The surrounding hills through a slit in a trench and the barrel of a gun (mid, long).
30 The watch-tower (long, 825).

■ **CARMEL NEWSREEL I-150** · August 20 1938
Children's daycamp visits the beach in Tel Aviv. Southern District Commissioner R E H Crosbie visits the Rishon Lezion winery. Scouts' camp near Tel Aviv.

□ PART A: TITLE: HOLIDAY CAMPS OF TEL AVIV PUPILS (335')

כותרת: קייטנות לתלמידי בתי-ספר העממיים על שפת הים, בתל-אביב

1 The children getting off buses (mid, long, 25).
2 A bugler (mid, 32).
3 The children leaving huts on the beach and falling in for roll-call. The children each stand at attention when their names are called (long, mid, 82).
4 The children exercise on the beach (mid, long, 124).
5 The children bathe in the sea and then shower (mid, long, 172).
6 Bringing food and setting the tables (mid, 193).
7 The children eating (c.u., long, 221).
8 Arts and crafts (mid, 279).
9 The children resting - playing in the sand, reading, playing chess, sleeping (long, 300).
10 Singing (long, 319).
11 The buses bringing the children home. Children waving from the bus windows (mid, 335).

□ PART B: TITLE: VISIT OF THE DISTRICT COMMISSIONER MR CROSBY [sic] AT RISHON WINE PRESSES (54')

כותרת: בקור מושל מחוז, מר קרוסבי ביקבי ראשון-לציון

1 Southern District Commissioner R E H Crosbie and entourage tour the winery (long, 50).
2 A toast (long, 54).

□ PART C: SCOUTS FROM TEL AVIV SCHOOLS (270')
1 General view of the scouts' camp in an empty field in the Tel Aviv area (long, 24).
2 The scouts coming to roll-call. Pan of the scouts and raising of the flag. A scout reads aloud near the flag. At attention, at ease and dismissed (long, 112).
3 The scouts playing games, using blindfolds (long, 140).
4 A group of scouts tossing a child up in the air and catching him in a tarpaulin (long, 166).

5  First aid practice (long, 185).
6  Semaphore practice (long, 214).
7  Singing and banging plates, cups and spoons. Distributing food (mid, 242).
8  A bugler at sunset. Sitting near the tents and singing (mid, long, 262).
9  A scout on watch, patrols between the tents, carrying a long stick (long, 270).

■ **CARMEL NEWSREEL I-151** · August 27 1938
An entire newsreel dedicated to the Hula Valley. Bedouin cutting, transporting and weaving papyrus reeds into mats. The Malaria Research Station of the Hebrew University provides medical treatment for the Arab residents. Water buffalo in the swamps.

□ PART A: TITLE: PREPARING PAPYRUS REEDS FOR MATS (510')

כותרת: תעשיית מחצלות בעמק החולה

1  The Hula swamps and vegetation. Bedouin.
2  Water buffalo.
3  Bedouin on bundles of cut reeds floating through the vegetation. A close-up of a bundle of cut papyrus reeds.
4  A sign in front of a tent: "Malaria Research Station of the Hebrew University". שלט: תחנה לחקירת המלריה של האוניברסיטה העברית
5  Bedouin leaving the Malaria Research Station tent.
6  Bedouin bringing children - their heads wrapped in black cloth - to the research station.
7  Doctors examine the children. Taking a blood sample.
8  Bedouin and bundles of cut reeds floating on the water.
9  The Jordan River (long).
10  One of the Jordan's sources. The shallow river bed causing the water to flood the area, creating the Hula lake (long).
11  General view of the Hula lake (long).
12  Bedouin sitting under a tree with the Hula Valley and lake in the background (long).
13  A Bedouin village on the shores of the lake (long).
14  The lake and mountains in the distance (long).
15  The Hula swamps and vegetation (long).
16  Water buffalo (long).
17  Bedouin children in the water with water buffalo (long).
18  Papyrus reeds in the water (long).
19  Cutting the reeds (long).
20  Arranging the reeds in bundles (mid).
21  Trimming the bundles - preparing to float them to the village (mid).
22  Bedouin on floating bundles of reeds. A close-up of a floating bundle of reeds and knife on top of the bundle (long, c.u.).
23  The legs of one of the men floating the reeds (mid).
24  General view of the lake and the Bedouin floating the reeds in close single file (long).
25  The Bedouin taking the bundles of reeds out of the water and to the village (long).
26  A loom and men carrying bundles of reeds in the background (mid).
27  Separating the papyrus fibres (mid).
28  A woman weaving (mid, long).
29  The woman cuts the finished mat from the loom and brings it to her husband (mid, long).
30  Pan of the village. Bedouin and a pile of mats in the centre of the village (long, 510).

■ **CARMEL NEWSREEL I-152** · September 3 1938
The establishment of the settlement of Ein Hamifratz - including armed ghaffirs (Jewish Settlement Police), building the Tower and Stockade settlement and fortifications, celebrating its completion. 5th year anniversary of Ein Hamifratz 1933, including the fields, the settlement, the cowshed, the adorable children. The original soundtrack includes a song recounting the story of Ein Hamifratz.

□ PART A: TITLE: FOUNDATION OF "EIN HAMIFRATZ" NEW SETTLEMENT. TITLE IN HEBREW: *THE SONG OF ALIYAH TO EIN HAMIFRATZ*, MUSIC MOSHE WILENSKY (619')

כותרת: הקמת ישוב חדש עין המפרץ. כותרת שנייה: שיר עלית עין המפרץ - בנין טננבוים, מוסיקה מ. וילנסקי

1  General view of Kiryat Yam (long, 33).
2  The night before the settlement is built; trying a generator, loading shack frames, children loading various equipment - shovels, hoes, watering cans, wheelbarrows, etc (long, 91).
3  The settlement site - swamps and barren land.
4  A clock showing the time: 04:00 (mid, 115).
5  Ghaffirs (Jewish Settlement Police) and other guards set out in a tractor and on horseback in the dark (long, 126).
6  The ghaffirs arrive at the site in armoured cars and trucks. The ghaffirs fall in, receive orders and spread out (long, 193).
7  A clock showing the time: 04:30 (c.u., 198).
8  Volunteers set out in trucks (long, 227).
9  The trucks cross Wadi Na'aman and arrive at the settlement site (long, 247).
10 Volunteers (men and women) get out of the trucks and unload equipment and shack frames (mid, 276).
11 Clearing the site with hoes (long, 292).
12 Beginning construction (long, 311).
13 A clock showing the time: 05:30 (c.u., 313).
14 Laying pipes in Wadi Na'man, over which a bridge will be built (mid, 334).
15 Building a shack and a barbed wire fence (mid, long, 367).
16 The tower is brought and raised (c.u., mid).
17 "Habimah" actor Aaron Meskin bangs a stake into the ground with a mallet (mid, 409).
18 The perimeter wall is filled with gravel (long, 428).
19 A tractor ploughing (long, 440).
20 Avraham Herzfeld speaks with volunteers (mid, 447).
21 Constructing a bridge on Wadi Na'aman (long, 484).
22 A clock showing the time: 08:30 (c.u., 486).
23 Completed shacks are taken across the bridge by tractor (long, 515).
24 Eating (mid, 528).
25 The shacks arrive at the settlement site (long, 530).
26 Herzfeld speaks (long, 566).
27 Dancing hora (long, 592).
28 Herzfeld dancing (mid, 603).
29 A model of the camp and its defences (long, 619).

■ **CARMEL NEWSREEL I-153** · September 10 1938
Citrus export from Tel Aviv Port. Ships arriving, loading crates of citrus fruits, unloading cargo and passengers.

□ PART A: TITLE: FIRST DISPATCH OF LEMONS AT TEL AVIV PORT (129')
1  TITLE IN HEBREW: A NEW RECORD FOR TEL AVIV PORT: ELEVEN SHIPS.

כותרת: שיא חדש לנמל ת"א: 11 אוניות

2  A crowd at the port, waving to arriving passengers (mid, long, 30).

3   A ship and passengers on deck (long, 42).
4   Crates of oranges on board the ship. A boat bringing crates to the ship. Passengers on a boat leaving the ship (mid, 88).
5   Loading and unloading cargo. A crowd, a banner and decorative flags (long, 129).

■ **CARMEL NEWSREEL I-154** · September 17 1938
Industrial, agricultural and residential development in the Zebulun Valley, 1928 and 1938.

▫ PART A: TITLE: THE DEVELOPMENT OF EMEK ZEVULUN (631')

כותרת: 10 שנות התפתחות עמק זבולון

1   TITLE IN HEBREW: MUSIC - EMMANUEL PUGCHOV WITH THE YOUTH DRAMATIC GROUP.

כותרת שנייה: מוסיקה - עמנואל פונג׳ וכ בהשתתפות חברי האלפן הדרמתי לנוער תל-אביב

2   TITLE IN HEBREW: BEFORE 1928     כותרת שלישית: לפני שנת 1928
3   A map of the Zebulun Valley and Acre Bay (36).
4   General view of the Zebulun Valley (pan, long, 60).
5   Sand dunes and swamp land (long, 97).
6   Jewish National Fund swamp drainage operations (mid, 106).
7   Menachem Ussishkin and journalists observe the drained swamp land, and a general view of the drained area (long, 134).
8   TITLE: 1938 (139).
9   Driving along a tree-lined road (long, 165).
10  The industrial zone (long, 174).
11  Factory smokestacks (c.u., 183).
12  Various industrial buildings (long, 197).
13  General view of Kiryat Bialik (long, 214).
14  Driving through one of the towns in the Zebulun Valley (long, 267).
15  Kiryat Haim, homes with gardens and lawns (long, 282).
16  Interior of large textile plant (long, 323).
17  Wagons on a bridge. Brick production - a machine putting bricks in a large kiln, removing them, a warehouse (mid, 382).
18  Casting bath-tubs (long, 405).
19  Manufacturing large pipes (long, 422).
20  A school (long, 468).
21  A tractor ploughing a field (mid, 506).
22  Digging a ditch with hoes (long, 527).
23  Ostrower plant nursery, child pushing wheelbarrow (long, 559).
24  Running water and irrigation ditches (long, 606).
25  Stacking bales of hay (mid, 610).
26  Work at a textile plant (long, 631).

■ **CARMEL NEWSREEL I-155** · September 24 1938
Inauguration of the Tel Aviv airport at Sdeh Dov, which opens routes between Tel Aviv, Haifa and Beirut, in the hope that air travel will be safer than travelling over land. Imported trucks arrive at the Tel Aviv port, where they are unloaded and assembled. Levelling off sand dunes in North Tel Aviv, a joint project of the Tel Aviv Municipality and the Jewish Agency to create jobs for the unemployed. The Haifa District Commissioner Edward Keith-Roach visits Haifa fire station.

▫ PART A: TITLE: INAUGURATION OF TEL AVIV AERODROME (143')

כותרת: חנוכת שדה התעופה ת״א

1   A crowd. Pan of the airfield (long, 18).

2  Tel Aviv Mayor Israel Rokah speaks (mid, 32).
3  Standing near an airplane (mid, 89).
4  An airplane taking off (long, 61).
5  TITLE IN HEBREW: IN HAIFA (64).
6  The airplane lands at Haifa. People getting out of the airplane (mid, 128).
7  Haifa District Commissioner Edward Keith-Roach and entourage (mid, 143).

□ PART B: TITLE: UNLOADING HEAVY GOODS AT TEL AVIV PORT (109')
כותרת: פריקת סחורות כבדות בנמל ת"א
1  A boat reaches the docks and large crates are unloaded (long, 28).
2  Crates are unloaded from a ship and loaded onto a boat (long, 37).
3  The crates are opened. They contain truck motors (mid, 66).
4  Truck bodies are removed from crates and assembled trucks leave the port in single file (long).
5  A crane hoisting a large crate marked "International Motor Trucks" (long, 109).

□ PART C: TITLE: PLAINING OF SANDHILLS AT TEL-AVIV (239')
כותרת: יישור החולות בצפון תל-אביב
1  General view of the area being levelled off (long, 23).
2  Workers arriving (mid, 32).
3  Pan of the sand dunes and workers filling wagons with sand (long, 61).
4  Emptying the wagons on low ground (mid, 70).
5  Various shots of workers (men and women) working in the sand (long, mid, 150).
6  Pushing the wagons filled with sand. A ghaffir (Jewish Settlement Police) guard at his post on the site (mid, 162).
7  Emptying the wagons (mid, 175).
8  A guard house (long, 184).
9  The levelled ground (pan, long, 196).
10  Pushing wagons.
11  A bell is rung (long, 231).
12  The workers leave the site (mid, 239).

□ PART D: TITLE: VISIT OF THE DISTRICT COMMISSIONER AT THE HAIFA FIRE BRIGADE (140')   כותרת: בקור מושל מחוז הצפון בתחנת מכבי-אש בחיפה
1  District Commissioner Edward Keith-Roach arrives. A crowd, including many children, lines the street (long, 44).
2  The District Commissioner speaks with notables (mid, 57).
3  Seated guests (mid, 69).
4  Various fire-fighting techniques are demonstrated as the crowd looks on (121).
5  A fireman jumps from a tower onto a tarpaulin held by his colleagues (long, 140).

■ **CARMEL NEWSREEL I-156** · October 1 1938
Labour and social welfare in Haifa: quarries, roadwork, construction; work at the docks, on boats and in factories; workers' housing and child care. Construction work at Haifa, including quarries, docks and factories.

□ PART A: TITLE: WORKER'S LIFE AT HAIFA (817')
כותרת: היומן מוקדש לפועל העברי בחיפה
1  TITLE IN HEBREW: MUSIC: MOSHE WILENSKY, SINGING: YOSEF GOLAND (24).   כותרת שנייה: המוסיקה: משה וילנסקי, השירה - יוסף גולנד
2  General view of Haifa. Dissolve to various streets in Haifa (long, 77).
3  The bridge over Wadi Salib (long, 97).

## Carmel Newsreels: Series 1

4 TITLE IN HEBREW: "IN QUARRIES" (102).  כותרת: "בחצץ"
5 Stone and lime quarries (long, 125).
6 Work at the quarries. A train carrying gravel (142).
7 TITLE IN HEBREW: "ON ROADS" (144).  כותרת: "בכביש"
8 Road construction (mid, 176).
9 TITLE IN HEBREW: "IN CONSTRUCTION" (178).  כותרת: "בבנין"
10 Construction work (mid, 196).
11 TITLE IN HEBREW: "AT THE DOCKS" (198).  כותרת: "בנמל"
12 Jews from Salonika working at the docks: loading and unloading cargo (mid, 224).
13 TITLE IN HEBREW: "AT SEA" (227).  כותרת: "בים"
14 Boats leaving the port and work on the boats (mid, 314).
15 Sailors on boats (mid, 347).
16 TITLE IN HEBREW: "IN FACTORIES" (350).  כותרת: "בבתי חרושת"
17 Smokestacks, the "Vulcan" metalworks, casting bath-tubs. An electrical wire factory (426).
18 Various shots of the "Shemen" oil and soap factory (long, mid, 489).
19 Workers leaving the factory and boarding buses (long, 508).
20 The buses - with latticed windows against attack - and workers boarding (long, 539).
21 Buses leaving the factory gates under ghaffir guard (long, 539).
22 The new workers' neighbourhood of Kiryat Amal (long, 583).
23 TITLE IN HEBREW: "CHILDCARE" (587).  כותרת: "טפול בילד"
24 Looking after children and infants (mid, long, 674).
25 The Histadrut building. Dissolve to other buildings - a cinema, an amphitheatre (long, 720).
26 Workers' parade (long, 746).
27 General view of lower Haifa and the Carmel (pan, long).
28 Workers' parade (long, 817).

■ **CARMEL NEWSREEL I-157** · October 8 1938
The *SS POLONIA* arrives in Tel Aviv, carrying immigrants. A memorial ceremony for Tel Aviv Mayor Meir Dizengoff. Completing a students' building at the Technion in Haifa. The Olberg puppet theatre performs *The Clown*.

□ PART A: TITLE: SS "POLONIA" AT TEL AVIV PORT (108')
כותרת: התחלת השנה - התחלת עליה בנמל ת"א
1 Dignitaries board the ship. Immigrants on deck (long, 43).
2 British and Jewish Agency passport control. The deck (mid, 79).
3 Immigrants leaving the ship. Immigrants on the dock (mid, 108).

□ PART B: TITLE: IN MEMORIAM MEIR DIZENGOFF (112')
כותרת: אזכרת דיזנגוף
1 Carrying a wreath. The procession passes by (mid, 65).
2 A crowd at the cemetery. A cantor praying (long, 112).

□ PART C: TITLE: A STUDENTS' HOME AT HAIFA (146')
כותרת: בנין מועדון הסטודנטים בטכניון בחיפה
1 The students' building during the final stages of construction (long, mid, 146).

□ PART D: TITLE: OLBERG'S NEW PUPPET THEATRE *MUKION* (308')
כותרת: תיאטרון הבובת "מוקיון" בהנהלת דב ושושנה אולברג בתל אביב
1 Puppet show and children in the audience enjoying the show (mid, long, 291).

2   Behind the scenes during the performance (long, 308).

■ **CARMEL NEWSREEL I-158** · October 21 1938
The High Commissioner Sir Harold MacMichael returning to Palestine by airplane. Dr Oscar Grinbaum, President of the Zionist Organisation of Austria, arrives as a new immigrant. Target shooting competition between members of the Jewish Hunters' Society and British soldiers.

□ PART A: TITLE: THE HIGH COMMISSIONER RETURNS TO PALESTINE (153')

כותרת: הנציב העליון חוזר ארצה. (8)

1   Pan of airfield at Atarot, a ghaffir guarding (mid, long, 45).
2   People arriving to greet High Commissioner MacMichael (mid, 55).
3   Small propeller plane lands, the Commissioner and his wife disembark and are received by Mr Eliashar and Mr Edleson, directors of Palestine Airway Ltd (mid, long, 125). Written on side of plane: 'PALESTINE AIRWAY LTD.'.
4   The Commissioner shakes hands with Mr Johnson, the Mandate Treasury Minister and enters his car (mid, 153).

□ PART B: TITLE: OSCAR GRINBAUM ARRIVED AT PALESTINE (67')

כותרת: ד"ר אוסקר גרינבוים עולה בנמל ת"א. (6).

1   Crowd on the dock waiting (long, 14).
2   Dr Grinbaum getting off small boat and going up to the dock at Tel Aviv (long, 31).
3   Walking with receiving crowds (long, 49).
4   A line of scouts greets him (long, 67).

□ PART C: TITLE: SHOOTING COMPETITION WITH HUNTING GUNS AT HAIFA.
1   TITLE IN HEBREW: SHOOTING COMPETITION BETWEEN THE HUNTING ASSOCIATION AND THE BRITISH ARMY (145').

כותרת: התחרות בקליעה למטרה בין אגודת הצײדים והצבא. (9).

2   People arriving at the shooting range (long, 18).
3   Structure with two flags - British and Zionist. Afterwards, four flags of the British division, the Zionist flag, the British flag and the hunting association flag (long, mid, 37).
4   People arriving at the shooting range, sitting on benches outside (long, 58).
5   Targets. Two people shooting. The judges. Sign: COLONIAL SMALL-BORE MATCH PALESTINE TEAM (108).
6   Scorekeeper writing on blackboard. The crowd.
7   Lying on stomachs, shooting. Crowd (mid, long, 145).

■ **CARMEL NEWSREEL I-159** · October 29 1938
Aviation in Palestine including the building and flying of gliders, and the servicing of propeller aircraft at Afikim. Stunning aerial photography of the Jezreel Valley, the Sea of Galilee, the Jordan Valley, Nahalal, Tower and Stockade settlement and Tel Aviv.

□ PART A: TITLE: PIONEERS OF THE AIR IN PALESTINE, MUSIC BY M. WILENSKY, *THE SONG OF AVIATION*, LYRICS BY LEA GOLDBERG (274')

כותרת: כבוש האויר בארץ ישראל, מוסיקה: מ. וילנסקי, מילים: שיר התעופה, לאה גולדברג. (21)

1   Young men working on gliders (mid, 36).
2   Young men building gliders (long, 97).
3   An engineer supervising construction (mid, 103).
4   The glider, with one young man aboard, is pulled along by a rope and then takes off (long, 118).

5   Hangar at Afikim, Aviron Co., servicing planes. Ben Ya'akov standing next to one of the technicians (mid, 140).
6   Continuing work on planes (mid, 156).
7   Tsur (Zuckerman), the first director of Lod Airport, servicing a plane (mid, 162).
8   Planes on runway (at Afikim) (long, 180).
9   Assembling wings (long, 194).
10  Fuelling the plane. Plane ready for take-off. Man spins propeller (by hand) and the plane takes off (long, mid, 274).

□ PART B: AERIAL VIEWS OF THE JORDAN VALLEY, THE SEA OF GALILEE AND NAHALAL (390')
1   Aerial views (song begins here) (long, 113).
2   Scenery, pilots in planes (Tsur is one of the pilots) and titles:
    TITLE: EMEK JORDAN           כותרת: עמק הירדן
    TITLE: LAKE OF GENNESARET [sic]    כותרת: ים כנרת וסביבתו
    TITLE: NAHALAL               כותרת: נהלל
3   View of train. The Jezreel Valley, Nahalal (long, 213).
4   Coastal plain. Plane landing (mid, long, 245).
5   TITLE IN HEBREW: ON THE WATCH        כותרת: בשמירה
6   Plane taking off for defence purposes, to establish contact with Tower and Stockade settlements. The plane circles above a watch-tower.
7   Woman, with binoculars, on watch-tower. Message dropped from plane, picked up and read by a man (291).
8   Repeated aerial view of previous scenes, with addition of titles and good aerial footage of Tel Aviv (390).

■ CARMEL NEWSREEL I-160 · November 5 1938
Exhibition of diaspora Zionist youth movements. Swimming competition in Tel Aviv. Fund-raising effort for national defence charity fund, Kofer HaYishuv.

□ PART A: TITLE: KEREN KAYEMET EXHIBITION AT TEL AVIV (192')
1   TITLE IN HEBREW: EXHIBITION OF DIASPORA ZIONIST YOUTH AT THE JEWISH NATIONAL FUND BUILDING IN TEL AVIV.

כותרת: תערוכת "הנוער הציוני בגולה" בבית הקק"ל בת"א (8)

2   Exterior of Keren Kayemet building (long, 18).
3   Poster at exhibit (in Hebrew): "For the Jewish People, countries are divided into two types - those that expel them and those that won't let them in" (Chaim Weizmann).

ציתות מחיים ויזמן, תלוי על הקיר: "בשביל העם היהודי, מתחלק העולם לשני סוגים של ארצות: מהן שמגרשים אותם ומהן שאין נותנים להם לבוא שמה."

4   Pan of refugee photos, on wall. Shots of youth movement symbols with Hebrew names: Brit Kana'im, Torah V'Avodah, Bnei Akiva, Maccabi, Maccabi Hatzair, Hadassah Hatzeira, Hanoar Hatzioni, Hashomer Hatzair, Dror, Gourdonia (192).

סמלים של תנועות נוער: ברית קנאים, תורה ועבודה, בני עקיבא, מכבי, מכבי הצעיר, הדסה הצעירה, הנוער הציוני, השומר הצעיר, דרור, גורדוניה.

□ PART B: COURSE FOR UNEMPLOYED SECRETARIES IN JERUSALEM

□ PART C: TITLE: SWIMMING MATCH AT TEL AVIV (172')
1   TITLE IN HEBREW: COMPLETION OF THE SWIMMING SEASON BY THE

PALESTINE MARITIME LEAGUE IN TEL AVIV.

כותרת: סיום עונת השחיה ע"י חבל ימי לישראל בת"א (8).

2 Flag of swimming group (14).
3 Young men and women, some young boys, (in bathing suits) march around a swimming pool. Man giving instructions over a megaphone (long, 55).
4 Racing dives, swimming crawl (long, 89).
5 Another race, judges (131).
6 Diving competition (mid, 172).

☐ PART D: TITLE: PUBLIC SUBSCRIPTION FOR "KOFER HAISHUW" [sic] (132')

כותרת: מפקד "כופר הישוב" בת"א (7).

1 Poster advertising charity drive for Kofer Hayishuv, pre-state fund for defence (15).
2 People lined up, donating assorted items, at a table (mid, 35).
3 TITLE IN HEBREW: IN HAIFA.     כותרת: בחיפה
4 Large crowd in outdoor amphitheatre. Meeting for Kofer HaYishuv. Large picture of stylised figures on arch framing stage (long, 71).
5 Speech from podium. Among people on stage are: Uriel Friedland (owner of "Shemen" factory), Yosef Almogi (later Mayor of Haifa) (mid, 82).
6 Crowd listening to speeches. Woman from Kibbutz Yagur speaking. Crowd listening. Car with poster advertisement on front (long, 132).

■ **CARMEL NEWSREEL I-161** · November 12 1938
Massive flooding in Tel Aviv. The Hebrew newspaper *Hacarmel* is printed in Haifa. Girls working on an agricultural training farm in Jerusalem.

☐ PART A: TITLE: THE LAST RAINS IN PALESTINE (211')

כותרת: השטפון בארץ (6)

1 Streets of Tel Aviv covered in water (long, 31).
2 Assisting persons to evacuate flooded houses. Car driving in water. Uprooted trees. Overturned car. Car driving in water (mid, 111).
3 Long line of people waiting their turn to go on a rowing boat across the street. Man lifting woman out of boat and placing her on the pavement (long, 151).
4 TITLE IN HEBREW: PRESS TOUR OF FLOOD-DAMAGED SITES (158).

כותרת: סיור עיתונאים במקומות הנגועים מהשטפון

5 Reporters, some dressed in suits and ties, looking at damaged sites, overturned cars, ruins (mid, long, 211).

☐ PART B: TITLE: THE HAIFA FIRST HEBREW NEWSPAPER (45')

כותרת: "הכרמל" - העיתון היומי הראשון בחיפה (9)

1 Printing presses printing the newspaper (mid, 19).
2 Editors looking at first edition (mid, 33).
3 The first edition (c.u., 40).
4 Newsboys selling the newspapers on street (long, 45).

☐ PART C: AGRICULTURAL TRAINING FARM IN JERUSALEM (21')
1 Girls hoeing in orchard (long, 21).

■ **CARMEL NEWSREEL I-162** · November 19 1938
The first agricultural farm of the Women Workers Union (Mo'etzet HaPoalot) at Nahalat Yehuda. Tel Aviv Mayor Israel Rokah on an inspection tour of sites damaged by flooding. Preparation of an exhibition, to be shipped to New York, dealing with life in Palestine.

□ PART A: TITLE: THE FIRST GIRLS FARM IN PALESTINE (98')

כותרת: ראשון למשקי הפועלות בנחלת יהודה (8)

1  Hebrew sign: Council of Working Women (24).
2  Entrance to a building on the farm, dissolve to second building (long, 40).
3  General view of the farm and the surroundings (long, 44).
4  Agricultural work in the outdoor nursery. Field of saplings. Girls picking and packing saplings. Loading crates onto wagon (long, 98).

□ PART B: TITLE: THE MAYOR OF TEL AVIV VISITING THE FLOOD PLACES (40')

כותרת: ראש עירית תל-אביב מבקר במקומות השטפון (6)

1  Mayor Israel Rokah and his entourage visiting flood-damaged sites (mid, long, 40).

□ PART C: TITLE: THE PREPARATION FOR THE NEW YORK EXHIBITION (303')

כותרת: הכנות לקראת תערוכת ניו-יורק (7)

1  Pan of model of exhibition (long, 29).
2  People looking at display of the symbols of the Twelve Tribes. Individual shots of the symbol of each Tribe (c.u., 94).
3  Crowd looking at exhibits. Preparations for the exhibits. Building model of swamps, map of Israel, exhibits of produce by season, large sculpture of man, sculptor on ladder finishing face, map hanging on the wall (mid, 303).

■ **CARMEL NEWSREEL I-163** · November 26 1938

Women working in the production of clay flower pots at Yagur. Life in the Kurdish immigrant settlement of Alroy in the Jezreel Valley. Completion of a Mekorot water-pumping station, bringing water to the western Jezreel Valley. Violinist Hela Jamm plays *Spanish Dance* by Manuel de Falla.

□ PART A: TITLE: MAKING FLOWERPOTS (154')

כותרת: לומען-טאפ אויסרבייטונג

1  Woman pushing clay into mixer. Woman bringing clay in wheelbarrow. Women operating machine that shapes clay into flower pots.
2  Woman operating pottery wheel. Close-up of her bare feet spinning the wheel. Close-up of pot forming in her hands.
3  Women placing pots on shelves. Checking piles of pots (154).

□ PART B: TITLE: THE ALROY SETTLEMENT AT EMEK YIZREEL (202')

1  TITLE IN HEBREW: ALROY, SETTLED BY KURDISH IMMIGRANTS, IN THE JEZREEL VALLEY.   כותרת: ישוב עולי קורדים "אלרואי" בעמק יזראעל (8)
2  General view of undeveloped settlement (long, 25).
3  Line of men digging trench. Close-up of grey-bearded man (68).
4  Woman walking with tray on her head (mid, 81).
5  Barefoot woman digging in dirt. Two women sitting on ground pounding flour with wooden mallets. Woman putting straw into oven. Woman forming dough into pita and placing it in oven.
6  Guard standing. Guard riding on donkey (mid, long, 167).
7  Kindergarten (c.u., mid, 202).

□ PART C: TITLE IN HEBREW: COMPLETION OF WORK ON MEKOROT WATER SYSTEM FOR THE WESTERN JEZREEL VALLEY (146')

כותרת: סיום עבודות הספקת המים לעמק יזרעאל המערבי "מקורות" מזרימה את מימיה לאדמת עמק יזרעאל (10)

1  Directors of Mekorot Water Company, headed by Levi Eshkol, showing reporters the finished water works, by the large reservoir (long, 46).

2   Assorted works (long, 68).
3   Pan of the Jezreel Valley (long, 102).
4   Pumping station, turning on the pump, large stream of water coming out of pipe (long, mid, 146).

□ PART D: TITLE: THE VIOLINIST HELA JAMM PLAYS *SPANISH DANCE* BY M. DE FALLA. PIANO M. TAUBER (187')

כותרת: הכנרת הלה ים מנגנת "ריקוד ספרדי" מאת מ. פלא. הפסנת. מ. טאובר, מנהל הקונסרבטוריון. (10)

1   Hela Jamm playing violin (mid, 65).
2   Continues playing (c.u., 66).
3   Finishes playing (mid, 187).

■ CARMEL NEWSREEL I-164 · December 3 1938
Extensive coverage of the benefits of the programmes of the HaNoar Ha'oved youth movement.

□ PART A: TITLE: THE LIFE OF THE YOUTH WORKERS IN NAAN (822')

כותרת: הנוער העובד בחיים ובעבודה ובהגשמה

1   TITLE IN HEBREW: ACCOMPANIED BY THE YOUTH WORKER'S ORCHESTRA AND CHOIR FROM THE BOROCHOV NEIGHBOURHOOD.

כותרת: ליווי ע"י תזמורת ומקהלה של חברי הנוער העובד בסניף שכונת בורוכוב

2   Pan of Tel Aviv neighbourhood (long, 25).
3   Dissolves of various parts of Tel Aviv lit up at night (long, 41).
4   A boy sleeping on a bench in the park. Another boy sleeping inside a large pipe, another sleeping on the floor. Children crowded together in a room (the shots repeat themselves).
5   A little boy wakes up and starts to put on his socks with holes in them (mid, c.u., 96).
6   Youths gathered at a HaNoar Ha'oved meeting listen attentively to a female counsellor (mid, c.u., 133).
7   At the gathering in Ben Shemen. A male counsellor reads aloud from a book. Dissolves on the faces of the listening youth (mid, long, 189).
8   Youths ascend the outdoor stairs of a building (mid, 208).
9   The youths working on various machines at the Max Fein Vocational School (c.u., 229).
10  Boys working in the carpentry workshop (mid, 268).
11  A boy working in the garage (mid, 287).
12  Soldering (mid, 305).
13  Young women cutting and sewing (mid, c.u., 338).
14  Boys fixing boats and performing various nautical duties (mid, c.u., 365).
15  Young women working with children at day-care (long, 376).
16  Mechanical work on vehicles (long, 386).
17  At the instructional farm; shots of harvesting, trimming, working with the cows, milking. Picking fruit in the orchard (long, 463).
18  Outdoor sing-along. Group confidence building games (long, 502).
19  Group calisthenics (long, 520).
20  Practical exercises, including scaling a wooden wall and carrying "the wounded" on planks (mid, 593).
21  The youths marching in formation over a hill and towards the camera (long, 622).
22  Pan of Kibbutz Na'an (long, 649).
23  Youths sitting near a table and taking notes from the counsellor at the seminar (mid, 678).

24 Two girls enjoying recreational reading. Students sitting near desks in a classroom (mid, c.u., 719).
25 Studying and eating at the same time (mid, 736).
26 Children writing on the blackboard. Handing out books in the library (mid, 743).
27 A soccer game.
28 Running and playing near bicycle riders (mid, 760).
29 A female counsellor addressing the youth and telling them about the benefits of the HaNoar Ha'Oved programme (long, 822).

■ **CARMEL NEWSREEL I-165** · December 10 1938
Kibbutz Mishmar-Zebulun helps in the construction of the Na'aman clay and brick factory near Acre.

□ PART A: TITLE IN HEBREW: HASHOMER HATZAIR KIBBUTZ MISHMAR ZEBULUN GOES TO CONSTRUCT THE 'NA'MAN' FACTORY NEAR ACRE (306')

כותרת: קבוץ השומר הצעיר משמר-זבולון עולה להקמת בית חרושת "נעמן" ע"י עכו

1 TITLE IN HEBREW: *THE SONG OF THE CLAY*, MUSIC: M. WILENSKY, SUNG BY YOSEPH GOLAND.

כותרת שניה: "שיר החימר". מוסיקה: מ. וילנסקי. הושר ע"י יוסף גולנד

2 Sand dunes at the place where Ein Hamifratz was settled. Close-up of Joshua Porter, one of the founders of Ein Hamifratz, examining the sand (mid, 41).
3 Swamps and barren land. Porter examining the clay soil. An expert examines the sand (c.u., 77).
4 Dissolve to a brick which is being examined by someone (mid, 89).
5 Guards near sand dunes at the site of construction of the Na'aman factory.
6 Building the tower and fence.
7 The crowd near the huts and the tower (long, 114).
8 The founders stand near the cornerstone with the audience (mid, 129).
9 One of the founders addressing the audience (mid, long,147).
10 Close-up of the cornerstone and the title of ownership. The parchment is put into a bottle and then placed into the cement (c.u., 212).
11 Demonstrating operation of the kiln (mid, 229).
12 Fired and finished products that were manufactured at the factory (mid, 236).
13 The audience leaves.
14 TITLE IN HEBREW: "WITH THE RISING OF THE SUN ANOTHER WILDERNESS AWAITS". כותרת: עם הנץ החמה עוד שממה
15 Overview of the barren land. A convoy (long).
16 Building a tower and fence for the factory.
17 The site is constructed (long, 306).

□ PART B - BUILDING THE NA'AMAN FACTORY (155')
1 Construction work. Clearing out the area before the construction (long, 39).
2 Shot from above and below of the tower going up (mid, 49).
3 Building the huts (mid, 71).
4 Baskets of gravel are passed from one person to another and are poured into the mix for the wall (mid, 124).
5 View of the tower seen from the walls (long, 131).
6 Mixing cement. View of the tower with boulders around it (155).

■ **CARMEL NEWSREEL I-166** · December 17 1938
Building the new Tel Aviv market including views of Tel Aviv. Receiving diplomas at the Zebulun Naval Course in Tel Aviv. Jewelry is donated in support of the national defence charity drive, Kofer Hayishuv. Scenes from the children's Chanukah play, *The Candles Speak*.

Carmel Newsreels: Series 1    139

□ PART A: TITLE: THE BUILDING OF THE NEW MARKET IN TEL AVIV (79')
כותרת: השוק המרכזי בת"א בבנינו (8).
1    General view, Aliyah Street. Assorted views (long, 79).

□ PART B: TITLE: ZEBULUN ROWING COMPETITION IN TEL AVIV (113)
1    TITLE IN HEBREW: DISTRIBUTION OF DIPLOMAS TO GRADUATES OF THE ZEBULUN NAVAL SCHOOL IN TEL AVIV.
כותרת: חלוקת התעודות לגומרי קורס בבי"ס ימי "זבולון" בת"א (9).
2    Decorated flagpole (long, 21).
3    Long view of the area, crowds gathering (48).
4    Speaker (mid, 57).
5    Distributing diplomas, shaking hands (mid, 81).
6    Principal speaking (mid, 90).
7    Graduation march (pan, long, 113).

□ PART C: TITLE: JEWELLERY PUBLIC DONATIONS FOR KOFER HAISHUV (257')
כותרת: מפעל התכשיטים ל"כופר הישוב" (8).
1    Armoured cars in the street (24).
2    Crowd gathering to observe how the jewelry is unloaded (45).
3    Bank Igud LeYisrael building. Bringing jewelry into the bank (mid, 66).
4    Female volunteers sorting jewelry on tables (mid, 84).
5    Dissolve to pieces of jewelry. Signing for special cartons (mid, 125).
6    Sorted jewelry passed hand to hand into bank vault (223).
7    Close-up of jewelry and sale (c.u., mid, 257).

□ PART D: TITLE: *THE CANDLES SPEAK*: CHANUKAH PLAY AT THE CONSERVATOIRE MICHAEL TAUBE (211')
1    TITLE IN HEBREW: PLAY BY ALIZA TAUBE. WORDS BY EPHRAIM TRUCHE. MUSIC BY MORDECHAI STRUMINSKY.
כותרת: קטע מתוך "הנרות מספרים" מוצג ע"י קונסרבטוריון, מיכאל טאובה. מחזה: עליזה טאובה. מלים: אפרים טרוכה. מוסיקה: מרדכי סטארומינסקי. (12).
2    Children dressed up as candles, among them Yoel Zilberg as a boy (c.u., 40).
3    Orchestra and choir below. Candles singing above (long, 211).

■ **CARMEL NEWSREEL I-167** · December 25 1938
Memorial service for Eliezer Ben Yehuda (which took place at the Ben Yehuda home in the Jerusalem neighbourhood of Talpiot December 14 1938), including shots of his study and his manuscripts. A Wizo handicrafts bazaar. The Tel Aviv Zoo. A parade in Tel Aviv.

□ PART A: MEMORIAL SERVICE FOR ELIEZER BEN YEHUDA (195')
1    A portrait of Eliezer Ben Yehudah (mid, 12).
2    Sign "The day is short and the task is great". Shots of his study: books, desk, furnishings (c.u., 53).
3    Manuscripts (c.u., 115).
4    A large crowd in procession (long, 161).
5    Man speaking. Honour guard (mid, 179).
6    Mrs Ben Yehuda giving a speech (mid, 188).
7    A statue of Ben Yehuda (c.u., 195).

□ PART B: A WIZO BAZAAR FOR POOR CHILDREN (131')
1    General view of the bazaar. Women selling (long, 41).
2    Women weaving (mid, 60).

3   Completed handicrafts, embroidery, child playing with toys (mid, 131).

□ PART C: THE NEW ZOO (188')
1   General view of the Tel Aviv Zoo (long, pan, 41).
2   Feeding the bears (mid, 85).
3   Keeper with lions; a cub kissing him (mid, 125).
4   Keeper with tiger (mid, 156).
5   Keeper with hyena (mid, 175).
6   First owner of the Zoo on Yarkon Street, Tel Aviv, playing with a parrot (c.u., 183).
7   Small parrot (188).

□ PART D: ZION FLAG PARADE IN TEL AVIV (159')
1   View of the parade (long, c.u., 17).
2   Leaders giving speeches. Crowd listening (long, mid, pan, 58).
3   Choir singing (68).
4   Raising the flag (91).
5   Receiving the flag. Passing it, handshaking (134).
6   The audience watching paraders marching in place (general, pan, 159).

■ **CARMEL NEWSREEL I-168** · January 28 1939
The steamer *MIRIAM* arrives in Tel Aviv Port. The new government hospital (today Rambam Hospital) in Haifa. Hapoel Rowing Competition on the Yarkon River. The inauguration of the new airline from Lod to Beirut.

□ PART A: TITLE: THE STEAMER *MIRIAM* IN TEL AVIV HARBOUR (109')
כותרת: קבלת פנים לאוניה העברית החדשה "מרים" בנמל ת"א (60).
1   The guests arriving (long).
2   Sailor by the steering wheel. Ship at sea. Mast (mid, 37).
3   Boarding the ship (mid, 51).
4   Journalists receiving information about the ship (mid, 93).
5   View of ship. Mast (c.u., 109).

□ PART B: TITLE: INAUGURATION OF THE GOVERNMENT HOSPITAL AT HAIFA (126')            כותרת: פתיחת ביה"ח הממשלתי בחיפה (8).
1   General view of hospital (today, Rambam Hospital) (long).
2   Guests and officials arriving at the new hospital decorated with the British flag.
3   The crowd is seated (long, 74).
4   Mayor of Haifa, Hassan Bey Shukri, making a speech (mid, 87).
5   The High Commissioner Sir Harold MacMichael speaking. Crowd listening (mid, long, 103).
6   The Commissioner saying goodbye to the director of the hospital, entering car, leaving the site (mid, 126).

□ PART C: TITLE: ROWING COMPETITION BY "HAPOEL" - TEL AVIV (114')
כותרת: תחרות שיט של "הפועל" על הירקון (8).
1   Taking sailing boats into the water (long, 33).
2   A crowd by the Yarkon River (mid, 42).
3   Drums and the beginning of the rowing competition, crowds (long, 62).
4   Honour guard. Man making speech, crowd (long, 96).
5   Mordechai Nemirovsky (Namir), later Mayor of Tel Aviv (mid, 103).
6   Zalman Aranne (Aharonowitz) speaking (mid, 108).
7   Crowd (long, 114).

□ PART D: TITLE: THE INAUGURATION OF THE NEW AIRLINE LUDD-BEIRUTH [sic] (111')
1   TITLE IN HEBREW: THE OPENING OF THE HEBREW AIR SERVICE FROM ERETZ ISRAEL TO ABROAD.
כותרת: פתיחת שרות אוירי עברי מא"י לחו"ל (8).
2   Guests at the airport. Drinking toasts (long, mid, 33).
3   Plane taking off (mid, 50).
4   Aerial photography, fields and Tel Aviv, airplane (long, 74).
5   Airplane landing at Lod (98).
6   Passengers disembarking (long, 111).

■ CARMEL NEWSREEL I-169 · January 29 1939
Dr Benjamin Meisler (Professor Mazar) showing archaeological discoveries from the period of the Sanhedrin, found at excavations at Sheikh Abrek (Beit Shearim).

□ PART A: TITLE: ARCHAEOLOGICAL EXCAVATIONS AT SHEIKH ABREK (886')
1   TITLE IN HEBREW: THE DISCOVERY OF A SANHEDRIN CITY. EXCAVATIONS AT BEIT SHEARIM.   כותרת: גלוי עיר הסנהדרין. החפירות בבית שערים
2   TITLE IN HEBREW: UNDER THE SUPERVISION OF THE ARCHAEOLOGICAL DELEGATION OF THE HEBREW SOCIETY FOR THE STUDY OF PALESTINE AND ITS ANTIQUITIES.
כותרת: המתנהלות ע"י המשלחת הארכיאולוגית מטעם החברה העברית לחקירת א"י ועתיקותיה
3   TITLE IN HEBREW: LECTURER: DR BENJAMIN MEISLER (PROFESSOR MAZAR), DIRECTOR OF THE EXCAVATIONS (32).
כותרת: המרצה: ד"ר בנימין מייזלר (פרופ' מזר) מנהל החפירות
4   Givat Zayit, general view (long, 48).
5   Pan of excavations, uncovered sections, pavements and steps (long, 92).
6   Dr Benjamin Meisler (Mazar) with his assistants checking a map (109).
7   Cleaning pottery. Sorting pottery. Searching in the dust. Finding a jug. A child goes to tell Dr Meisler to come and inspect the jug. Dr Meisler and his assistants arrive to inspect. Measuring the site and marking on map (mid, 189).
8   Removing the jug from the ground (mid, 214).
9   Measuring the jug, pan on assorted vessels (mid, 234).
10  Finding a large, smooth stone which covers a hole. Placing a ladder in the hole and entering with work tools (mid, 295).
11  Inside the hole, discovering an arched opening to a room (mid, 325).
12  A boy digging and removing pottery (mid, 340).
13  Pottery cleaning area (mid, 365).
14  Pan of excavations in burial rooms (425).
15  Tombstone written in ancient Hebrew writing which states that the man was born abroad and requested to be buried in Beit Shearim (c.u., 435).
16  Entering the cave.
17  Cleaning a sarcophagus (c.u., 470).
18  Stone door opens and closes (c.u., 484).
19  An additional stone door opens and boy passes to the second room (c.u., 499).
20  Portion of a wall with the painting of a menorah. Tilt down to wall decorations. Through an opening, view of pottery cleaning (mid, 550).
21  Wall decorations. Meisler's assistant, archaeologist Pessach Bar Adon, coming out of one of the caves. Bar Adon showing decorations. Tilt down to a corridor to the burial rooms. Stone chair. Ark carved on wall (662).
22  Gathering pottery. Decorated pillars above the graves. Stone engravings (mid, 772).

23 Discovering stone door, opening it. Dr Meisler and Bar Adon entering (mid, 784).
24 Cleaning a mosaic floor. Putting pieces together. Finding engraved Hebrew letters (832).
25 Cleaning vessels (855).
26 Cleaning a mosaic floor (869).
27 Mosaic tiles (c.u., 886).

■ **CARMEL NEWSREEL I-170** · February 1939
The celebration of Tu B'shvat, at Kiryat Avodah, at the Yishuv Forest of Ma'aleh, at Haifa and at Ramat Gan.

□ PART A: TITLE: FIFTEENTH DAY OF SHVAT, KIRYAT AVODAH (77')
1 TITLE IN HEBREW: TU B'SHVAT - THE ALMOND TREE AND SUNSHINE BLOOM.
כותרת א': ט"ו בשבט. השקדיה פורחת ושמש פז זורחת. כותרת ב': ט"ו בשבט בקרית עבודה (10)
2 The place is decorated with a gateway and flags, children gather by the gate (long, 23).
3 All line up on the field (mid, 37).
4 Distributing seedlings to the children who go to plant them (long, 77).

□ PART B: TITLE: PLANTING OF THE "YISHUV FOREST" AT BAMA'ALEH (109')
כותרת: נטיעת "יער הישוב" (8)
1 Crowds gathering at the location of the forest (long, 51).
2 Yosef Weitz, from the Jewish National Fund, speaking to the crowd (mid, 75).
3 People planting trees (mid, long, 109).

□ PART C: TITLE: FIFTEENTH DAY OF SHVAT AT HAIFA (86')
כותרת: ט"ו בשבט בהר הכרמל (8)
1 An empty lot, children appear going to plant trees, line up. Speeches (long, 38).
2 Planting, hoe, parade, receiving bags of Tu B'shvat dried fruit (mid, long, 86).

□ PART D: TITLE IN HEBREW: TU B'SHVAT IN RAMAT GAN (335')
כותרת: ט"ו בשבט ברמת-גן (5)
1 A child reciting a poem (c.u., 51).
2 Singing in an amphitheatre (long, 83).
3 General view of stage with flags. Children on stage, girl reading (long, mid, 99).
4 Young girls presenting on stage, audience (106).
5 Avraham Krinitzi, Mayor of Ramat Gan, speaking, audience clapping (long, mid, 119).
6 Children marching on a path with seedlings and tools. Passing over a bridge (mid, 145).
7 Children walking in a park. Passing bridges and singing (long, 253).
8 Children at the planting site (mid, 268).
9 Planting (long, 303).
10 Krinitzi and Elimelech Rimalt, city educational director, observing (mid, 31).
11 Children planting (mid, 335).

■ **CARMEL NEWSREEL I-171** · February/March 1939
The opening of the Zuckerman House Community Centre at the settlement of Tzofit. The opening of the Egged bus station at Hadera. Assembly of the Palestine Maritime League, including the awarding of diplomas to naval academy graduates.

Inauguration of the Tel Aviv Yacht Club on the Yarkon River.

□ PART A: TITLE: OPENING OF THE ZUCKERMAN HOUSE AT TZOFIT (108')

כותרת: פתיחת בית עם על שם צוקרמן בצופית (8)

1   General view of Tzofit. Pan of the settlement (40).
2   Community centre with crowd. Crowd entering centre (long, 60).
3   Children marching with a flag and singing (mid, 74).
4   Crowd by the entrance (long, 84).
5   Planting a palm tree near the entrance (mid, 108).

□ PART B: TITLE: INAUGURATION OF THE EGGED STATION AT HADERA (61')

כותרת: חגיגת פתיחת תחנת "אגד" בחדרה (9)

1   General view of Hadera (pan, 30).
2   Crowd around the station (long, 38).
3   Banquet for Egged executives, speeches (mid, 51).
4   Cutting the ribbon, opening the station (mid, 61).

□ PART C: TITLE: PALESTINE MARITIME LEAGUE ASSEMBLY AT TEL AVIV (90')

כותרת: כנוס הנוער של חבל ימי לישראל (7)

1   Galina Coffeehouse, pan of tables with the Hebrew banner: Maritime League for Israel (long, 29).
2   Speeches (mid, 37).
3   Naval academy graduates. Little boy in sailor's uniform (c.u., 42).
4   Graduates receiving diplomas along with the little boy (long, 68).
5   Officers marching (long, 90).

□ PART D: TITLE: THE INAUGURATION OF THE TEL AVIV YACHT CLUB PREMISES (95')        כותרת: חנוכת מועדון השייטים בת"א (7)

1   Crowd seated outside club (mid, 20).
2   Man speaking to crowd holding a trophy in his hand (mid, 35).
3   Crowd listening to speaker (mid, 46).
4   Sailors lowering a boat into the Yarkon River (long, 60).
5   Boats sailing (long, 95).

■ **CARMEL NEWSREEL I-172** · February/March 1939
*Hora* song with shots of paving a road, orange groves, Tower and Stockade, shepherd and his flock. A holiday *Namal* dance. Tap-dancing performed by the Chocolate Trio.

□ PART A: TITLE: *HORA* SONG BY SARAH PETSHAFT (315')
1   TITLE IN HEBREW: MELODY BY VERDINA SHLONSKY.

כותרת: שיר "אלפי ידיים" ע"י שרה פטשפט. מנגינה: ורדינה שלונסקי (9)

2   The singer waiting for her cue to begin (mid, 101).
3   The singer sings (c.u., 198).
4   Background pictures for the song. Pan of a village (long, 209).
5   A mountain, clouds, scenery in Samaria (long, 230).
6   Levelling sand dunes in north Tel Aviv with the help of shovels. Paving a road (mid, long, 269).
7   Pan of orange groves (long, 285).
8   Raising a tower in a Tower and Stockade settlement (long, 296).
9   A shepherd with his flock (long, 306).
10  Children dressed in white sheets bringing holiday baskets of first fruits (315).

□ PART B: TITLE: *NAMAL DANCE* BY THE FRIDERBAUM STUDIO (110')
1   TITLE IN HEBREW: THE NAMAL HOLIDAY DANCE BY THE LASMAN SISTERS

FROM THE FRIDERBAUM STUDIO. MUSIC: SHULTZ HOUSE.

כותרת: "חג הנמל" רקוד ע"י אחיות לסמן מהסטודיו פרידבאום. מוסיקה:
בית שולץ (9)
2   The sisters dance (mid, long, 110).

□ PART C: TITLE: TAP DANCING BY THE CHOCOLATE TRIO. PIANO: L. AHARONOWICH (227')
1   TITLE IN HEBREW: *STREET CHILD* TAP DANCE BY THE TUVIA BROTHERS. PIANO: LEON AHARONOVITZ.

כותרת: "ילד הרחוב" רקוד סטפס ע"י אחים טוביה. ע"י פסנתר: ליאון
אהרונוביץ (10)
2   Brothers dance (mid, 62).
3   Another boy enters. Playful dance (mid, 227).

■ **CARMEL NEWSREEL I-173** · March 1939
The Rabbi of Sadigura, Rabbi Mordechai Friedman, is welcomed at Tel Aviv port by his Hassidim. The export of barrels of fruit juice. Maccabi Tel Aviv basketball game.

□ PART A: TITLE: THE RABBI OF SADIGURA ARRIVES TO PALESTINE (97').

כותרת: הרבי מסדיגורה בא לארץ (6)
1   The port of Tel Aviv, Rabbi Friedman arrives in a boat to the dock, comes ashore, handshaking, being received by men. Showing his passport to a policeman (mid, 63).
2   Rabbi Friedman leaving the port. Behind the gate, crowds of Hassidim waiting (mid, 81).
3   Departing through the gate, the Hassidim surround him (97).

□ PART B: TITLE: THE GREATEST JUICE EXPORT IN TEL AVIV HARBOUR (73').

כותרת: משלוח של מיצי הדר דרך נמל ת"א (7)
1   Barrels of juice on the dock. Rolling them on the dock (23).
2   The barrels roll to the boat. Pan of the boat. Crane lifting the barrels onto the boats (73).

□ PART C: TITLE: BASKETBALL MATCH BY MACCABI IN TEL AVIV (83').
1   TITLE IN HEBREW: MACCABI BASKETBALL GAME FOR THE NATIONAL ERETZ ISRAEL CHAMPIONSHIP.

כותרת: התחרויות של מכבי בכדורסל לקראת תואר רבנאות "א"י
2   Parade of players. A pan of the court (32).
3   The game (83).

■ **CARMEL NEWSREEL I-174** · March 1939
Cultivating bees at the Women's Farm in the Borochov neighbourhood of Tel Aviv. The arrival of author Max Brod from Prague. The construction of fishing boats in Nahariya. The 10th anniversary of the Wizo Mother & Child Clinic in Tel Aviv, including shots of a woman doctor and mothers nursing their babies.

□ PART A: TITLE: BEES CULTIVATION IN PALESTINE (27').

כותרת: רדיית דבש במשק הפועלות בשכ' בורוכוב
1   TITLE IN HEBREW: GATHERING HONEY IN THE WOMEN'S FARM IN THE BOROCHOV NEIGHBOURHOOD (27).

□ PART B: THE ARRIVAL OF MAX BROD (62')
1   Max Brod speaking beautiful Hebrew, how happy he is to be here, how sad he is about those who stayed behind in Czechoslovakia and how committed he is to building the land (62).

☐ PART C: TITLE: FISHING BOATS MANUFACTURING IN PALESTINE (73')
כותרת: בנין סירות דייג בנהריה (7)
1 General view of boatyard (26).
2 Building and repairing boats (mid, long, 56).
3 Heating the materials by steam, building (73).

☐ PART D: TITLE: TENTH ANNIVERSARY OF "THE MOTHER AND CHILD HOUSE" IN TEL AVIV (185')
כותרת: עשר שנות קיום "מוסד לטפול באם ובילד" של ויצו בת"א (9)
1 Women sitting and listening (22).
2 The building (30).
3 Taking care of babies (51).
4 Woman doctor taking care of baby (87).
5 Giving the babies to the mothers who modestly nurse them (108).
6 Nurses feeding the babies (mid, 121).
7 Teaching mothers how to prepare baby food. Nurses teaching infant care (185).

■ **CARMEL NEWSREEL I-175** · April 1 1939
The first anniversary of Kibbutz Eilon and Kibbutz Hanita, including footage of everyday life, scythes, ploughing, defence and an archetypal female image with bullets strung around her waist and a gun in hand.

☐ PART A: FIRST YEAR BIRTHDAY CELEBRATION OF EILON AND HANITA (346')
1 General view of Hanita Mountains. Dissolve to remains of ancient buildings. A ghaffir (Jewish Settlement Police) passes with a dog. Dissolve to a man passing by (50).
2 Cleaning area, burning thorns. A flowing stream, man bends down to drink, water pipe passing from stream to dining room. Starting up the generator. Water flowing from tap (mid, 122).
3 Hill with ancient structure. Guards shooting in Hanita (132).
4 People running out of kibbutz for counter-attack (138).
5 Kibbutz Eilon. Pan of hills, general view.
6 Levelling the land, corn harvest, planting tree, close-up of hand carrying scythe. Cutting corn (long, 198).
7 Ploughing with a horse. Men and women working in a vegetable garden (224).
8 General view of Kibbutz Eilon (235).
9 Guard (mid, 239).
10 Uprooting trees. Workers returning home (267).
11 By the hills (274).
12 Uprooting roots. Cleaning area (295).
13 Shot through opening of tent, two girls talking, flowers on table (307).
14 Signalling to Haifa from tower (326).
15 Men hoeing, man on stomach shooting. Woman kneeling in bushes, string of bullets around her neck, gun in hand, gets up to walk, bullets around waist.
16 Shepherd with sheep, young women with sheep, one sucks her finger (long).
17 Ploughing with horse. Man scything. Pan of wooden houses. Armoured car drives in (346).

■ **CARMEL NEWSREEL I-176** · April 8 1939
75th birthday of David Yellin. Dr Chaim Weizmann and David Ben Gurion arrive by boat at Tel Aviv port following talks in London. A window-dressing competition. Road construction by Histadrut workers in the north. Horse show in Jerusalem.

☐ PART A: TITLE: 75TH ANNIVERSARY OF DAVID YELLIN (39')
1 TITLE IN HEBREW: TO LONG LIFE - DAVID YELLIN - 75 YEARS OLD.

2   Yellin speaks to camera about the hard times for the Jewish People. He quotes from The Book of Isaiah.

☐ PART B: TITLE: DR WEIZMANN AND BEN GURION ARRIVE IN PALESTINE (39')
1   TITLE IN HEBREW: FOLLOWING TALKS IN LONDON.

כותרת: אחרי שיחות לונדון. ד"ר חיים וייצמן וד. בן גוריון חוזרים ארצה

2   Boat approaching Tel Aviv port (long, 19).
3   Policemen and welcoming crowds waiting on dock (32).
4   Paula Ben Gurion and daughter (mid, 39).

☐ PART C: TITLE: SHOW-WINDOW COMPETITION FROM PALESTINE PRODUCTION (105')
1   TITLE IN HEBREW: MADE-IN-ISRAEL. THE LABOUR OF OUR HANDS SHOWS FAITH IN THE LAND.

סמל תוצרת הארץ עליו כתוב: תוצר הארץ. ידינו אמונה הארץ.

2   TITLE IN HEBREW: ECONOMIC SELF-DEFENCE. SHOP-WINDOW COMPETITION.

כותרת שניה: התגונננותינו הכלכלית. התחרות חלונות ראווה בארץ

3   TITLE IN HEBREW: JERUSALEM (18).   כותרת שלישית: ירושלים.
4   A street in Jerusalem (general view) dissolve to a display window (long, 25).
5   Display window (33).
6   Silk, Assis products (mid, 45).
7   TITLE IN HEBREW: IN HAIFA.
8   Windows with Shemen products. Fabrics by Kaddenstein. Bags, jewelry (mid, 84).
9   Interior of auditorium. Award ceremonies for the shop window competition. Mayor Israel Rokah of Tel Aviv distributes certificates (105).

☐ PART D: TITLE: ROAD CONSTRUCTION IN THE NORTH AREA OF PALESTINE (138')
1   TITLE IN HEBREW: WORK CAMP OF HISTADRUT WORKERS IN THE NAFTALI MOUNTAINS (ON THE NORTHERN BORDER)

כותרת: מחנה העבודה של ההסתדרות העובדים הלאומים בהרי נפתלי (בגבול הצפון).

2   Pan of mountains.
3   Tents.
4   Workers on trucks, moving stones. Tractor.
5   Workers eating loaves of bread.

☐ PART E: TITLE: HORSE SHOW AT JERUSALEM (138')

כותרת: התחרות רכיבה בירושלים (6)

1   Crowds watching, riders preparing, band playing (25).
2   Race begins, jumping competition, crowd, games while riding (104).
3   The riders passing in a line (mid, 126).
4   Distribution of prizes to winners (138).

■ **CARMEL NEWSREEL I-177** · April 22 1939
Hapoel sports day in a stadium in Tel Aviv.

☐ PART A: TITLE: HAPOEL SPORT DAY IN TEL AVIV (434')
1   TITLE IN HEBREW: THE FIRST NATIONAL SPORTS MEETING OF HAPOEL.

כותרת: הכנוס הארצי הראשון של פלונות "הפועל" (8)

2   Decorated outdoor stage (long, 16).

3   Teams marching in through the gate of the stadium with band and flags (long, 47).
4   Parade with flags. Additional teams marching. Girls marching (mid, 83).
5   Teams marching (from above, mid, c.u., 119).
6   General view of the stadium (long, 127).
7   Teams at attention holding flags. Pan of the stadium and the teams (long, 154).
8   From the Hapoel Center, entering the stadium (mid, 167).
9   Dov Hoz giving a speech. The heads of Hapoel Center among them Zalman Aranne (Aharonovich) (c.u., 178).
10  Alexander Ziskind Rabinowitz in the crowd (c.u., 183).
11  The teams march to the stage (long, 323).
12  Split-screen, one side marching, the other side exercising (mid, c.u., 372).
13  Calisthenics demonstrations (c.u., 382).
14  The teams marching (long, 415).
15  The heads of Hapoel and the Histadrut (mid, 420).
16  Teams arranged on the field (long, 434).

■ **CARMEL NEWSREEL I-178** · April 29 1939
Palestine Track and Field Championship. Meeting of the League Against Tuberculosis. Jewish refugees from Germany disembarking at Tel Aviv port. Betar Youth camp at Kiryat Aryeh.

☐ PART A: TITLE: PALESTINE TRACK AND FIELD CHAMPIONSHIP (124')
1   TITLE IN HEBREW: THE 1939 NATIONAL ERETZ ISRAEL COMPETITION OF ATHLETICS

כותרת: התחרויות לרבנאות הא"י באתלטיקה קלה לשנת 1939 (8)

2   Participants from schools dressing in stadium, crowd (29).
3   Heads of sport, one gives speech, the judges stand (mid, 36).
4   Competition begins. Girls long distance running (mid, long, 78).
5   Girls long distance jumping (long, 96).
6   Relay race (long, 111).
7   Line of trophies on table (mid, 114).
8   Woman distributing trophies (mid, 124).

☐ PART B: TITLE: ANTI-TUBERCULOSE [sic] MEETING IN TEL AVIV (35')

כותרת: ועידת הליגה למלחמה בשחפת בת"א (7)

1   People around tables (mid, 18).
2   Dr Mordechai Levinstein speaking. Yitzhak Sadeh among audience (mid, 35).

☐ PART C: TITLE: JEWISH IMMIGRANTS FROM GERMANY ARRIVE AT TEL AVIV HARBOUR (37')   כותרת: פליטי גרמניה עולים בנמל ת"א
1   Taking a sick person ashore by stretcher.
2   Immigrants disembarking (mid, 37).

☐ PART D: TITLE: YOUNG BETAR CAMP IN KIRYAT ARYEH (151')

כותרת: מחנה בית"ר הצעירה בקרית אריה

1   Pan of tents.
2   Line-up of youth in uniforms being inspected by adults in uniforms.
3   Marching band, drums, trumpets.
4   Children of various ages marching (151).

■ **CARMEL NEWSREEL I-179** · May 6 1939
The opening of the Carmel Market in Tel Aviv. Club for Yemenite Jewish women in Rehovot. The aviation school in Lod and graduation of the pilot course.

□ PART A: TITLE: THE OPENING OF THE NEW MARKET IN TEL AVIV (114')

כותרת: פתיחת השוק העירוני החדש בת"א (8)

1 Carmel Market (Shuk Ha'Aliya) (12).
2 Market stalls. People buying from stalls (114).

□ PART B: CLUB FOR YEMENITE JEWISH WOMEN IN REHOVOT
1 Pan of crowd seated on ground.
2 Close-ups of faces.
3 Man speaking.
4 Crowd walking through field.
5 Man explaining something about crops. Pan of people listening.
6 Sitting around table.

□ PART C: FORMAL OPENING OF AVIATION SCHOOL IN LOD. GRADUATION OF ETZEL PILOT COURSE (83')
1 Crowd gathered by the Lod airport building (long, 10).
2 Fireman band playing (mid, 16).
3 A parade of Betar Youth club. Their leader tells them to sit. Taking turns by the flag (mid, 31).
4 A plane lands (mid, 56).
5 High Commissioner Sir Harold MacMichael speaks. Zvi Shechterman (later a member of Knesset) by his side (mid, 60).
6 Rabbi Moshe Avigdor Amiel speaking. MacMichael shakes hands with Rabbi Ben Zion Meir Chai Uziel's (mid, 75).
7 MacMichael giving diplomas, shaking hands (mid, 83).

■ **CARMEL NEWSREEL I-180** · May 20 1939
Flower exhibition in Tel Aviv. Members of Maccabi delegation to Australia lay a wreath at the memorial for the Australian soldiers who died fighting for Palestine during World War I. HaNoar Ha'oved celebrates Lag Ba'omer. Views of Hadassah Hospital on Mount Scopus.

□ PART A: TITLE: EXHIBITION OF FLOWERS IN TEL AVIV (61')

כותרת: תערוכת פרחים בת"א (8)

1 Crowd looking at flowers.
2 Sa'adia Shoshani giving a speech (mid, 28).
3 Close-ups of flowers (61).

□ PART B: TITLE: MEMBERS OF MACCABI ORGANIZATION PRIOR TO DEPARTURE FOR AUSTRALIA (71')

כותרת: משלחת "המכבי" לקראת נסיעה לאוסטרליה

1 The Maccabi contingent laying a wreath at the memorial for the Australian soldiers who fought in Palestine. Other members stand at attention (mid, 47).
2 At military cemetery in Tel Aviv. Saying goodbye to the Australian consul (mid, 71).

□ PART C: TITLE: TRADITIONAL CELEBRATION OF LAG BA'OMER BY NOAR HAOVED IN TEL AVIV (70')     כותרת: חג המעלות לנוער העובד
1 Boys marching with the flags towards a gate with Hebrew banner: "Gate of the Torah". Pan of three gates, with Hebrew banners: "Torah", "Work", "Life" (long, 39).
2 A young girl reading a poem, marching through the gate of "Work" (long, 70).

□ PART D: HADASSAH MEDICAL CENTER ON MOUNT SCOPUS (100')
1 General view of Mount Scopus Medical Center, Jerusalem.

2   Buildings from all angles with dissolves.

■ **CARMEL NEWSREEL I-181** · May 27 1939
Shavuot first fruit festivities in a Tel Aviv kindergarten, a commercial high school, Yahalom School in Ramat Gan, Kiryat Haim and Petah Tikva.

◻ PART A: TITLE: FRUIT OFFERING FESTIVITIES IN PALESTINE (104')

כותרת: חג הבכורים תרצ"ט

1   TITLE IN HEBREW: TEL AVIV KINDERGARTENS (12)

כותרת: כת"א גני ילדים (12)

2   Children presenting first fruits, marching and singing (long, mid, 54).
3   Teachers dancing on stage and the children lifting up their baskets as offerings (assorted shots, 104).

◻ PART B: TITLE IN HEBREW: SHAVUOT CELEBRATIONS AT A COMMERCIAL HIGH SCHOOL IN TEL AVIV (217')

כותרת: חג הבכורים בביה"ס למסחר כת"א (5)

1   Girls with flowers (mid, 17).
2   Girl singing (mid, 139).
3   A play on the stage, by girls (long, 190).
4   The crowd in the schoolyard. The students sit down, receiving fruit offerings (mid, 217).

◻ PART C: TITLE IN HEBREW: SHAVUOT CELEBRATIONS IN RAMAT GAN (72')

כותרת: חג הבכורים ברמת-גן

1   Children walking outside the Yahalom School. The school principal, Rimalter, giving a speech (long, 33).
2   Avraham Krinitzi, Mayor of Ramat Gan, giving a speech (mid, 38).
3   A boy giving a speech. Children bring him baskets of fruit (mid, 72).

◻ PART D: TITLE IN HEBREW: SHAVUOT CELEBRATIONS IN KIRYAT HAIM (75')

כותרת: חג הבכורים בקרית-חיים

1   A decorated gate with Hebrew banner: "Welcome to the Bearers of First Fruits" (mid, 6).
2   Children with drums, marching. Children with baskets (mid, long, 49).
3   Children bringing their baskets to the stage (mid, 75).

◻ PART E: SHAVUOT CELEBRATONS IN PETAH TIKVA (134')
1   Plaza in Petah Tikva. Schoolchildren gathering and marching (long, 33).
2   Boy riding a horse, followed by children with decorated signs riding a donkey, followed by children parading with first fruits (mid, long, 60).
3   A wagon laden with fruit, on the way to the Maccabi Field in Petah Tikva (mid, 66).
4   TITLE IN HEBREW: MAYOR SHLOMO STAMPFER (71).

כותרת: ראש העיר שטמפפר

5   Mayor Stampfer giving a speech (mid, 78).
6   Children dancing by the municipality with baskets (mid, long, 134).

■ **CARMEL NEWSREEL I-182** · June 8 1939
Extensive survey of the construction and celebrations upon the completion of Metzudat Ussishkin, one of the settlements established in reaction to the British White Paper of May 1939.

□ PART A: TITLE IN HEBREW: BUILDING METZUDAT USSISHKIN, DAFNA DAN
(818') כותרת: הקמת מצודת אוסישקין, דפנה דן
1 DISSOLVE TO TITLES IN HEBREW: MUSIC: M. WILENSKY, WORDS: EMANUEL HAROUSI, SINGING: YEHUDAH REJNITSAV.

כותרות: מוסיקה: מ. וילנסקי, מילים: עמנואל הרוסי, הזמרה: יהודה ריז׳נייצב

2 A map of the Galilee with two points marked on it: Kibbutz Dafna and Kibbutz Dan.
3 Pan of a kibbutz. Tower and Stockade.
4 TITLE IN HEBREW: "MEZTUDAT USSISHKIN" (c.u., 57).

כותרת: מצודת אוסישקין

5 Volunteers' cars (77).
6 Cars leaving Tel Hai (85).
7 Running water (90).
8 Taking pipes off trucks in order to build a bridge (122).
9 Trucks drive on provisional bridge carrying equipment and people (160).
10 Mounted guards near the bridge (168).
11 Iris shot of water, dissolve to running water (187).
12 The completed bridge. Trucks cross over it (201).
13 Taking off pre-fab walls and other building materials from the trucks (234).
14 Building and clearing the area (mid, long, 209).
15 The British District Commissioner for the north comes to see the construction work (mid, 303).
16 Continuation of the construction work. The view from Kfar Giladi (mid, 312).
17 The tower is brought in (318).
18 Dignitaries arrive at the site, among them is Mr Weiss followed by Menachem Ussishkin walking with Ezrachi (mid, 332).
19 Weiss explaining to Ussishkin (mid, 337).
20 The tower with a sign on it reading: "Your Fortress Menachem - is our Fortress" (mid, c.u., 349).
21 Ussishkin addressing an audience that includes Weiss and his son (357).
22 Weiss talking with Leib Jaffe and Ussishkin (mid, 361).
23 Approaching a completed site (mid, 357).
24 French military men and their female companions come to see the raising of the tower (mid, 379).
25 Guests come to the tower with welcoming sign in Hebrew (384).
26 Arabs from the area join their new neighbours in a meal eating inside a tent (mid, 387).
27 The local Arabs receiving key money and signing legal documents in the crowded tent.
28 Pouring coffee into cups and serving (430).
29 Ploughing the recently purchased land with horses (462).
30 Tractors ploughing (mid, 508).
31 Bedouins put up a tent.
32 Sheep are brought in.
33 Officials arrive at the ceremony (mid, 528).
34 Eating (535).
35 Ghaffirs help the Arabs put up the tents (567).
36 Arriving at the completed site (572).
37 High-ranking military officials (mid, 575).
38 Weiss and Ussishkin (mid, 580).
39 The nearly completed site (590).
40 Finding an ancient stone in the area and part of an ancient column (596).
41 The work is completed and everyone goes to eat and see the fortress (long, 609).

42 Menachem Ussishkin plants a tree on the site (mid, 624).
43 The food is brought out (long, 649).
44 Dignitaries enjoying the meal, among them are French officers (mid, 666).
45 Arabs around the tent (680).
46 Bedouin women and children. The women preparing food (711).
47 Building the wall around the settlement (mid, 717).
48 Bedouin women cooking (mid, 720).
49 Construction.
50 An Arab man grounding coffee.
51 Bedouin women cooking.
52 Arabs and Jews eating with their hands (mid).
53 Guests arriving at the completed site (774).
54 Interior of people seated next to tables as they listen to Leib Jaffe speaking. Ussishkin and others applaud (mid, 803).
55 The tower decorated with flags. Signalling that the fortress is completed (mid, 818).

■ **CARMEL NEWSREEL I-183** · June 1939
Ramat Gan, from the ground and the air, including shots of homes, gardens, factories and children.

▫ PART A: TITLE: RAMAT GAN ONCE AND TODAY (613')

כותרת: רמת-גן יפת הנוף - סיור בעיר הגנים (10)

1 Ramat Gan aerial photograph (long, 32).
2 Two riders on horses passing on the outskirts of Ramat Gan, houses surrounded by gardens (60).
3 Buses in the streets. Houses (88).
4 HEBREW TITLE: REST HOMES.   כותרת: בתי הבראה
5 Relaxing in the garden, eating (135).
6 Gardens. A bridge in the garden. Walking in the garden. Flowers. Children playing (184).
7 Factories, chimney (190).
8 Children playing in the park. Fish in water (246).
9 Factories - paper, paper bags, sweets, natural silk, furniture, socks, rope and fabric (Yerushalmi Bros.) (454).
10 Delivering a speech. Employment office. Distribution of work assignments (484).
11 Children eating (c.u., 508).
12 Building (518).
13 Movie theatres (530).
14 HEBREW TITLE: IF WAR SHOULD BEFALL US (536)

כותרת: והיה כי תקראנה מלחמות

15 Digging for antiquities. Caves (584).
16 Vacationers, sunset, guards going out on duty (613).

■ **CARMEL NEWSREEL I-184** · June 24 1939
An exhibition at the Montefiore Technical High School in Tel Aviv. Dedication of the Young Mizrachi House in Tel Aviv. Celebration on board SS HAR ZION in port.

▫ PART A: TITLE: TECHNICAL EXHIBITION OF THE MONTEFIORE SCHOOL IN TEL AVIV (191')

כותרת: לקראת התערוכה הטכנית של בי"ס מונטיפיורי בת"א (8)

1 Children building model airplanes (mid, 18).
2 Welding (long, mid, 56).
3 Working in electronics workshop. Radio. Electrical circuits (mid, 112).

4  People entering, looking at the exhibits. Aviation, radio, electronics (164).
5  Boy exhibiting gas masks with chemicals. People looking at exhibits (mid, 191).

☐ PART B: TITLE: DEDICATION OF BETH ZEIROTH MIZRACHI IN TEL AVIV (64')
כותרת: חנוכת בית צעירות מזרחי בת"א (7)
1  Exterior of house (pan, 18).
2  Visitors, interior. Men and women sitting separately. Speeches (42).
3  Women ironing, writing letters, relaxing (64).

☐ PART C: TITLE: FESTIVAL ON BOARD THE *SS HAR-ZION* (136')
1  TITLE IN HEBREW: THE NATIONAL CONFERENCE FOR THE HEBREW NAVY ON BOARD THE *HAR ZION*.
כותרת: הכנוס הארצי למען הצי העברי על האוניה "הר-ציון" (8)
2  A small boat with visitors, approaching the large ship. Visitors embarking (long, 31).
3  Pan from the mast to the ship (54).
4  Jewish flag (75).
5  Press conference (80).
6  Bar Kochbah (Meyerowitz) speaking. Crowd listening. Speeches (115).
7  Dancing hora on board (136).

■ **CARMEL NEWSREEL I-185** · July 1 1939
Ceremony and parade in Jerusalem on the occasion of the installation of Rabbi Ben Zion Meir Chai Uziel as chief rabbi.

☐ PART A: TITLE: CORONATION OF RABBI UZIEL IN JERUSALEM (205')
1  TITLE IN HEBREW: A HOLIDAY FOR THE PEOPLE OF ISRAEL. CORONATION OF RABBI BEN ZION MEIR CHAI UZIEL AS THE CHIEF RABBI OF ERETZ ISRAEL AND RISHON LEZION.
כותרת: יום חג לכנסת ישראל בארץ. הכתרת הרב בן-ציון מאיר חי עוזיאל כתור רב ראשי לא"י וראשון לציון.
2  The streets of Jerusalem decorated, Hebrew banner. Crowd accompanying Rabbi Uziel, going down an alley towards the Western Wall. People on rooftops observing (long, 35).
3  Rabbi Uziel speaking (c.u., 128).
4  Profile of Rabbi Uziel speaking (c.u., 205).

■ **CARMEL NEWSREEL I-186** · July 15 1939
Reporters touring the ship *NEA HELLAS* in Tel Aviv port. The *OFEK* ship leaves for Egypt. The Yemenite Jewish Youth Camp at Nahalal.

☐ PART A: TITLE: VISIT OF JOURNALISTS ON BOARD *SS NEA HELLAS* IN TEL AVIV HARBOUR (124')
1  TITLE IN HEBREW: A DIRECT LINE FROM ERETZ ISRAEL TO AMERICA.
כותרת: ביקור עתונאים באוניה "ניה הללס". קו ישר א"י - אמריקה (9).
2  Ship (long, 18).
3  Visitors going from small boat to larger ship (long, mid, 32).
4  Tilt to the mast (long, 46).
5  Reporters touring the ship. The captain receiving flowers. Raising the Jewish flag (mid, 93).
6  Captain speaking. Pan of the ship (long, 124).

□ PART B: TITLE: THE *OFEK* BOAT DEPORT [sic] EGYPT (88')

כותרת: סירת "אופק" מפליגה מצרימה (6)

1 Boat leaving Tel Aviv Port. Affixing a mezuzah with hammer (mid, 47).
2 Mast decorated with flags. View of ship (long, 58).
3 Boat leaving the port (long, 88).

□ PART C: TITLE: CAMP OF YOUNG YEMENITE IN NAHALAL (84')
1 HEBREW TITLE: YEMENITE YOUTH CAMP AT NAHALAL.

כותרת: מחנה הנער התימני בנהלל

2 Boys doing exercise on wooden horse (long).
3 Girl peeling fruit.
4 Young men playing chess (mid).
5 Young man pushing young woman on swing.
6 Eating around table.
7 Dancing hora, shot through crowd (long, 84).

■ **CARMEL NEWSREEL I-187** · July 23 1939
An aria from *Tosca* sung in Hebrew by Edith Della Pergola. Clara Imas whistles a Romanian folk tune. Episodes from Jewish history presented by the pupils of the Safra School.

□ PART A: TITLE: ARIA FROM *TOSCA* SONG BY DELLA PERGOLA, AT THE PIANO DR JOCHANAN PAGENER (250')

כותרת: קטע מ"טוסקה" בעברית ע"י אדית דילה פרגולה. ע"י הפסנתר ד"ר יוחנן פגנר (10).

1 Three shots of the opera singer singing (long, mid, c.u., 250).

□ PART B: TITLE: *DOINA* WHISTLE BY CLARA IMAS (211')
1 TITLE IN HEBREW: ROMANIAN FOLK SONG, *DOINA*, WHISTLED BY CLARA IMAS (9).    כותרת: "דוניה" שיר עממי רומני שריקה ע"י קלרה אימס
2 Clara playing piano (mid, 32).
3 Clara begins to whistle (mid, 131).
4 Close-up of whistling (176).
5 Clara whistling (mid, 211).

□ PART C: EPISODES FROM JEWISH HISTORY PRESENTED BY PUPILS OF THE SAFRA SCHOOL (446')

כותרת: פרשיות מתולדות ישראל ע"י בית הספר ספרא (9)

1 Gymnastics in the schoolyard (long, 20).
2 TITLE: BY THE WATERS OF BABYLON (24).    כותרת: על נהרות בבל
3 Girls performing (mid, 98).
4 TITLE: ROMAN PERIOD (107)    כותרת: תקופת רומא
5 Scene of Jewish delegation visiting Rome (long, mid, 246).
6 TITLE: BY THE WAILING WALL (252)    כותרת: על יד הכותל המערבי
7 Scene by the wall (mid, 351).
8 TITLE: IN THE VALLEY OF ISRAEL TODAY (358)

כותרת: בעמק בימים אלה ...

9 Scene about work and guarding (mid, 446).

■ **CARMEL NEWSREEL I-188** · July 1939
Degel Zion convention in Haifa. Unveiling the Bialik Memorial in Ramat Gan. Completion of the Mishmar HaMaccabi leadership course. First graduates of the Afikim Aviation School.

## 154    *Carmel Newsreels: Series 1*

☐ PART A: TITLE: DEGEL ZION CONVENTION AT HAIFA (104')

כותרת: כנוס ארצי של "דגל ציון" בחיפה. (7)

1. Marching with flags (32).
2. Young men lined up, holding flags. Leader of the Degel Zion movement shaking hands with the commander (long, 58).
3. Raising the flag. Placing pins on lapels. Procession (mid, 104).

☐ PART B: TITLE: UNVEILING OF THE CH. N. BIALIK PLAQUETTE AT RAMAT GAN (48')      כותרת: גילוי ציון ח. נ. ביאליק ברמת גן

1. Mayor Avraham Krinitzi unveiling the memorial and giving a speech. Audience standing (mid, 37).
2. Group of authors (among them Fishman) (mid, 48).

☐ PART C: TITLE: THE MISHMAR HAMACCABI TRAINERS FINISH THEIR COURSE (94')      כותרת: סיום הקורס למדריכי "משמר מכבי" באצטדיון בת"א

1. Parade (long, 29).
2. Running obstacle course, demonstrating games with ball, jumping over fences. Crowd observing. Climbing down ropes (long, 94).

☐ PART D: TITLE: AWARD OF CERTIFICATES TO THE FIRST GRADUATES OF THE AVIATION SCHOOL IN AFIKIM (114')

כותרת: חלוקת התעודות לגומרי בי"ס לטיס באפיקים (9).

1. Convoy of cars. A small airplane looking for a place to land (long, 36).
2. Aerial photo of the Sea of Galilee and Tiberias (long, 54).
3. Pan of graduates receiving diplomas (long, 69).
4. Dov Hoz, Yitzhak Gruenbaum and Yitzhak Ben Ya'akov (mid, 87).
5. Pilots receiving diplomas (mid, 93).
6. Gruenbaum and Hoz observing airplanes. A plane taking off and disappearing (mid, long, 114).

■ **CARMEL NEWSREEL I-189** · August 5 1939

The students of the Haifa Naval School sailing in Haifa Bay. The immigrant tent camp of the Gordonia Ma'apilim group at Atlit. Fisherman on the Yarkon River at the Reading Station. The Hapoel Sports Association inaugurates a new training boat. The Palestine Maritime League delivers new rowing boats from Germany to the sports association.

☐ PART A: TITLE: THE HAIFA NAUTICAL SCHOOL (92')

כותרת: בי"ס הימי ליד הטכניון העברי בחיפה (7).

1. The students in naval uniform, parading in the courtyard of the Technion. Flag-raising with British and Jewish flags (long, 43).
2. Marching towards the camera (c.u., 53).
3. Sailors taking sails out of storage and bringing them down to the boats, preparing to sail.
4. Sailing in Haifa Bay (mid, long, 92).

☐ PART B: TITLE: GORDONIA MAAPILIM GROUP ON THE SHORE OF ATLITH (145')      כותרת: קבוצת מעפילים "גורדוניה" בעתלית.

1. Immigrant tent camp on the beach (long, 38).
2. The immigrants taking their boats out to sea. Sailing (mid, long, 83).
3. Raising the sails (c.u., 107).
4. On the beach, women laying out nets to dry (long, 118).
5. The boats in the water (mid, 128).
6. Four women drying and repairing nets (c.u., 145).

☐ PART C: TITLE: READING GROUP, TEL AVIV (73')
כותרת: קבוצת "רידינג" בחוף הירקון בת"א (7).
1. Tents on the banks of the Yarkon River, in the background Reading Station Building (long, 17).
2. Fisherman repairing a net. Yarkon Bridge in the background.
3. Fishermen repairing nets with a string of camels passing by in the background (long, mid, 30).
4. Placing nets in the water from a rowing boat. Men on shore pulling the nets (long, mid, 73).

☐ PART D: TITLE: INAUGURATION OF THE TRAINING SHIP *CHAIM ARLOSOROFF* OF THE HAPOEL SPORT ASSOCIATION (81')
כותרת: חנוכת ספינת הלימוד "חיים ארלוזורוב" (9).
1. Ship anchored. Ceremonial line-up of Hapoel. Pan of crowd (long, 28).
2. Zalman Aranne (Aharonowitz) speaking to the crowd. View of line-up (mid, c.u., 39).
3. Distributing certificates (mid, 45).
4. Preparing the ship to sail, sailing past smaller Hapoel boats (mid, long, 81).

☐ PART E: TITLE: THE PALESTINE MARITIME LEAGUE IS HANDING OVER THE BOATS RECEIVED FROM GERMANY (72')
1. TITLE IN HEBREW: CEREMONY OF THE HANDING OVER OF 21 BOATS TO THE SPORT ASSOCIATION BY THE PALESTINE MARITIME LEAGUE.
כותרת: טקס מסירת 21 סירות מגרמניה לאגודת הספורט בארץ ע"י חבל ימי לישראל (12).
2. Boats on the shore. Men in sailor suits, some in vests, near the boats. A representative from the Sport Association is inspecting (long, 44).
3. Taking the boats to the Yarkon River (mid, long, 65).
4. General view of the Yarkon with people rowing the boats (long, 72).

■ **CARMEL NEWSREEL I-190** · August 11 1939
Yishuv representatives depart for the Geneva Congress. Mayor Shlomo Stampfer of Petah Tikvah speaking at the cornerstone laying ceremony of a school for workers' children. Dedication of a Wizo building in Hadera.

☐ PART A: TITLE IN HEBREW: ERETZ ISRAEL REPRESENTATIVES TO THE GENEVA CONGRESS (84')      כותרת: צירי א"י לקונגרס בג'נבה (7).
1. Eliezer Kaplan, Yitzhak Gruenbaum, sitting on the plane.
2. Winding up the plane, the plane takes off (mid, long, 84).

☐ PART B: LAYING CORNERSTONE FOR A SCHOOL FOR CHILDREN OF WORKERS IN PETAH TIKVA (62')
כותרת: הנחת אבן-הפינה לבנין בי"ס לילדי עובדים כ-4 בתי חינוך בפתח-תקוה. (10).
1. Laying concrete by the guests.
2. Mayor Shlomo Stampfer speaking before the guests (62).

☐ PART C: DEDICATION OF WIZO DAY CAMP BUILDING, HADERA (88')
כותרת: חנוכת בית הקיטנות ע"י ויצו בחדרה.
1. An audience of adults and children listening to a female speaker.
2. Raising the Jewish flag.
3. Distribution of books.
4. Signalling with flags.
5. Assorted running games (88).

■ **CARMEL NEWSREEL I-191** · August 19 1939
Harvest in the Jezreel Valley, including farming, sheaves of wheat and celebrations at Merhavia. Singer Yehuda Rojnitsav.

□ PART A: TITLE: *HARVEST IN EMEK*. MUSIC: M. WILENSKY. TEXT: EMANUEL HARUSY. THE SINGER: J. RIAZANCEW (545')

כותרת: קציר בעמק יזראל. מוסיקה מ. וילנסקי. שיר הקציר מאת עמנואל הרוסי. הזמר יהודה רוז'ניצב. (34)

1 General view of the Jezreel Valley from Givat Zeid. Close-up of son of Alexander Zeid, a young man, sitting on a horse (45).
2 Field of wheat blowing in the wind.
3 Daughter of Tsvi Lieberman, a young woman, in the wheat field. Close-up of her face (71).
4 View of guards on horseback returning from guard duty through a field (mid, 76).
5 A combine, accompanied by a guard on horseback going out to the field (long, 103).
6 Young boy sitting on a farm machine pulled by two horses (c.u., long, 128).
7 A young man sharpening his scythe, cutting wheat. A line of harvesters (mid, c.u., 154).
8 Young man with pitchfork, gathering the harvest, loading the wagon. The wagon goes (mid, 178).
9 Pan of field. A combine approaches in the distance. Assorted views of combine. Young man closing sacks and throwing them from the combine. Combine moving, leaving behind straw and sacks (c.u., long, 288).
10 Young man with horse gathering the harvest into piles, loading them onto a wagon (long, 331).
11 A ghaffir guarding the sacks in the field (mid, 335).
12 Short shot of young woman. Arranging the bales into stacks. Horse circling, tied by rope, powering machine which makes bales (mid, long, 375).
13 General view of Merhavia. Dissolve to bales and pan of sacks. Warehouse (mid, 395).
14 Decorated tower. Slogan on Hebrew banner: "The Seed of the Harvest will Never Cease" (mid, 408). סיסמא על דגל: זרע קציר לא ישבת.
15 Guards on horses. Decorated wagons follow them to the field to celebrate the harvest festival. Wagon with children. Parade with sickles, girls with sheaves of wheat, youth orchestra (mid, long, 467).
16 Decorated combine. Youth carrying fruits. Wagon with lambs. Wagon with adorable babies (mid, long, 498).
17 Decorated tractors and cars passing. Wagon with children with recorders (mid, 517).
18 General view of Merhavia celebrating (long, 523).
19 Girls with sheaves of wheat dancing. Crowd watching (long, 545).

■ **CARMEL NEWSREEL I-192** · September 2 1939
A sailing competition between Haifa and Tel Aviv. A nursery school for children of working mothers is built in Hadera. Physical education training in Palestine.

□ PART A: SAILING COMPETITION BETWEEN TEL AVIV AND HAIFA (78')

כותרת: תחרויות שייט בין חיפה ותל-אביב (7).

1 The port of Haifa. The decorated building of the Zebulun nautical school (long, 42).
2 Boats sailing in the competition. Someone speaking before an audience on the shore (mid, 78).

□ PART B: NURSERY SCHOOL FOR CHILDREN OF WORKING MOTHERS (84')
כותרת: בנין גן-ילדים לילדי אמהות עובדות בחדרה. (8).
1  The exterior of the building. Nursery schoolchildren enter the building (long, 21).
2  Mothers and their children playing various games (mid, long, 36).
3  The children help with the construction of the building. Playing in the sand, carrying pails and pushing the wheelbarrow (mid, 84).

□ PART C: PHYSICAL EDUCATION IN ISRAEL (192')
כותרת: הכשרה גופנית בארץ.
1  The sportsmen leave their shacks and arrange themselves in lines in the courtyard for inspection (mid, 35).
2  General calisthenics. A running game (mid, long, 60).
3  Jumping over fences (long, 63).
4  Carrying "the wounded" on wooden planks (long, 99).
5  Lining up for inspection and exercises (long, 127).
6  Running to strategic points (long, 138).
7  Pan of the camp and its tents (long, 149).
8  Lining up next to the tents and performing exercises. Running and falling down.
9  Stick-fights while horseback riding (192).

■ **CARMEL NEWSREEL I-193** · September 9 1939
Ceremonial roof-raising of an orphanage in Ramat Gan. The official laying of the foundation for a religious school in Netanya. Swimming competition between the Haifa branch of Maccabi and the Tel Aviv branch in Bat Galim.

□ PART A: FESTIVE ROOF-RAISING CEREMONY FOR A NEW ORPHANAGE IN RAMAT GAN (152')   כותרת: טקס חגיגי של יציקת גג לבית יתומים ברמת-גן. (7).
1  Pan of construction work (mid, 25).
2  The orphans, escorted by women, arrive at the ceremony (mid, 50).
3  Preparing the roof as the children look on (mid, 88).
4  On the roof (mid, long, 121).
5  Children coming out of the building (mid, 152).

□ PART B: LAYING THE FOUNDATION STONE FOR A RELIGIOUS SCHOOL IN NETANYA (67')     כותרת: אבן הפינה לתלמוד - תורה החרדי בנתניה. (7).
1  Rabbi Ben Zion Meir Chai Uziel arrives and addresses the audience. Other rabbis are seated (mid, c.u., 35).
2  The seated rabbis, among them Rabbi Uziel (mid, 44).
3  Rabbi Uziel speaking.
4  The audience rises and listens (mid, 67).

□ PART C: SWIMMING COMPETITION BETWEEN THE TEL AVIV AND HAIFA BRANCHES OF MACCABI (216')
כותרת: התחרות שחיה בין מכבי חיפה - ת"א בכת-גלים. (8).
1  View from above of the pool and the audience. Maccabi officials arrive (mid, 33).
2  The swimmers dive into the pool and start to swim. The audience watching the various types of strokes (long, 107).
3  Water polo (mid, 148).
4  Diving off a diving board. Two divers jump at once (mid, 216).

■ **CARMEL NEWSREEL I-194** · September 16 1939
Civil defence exercise of air raid precautions and learning how to use gas masks.

Physical education camp for young women in Kfar Vitkin. Religious youth camp of Bnei Akiva in Bnei Brak.

☐ PART A: TITLE: AIR RAID PRECAUTIONS DISPLAY BY MAJOR A. D. SPARK N.C. (130')     כותרת: הצגתו של המאיור כהתגוננות נגד התקפת - אויר (9).
1  The Major speaking on a megaphone, people wearing gas masks. The Major demonstrating defence against gas (long, 46).
2  The Major puts an object in the middle of the courtyard and then explodes it (mid, 70).
3  The Major wearing a gas mask. People with gas masks and long sticks check the ground (mid, 95).
4  Continuing demonstration. Spreading cleaning agent (long, 130).

☐ PART B: TITLE: PHYSICAL EDUCATION CAMP (208')
1  TITLE IN HEBREW: ACTIVITIES OF THE PHYSICAL TRAINING DEPT. AFFILIATED WITH THE VA'AD LEUMI; PHYSICAL EDUCATION YOUTH CAMP AT KFAR VITKIN
כותרת: מפעולות המחלקה להכשרה גופנית שע"י הועד הלאומי מחנה הנוער לתרבות הגוף בכפר ויתקין (10).
2  Girls jumping over walls or obstacles (mid, 22).
3  Girls running bent over (mid, 29).
4  Girls carrying "wounded" on stretchers, giving first aid (long, 52).
5  Group running around the field (c.u., mid, 83).
6  Marching girls, calisthenics. Running obstacle course (long, mid, 208).

☐ PART C: TITLE: THE RELIGIOUS YOUTH CAMP OF BNEI AKIBA AT BNEI BRAK (189')     כותרת: מחנה הנוער הדתי בני עקיבא בכני ברק (7).
1  A boy washing. Boys, wearing tallit katan, running out of their tents and washing (mid, c.u., 27).
2  Flag-raising. Trumpet blowing (mid, 44).
3  Boys praying with prayer shawl and phylacteries. Reading from Torah scroll.
4  Scouting activities. Building tents (165).
5  Learning Mishnah inside a tent (mid, 189).

■ **CARMEL NEWSREEL I-195** · September 30 1939
The establishment of a new Tower and Stockade settlement, Kfar Netter, including the raising of the watchtower. Swimming lessons for schoolchildren in a pool.

☐ PART A: KFAR NETTER, A NEW SETTLEMENT (129')
כותרת: כפר נטר נקודת ישוב חדשה (8).
1  Pan of housing construction (assorted shots, 71).
2  People talking among themselves (c.u., 77).
3  Continuing the construction work (long, 86).
4  Raising the watchtower (long, 103).
5  Building wooden houses (long, 110).
6  Sitting before long tables, someone speaking (mid, 124).
7  A child on the tower (mid, 129).

☐ PART B: THE END OF A SWIMMING COURSE FOR SCHOOLCHILDREN (148')
1  The swimmers around the pool (mid, 12).
2  Swimming with kickboards in the pool (mid, 55).
3  Diving under the water. Someone getting out of the water (mid, 104).
4  Lesson in life-saving techniques (mid, 133).
5  Receiving certificates (mid, 148).

■ **CARMEL NEWSREEL I-196** · October 7 1939
15th anniversary of Hanoar Ha'oved. Mass naturalisations in Tel Aviv. Exhibition of air raid precaution accessories, including gas masks for civil defence.

□ PART A: TITLE IN HEBREW: FIFTEENTH ANNIVERSARY OF HANOAR HAOVED (85')　　　　　　　　　　　　　　　　　כותרת: ט"ו שנים הנוער העובד.
1　Exhibition of Hanoar Ha'oved in the Borochov neighbourhood.
　　　　　　　　　　　　כותרת: תערוכת הנוער העובד בשכונת בורוכוב (15).
2　Exhibition hall (85).

□ PART B: TITLE: MASS NATURALIZATIONS IN TEL AVIV (62')
　　　　　　　　　　　　　　　　　　כותרת: התאזרחות המונית בת"א (6).
1　Pan of Allenby Street. Long line outside naturalisation bureau (long, 26).
2　People standing, sitting on chairs, woman knitting (long, 62).

□ PART C: TITLE: EXHIBITION OF THE AIR RAID PRECAUTION ACCESSORIES (224')　　　　　　　　　　כותרת: תערוכת התגוננות נגד התקפות אויר (10).
1　Equipment for protection against gas. Gas masks and dummies dressed in clothes against gas warfare (mid, 25).
2　Signs about the dangers of gas. Equipment (mid, 42).
3　Gas bomb (mid, 54).
4　Sketches of buildings (mid, 66).
5　Protective tents, sketches of shelters. Signs.
6　Demonstration of an explosion and protective equipment. Signs.
7　Protective garments and gas masks (174).
8　Demonstrating putting on gas masks (c.u., 203).
9　Dummy wearing protective garments (mid, 224).

■ **CARMEL NEWSREEL I-197** · October 14 1939
A parade for the first anniversary of the Civil Guard in Tel Aviv. Training of Maccabi Hatzair youth leaders in Rehovot. Parade of Jewish Brigade Officers.

□ PART A: TITLE: THE ANNIVERSARY CELEBRATION OF THE CIVIL GUARD AT TEL AVIV (64')　　　　　　　　　　　　　כותרת: שנה למשמר האזרחי
1　Mayor Israel Rokah presents the flag to the commander of the Civil Guard. The Civil Guard marching in the Tel Aviv stadium (mid, 52).
2　Mayor speaking to crowd (c.u., 57).
3　The Civil Guard marches past (mid, 63).
4　The Civil Guard accompanied by a band march down Allenby Street in Tel Aviv (long, 64).

□ PART B: TITLE: END-OF-COURSE CELEBRATION, THE YOUNG MACCABI TRAINERS AT REHOVOT (138')
　　　　　　　כותרת:סיום הקורס הארצי של מדריכי מכבי הצעיר ברחובות (8).
1　General view of the tent camp of the trainers (19).
2　Training exercises, young men running, climbing poles, jumping over obstacles, crawling under obstacles, balancing on a beam (138).

□ PART C: PARADE OF JEWISH LEGION OFFICERS (81')
1　Marching with banners which proclaim in Hebrew: "For the Jewish Legion" (59).　　　　　　　　　　　　　　　　　　שלט: למען הגדוד העברי
2　The parade passes in Mugrabi Square (81).

■ **CARMEL NEWSREEL I-198** · October 28 1939
Women demonstrating first aid techniques at a Magen David Adom branch in Ramat Gan. Graduation ceremonies of the first class of the School of Law and Economics in Tel Aviv. The picking and packing of citrus fruit. Infant care in Rehovot. An after-school club for children in Jerusalem.

□ PART A: TITLE: THE OPENING OF MAGEN DAVID ADOM BRANCH AT RAMAT GAN (102')
1　TITLE IN HEBREW: THE OPENING OF THE BRANCH OF MAGEN DAVID ADOM IN THE BOROCHOV NEIGHBOURHOOD IN RAMAT GAN

כותרת: פתיחת סניף מגן דוד אדום שכ' בורוכוב כר"ג והסביבה (7).

2　Women demonstrating first aid, care of wounded, artificial respiration, bandaging (55).
3　The heads of Haganah with heads of Magen David Adom inspecting parade (long, 69).
4　Distribution of certificates to young women who have completed the para-medical course (102).

□ PART B: TITLE: AWARD OF CERTIFICATES TO THE FIRST GRADUATES OF THE SCHOOL OF LAW AND ECONOMY [sic] AT TEL AVIV (72')

כותרת: סיום המחזור הראשון כביה"ס למשפט וכלכלה בת"א (8).

1　Ceremonies in the courthouse in Tel Aviv. Audience and judges, speeches. Applause.
2　Distribution of diplomas to the new lawyers, including one woman (72).

□ PART C: TITLE: THE CITRUS SEASON FRUIT IN PALESTINE (49')

כותרת: עונת פרי הדר החלה (5).

1　Women picking citrus fruit (dissolve, mid, 19).
2　Packing fruit in crates (long, 27).
3　Donkeys carrying the crates to the packing house (42).
4　Women wrapping the fruit (long, 49).

□ PART D: TITLE: THE BABY HOME AT REHOVOT (84')

כותרת: בית תינוקות ברחובות (6).

1　General view of building (long, 15).
2　Close-ups inside the home, baby crying, woman approaches, picks up, bathes the baby in a tub (40).
3　Women feeding babies (c.u., mid, 58).
4　Babies sitting on potties (mid, 68).
5　A row of cribs; close-up of baby sleeping (84).

□ PART E: TITLE: AFTERNOON CHILDREN'S CLUB IN JERUSALEM (70')

כותרת: קלוב ילדים בירושלים (8).

1　Children entering (mid, 16).
2　Sitting in classroom, going up to the board, close-up of a girl writing (32).
3　Children doing homework, arts and crafts (mid, 53).
4　Children exercising in a group (mid, 70).

■ **CARMEL NEWSREEL I-199** · November 11 1939
A roller-skating competition for children in Tel Aviv. Shepherding sheep in Mishmar Ha'Emek. An after-school club for children in Tel Aviv.

□ PART A: ROLLER SKATES COMPETITION IN TEL AVIV (159')
1　Children skating in a race. Crowds watching. Young men doing fancy skating (120).

2   Circle dance on skates (159).

□ PART B: TITLE: THE JEWISH SHEPHERD (43')
כותרת: הרועה העברי כמשמר העמק (8).
1   A shepherd (appears to be a girl) and flock pass by the camera. A girl on a donkey is accompanying the sheep (43).

□ PART C: TITLE: TEL AVIV CHILDREN IN THE AFTERNOON HOURS (140')
כותרת: מועדון לילדי תל אביב בשעות אחרי הצהרים (5).
1   Pan of children eating, drinking. Little girls washing dishes. Little boy clearing counter (mid, 56).
2   Preparing lessons. Assorted close-ups.
3   Woman reading story to children.
4   Nurses bandaging boy's hand.
5   Boy making toy house (117).
6   Children playing "blind man's bluff". Close-ups of laughing faces (140).

■ **CARMEL NEWSREEL I-200** · November 18 1939
Refugee children arriving at the Ahava agricultural school in Kiryat Bialik. Refugee children in a camp on the beach in Netanya. Illegal immigrants from the ship *PARITA* released from Sarafend Detention Camp.

□ PART A: TITLE: HOME FOR CHILDREN "AHAVA" AT KIRYAT BIALIK (301')
כותרת: בית ספר אהבה בקרית ביאליק (20).
1   Entrance to school. A pan of the farm and buildings (long, 104).
2   Youth, coming from port, disembarking from buses at the school (long, 59).
3   Sitting by long tables, outside, two boys playing stringed instruments (possibly the balalaika) (long, 75).
4   Girl in apron ringing bell. Youth walking past the dining room (long, 127).
5   Boy working in woodshop (long, 146).
6   Working with cows, milking, girl feeding caged chickens (long, 181).
7   Boy ploughing with horse. Girls picking vegetables. Harvesting clover (long, mid, 228).
8   Picking vegetables. Outdoor lessons around long tables (mid, 301).

□ PART B: TITLE: THE CHILDREN'S CAMP AT NETANYA (189')
כותרת: המחנה בנתניה. (6).
1   Young children, some with shaven heads, walk past; some salute the camera. Children, now in bathing suits, run out of a small wooden building towards an outdoor shelter with long tables (long, 87).
2   Children running down to beach in Netanya. Playing in the water (long, 113).
3   Children on the beach, dancing hora, shot from above. Children exercising. Children in a circle being given milk in little glass bottles (mid, 163).
4   Pan of beach and Mediterranean Sea. Close-ups of individual children's faces. Group of faces (c.u., 189).

□ PART C: IMMIGRANTS FROM THE SHIP *PARITA*, LIBERATED FROM PRISON (107')
1   Group of men in European clothing, crowded around a man speaking, outside a warehouse building (long).
2   Men gathering luggage, lining up, walking through gate, past camera (mid).
3   Men dancing hora. Surrounded by men watching (long).
4   Boarding transport vehicles, loading luggage on top (long, mid).
5   Vehicles on city street. Men being greeted by crowd. Couple kissing passionately. Bearded man holding small Torah scroll, wrapped in tallit (107).

## CARMEL NEWSREEL I-201 · November 25 1939
Volunteers for the Czech Army, at Sarafend Army Camp, before they leave for the front. First anniversary celebrations for Kfar Geulim. A ghaffir (Jewish Settlement Police) parade in Jerusalem.

☐ PART A: TITLE: THE HANDLING [sic] OVER OF THE FLAG TO THE CZECH VOLUNTEERS BEFORE THEY LEAVE FOR THE WAR FRONT (291')

כותרת: טכס מסירת דגל למתנדבים לצבא הצ׳כי בסרפנד לפני צאתם לחזית (10).

1. General view of Sarafend and the volunteers, mainly in civilian dress (32).
2. Standing in line, plates and cups in hand, to get food. Eating (mid, long, 59).
3. The volunteers, in civilian clothes, marching, lined up (long, 86).
4. Speech. A colonel standing next to the speaker (mid, 106).
5. The Czech consul speaks in Czech (162).
6. The volunteer soldiers and commanders stand at attention (203).
7. Volunteer brings a flag and passes it to three volunteers. Kissing flag. Standing at attention (long, 250).
8. Army officers in uniform inspecting the line-up. The flag passes between the lines. Marching past the podium (291).

☐ PART B: TITLE: ANNIVERSARY FESTIVITIES AT KFAR GEULIM (61')
1. TITLE IN HEBREW: ONE YEAR ANNIVERSARY CELEBRATION OF THE SETTLEMENT OF KFAR GEULIM IN THE NORTHERN SHARON AREA.

כותרת: חגיגה למלאות שנה להתישבות לכפר גאולים למקום התישבותו בשרון הצפוני (9).

2. Flags on tower building (tilt down). Speakers on porch of tower.
3. Crowd below listening. Close-up of speakers, possibly including Pinchas Sapir (44).
4. Group dancing hora, shot from above.
5. Pan of a newly planted orchard (long, 61).

☐ PART C: GHAFFIR (JEWISH SETTLEMENT POLICE) PARADE IN JERUSALEM (96')
1. Line-up of policemen. Marching in lines. Parade exercises with rifles (long, 44).
2. Commanders observe parade exercises. Inspect rows (long, 69).
3. Marching (mid, 96).

## CARMEL NEWSREEL I-202 · December 1939
Laying of foundation stone for boat station at Zebulun Sailing Club in Herzliyah. A school kitchen and cafeteria run by the Parents' Committee of a Tel Aviv school. Scouts' activities in Haifa.

☐ PART A: TITLE: THE LAYING OF THE CORNERSTONE OF THE ZEBULUN BOAT STATION AT HERZLIYAH (78')

כותרת: הנחת אבן-הפינה לתחנות סירות "זבולון" בהרצליה (9).

1. View of beach, including ocean. Youth waving flags and banners, followed by large crowd, including Zebulun members (long, 46).
2. Speech. Laying the stone. Crowd watching (long, 78).

☐ PART B: TITLE: THE PUBLIC SCHOOL PUPILS' KITCHEN AND LUNCH ROOM AT TEL AVIV (94')

כותרת: מטבח והמסעדות של ועד ההורים המרכזי שע"י בתי ספר עממים בתל אביב

1. Preparing meals in large pots at central kitchen. Putting food in containers and

loading on trucks for distribution to schools (mid, 49).
2  Groups of children sitting around tables, getting food and eating. Assorted pans (mid, long, 94).

□ PART C: TITLE: THE BOY SCOUTS' PARADE AT HAIFA (149')
כותרת: מפקד הצופים בחיפה (8)
1  Boy and girl scouts exercising (mid, 46).
2  Scouting activities. Making tents from blankets and stones.
3  Flag-raising (mid, 102).
4  First aid practice. Girls carrying girl on stretcher, bandaging (mid, 121).
5  Learning how to signal with flags (mid, 149).

■ **CARMEL NEWSREEL I-203** · December 1939/January 1940
Funeral of Zionist leader S Van Vriesland. Laying of foundation stone of central buildings in Tsur Moshe. Sowing ceremonies in Kibbutz Karit at Kfar Menachem.

□ PART A: TITLE: THE FUNERAL OF MR VAN VRIESLAND (51')
כותרת: לוויית ז. ואן פריזלנד ז"ל (6)
1  Pan of large crowd of European-looking men in suits and hats crowded in street around hearse.
2  Boys in sailor tops carrying wreaths followed by crowd (long, 51).

□ PART B: TITLE: LAYING OF FOUNDATION STONE OF THE FIRST HOUSES IN TSUR MOSHE (85')    כותרת: הנחת אבן הפינה לבתים הראשונים בצור-משה (7)
1  Crowd gathering around welcome banner in empty field (long, 40).
2  Signing document. Menachem Ussishkin speaking (long, 40).
3  Crowd watching as hole is dug for cornerstone. Several members of crowd shovel in dirt. Eating around tables (85).

□ PART C: TITLE: SOWING FESTIVITIES OF THE KRITH KIBBUTZ AT KFAR MENACHEM (139')    כותרת: חגיגת הזריעה של קבוץ "כרית" בכפר מנחם. (8)
1  Trucks full of people arriving (mid, 41).
2  Sitting around tables outside (mid, 55).
3  Speech, choir (mid, 69).
4  Tractors with planting attachments drive out to the field, accompanied by the crowd (mid, 96).
5  The machine planting, crowd walks behind, including man carrying a camera (c.u., mid, 139).

■ **CARMEL NEWSREEL I-204** · December 1939/January 1940
Inauguration of an orthodox youth village, near Kfar Hassidim. Reunion of immigrants from *SS RUSLAN*. Car accident on the Haifa-Tel Aviv highway. Parade and sports exhibition of Hapoel, Tel Aviv.

□ PART A: TITLE: THE INAUGURATION OF AN ORTHODOX YOUTH FARM NEAR KFAR HASSIDIM (30')    כותרת: חנוכת כפר הנוער הדתי ע"י כפר-חסידים (7).
1  Pan of the buildings in the village (long, 17).
2  Buses on the way to the village (long, 30).

□ PART B: TITLE: IMMIGRANTS FROM *SS RUSLAN* CELEBRATING THEIR REUNION (54')    כותרת: פגישה חגיגית של עולי "רוסלאן" בתל-אביב (8)
1  A hall filled with tables. Prosperous-looking middle-aged people around the tables (54).

164   *Carmel Newsreels: Series 1*

☐ PART C: TITLE: ACCIDENT ON THE HAIFA-TEL AVIV ROAD (46')

כותרת: תאונת דרכים בכביש חיפה תל-אביב (6).

1   A van and cars wrecked by side of road (long, 46).

☐ PART D: TITLE: PARADE OF THE HAPOEL IN TEL AVIV (115')

כותרת: מסדר חניגי של "הפועל" בת"א (6).

1   Members of Hapoel entering the field for a line-up (mid, 40).
2   Various teams, some in uniform, including children, marching in. Crowd watching (mid, 58).
3   A line of young people with flags (long, 64).
4   General exercising. Boxing. Jumping over obstacles. Fencing (mid, 106).
5   Marching (long, 115).

■ **CARMEL NEWSREEL I-205** · January 1940
Press conference at the Yahalom oven factory in Tel Aviv. Tigers in Tel Aviv Zoo.

☐ PART A: TITLE: JOURNALISTS VISIT THE NEW OVEN FACTORY AT TEL AVIV (116')   כותרת: ביקור עתונאים בכית חרושת לתנורים "יהלום" בתל-אביב (9).

1   Journalists around table. Someone giving explanation of products (long, 28).
2   Stages of production, including welding, painting, baking (mid, 106).
3   Director exhibiting finished product (mid, 116).

☐ PART B: TITLE: NEWS IN THE TEL AVIV ZOO (48')

כותרת: פנים חדשות בגן החיות בתל-אביב (7).

1   The zoo-keeper playing with two tigers (mid, c.u., 48).

■ **CARMEL NEWSREEL I-206** · January 1940
A project of the Municipality of Ramat Gan, encouraging citizens to raise vegetables as part of the war effort.

☐ PART A: TITLE: EXEMPLARY VEGETABLES GROWING IN RAMAT GAN FOR EMERGENCY TIME. MUSIC: M. WILENSKI (539')

כותרת: מצוק העתים / מפעל ירקות למופת לשעת-חרום ברמת-גן. מוסיקה: משה וילנסקי. (19).

1   Printing presses printing newspapers. Hebrew newspaper headlines urging civil co-operation in time of crisis. *Davar, Ha'aretz, Haboker* (mid, 41).
2   Hebrew poster from the Ramat Gan Municipality urging the growing of vegetables on open lots (long, 70).
3   Poster announcing a tour of gardens (long, 88).
4   Erecting barbed wire fences around empty lots. Ploughing, planting, working (long, 134).
5   Pan of the vegetable garden. People going out to work in the garden. Chopping down trees in deserted orchards (long, 180).
6   HEBREW TITLE: "HE WHO PLANTS IN TEARS, REAPS IN JOY".

כותרת: הזורעים בדמעה ברינה יקצורו (192).

7   Plots of ripe vegetables, water sprinklers and ditch irrigation (mid, long, 265).
8   Picking vegetables (mid, 321).
9   Pan of empty lots in Ramat Gan planted with vegetables (long, 341).
10  Group touring vegetable gardens.
11  Avraham Krinitzi, Mayor of Ramat Gan, calling citizens to grow vegetables.
12  Horse-drawn wagons laden with vegetables (mid, 384).
13  Dining room for needy.
14  Adults eating in a restaurant.
15  Bringing cooked vegetables to children (mid, long, 440).

16  Vegetable cooking lesson (mid, 470).
17  Meals ready for children. Schoolchildren getting food and eating (mid, 479).
18  TITLE IN HEBREW: "HOW GOOD IS A MEAL OF VEGETABLES AND THE LOVE OF GOD" (514).   כותרת: טוב ארוחת ירק ואהבה שם.
19  Preparing seedlings. Men and women working in vegetable garden (mid, 539).

■ **CARMEL NEWSREEL I-207** · January 27 1940
Planting a Tu B'shvat forest in memory of Zusia Shechory at Kfar Chaim. Schoolchildren planting trees. New worker settlement at Heftzibah near Hadera. Tiberias Hot Springs.

□ PART A: TITLE: FIFTEENTH OF SHEVAT CELEBRATIONS (115')
1  TITLE IN HEBREW: HOLIDAY OF TREE PLANTING. PLANTING IN THE FOREST IN MEMORY OF ZUSIA SHECHORY AT KFAR CHAIM IN HEFER VALLEY.
כותרת: חג הנטיעות בארץ. נטיעת יער על שם זוסיה שחורי בכפר חיים עמק חפר
2  Children marching with seedlings in their hands. Little children with crowns of flowers (mid, 43).
3  Family of Zusia Shechory, friends and members of the Haganah planting trees (mid, 76).
4  Little children planting seedlings in a field (mid, 115).

□ PART B: TITLE IN HEBREW: IN RAMAT GAN (86')   כותרת: ברמת גן
1  Students with seedlings in their hands, go to plant (long, 25).
2  By a gate, three youths speaking to group (mid, 46).
3  Children planting trees, assorted angles (mid, 86).

□ PART C: TITLE: BEGINNING CONSTRUCTION OF WORKERS SETTLEMENTS AT HEFTZIBAH, NEAR HADERA (103')
כותרת: לקראת ישוב פועלים חדש בחפציבה (ע"י חדרה) (9).
1  Crowd walking.
2  Camels laden with wooden boxes.
3  Guests arriving and looking at the settlement under construction.
4  Close-up of two guests speaking to each other.
5  Pan of crowd (71).
6  Laying the foundation stone.
7  Each guest throwing cement into the hole (92).
8  General view of area. Guest walking on the road, surrounded by sand dunes (103).

□ PART D: TITLE: THE SEASON AT HAMEI TIBERIAS (TIBERIAS HOT SPRINGS) (106')   כותרת: עונת הרחצה בחמי טבריה
1  General view of Tiberias (long, 35).
2  Tiberias Hot Springs. Garden outside the bathhouse (61).
3  Bus arrives, bathers getting off bus and entering bathhouse (106).

■ **CARMEL NEWSREEL I-208** · February 3 1940
A hike around Kibbutz Nir David (Tel Amal) on its third birthday, including fishponds, chickens and vineyards, with the mountains of Gilboa in background.

□ PART A: TITLE: 3RD ANNIVERSARY OF TEL-AMAL, SONG *TEL-AMAL* BY N. ALTERMAN (456')
כותרת: שלוש שנים להתישבות החדשה "ניר-דוד (תל-עמל)" הכבורה בנקודות החדשות. שיר תל-עמל: נתן אלתרמן. מוסיקה: מרדכי זעירא (24).

1  TITLE IN HEBREW: MUSIC BY MORDECHAI ZEIRA.
2  TITLE IN HEBREW: HIKE FROM BEIT ALPHA TO TEL AMAL.

כותרת: טיול מבית אלפא לתל-עמל (29).

3  General view. Students going down to the fishponds (long, 89).
4  Group leader talking to youth (mid, 91).
5  Fishponds. Group walks past ponds and arrives at Kibbutz Nir David (long, 130).
6  Group enters the kibbutz. Cows. The mountains of Gilboa in the background (long, 145).
7  Pulling full nets out of water (long, 169).
8  Sitting by fishponds (long, 192).
9  Group leader speaking (c.u., 202).
10  The youths listen to him (mid, long, 230).
11  The stream, plants, Mount Gilboa (long, 235).
12  Group leader continues talking (c.u., 251).
13  Youths listening. Fishermen working in background. Bringing in nets (long, 342).
14  Walking by fish ponds (long, 350).
15  Girls working in vineyard (long, 371).
16  Taking care of chickens (mid, 387).
17  Leader talking. Ducks in stream. The group swimming. General view of stream (mid, long, 446).
18  By a memorial (long, 456).

■ **CARMEL NEWSREEL I-209** · February 11 1940
Floods in Tel Aviv. Innovation in chicken raising at Mikveh Israel. Gas mask distribution to children.

☐ PART A: TITLE: THE LAST FLOOD AT TEL AVIV (85')

כותרת: השטפון האחרון בסביבות תל אביב (8).

1  Pan of the Montefiore neighbourhood covered in water. Horse-drawn carriage driving through water (long, 43).
2  People standing. A box floating on the water, being pulled by current. People lined up for boat to other side of street (long, 66).
3  Firemen carrying women on their shoulders. Houses in the water (mid, long, 85).

☐ PART B: TITLE: INNOVATION...CHICKEN COOP...ISRAEL (47')
1  TITLE IN HEBREW: AN INNOVATION AT MIKVEH ISRAEL - EYEGLASSES FOR THE CHICKENS.

כותרת: חידוש בלול במקווה ישראל. משקפיים לתרנגולות (9).

2  Close-up of chickens with glasses. Man holding glasses. Lots of chickens with glasses (c.u., 47).

☐ PART C: TITLE: DISTRIBUTION OF GAS MASQUES [sic] FOR TEL AVIV CHILDREN (67')      כותרת: חלוקת מסכות גאז לילדי בי"ס בת"א (7)
1  Children trying on gas masks. Children standing in line (mid, c.u., 37).
2  Children wearing gas masks (c.u., 51).
3  A fire engine leaving. A very cute little boy speaks (c.u., 67).

■ **CARMEL NEWSREEL I-210** · February 24 1940
Inauguration ceremonies for new roads in Kfar Saba. Former British High Commissioner Sir Herbert Samuel visiting in Tel Aviv. Ceremony on the occasion of the completion of the first 40 houses in Kiryat Ono (Kfar Ono). Australian and New Zealand Armed Corps in Tel Aviv.

□ PART A: TITLE: FESTIVITIES FOR THE OPENING OF THE NEW ROADS IN KFAR SABA (149')   כותרת: חגיגת הפתיחה של הכבישים החדשים בכפר סבא (10).
1   Spectators, children lining up (long, 14).
2   People arriving, among them Pinchas Sapir. Children carrying palm branches (long, 51).
3   General view. Children in the square, lined up for parade. Pan of Kfar Saba streets lined with children doing gymnastics (long, 98).
4   Speaker with megaphone on roof. Gymnastics (long, 109).
5   Heads of the police. Dignitaries approach ribbon and cut it (mid, 129).
6   Guests planting trees next to road (mid, 149).

□ PART B: TITLE: VISCOUNT HERBERT SAMUEL AT TEL AVIV (64')
כותרת: לורד הרברט סמואל בת"א (9).
1   Tall building. Sir Herbert Samuel received by hosts, including Tel Aviv Mayor Israel Rokah. Samuel enters building. Shaking hands (c.u.).
2   Samuel entering car after tour (64').

□ PART C: INAUGURATION OF THE FIRST 40 HOUSES IN KIRYAT ONO (71')
כותרת: חנוכת 40 הבתים הראשונים בכפר אונו
1   General pan of Kiryat Ono and the first houses (long, 19).
2   Residents by their houses. Gathering together for the celebration.
3   Placing cement for the cornerstone of additional houses (long, mid, 64).
4   People sitting at tables (long, 71).

□ PART D: TITLE: VISITORS FROM THE OTHER SIDE OF THE GLOBE: AUSTRALIANS IN TEL AVIV (52')   כותרת: החיילים האוסטרלים בת"א
1   A line of buses filled with soldiers, arriving at the exhibition field.
2   Soldiers leaving buses and walking around the streets of the city (long, 52).

■ **CARMEL NEWSREEL I-211** · February/March 1940
High Commissioner Sir Harold MacMichael visits Petah Tikva. The mechanised dairy industry, including milking, processing and the milk reaching the consumer. Making improvements on the beach facilities at Tel Aviv.

□ PART A: TITLE: HIS EXCELLENCY, THE HIGH COMMISSIONER FOR PALESTINE VISITING PETAH TIKVA (39')   כותרת: ביקור הנציב העליון בפתח תקוה (8).
1   High Commissioner MacMichael received by Mayor Shlomo Stampfer. They enter the municipal hall.
2   Greeted by crowds on their way out (long, 39).

□ PART B: TITLE: THE MILK PROCESSING IN THE DAIRIES OF PALESTINE (224')
כותרת: מן הרפת לצרכן - ייצור החלב בארץ
1   Large cowshed. Men and women coming to milk cows. Close-up of hand milking (57).
2   Pouring milk into containers. Loading containers onto a truck. Truck driving, arriving at new Tnuva dairy plant, on the Petah Tikva road (long, 102).
3   Pouring the milk into troughs (long, 122).
4   Mechanised production line, assorted machinery (long, 152).
5   Bottles filled with cream and milk (c.u., 177).
6   Machinery (long, 202).
7   People eating milk products in a restaurant. Women and a girl drinking milk (mid, 224).

□ PART C: TITLE: IMPROVEMENTS ON THE SEA-SHORE AT TEL AVIV (80')
כותרת: לקראת שיפורים על שפת הים בת"א
1   Large crowd on Tel Aviv beach (long, 18).
2   Beach promenade. Beach improvements. Work on pavements and gardens (long, 80).

■ CARMEL NEWSREEL I-212
Number omitted in the original listing.

■ CARMEL NEWSREEL I-213 · March 30 1940
The raising of sheep on a kibbutz in the Jezreel Valley. Lovely footage interspersed with relevant biblical verses, including shots of children with sheep, sunrise and a view of Mount Hermon.

□ PART A: TITLE: *THE JEWISH SHEPHERD*. MUSIC M. WILENSKY (560').
1   TITLE IN HEBREW: WORDS; YA'AKOV RIMON. SINGING; SHELI SHARONA.
כותרת:"הרועה בגליל" דיסולב לכותרת: מוסיקה: מ.וילנסקי. דיסולב -
מלים: יעקוב רימון, שירה: שלי שרונה.
2   TITLE: FOR THE MEN ARE SHEPHERDS FOR THEIR TRADE HATH BEEN TO FEED CATTLE; AND THEY HAVE BROUGHT THEIR FLOCKS AND THEIR HERDS. (Genesis 46:32). TITLE: AND ABEL WAS A KEEPER OF SHEEP BUT CAIN WAS A TILLER OF SOIL. (Genesis 4:2)
כותרת: "והאנשים רעו צאן כי אנשי מקנה היו וצאנם ובקרם וכל אש להם הביאו".(בראשית מו:32). דיסולב לפסוק אחר: "ויהי הבל רועה צאן וקין היה עובד אדמה" (בראשית ד:3).
3   TITLE IN HEBREW: "IF YOU DO NOT KNOW, OH FAIREST AMONG WOMEN, FOLLOW IN THE TRACKS OF THE FLOCK AND PASTURE YOUR KIDS BESIDES THE SHEPHERD'S TENT". (The Song of Songs 1:8).
כותרת: דיסולב ל - "אם לא תדעי לך היפה בנשים, צאי לך בעקבי הצאן ורעי את גדיתיך על משכנות הרעים" (שיר השירים א:8).
4   TITLE IN HEBREW: "FIFTY YEARS AGO, THERE WAS ONLY ONE HEBREW FLOCK IN THE LAND OF ISRAEL, WITH 60 HEAD OF SHEEP".
5   TITLE IN HEBREW: "AND SINCE THE BEGINNING OF THE GREAT ALIYAH, AFTER WORLD WAR, KEREN HAYESOD BEGAN THE GREAT PROJECT OF SETTLING ON KEREN KAYEMET LAND, SHEEP RAISING HAS BEEN MADE A WORK BRANCH ON THE KIBBUTZ FARMS OF JEZREEL VALLEY".
לפני חמישים שנה, היה רק עדר עברי אחד בארץ ישראל, ובו 60 ראשי צאן. ומהתחילה העליה הגדולה אחרי המלחמה העולמית האחרונה, וקרן היסוד במפעל התחילה ההתישבותי הגדול על אדמת הקרן הקימת הוכנס ענף של גידול צאן לרוב המשקים הקיבוציים שבעמק יזראל.
6   Sunrise. Sheep in pens (long, 97).
7   The shepherds enter and milk the sheep (mid, long, 130).
8   Sunrise. The shepherd opens the gate and the sheep leave. The sheep dog chases the sheep out of the pen. The shepherd followed by sheep (240).
9   The dog gathers the wandering sheep according to shepherd's instructions (long, mid, 260).
10  Sheep going down to the water, drinking and resting. Dog resting (mid, long, 319).
11  The shepherd eating and sharing his food with the dog (mid, 342).
12  The shepherd playing the recorder, surrounded by sheep (mid, c.u., 399).
13  The shepherd approaches a sheep giving birth and helps her. The lamb stands up immediately and nurses. The shepherd takes the lamb and brings it to the

kibbutz and puts it in the nursery. Children watching (mid, 489).
14  The guard opens the gate and the children run in to play with the lamb. Boy holding sheep (mid, long, 500).
15  Sunset through the palm trees. View of Mount Hermon. Flocks return home (long, 550).
16  TITLE: THE LORD IS MY SHEPHERD... (Psalm 23:1-2).
17  Map showing growth of sheep industry over time (560).

■ **CARMEL NEWSREEL I-214** · April 6 1940
Laying of the foundation stone for Kfar Masaryk attended by consul F Necas of Czechoslovakia. Demonstration of the Fire Brigade at Ramat Gan. A sports gathering of ghaffirs (Jewish Settlement Police) in Petah Tikva. Supreme Court Judge Alan Rose arrives in court in Tel Aviv. Inauguration ceremonies of Gan Yehuda park, named after Yehuda L Matman-Cohen.

☐ PART A: TITLE: THE FOUNDATION OF KFAR MASARIK (105')

כותרת: יסוד כפר מאסאריק (5).

1  Crowd entering. Gate with welcome sign. The consul of Czechoslovakia, Mr F Necas, arrives with entourage (long, 28).
2  Man speaking. Crowd listening. Banner on platform says in Hebrew: "Truth will win". "PRAVDA VITEZI!" (long, 60). שלם: האמת תנצח
3  Arab with keffiyeh speaks to crowd. Crowd walks in direction of cornerstone laying. Different people place bricks (long, 88).
4  Crowd seated around tables, eating (long, 105).

☐ PART B: TITLE: PARADE OF THE FIRE BRIGADE AT RAMAT GAN (93')

כותרת: טקס מסירת דגל לגדוד מכבי אש ברמת-גן (9).

1  Pan of a line-up of firemen. Mayor Avraham Krinitzi arrives with head of fire brigade (mid, long, 28).
2  Pinning a medallion with the fire brigade symbol on Krinitzi.
3  Distributing certificates. Passing the flag to the fire brigade (long, 70).
4  Demonstration of fire-fighting techniques with real fire (long, 93).

☐ PART C: TITLE: JSP (Jewish Settlement Police) THE SHARON COY'S SPORTS DAY AT PETAH TIKVA (80')

כותרת: כנוס ספורטיבי של נוטרי הגדוד השרון בפ"ת (9).

1  Parade of ghaffirs, dressed in sports clothing. The commander approaches an individual and points to him. Order given to begin (long, mid, 26).
2  Running (long, 45).
3  Running race shot from above (long, 52).
4  Shot-putting, running (long, 70).
5  Sack race (mid, 80).

☐ PART D: TITLE: HIS HONOUR JUSTICE A. ROSE ON HIS ARRIVAL (27')

כותרת: ביקור ה. מ. שופט העליון בבית-משפט בתל-אביב (8).

1  Police honour guard (among them Officer Sharaf) receiving the Supreme Court judge as he enters courtroom (mid, 27).

☐ PART E: OPENING OF A PUBLIC GARDEN AT RAMAT GAN (110')

כותרת: פתיחת גן יהודה ברמת-גן ע"ש ד"ר י.ל. מטמן-כהן ז"ל (8).

1  General view of park to be named in memory of Yehudah L Matman-Cohen (long, 25).
2  Woman uncovers sign in Hebrew: "Gan Yehuda". Close-up of sign (mid, c.u., 36).

3   Someone opens the garden, guests entering garden (mid, 55).
4   Corner with water sprinkler irrigating (mid, 110).

■ **CARMEL NEWSREEL I-215** · April 20 1940
A general view of Rehovot in honour of its 50th anniversary, including orchards, citrus factory and the Weizmann Institute.

□ PART A: TITLE: REHOVOT, THE BIG PRIVATE VILLAGE IN THE PLANTATION ZONE CELEBRATES ITS 50TH ANNIVERSARY 1890-1940. MUSIC: M. WILENSKY (823').
1   TITLE IN HEBREW: WORDS: LEAH GOLDBERG. SINGING: SHELI SHARONA.

כותרת: רחובות בת 50. מוסיקה: מ. וילנסקי. מילים: לאה גולדברג. שירה: שלי שרונה.

2   Signs in Hebrew and English: Border of Rehovot, Drive Slowly. Local Council Rehovot. Signs in Hebrew: Train Station. Bus Station.
3   Pan of Rehovot. Parade of local schoolchildren. Spectators on porches and roofs. Mayor of the municipality watching from the balcony of the Municipal hall as the children pass (long, mid, 84).
4   TITLE: THE FOUNDER AND THE FIRST SETTLERS (88).

המיסדים והמתישבים הראשונים.

5   Founders standing on steps of building as the young people pass. Pan of the founders including close-ups of faces (c.u., long, 110).
6   Children marching. Seated spectators (long, mid, 149).
7   Stills of Rehovot in its first years. A few houses. Fields and a house (mid, 197).
8   Pan of city. Houses by an orchard and buses (long, 227).
9   Municipal building.
10  Assorted institutions, the Great Synagogue, the Municipality (mid, 275).
11  Pan of the orchards around Rehovot (long, 311).
12  Workers harvesting in the orchards (c.u., long, 340).
13  Sorting and wrapping fruit in the packing house (long, c.u., 363).
14  Sign on factory in Hebrew and English: Jaffora. Pan of the factory. Workers working on piles of fruit in machinery (mid, 400).
15  Sign on factory in Hebrew and English: Pri-peri. Pan of factory. Hand-squeezing orange juice. Juice poured into barrels (mid, 424).
16  Train station. Workers unloading citrus fruit and moving it to a large storage facility (mid, 449).
17  General view of Rehovot (mid, 466).
18  TITLE: AGRICULTURAL EXPERIMENT STATION.

כותרת: תחנה למחקר החקלאות (489).

19  Entrance to the Weizmann Institute. Buildings, grounds (long, 519).
20  Sign on building in Hebrew and English: Daniel Research Institute. Pan of the garden and buildings (mid, long, 551).
21  Interior view of laboratory. Assorted research equipment (mid, long, 593).
22  General view of Rehovot (long, 637).
23  Neighbourhoods in Rehovot. Givat Brenner. Pan of various sites in city (mid, 737).
24  Police car and parade of ghaffirs (long, 252).
25  Youth marching in the street. People standing on the balcony of the municipality (mid, 774).
26  General calisthenics exhibition (long, 823).

■ **CARMEL NEWSREEL I-216** · April 27 1940
An entire newsreel devoted to showing the life of volunteers in the Auxiliary Military Pioneer Corps at Sarafend army camp.

□ PART A: A PORTRAIT OF THE DAILY ROUTINE OF THE AUXILIARY MILITARY PIONEER CORPS IN SARAFEND ARMY CAMP (638')
1   The symbol of the Pioneer Corps: a pick crossed by a shovel and a gun with a crown on top and a banner underneath: LABOR OMNIA VINCIT (work conquers all).
2   TITLE: THIS FILM IS ENTIRELY DEVOTED TO THE DAILY LIFE OF THE AUXILIARY MILITARY PIONEER CORPS, SOMEWHERE IN PALESTINE.

כותרת: יומן מוקדש לחיי יום יום של חייל העזר החלוץ הארצי אי-שם בארץ.

3   Dissolve to TITLE: BY THE KIND PERMISSION OF THE G.O.C. IN PALESTINE AND TRANSJORDAN (29')

כותרת: ברשותו האדיבה של המפקד הצבאי בארץ ובעבר הירדן.

4   Parade of Pioneer Corps down a crowded street in Tel Aviv, carrying a banner in Hebrew calling on others to join them (long, 34).
5   Men in civilian clothes in Sarafend, march past camera, man in uniform gives them orders (long, mid).
6   Line-up of men in uniform being inspected by officer. Doing marching exercises (shot from various angles) (long).
7   Interior of gym. Men in sleeveless vests and shorts doing exercises, jumping jacks, stretches, sit-ups, leg lifts (long, mid).
8   Men in uniform (short trousers) lined up for inspection (mid).
9   Officer giving commands in English which is hard to understand. Second officer issuing commands in English with a South African accent (c.u.).
10  Soldier saluting (mid).
11  Pan of men in uniform seated as if for group photo.
12  Men in uniform picking up picks and shovels, starting to dig trenches as officers direct.
13  Later in the day, men up to their waists in the trenches they are digging (long, mid).
14  Men marching through finished trenches. Re-enacting battle in trenches (long, mid).
15  Money pouring onto table. Pan of men in line for pay. Saluting and receiving pay from seated officers.
16  Pan of men with metal bowls lined up for food. Receiving food from large pots. Seated at table (long, mid).
17  Men lined up at canteen. One lights a cigarette. One buys a beer. Pan of room with many tables full of relaxing soldiers (mid, long).
18  Soldiers lined up with guns, marching with guns. Pan of large groups of soldiers at attention.
19  Scottish band, with men in kilts, marches by (mid, 638).

■ **CARMEL NEWSREEL I-217** · May 4 1940
Horse racing in Ramat Gan. Opening of the Talpiot Market at Hadar Hacarmel in Haifa. Haifa ladies knitting for a soldiers' party in Haifa. Australian and New Zealand Armed Corps in Tel Aviv.

□ PART A: HORSE RACING IN RAMAT GAN (182')
1   Riders gathered by Napoleon Hill (mid, 26).
2   Shapiro appears on his horse (mid, 32).
3   Pan of Napoleon Hill with large crowd including Arabs. British and Jewish flag. Band playing (long, 57).
4   Horse ranch owner Eliyahu Gordon appears on horseback. The race begins (long, 70).
5   The race (from different angles) (long, 118).
6   Second race (long, 171).
7   Prize given to Gordon, the winner. He holds up the horse statuette (mid, 178).

8   General view of Napoleon Hill with crowd (long, 182).

□ PART B: TITLE: OPENING OF THE NEW MARKET "TALPIOT" AT HADAR HACARMEL IN HAIFA (136')

כותרת: פתיחת השוק החדש - תלפיות בהדר הכרמל בחיפה.

1   General exterior view of the market buildings which look like a multi-storey modern office building (long, 53).
2   Interior of building. The electrical circuit board (mid, 66).
3   Well-dressed crowd lined up for opening ceremony. Crowd seated.
4   Officials speaking from a podium. Uriel Friedland speaking (long, mid, 94).
5   White-bearded rabbi hangs mezuzah (mid, 100).
6   General views of stands full of vegetables, people buying. Empty stands (long, 136).

□ PART C: HAIFA LADIES KNITTING PARTY FOR THE FIGHTING MEN (79')

כותרת: נשי חיפה למען אנשי הצבא הבריטי.

1   Well-dressed women lined up, choosing wool. Women knitting, seated on sofas and chairs in a large room (mid, 70).
2   Sailor in sailor suit holds wool as woman winds ball (mid, 79).

□ PART D: ANZACS DAY AT TEL AVIV (109')
1   The ANZACS (Australian and New Zealand Armed Corps) marching down the street in Tel Aviv, band (long, 17).
2   Mayor Israel Rokah and the ANZACS Commander pass through lined up troops (mid, 23).
3   Dizengoff Circle. Pan of soldiers lined up (long, 42).
4   Soldiers marching down street (long, 84).
5   Australian soldiers lined up. Commander giving orders. Pan from commander to Mayor Rokah (mid, long, 100).
6   Soldiers marching down street (long, 109).

■ **CARMEL NEWSREEL I-218** · May 18 1940
Exhibition on the history of transportation in Palestine.

□ PART A: THE HISTORY OF TRANSPORTATION IN PALESTINE (614')
1   Small open bus full of people pulls up. Exterior of exhibition hall (mid, long).
2   Speaker on podium. Audience listening (long, 22).
3   People walking through exhibition hall looking at posters, exhibits including agricultural tools (mid, 112).
4   TITLE IN HEBREW: THE HISTORY OF TRANSPORTATION IN THE LAND

תולדות התחבורה בארץ.

5   The title is the cover of a book which opens to show a still of camels with the year 1900.
6   Page turns to 1910. Still of man with whip, driving horse-drawn carriage comes to life, he whips horses, carriage travels (mid).
7   Page turns to 1914. Same man posed in front of open motor vehicle with seven or eight passengers. He winds it up from up front and then drives, honks horn.
8   Page turns to 1940. A street with a bus. The bus drives down the street (long, 133).
9   Cargo being unloaded from large ship, placed on smaller boats.
10  Men working on truck. Truck without back drives by (long, 161).
11  Interior of machine shop where parts for cars are made (mid, 193).
12  Putting parts together (long, 201).
13  Little white sports car pulling towing jack with sign in English, OLYMPIA GARAGE, pulls up to larger black car and tows it.

14  Retreading tires (mid, 282).
15  Interior machine shop for car parts. Exhibition of parts (mid, 312).
16  Industry for building bus cabins. Stages of production until final product (mid, 415).
17  Testing brakes (mid, 425).
18  Bus on crowded street, drives past shop fronts. Interior of bus, driver at wheel. People disembarking from bus (mid, long, 532).
19  Assorted shots of buses. Convoy of buses (long).
20  Bus drives through hills in the Galilee. Comes to street with sign on wall in Hebrew and English "Safed".
21  Bus driving through hills. Convoy of buses in large outdoor station with sign in Hebrew and English, "Egged". Buses drive through streets. Sign in Hebrew in window of bus "Gan Yavneh". Second bus with sign "Be'er Tuvia".
22  Convoy of trucks. Truck full of bales of hay (614).

■ **CARMEL NEWSREEL I-219** · May 1940
Annual mounted sports competition by the ghaffirs (Jewish Settlement Police) in Tel Aviv. Sports competitions between the Jewish schools in Zichron Ya'akov, Petah Tikva, Afula and Jerusalem.

□ PART A: ANNUAL MOUNTED SPORTS BY THE JEWISH SETTLEMENT POLICE AT TEL AVIV (105')

כותרת: תחרות רכיבה כת"א של משטרת הישובים העבריים בארץ.

1  Ghaffirs on horses lined up for start of race (long, 19).
2  They ride, then jump off their horses, shoot at bottles, jump back on their horses (long, 58).
3  The table with judges, officers and prizes (mid, 64).
4  Horses jumping over hurdles. The crowd clapping. A string of British and Jewish flags (long, 105).

□ PART B: SPORTS COMPETITIONS BETWEEN THE JEWISH SCHOOLS IN PALESTINE (295')        כותרת: כינוס הספורט
1  TITLE IN HEBREW: SHOMRON REGION IN ZICHRON YA'AKOV (12).
              כותרת: מחוז השומרון בזכרון-יעקב.
2  Children lined up on the field. Crowd (long, 35).
3  Children running a race (long, 48).
4  TITLE IN HEBREW: SHARON REGION IN PETAH TIKVA (long, 53).
              כותרת: מחוז השרון כפ"ת.
5  Students enter the field. Young men and women lined up by a swimming pool. At a sign they dive and race (long, 124).
6  The judges' table. Close-up of swimming. Woman demonstrating life-saving swimming holds (mid, 148).
7  TITLE IN HEBREW: JEZREEL VALLEY REGION IN AFULA (154).
              כותרת: מחוז העמק בעפולה.
8  Youth marching with flags onto a playing field (long, 186).
9  Relay race. Handball game (long, 226).
10  TITLE IN HEBREW: JERUSALEM (229).
11  Girls and boys racing and long-jumping (long, 267).
12  Line-up on the playing field. Speaker (mid, 289).
13  Smiling youth holding large round prize medal (mid, 295).

■ **CARMEL NEWSREEL I-220** · June 1 1940
An entire newsreel devoted to varied youth activities in Palestine with many titles praising youth and its role in the Zionist dream.

□ PART A: TITLE: THIS NEWS FILM IS BEING SHOWN IN CONNECTION WITH YOUTH WEEK (501')　כותרת: שבוע הנוער.
1. TITLE IN HEBREW: HERZL TO THE STUDENTS FROM THE LETTER OF 1904　כותרת: הרצל לתלמידים מתוך אגרת 1904.
2. A handwritten page of Herzl's letter of 1904 to the students, dissolve to portrait of Herzl.
3. TITLE: PALESTINIAN YOUTH MAKES HERZL'S DREAM A REALITY (51).　כותרת: הנוער הא"י מקיים את צוואתו של הרצל.
4. TITLE: AND IS FAITHFUL TO THE IDEAL OF THE UP-BUILDING OF THE HOMELAND.　כותרת: ושומר אמונים לבנין מולדתו.
5. Boy blowing a trumpet. Group of boys blowing trumpets (c.u.,63).
6. TITLE: MACCABI (67).
7. Members of Maccabi marching, doing exercises (long, 89).
8. Members of Hapoel enter playing field (long, 112).
9. Boy blowing trumpet. General view of camp. Flag-raising. Youth marching (long, mid, 138).
10. Young men in sailor suits rowing in boat (mid, 145).
11. Sailors lined up (long, 155).
12. Youth marching to field (long, 167).
13. Betar Youth (in dark shirts and ties) marching (long, 181).
14. Construction of Beit Hadar. Factory work (including young woman working).
15. Children asleep in a shack. They wake up and go outside (mid, 231).
16. Two of the children pull a small wagon with sign in Hebrew: The Market Taxi.
17. Boy selling newspapers. Boy shining shoes (mid, 251).
18. Group of youths studying outside. Teacher (long, 271).
19. TITLE: ZIONIST YOUTH EXHIBITION IN THE DIASPORA (283).　כותרת: תערוכת הנוער הציוני בגולה.
20. Children at the exhibit. Posters (mid, 308).
21. TITLE: AT CAMP MACCABI HAZAIR AT KIRYAT ARIEH (315).　כותרת: מחנה מכבי הצעירה.
22. Flag-raising in camp. Man reads from book and youth stand at attention (mid, 344).
23. Pan of assorted sights in the camp. First aid station. Cooking on open fire (mid, 410).
24. Young girls in a tent (mid, 416).
25. Group of youth exercising in the forest (long, 428).
26. TITLE: THE YOUTH OF TODAY ARE THE MEN AND WOMEN WHO WILL INHERIT TOMORROW (441).　כותרת: הנוער הוא גרעין הדור הבא.
27. TITLE: WELL TRAINED YOUTH MEANS ZIONIST UNITY (454).　כותרת: חינוך הנוער הדרך לליכוד הציונית.
28. TITLE: HELP THEM TO GO FROM STRENGTH TO STRENGTH (470).
29. TITLE: YOUTH CALLS TO YOU FOR HELP (485).　כותרת: קומו לעזרת הנוער.
30. Youth of assorted ages march past camera (mid, 501).

■ **CARMEL NEWSREEL I-221** · June 15 1940
80th birthday for Dov Ariel Leibowitz, member of the BILU and a founder of Gedera. Sports competition between the Jewish schools in Palestine. Lag Ba'omer celebration at Mount Meiron near Safed.

□ PART A: TITLE: A LINK WITH THE BILUIM. 80 YEAR OLD D. A. LEIBOVITZ. THE BILUIM WERE A GROUP OF STUDENTS IN RUSSIA WHO LEFT THEIR STUDIES TO COME TO PALESTINE AS THE FIRST PIONEERS, MORE THAN 60 YEARS AGO (53')　כותרת: הביל"וי ד.א. ליבוביץ בן 80.

1 Close-up of Leibowitz's face (20).
2 Leibowitz walking by his shack in Gedera accompanied by another elderly man (possibly Tsvi Horovitz) (long, 29).
3 Moshe Smilansky speaking at the 50th anniversary celebration in Gedera in 1935 (see **CARMEL NEWSREEL I-001**) (mid, 38).
4 Leibowitz handing his grandson a hoe. The grandson and the hoe (mid, c.u., 53).

□ PART B: TITLE: SPORT COMPETITIONS BETWEEN THE JEWISH SCHOOLS IN PALESTINE (214').

כותרת: כנוס הספורט של בתי הספר עממים והתיכוניים בארץ.

1 TITLE IN HEBREW: AT TEL AVIV (12). כותרת: בתל-אביב.
2 Young men ready to race, racing. Another group racing (long, 39).
3 Young men, with light backpacks, in a fast walking race. Crowd watching (mid, long, 74).
4 Young woman throwing a ball. Men's shot-put (long, mid, 100).
5 TITLE IN HEBREW: HAIFA (103). כותרת: חיפה.
6 Long-jump (long, 117).
7 Relay race. Crowd. Young women's relay race (long, 158).
8 TITLE IN HEBREW: TIBERIAS (161). כותרת: טבריה
9 Crowd seated. Students lined up on playing field. Seated by the Sea of Galilee. Swimming (mid, long, 214).

□ PART C: TITLE: CELEBRATION OF LAG BA'OMER AT MOUNT MEIRON, NEAR SAFED. THIS YEAR AS IN PREVIOUS YEARS, CROWDS GATHERED AT MEIRON, CELEBRATE THE FESTIVAL ASSOCIATED WITH RABBI SIMON BAR YOCHAI (178') כותרת: חגיגות ל"ג בעומר במירון.
1 Crowd arriving at the synagogue. Trucks pulling up. Crowd including Arabs (long, 48).
2 Crowd of bearded orthodox men, pushing to enter.
3 Screen full of heads with hats (mid, 65).
4 General view of the grave (long, 70).
5 Men lighting a torch and singing (mid, 94).
6 The lighted torch. Men praying (mid, 113).
7 Procession bringing a Torah scroll (mid, long, 139).
8 The crowd dancing. Soldiers and Hassidim. Children on shoulders (mid, long, 178).

■ **CARMEL NEWSREEL I-222** · June 22 1940
Preparatory civil defence activities in Palestine. Anniversary of the death of Dr Moshe Glickson with shots of Tower and Stockade settlement. The BILU settlement of Gedera.

□ PART A: TITLE: A.R.P. ACTIVITIES: TRENCHES ARE BEING DUG IN GARDENS AND OPEN SPACES AND A.R.P. SHELTERS ARE BEING CONSTRUCTED THROUGHOUT THE COUNTRY (175') כותרת: פעולות הננה פאסיבית בארץ.
1 Sign in Hebrew: Citizen prepare while there is still time. The advisor for civil defence. פלקט: אזרח היכון בעוד מועד. יועץ הסוכנות לעניני הג"א
2 Second sign in Hebrew: Preparation of a shelter in an existing house (27).

פלקט שני: התקנת מקלט בבית קיים.

3 Placing sandbags outside doors of houses. Construction (long, 52).
4 Drawing of a shelter in a yard.
5 Men, women and children digging holes (c.u., long).
6 Construction of shelters.

7   Interior of incompleted shelter. People entering (long, 159).
8   Posters and pamphlets on first aid (c.u., 175).

◻ PART B: FIRST ANNIVERSARY OF THE DEATH OF DR GLICKSON (55')
1   Pan of typical early kibbutz, Tower and Stockade. Interior of tents. Crowd going to memorial ceremony.
2   Crowd seated. Dr Yitzhak Gruenbaum speaking. Crowd listening (long, 55).

◻ PART C: GEDERA, A BILU SETTLEMENT (150')
1   General view of Gedera (long, 13).
2   Streets, gardens, houses with greenery (long, 79).
3   Guest House. Guests relaxing in garden (long, 97).
4   Children playing in sand. Doves flying over Gedera (long, 150).

■ **CARMEL NEWSREEL I-223** · June 29 1940
Life of Yemenite Jews in Palestine, showing various aspects of life and work, including wedding with traditional dances.

◻ PART A: TITLE: THE LIFE OF YEMENITE JEWS IN PALESTINE (548')

כותרת: מחיי יהודי תימן בארץ ישראל

1   Yemenite men working in tile factory (mid, long, 39).
2   Yemenite women embroidering. Close-up of embroidery (mid, 52).
3   Goldsmiths. Close-ups of jewelry and faces (c.u., mid, 79).
4   Boy closing crates of citrus fruits (mid, 87).
5   Employment office of Yemenite association. Typing, waiting in line (long, 120).
6   School for Yemenite immigrant children. Children leaving classroom. Children seated in classroom, writing. Boy standing by blackboard. Teacher approaches students (mid, long, 156).
7   Traditional Torah study group. Children sitting on the ground. Teacher and children by a table inside. Close-up of teacher. Close-up of children learning (c.u., mid, 192).
8   Third school classroom, student standing by teacher (mid, 223).
9   Elderly men engaged in traditional study in synagogue (mid, long, 267).
10  Youth marching in sports uniform (mid, long, 276).
11  Yemenite workers constructing building (mid, 293).
12  Yemenite quarter in Jerusalem (long, 315).
13  Porters (mid, 321).
14  Yemenite women in the 'Market for Cleaning Women' (mid, 324).
15  Women preparing felafel. Different kinds of work (mid, 335).
16  At sea, a boat approaches. Yemenite immigrants alighting. Being received by the Jewish Agency. Leaving the port for Rehovot. First meal (mid, long, 402).
17  General view of Moshav El Yashiv. Elderly man descending steps (long, mid, 431).
18  Harvesting wheat with a scythe (mid, 437).
19  Working in a chicken coop (mid, 461).
20  Grinding wheat between stones (mid, 466).
21  Boy and two men working in vegetable patch (mid, 478).
22  Two men talking (mid, 483).
23  Bride and groom under bridal canopy (c.u., 533).
24  Bringing the groom into the wedding hall. Bringing in the bride (mid, 548).
25  Taking bride to wedding canopy.
26  Group of men in traditional Yemenite dress, singing and clapping. Two men stand up and dance. Women clapping (548).

■ **CARMEL NEWSREEL I-224** · 1941
Afforestation, including barren hills, planting saplings and enjoyment of full-grown forests.

□ PART A: AFFORESTATION (620')
1  Pan of barren hills (long, 12).
2  Pan of cracked, parched land (long, 28).
3  Two hikers, climbing on barren hills and sitting down. Pan of hills. Hikers continue walking (120).
4  Building terraces on the hillside, to prevent erosion (long, 139).
5  Digging holes for planting. One man digs the hole. The next places the sapling. And the third covers with soil. Donkey pulling cart with saplings (long, mid, 181).
6  Unloading crates of saplings (mid, 188).
7  Planting saplings. Saplings between rocks (long, 214).
8  Young forest (mid, 230).
9  Nursery. Women loading saplings into crates (long, 259).
10 Hills, close-up of young man preparing the area for planting (273).
11 Close-up of girl pointing out the forest from afar. Pan of the hills covered with trees and hikers entering the shade of the forest (351).
12 Group leader explaining to youth about the care and pruning of trees (mid, 379).
13 Pruning and thinning trees in the forest (mid, 401).
14 Cutting down large trees for industry, loading them onto trucks. Sawmill.
15 Joseph Weitz walking through the forest (463).
16 Road passing through Ginegar forests (long, 472).
17 General view of the valley, shot from between the trees (long, 480).
18 Kindergarten children playing with their teacher in a forest (long, 518).
19 Two hikers climbing the hill and sitting in the forest, looking at the pine trees around them (long, mid, 551).
20 Children climbing on rocks, teacher leading discussion among the trees (mid, 577).
21 Road between the trees (mid, 592).
22 TITLE: FRESH SPROUTS FROM THE OLD STEM.
23 Mr Weitz (the father) showing new branches growing from old tree trunks (mid, 610).
24 Iris shot of forest (long, 620).

■ **CARMEL NEWSREEL I-225** · 1941
An ode to Tel Aviv featuring street scenes, park scenes, a civil defence emergency drill, work in assorted industries and an air raid alarm.

□ PART A: TITLE: *TEL AVIV*. SONG *TEL AVIV*: EMANUEL HARUSSI.
1  TITLE IN HEBREW: EMANUEL HARUSSI, WORDS. MUSIC: M. ZEIRA. SINGER: YOSEF GOLAND (955')

כותרת: תל-אביב. דיסולב לכותרת שניה: שיר ת"א, ע. הרוסי, מילים.
מוסיקה: מ. זעירא, הזמר: יוסף גולנד. (23)

2  Fountain at Dizengoff Circle (long, 28).
3  Buses leaving station in the morning (long, 50).
4  Waiting in line for buses (mid, 58).
5  Moshavot Square, cars, streets with cars and double decker bus. Getting in and out of cars. Soldiers in the street (long, 118).
6  Shot from bus window: streets of the city. Dissolve to streets of the city, shot from above (long, 200).
7  Kamentzer coffee house. People sitting outside around tables. Soldiers (long, 209).
8  People reading from announcement board. Newspaper stand (long, 218).
9  Close-up of newspapers, Hebrew names: *Haga, Beit Ya'akov, Hatsofeh, Amerikaner*. People at bookstalls (c.u., 253).
10 TITLE: A.R.P. PRACTICE (253).   כותרת: תמרון אזעקה

11 Civil defence guards. A house on fire. Civil guard going out in cars, setting up road blocks. Nurses and medics running with medical equipment, entering the burning building. Fireman in fire trucks (long, 330).
12 Operating fire-fighting equipment (c.u., 345).
13 Head of Civil Defence Guards, Yerushalayim Segal and the Regional Governor, with Dov Hoz, watching the drill (mid, 350).
14 Evacuating "wounded" onto a bus, through the window (mid, 361).
15 Stalls in the new vegetable market (mid, 378).
16 Factory smokestacks (long, 383).
17 Dissolve to interior of candy factory. Women packing. Machines working (long, 438).
18 Knitting machines. Looms weaving (long, 481).
19 Dissolve to woodworking factory. Machines working wood (long, 527).
20 Interior of chocolate factory with machinery working (long, 572).
21 Assorted activities in oil factory (long, 588).
22 Soap factory. Razor blade factory (long, 670).
23 Yitzhar factory (long, 674).
24 Tnuva trucks leaving Tnuva (long, 702).
25 Wholesale market. Signs on wall: TNUVA.
26 Packing and selling vegetables and eggs (long, 738).
27 People in outdoor café (long, 742).
28 Air raid alert. People running to shelters (long, 769).
29 Street scene including traffic, soldiers (long, 779).
30 Pan of posters in Hebrew on notice board: Hakoach Tel Aviv against Tsion Tel Aviv; Maccabi Tel Aviv; Children's Fund; Devora Bertonov Performs; Happy Battalion; Habimah presents "Glorious, Miracle Worker" (800).

מודעות: הכח ת"א נגד ציון ת"א. משטרת שכונה, מכבי ת"א. קרן הילד. דבורה ברטונוב בהופעת יחיד. הגיס העליז. הבימה: גלוריוס בעל הנס.

31 Crowd inside theatre (mid, 803).
32 Square in front of Mugrabi movie theatre. Boats on the ocean (long, 822).
33 Promenade by ocean. People walking (long, 835).
34 Modern housing (with dissolves) (long, 850).
35 Assorted shots of gardens. Rothschild Boulevard. Children playing in parks. General view of parks. Fountain in Dizengoff Circle (long, 955).

■ CARMEL NEWSREEL I-226 · 1941
The Teheran children, rescued from Nazi-occupied Europe, arrive in Palestine by train and are met by a crowd including Henrietta Szold and many children. Keren Hayesod photography exhibition depicting military and civilian life in Palestine. Jewish National Fund Serviceman's Forest at Ma'aleh Hahamisha. The children of soldiers at a hostel in Bnei Brak. A Jewish military parade in Tel Aviv.

□ PART A: THE "TEHERAN" CHILDREN ARRIVE IN PALESTINE (217')
1 TITLE IN HEBREW: LAST STOP, MRS SZOLD IS WAITING ON THE PLATFORM. כותרת: התחנה האחרונה, הגב' סאלד מחכה על הרציף.
2 A train approaches the platform. The children (rescued from Nazi-occupied Europe) are seated on the train. The wheels of the train and another shot of the children (mid, 35).
3 The crowd waiting on the platform applauds and waves as the train comes in. A shot taken from the train. The children aboard the train wave to the crowd. The crowd (mid, long, 54).
4 Henrietta Szold standing on the platform. The children looking out of the train windows.
5 Children on the platform with banners in Hebrew: For ours is this Land of Israel; Nevertheless and in spite of everything - Eretz Israel (mid, 81).

כתובות: כי לנו זאת א"י; אף על פי כן ולמרות הכל ארץ ישראל

6   Mothers and infants. Children around Mrs Szold. The train stopping. Children holding flowers. Children on the train waving flags. The children get off the train - wearing hats. Sick and small children are carried (mid, c.u., 188).
7   Buses take the children to their final destinations. Henrietta Szold speaking with the children (mid, 217).

□ PART B: TITLE IN HEBREW: JNF SERVICEMEN'S FOREST PLANTED AT MA'ALEH HAHAMISHA (106')

כותרת: יער החייל של הקק"ל נטע במעלה החמשה

1   A gate and banner in Hebrew: And they Shall Beat Their Swords into Plough Shares (The Book of Isaiah 2:4).   כתובת: וכתתו חרבותם לאיתים
2   Soldiers arriving (long, 26).
3   Servicemen and women listening to a speaker.
4   The soldiers plant trees. Fade-out (mid, long, 106).

□ PART C: TITLE: WHILE FATHER FIGHTS AND MOTHER WORKS, THEIR CHILDREN STAY IN HOSTELS (107')

כותרת: ילדי החיילים מתחנכים במעון לילדי המגוייסים בכני-ברק מיסודה של מגבית ההתגייסות

1   A teacher reads to the children (long, 29).
2   The children eat under a teacher's supervision. Various shots of the children eating (c.u., mid, 54).
3   The children go to their bedroom and lie down on their beds (fully dressed) (mid, 76).
4   Children having a discussion with a teacher (85).
5   A soldier picks up and plays with his son. Other children. Fade-out (mid, 107).

□ PART D: TITLE IN HEBREW: AT THE KEREN HAYESOD PHOTOGRAPHY EXHIBITION: *THE PEOPLE OF THE LAND* (78')

כותרת: בתערוכת קרן היסוד "פני עם הארץ"

1   Banner in Hebrew: "At Arms and at Work - Face of a Land and a People".
   כתובת: לנשק ולמשק פני ארץ ועם; קרקע והתיישבות
2   Pan of exhibits labelled: "The Jewish Soldier". Another in Hebrew: "Land and Settlement" (long).   כבובת: קרקע והתיישבות
3   People looking at the photographs - including a soldier in uniform.
4   The photographs.
5   A group of soldiers. A Jewish soldier. Fade-out (long, mid, 78).

□ PART E: TITLE: JEWS IN UNIFORM JEWISH BATTALIONS PARADE IN TEL AVIV (34')   כותרת: חיילים וחיילות עבריים עוברים בסך ברחובות תל-אביב
1   The parade. People lining the streets. Officers go by in cars.
2   The soldiers marching (long, 34).

■ **CARMEL NEWSREEL I-227**
The Fourth National Assembly (communal governing council of the Yishuv) opens on Mount Scopus, shots of various Zionist leaders. Refugees from the Balkans arrive at Atlit Internment Camp still wearing yellow stars on their clothing. Memorial service for WWI pro-British *NILI* spy-ring member Sarah Aaronsohn in Zichron Ya'akov. Ambulances donated by American Magen David Adom for Palestine arrive. The second Sea of Galilee Swimming Marathon. Refugees arrive in Haifa aboard the *GUINE*.

□ PART A: OPENING OF THE FOURTH NATIONAL ASSEMBLY ON MOUNT SCOPUS (148')

1. A bus arrives. Pan of a building and a banner in Hebrew: The 4th National Assembly. שלט: אסיפת הנבחרים ה-4.
2. People entering the building, including Rabbi Yitzhak Herzog, David Hacohen, Yitzhak Gruenbaum and Aharon Zisling (mid, 43).
3. Yitzhak Ben Zvi, Yosef Sprinzak and David Remez enter the building.
4. Pan of the building and flags (long, 65).
5. The interior of the building. Ben Zvi speaking (mid, 86).
6. The press table - among the journalists is Yishayahu Klinov of *Ha'aretz*. Rabbi Herzog speaking (mid, 104).
7. The assembly (long, 111).
8. David Ben Gurion speaking. Seated among the crowd are: newspaper editors Eliezer Lubrani, David Hacohen and Golda Myerson (Meir) (mid, 124).
9. A young man speaking (he was a British officer and was court martialled for his speech) (mid, 131).
10. The promenade on Mount Scopus. Pan of the building and banner (long, 148).

□ PART B: TITLE: REFUGEES FROM THE BALKANS END THEIR WANDERINGS (167') כותרת: פליטי חרב מארצות הבלקן

1. A train arrives in Atlit. Refugees from the European concentration camps wave from the train. A Jewish flag. The refugees are met by relatives (mid, 41).
2. The refugees with yellow stars of David on their clothing (mid, 54).
3. Emotional meetings with relatives (mid, 74).
4. A refugee is transferred from a stretcher to an ambulance (mid, 88).
5. Individual refugees (mid, 94).
6. Distributing food to the refugees (mid, 117).
7. Refugees and relatives standing near the train (long, 126).
8. Packages are loaded onto buses to be taken to the [Atlit internment] camp (167).

□ PART C: TITLE: MEMORIAL SERVICE FOR SARA AARONSON ZICHRON YA'AKOV (131') כותרת: עליה לקברה של שרה אהרונסון

1. A gate with a banner in Hebrew: "The Eternal One of Israel Will Not Lie" ("NILI": the password of Aaronsohn's pro-British spy-ring active in Ottoman Palestine during World War I). People bringing memorial wreaths. The Maccabi flag (long, 18).
2. A procession in Zichron Ya'akov. A crowd, including many youths (long, 33).
3. A large crowd at the cemetery, including veteran Zichron Ya'akov residents (long, 57).
4. A crowd near Aaronsohn's grave (long, 83).
5. Sarah Aaronsohn's house in Zichron Ya'akov (mid, 93).
6. A procession in Zichron Ya'akov (long, 111).
7. A speaker (mid, 131).

□ PART D: TITLE: AMERICAN MAGEN DAVID FOR ISRAEL INCORPORATED SENDS AMBULANCES TO PALESTINE (147')

כותרת: "מגן דוד אדום" באמריקה למען מגן דוד אדום בארץ

1. Opening crates, removing the ambulances at the port and leaving the customs office (mid, 33).
2. Magen David Adom headquarters. A speaker and Rabbi Ben Zion Meir Chai Uziel (mid, 46).
3. A Red Cross representative. Rabbi Yitzhak Herzog. The crowd applauding (long, 57).
4. Rabbi Uziel speaking (mid, 61).
5. Magen David Adom nurses standing at attention. Guests passing by Magen David Adom volunteers standing at attention near ambulances (long, 108).

6   Close-ups of two nurses (c.u., 113).
7   The interior of an ambulance. The ambulances drive by (long, 147).

▫ PART E: TITLE IN HEBREW: THE SECOND MARATHON SWIMMING ACROSS THE SEA OF GALILEE (279')    כותרת (חסרה): צליחת הכנרת ה-2
1   General view of the Sea of Galilee (long, 13).
2   A map of the sea with arrows marking Ein Gev and Tiberias (mid, 18).
3   Ein Gev beach seen from the lake (long, 30).
4   A crowd gathering on Ein Gev beach. Swimmers have drops put in their eyes and their bodies oiled (mid, 59).
5   A woman (later to take first place) rubbing her body with oil (mid, 59).
6   General view of the beach at Ein Gev and the crowd. Boats sailing near shore in single file (long, 82).
7   The race begins. The swimmers are accompanied by boats. The judges in a motor boat (mid, 106).
8   A map with a line showing the route of the marathon - from Ein Gev to Tiberias (9 km) (long, 116).
9   Swimmers and boats in the water. Close-up of the winning swimmers (a man and a woman) (c.u., 144).
10  The judges observing the swimmers from aboard a boat (long, 161).
11  A swimmer is handed something to eat from a boat. Various shots of swimmers (long, 196).
12  Tiberias beach and a welcome sign in Hebrew. The swimmers nearing the beach. The winner is applauded as he comes ashore (long, 218).
13  One of the winners (a woman) comes ashore (mid, 254).
14  General view of the Sea of Galilee shoreline (long, 279).

▫ PART F: TITLE: FROM ALL PARTS OF THE DIASPORA TO THE NATIONAL HOMELAND REFUGEES ARRIVE ON THE PORTUGUESE SHIP *GUINE* (143')
כותרת: מארבע כנפות הארץ לחופי המולדת: האניה "גואינה" מגיעה ארצה
1   The ship enters Haifa Port (long, 17).
2   Various shots of passengers waving and looking towards shore (mid, long, 59).
3   Children aboard the ship (mid, 92).
4   Taking an ill passenger off the ship on a stretcher and into an ambulance (mid, 108).
5   The passengers disembark and leave the port on buses (mid, 143).

■ CARMEL NEWSREEL I-228
High Commissioner Sir Harold MacMichael visits Hebrew University and is received by Dr Judah Magnes and Henrietta Szold. Dr Chaim Weizmann arrives in Palestine, reviews Jewish recruits and attends industrialists' conference. A Torah scroll is presented to the Jewish Brigade. Chanukah candles are lit by Cantor Delin at Tel Aviv's Great Synagogue. Dr Weizmann visits Nahalal.

▫ PART A: TITLE: H.E. THE HIGH COMMISSIONER VISITS HEBREW UNIVERSITY AND HADASSAH UNIVERSITY HOSPITAL (190')
כותרת: ה.מ. הנציב העליון באוניברסיטה העברית ובכיה"ח האוניברסיטאי - "הדסה"
1   High Commissioner MacMichael gets out of his car and is received by Dr Magnes. They walk towards the entrance where a crowd awaits the High Commissioner and applauds as he approaches (long, 42).
2   The High Commissioner, Dr Magnes and entourage visit the various buildings of the university (mid, 74).
3   General view of Jerusalem from Mount Scopus. The High Commissioner and

Dr Magnes look at the view.
4   The High Commissioner and Dr Magnes visit university buildings. They enter the Nursing School, where they are received by Henrietta Szold (long, mid, 173).
5   The High Commissioner at the university amphitheatre (mid, 190).

☐ PART B: PALESTINE WELCOMES DR WEIZMANN. JEWISH BRIGADE RECRUITS MARCH TO MEIR PARK IN TEL AVIV WITH DR WEIZMANN (216')
1   TITLE: SPEEDING RECRUITS FOR THE JEWISH BRIGADE (8).
כותרת: המתגייסים לחטיבה היהודית הלוחמת צועדים למסדר בגן מאיר בתל-אביב.
2   The recruits march through the streets of Tel Aviv, preceded by a marching band. Young men march with placards, firemen and civil guardsmen marching in uniform (long, 98).
3   Pan of the recruits in Meir Park. A band is playing. Dr Weizmann and his entourage, including Moshe Shertok (Sharett), arrive and walk through the ranks of the recruits. The commander of the Jewish Brigade (mid, long, 124).
4   Yitzhak Ben Zvi speaks and Tel Aviv Mayor Israel Rokah speaks (mid, 161).
5   Dr Weizmann speaks (mid, 216).

☐ PART C: TITLE: DR C. WEIZMANN AT INDUSTRIALISTS' CONFERENCE, TEL AVIV (73')   כותרת: ד"ר חיים וויצמן בועידה של התאחדות בעלי התעשיה
1   The industrialists' association hall and those attending the conference (long, 12).
2   The British and Jewish flags flying outside the building. Inside the hall Weizmann is applauded (long, 42).
3   Weizmann addresses the industrialists (long, 58).
4   The industrialists applaud as Weizmann leaves (long, 64).
5   A large crowd cheers Weizmann as he leaves the building (mid, 73).

☐ PART D: TITLE: SCROLL OF LAW DEDICATED FOR JEWISH BRIGADE (58')
כותרת: ספר תורה לחטיבה היהודית הלוחמת
1   Soldiers and a chaplain stand opposite the holy ark, holding Torah scrolls. A cantor recites a prayer (mid, 30).
2   Two soldiers hold a flag. David Zvi Pincas speaks (mid, 43).
3   The chaplain holds a Torah scroll and soldiers are seated in the pews (long, 53).
4   The cantor recites a prayer (long, 58).

☐ PART E: CANTOR DELIN LIGHTS CHANUKAH CANDLES AT THE GREAT SYNAGOGUE IN TEL AVIV (201')
1   TITLE IN HEBREW: LIGHTING CHANUKAH CANDLES AT THE GREAT SYNAGOGUE (8).   כותרת: הדלקת נרות חנוכה בבית-הכנסת הגדול
2   Interior of synagogue. Cantor Delin standing in front of the candles and reciting blessings. Among the congregation is Moshe Shertok (Sharett).
3   Delin lights the candles (c.u., 85).
4   The synagogue candelabra and windows. Delin sings. Synagogue lights. The congregation praying. The candelabra and other candelabra outside the synagogue (mid, 160).
5   Delin lighting the candles (c.u., 201).

☐ PART F: DR WEIZMANN AT NAHALAL (89')
1   General view of Nahalal (long, 5).
2   A welcome banner, people looking out of windows and a sign in Hebrew on

the town hall: The People Bless the President (mid, 19).

כתובת על בית העם: לנשיא ברכת העם

3   A detail of soldiers. Dr Weizmann and entourage arrive, Weizmann greets the detail commander (c.u., 29).
4   Weizmann converses with the soldiers and officers. With Weizmann are Eliezer Kaplan and Avraham Herzfeld (with bandaged hand) (long, mid, 61).
5   Weizmann speaking with Herzfeld (c.u.). Weizmann is applauded and presented with a bouquet of flowers (mid, 89).

■ **CARMEL NEWSREEL I-229** · 1945
Professor Yosef Klausner is honoured by the city of Ramat Gan. David Ben Gurion addresses the Tel Aviv Journalists' Club on the remnants of European Jewry. Dr Chaim Weizmann visits the Haifa Nautical School. The Fourth Zionist Conference in Tel Aviv - Weizmann, Ben Gurion and Yosef Sprinzak speak. Launching a fishing boat named *VICTORY*. Canadian Wizo children's village near Even Yehuda.

□ PART A: TITLE: PROFESSOR KLAUSNER - FREEMAN, OF RAMAT-GAN (51')

כותרת: פרופסור קלויזנר - אזרח כבוד של רמת-גן

1   Mayor Avraham Krinitzi standing near a table and addressing the crowd. A municipal official holds up a scroll on which "Professor Klausner - Honorary Citizen of Ramat Gan" is written in Hebrew (mid, 28).

כתובת על גבי קלף: אזרחות כבוד לפרופסור קלויזנר

2   Krinitzi presents the scroll to Professor Klausner, who shakes the Mayor's hand. The crowd applauds (long, 40).
3   Professor Klausner speaks. The crowd applauds (long, 51).

□ PART B: TITLE: D. BEN GURION SPEAKS ON REMNANTS OF JEWRY AT THE JOURNALISTS' CLUB TEL-AVIV (76')

כותרת: דבר שארית הפליטה מר ד. בן-גוריון במועדון העתונאים בתל-אביב

1   Ben Gurion speaks to journalists seated around tables (long, 34).
2   Ben Gurion speaking. He speaks of the need to save survivors and transfer Jews from Arab lands (c.u., 76).

□ PART C: TITLE: DR WEIZMANN AT HAIFA NAUTICAL SCHOOL (77')

כותרת: הנשיא ח. וייצמן בבית הספר הימי בחיפה

1   Raising flags. As Weizmann arrives at the ceremony, drummers begin to play. Weizmann reviews the students' ranks (long, 28).
2   Students march by. A crowd watches the students on parade (long, 77).

□ PART D: THE FOURTH ZIONIST CONFERENCE (119')
1   The "Esther" Cinema in Tel Aviv. A banner in Hebrew on the building: The Fourth Zionist Conference. Loudspeakers mounted on the building. Delegates (long, 18).
2   A long line near the cinema. Delegates present their invitations. Delegates pass between rows of civil guards. Weizmann arrives. Graffiti in Hebrew on the building: Remember! (long, 51).
3   The interior of the cinema. Weizmann addresses the conference (long, 74).
4   Ben Gurion speaks. The delegates (long, 104).
5   Yosef Sprinzak speaks (long, 119).

□ PART E: TITLE: LAUNCHING OF "VICTORY", A "NACHSHON" FISHING VESSEL (86')

כותרת: חנוכת "נצחון" ספינת דיג חדשה של "נחשון"

1   The new boat - decorated with flags. A woman speaking (long, 13).
2   Another speaker. The crowd moves towards the boat (long, 40).

3   A woman carrying a plaque on which "Nachshon" is written in Hebrew. Yitzhak Tabenkin affixes the plaque to the side of the boat. A crowd standing near the boat, including Yosef Sprinzak (long, mid, 86).

□ PART F: TITLE: CANADIAN HADASSAH (WIZO) CHILDRENS VILLAGE NEAR EVEN YEHUDA AS FIRST FURROW PLOUGHED (129')

כותרת: כפר ילדים ליד אבן-יהודה מקימה הפדרציה הקנדית של ויצ"ו

1   Pan of the area (long, 29).
2   A gate at the entrance to the village. Children walking in orderly fashion (mid, long, c.u.).
3   Seated guests and a woman addressing them (c.u., long, 37).
4   Another speaker. Pan-tilt of the area. A woman addresses the children and guests (c.u., long, 86).
5   A tractor ploughing and children following it and singing (mid, 129).

■ **CARMEL NEWSREEL I-230** · March-April 1945
Funeral of Henrietta Szold at Hadassah nursing school on Mount Scopus. Tiberias hot springs spa. The Chief Rabbinate proclaims fast and mourning - prayers at Jerusalem's Hurva Synagogue. The settlement of Dafna in 1940 at its establishment, and in 1945 at its 5th anniversary.

□ PART A: HENRIETTA SZOLD, MOTHER OF THE YISHUV, IS NO MORE (170')
1   A crowd walking towards the nursing school on Mount Scopus (long, mid, 12).
2   Henrietta Szold's bier on the ground - candles and a nurses' honour guard. A crowd inside the building (long, 24).
3   The funeral - a large crowd attending (long, 45).
4   Flashback: Henrietta Szold at the inauguration of a Youth Aliyah institution - hands are purified with water and a mezuzah is fixed to the doorpost (mid, 78).
5   Henrietta Szold speaking with children at the institution (long, mid, 101).
6   A large crowd at the funeral: Rabbi Uziel, the director of the nursing school, nurses, diplomats, army officers. A flag is lowered to half-mast (mid, 170).

□ PART B: TITLE: SEASON OPENS AT TIBERIAS HOT SPRINGS (213')

כותרת: חמי טבריה בעונה

1   A sign in Hebrew in the window of a bus: Tiberias. The bus descending along a winding road. Tiberias appears in the distance. Pan of Tiberias (fade-out) (long, c.u., 46).
2   A hot-spring in Tiberias. The hot water is collected in pools (c.u., 63).
3   Near the Tiberias hot springs. Visitors get off the buses. The entrance to the springs (long, 81).
4   A men's pool at the springs (long, 88).
5   Steam-emitting devices. Men and women inhaling steam (mid, 105).
6   A sign in Hebrew: Mineral Water. Tilt down to a woman drinking (mid, 112).
7   A Tiberias scene (long, 129).
8   A large restaurant on the water (long, 146).
9   Hotels and a café (long, 161).
10  Gardens and playgrounds (long, 178).
11  Gardens - people relaxing in the shade (fade-out) (long, 213).

□ PART C: TITLE: PALESTINE'S RABBINATE PROCLAIMS FAST AND MOURNING (172')

כותרת: רבני א"י מכריזים על אבל

1   A crowd outside Jerusalem's Hurva Synagogue. The men enter the synagogue (mid, 29).
2   Torah scrolls are removed from the holy ark (mid, 54).

3   The congregation sits on the synagogue floor (a sign of mourning). A cantor recites a prayer (long, 79).
4   Chief Rabbi Yitzhak Herzog ascends the steps to the holy ark and standing at the pulpit, addresses the congregation (long, 95).
5   Pan of the congregation praying (long, 134).
6   A crowd coming out of the synagogue - including diplomats wearing top hats (long, 172).

□ PART D: THE SETTLEMENT OF DAFNA CELEBRATES ITS FIFTH ANNIVERSARY (224')
1   1940 - a convoy of settlers makes its way towards Dafna. The convoy arrives and equipment is unloaded (mid, long, 36).
2   Ploughing (long, 44).
3   Putting up shacks (long, 49).
4   A model of a Tower and Stockade settlement (dissolve) (long, 55).
5   1945 - the watchtower at Dafna. Various scenes at Dafna (long, 74).
6   Pools of water and waterfalls. Running water (long, 99).
7   Settlers working in the greenhouses (mid, 112).
8   Boating on the Jordan River (long, 121).
9   Cows in the cowshed. Piling hay for the livestock. Work in the cowshed and yard (mid, long, 144).
10  Flocks of sheep are taken past the kibbutz buildings to pasture (long, 189).
11  The shepherd and flock near a stream (mid, 218).
12  Running water (fade-out) (long, 224).

■ CARMEL NEWSREEL I-231
The High Commissioner, Lord Gort, visits Netanya. Jewish Relief Commandos (UNRRA) depart from Tel Aviv on their way to Greece. A camp housing Yemenite Jewish immigrants. A tour of the Galam corn by-products factory in Karkur. A Torah scroll is presented to the Bnei Akiva (religious Zionist youth movement) yeshiva (religious school) in Kfar Haroeh. Springtime in the foothills of the Hermon - streams, waterfalls, flowers, animals, children and the snowcapped Mount Hermon.

□ PART A: THE HIGH COMMISSIONER VISITS NETANYA (36')
1   The High Commissioner and entourage walking with Ovad Ben-Ami, Mayor of Netanya.
2   Shots of the beach and municipal gardens (36).

□ PART B: TITLE: JEWISH RELIEF COMMANDOS (UNRRA) OFF FOR GREECE (107')   כותרת: פלוגות הסעד של הישוב יוצאות ליוון (אונרא)
1   A farewell ceremony at the Jewish Agency building. The relief unit standing with flags. One of the soldiers addresses the crowd, seated at tables. Journalists taking notes (mid, 41).
2   A man in uniform speaks and is followed by another speaker (mid, 61).
3   A flag is presented to the departing soldiers. The anthem is sung (long, 107).

□ PART C: TITLE: SETTLEMENT OF YEMENITE IMMIGRANTS (58')
כותרת: שכונת עולי תימן
1   Pan of a large tent camp (long, 18).
2   Various shots of the housing area (mid, long, 33).
3   Various shots of Yemenite Jews in their homes, fathers and children. Children playing in the sand (mid, 58).

□ PART D: TITLE: RAMAT YOHANAN J.S.P. POST OPENED (75')
כותרת: חנוכת תחנת הנוטרים של גוש רמת יוחנן

1. British and Jewish flags flying over the station (mid, 20).
2. Ghaffirs (Jewish settlement police) on parade. Their British commander approaches and the ghaffirs stand at attention. Faces of ghaffirs wearing "Australian" hats (mid, long, 40).
3. The ghaffirs stand at attention as their commanding officer enters the station (mid, 75).

☐ PART E: TITLE: INDUSTRY. GALAM FACTORY KARKUR (143')

כותרת: בתעשיה. כותרת שנייה: בית חרושת "גלעם", ברכור

1. Fade-in to a general view of the factory. Officials and journalists arrive. They are taken by the manager on a tour of the factory. Tilt to corn (mid, long, 45).
2. Sacks of corn. A worker pours corn into a conduit. Various stages in the manufacture of glucose and starch from corn (mid, 134).
3. The finished product is tested in laboratory (mid, 143).

☐ PART F: TITLE: SCROLL OF THE LAW PRESENTED TO THE YESHIVA COLLEGE "BNEI-AKIVA" OF KFAR-HAROEH (69')

כותרת: ספר תורה לישיבת בני עקיבא בכפר הרואה

1. Fade-in to Kfar Haroeh. Dissolve to the yeshiva building. Boys come out of the yeshiva, carrying flags. Boys walking in a group (mid, 43).
2. Rabbis stand holding Torah scrolls. The rabbis begin to proceed, under a canopy, to the yeshiva. The crowd follows (mid, 66).
3. Girls strew the path with flowers (long, 69).

☐ PART G: TITLE (decorated with flowers): SPRINGTIME... IN THE HERMON FOOTHILLS (194')

כותרת (מקושטת בפרחים): אביב לרגלי החרמון

1. Clouds above Mount Hermon. General view of the snowcapped mountain through the clouds. Sunrise and a stream (long, 36).
2. General view of the Galilee and snowcapped Mount Hermon. Sprouting vegetation, blossoming trees, a swollen Jordan River and waterfalls, young chicks in a coop, running sheep, birds in flight and children running among flowers.
3. Children playing in the undergrowth and dancing. Bird watchers. Children playing near waterfalls. Water flowing (long, mid, 194).

■ CARMEL NEWSREEL I-232 · 1945

Mikveh Israel Agricultural School celebrates its 75th anniversary. Building the hilltop settlement of Kibbutz Menara. Leather manufacture at Elion tannery. Housing for Kiryat Amal workers. Hapoel athletic competition in the Sharon region. Victory day celebration in Jerusalem.

☐ PART A: TITLE: MIKVEH ISRAEL AGRICULTURAL SCHOOL'S 75TH ANNIVERSARY HARVEST COMPETITION (147')

כותרת: בית-הספר החקלאי מקוה ישראל ביובלו - תחרות בקציר

1. Riding on wagons. The Mikveh Israel school band marches after the wagons to the competition site (long, 27).
2. The competition: a row of boys and girls harvesting with scythes, as a crowd looks on (c.u., mid, 91).
3. Boys and girls gather the freshly cut clover and load sheaves onto wagons (long, 119).
4. The harvesters return and wet their scythes (c.u., long, 136).
5. Pan of the crowd and boys and girls returning to the school on a wagon (long, 147).

☐ PART B: THE MOUNTAIN SETTLEMENT OF KIBBUTZ MENARA (83')

1   TITLE: SETTLEMENT. SECOND TITLE: RAMIM-MENARA (8').

כותרת: בהתיישבות. כותרת שנייה: רמים-מנרה התיישבות בהרים

2   Rocky mountain at Kibbutz Menara (long, 29).
3   Removing stones and using horses to drag them away (mid, 63).
4   Removing stones on a terraced hill (long, 75).
5   The summit of Mount Menara. The houses of Menara (long, 83).

□ PART C: TITLE: INDUSTRY, LEATHER PRODUCTION AT THE ELION TANNERY (224')     כותרת: בתעשיה. כותרת שנייה: עיבוד עורות
1   Building the tannery (long, 12).
2   Taking skins and placing them in vats (long, 35).
3   The tanning process from the vats to cleaning with various machines.
4   Embossing the tannery seal and arranging the leather for shipment (long, 205).
5   Workers leaving the factory at the end of the day (long, 224).

□ PART D: TITLE: HOUSING. KIRYAT AMAL FOUNDED BY SHICHUN WORKMEN'S HOUSING CO. (95')     כותרת: בשכון. כותרת שנייה: קרית עמל
1   General view of the hills near Givat Zeid.
2   Manufacturing concrete blocks for construction.
3   Close-up of a row of houses under construction.
4   General view of the houses and street.
5   Various shots of children (mid, long, 95).

□ PART E: TITLE: SPORT. SHARON RELAY RACE BY HAPOEL (150')

כותרת: בספורט. כותרת שנייה: מירוץ השרון של "הפועל"

1   The athletes, including soldiers, line up and receive participation cards (long, 40).
2   The race begins. Runners on the road, followed by cars. A relay race. The judges drive by in cars (long, 110).
3   Entering the town at the end of the race (long, 134).
4   Athletes and spectators (long, 150).

□ PART F: VICTORY DAY CELEBRATIONS IN JERUSALEM (186')
1   Newspaper headlines proclaim the end of the war - *Davar*, *Ha'aretz*, *Haboker*, *The Palestine Post*: EUROPEAN WAR OVER: VICTORY DAY TODAY. Another headline in Hebrew: The Jews of Palestine Demonstrate Their Joy and Demands (16).     כותרת בעתון: הישוב מפגין את שמחתו ותביעתו
2   General view of Jerusalem from Mount Scopus (long, 21).
3   Crowds march through the city with placards (long, 40).
4   The Jewish Agency building flying British and Jewish flags (mid, 48).
5   General view of Jerusalem and the crowds in the streets. Marching with placards in Hebrew: "Free Immigration for Jews to Their Homeland" (long, 64).     פלקט: עליה חפשית ליהודים למולדתם
6   Youth carrying placards (mid, 72).
7   A large crowd in front of the Jewish Agency building (long, 83).
8   Yitzhak Ben Zvi addresses the crowd (mid, 90).
9   Marching with placards in Hebrew: "Free Haganah Prisoners"; "Through Thy Blood Thou Shalt Live"; "Immediate Immigration"; "Down With the White Paper"; "The Entire Land for Jewish Settlement"; "Clandestine Immigration Will Continue" (long, 129).

פלקטים: שחרור מידי לאסירי ההגנה; בדמיך חיי; עליה מיד; הלאה הספר הלבן; הארץ כולה להתיישבות העם; המעפילים יעפילו.

10  Marching with placards (long, 186).

## 188  Carmel Newsreels: Series 1

### ■ CARMEL NEWSREEL I-233
Moshe Shertok (Sharett) addresses a journalists' convention. A plague of locusts at Kibbutz Massada. Jewish prisoners of war from Palestine return home.

□ PART A: TITLE: JOURNALISTS' CONVENTION (61')

כותרת: העתונאים באסיפתם

1. The journalists seated in the convention hall. Dr Ezriel Karlebach addresses the convention. Another speaker. Moshe Shertok (Sharett) seated in the hall (long, 37).
2. Shertok speaks (long, 45).
3. Applause (long, 61).

□ PART B: TITLE: THE LOCUST INVASION (189')  כותרת: ויעל הארבה
1. TITLE: MASSADA FOUNDED BY KEREN HAYESOD (9).

כותרת: זו מסדה מיסודה של קרן היסוד

2. A kibbutz member working in a field, suddenly sees locusts in flight (c.u., 18).
3. A "cloud" of locusts. The kibbutz member running. Many locusts (long, 52).
4. The other members come out of the dining room and look at the sky and the locusts. The members then look at the growing plants and vegetables (c.u., mid, 82).
5. Children, enjoying the excitement, running through a cloud of locusts (mid, 107).
6. Children hold fistful of locusts.
7. A locust lays her eggs.
8. Bushes covered with locusts (mid, 141).
9. A pair of mating locusts is held up and pointed to. A hand pulls on one of the two locusts, pulling it apart (mid, 160).
10. Female locusts laying eggs on the ground (mid, 189).

□ PART C: FROM CAPTIVITY TO THE HOMELAND (158')
1. Houses decorated with banners and flags. Tilt down to crowds filling the street. A convoy of military trucks appears. The crowd runs towards the soldiers. Relatives and friends embrace (mid, 43).
2. Tables are prepared for the celebration (long, 45).
3. A banner in Hebrew on a building: "Zion Shall be Redeemed With Judgment and her Returning Sons with Righteousness". Tilt down to a choir and the crowd. Pan of tables set for the soldiers and their families (long, 73).

כתובת: ציון במשפט תפדה ושביה בצדקה

4. Soldiers and their families eating (c.u., 87).
5. The choir. Officers and soldiers (long, 102).
6. Pan of the tables from above. Close-up of Yitzhak Ben Zvi sitting near an officer (c.u., long, 121).
7. Tel Aviv Deputy Mayor Eliezer Perlson speaks (mid, 127).
8. Moshe Shertok (Sharett) speaks. The crowd applauds.
9. Journalists taking notes. Men and women in uniform at the tables (mid, 148).
10. A barrack. Soldiers arranging their kits (long, 158).

### ■ CARMEL NEWSREEL I-234
A military parade in Jerusalem in honour of the birthday of King George VI. Inauguration of a Maccabi sports club swimming pool in Rehovot. A rowing competition on the Yarkon River. Kibbutz Sha'ar Ha'amakim celebrates its 10th anniversary.

□ PART A: TITLE: H.M. THE KING'S BIRTHDAY PARADE IN JERUSALEM (149')

כותרת: יום הולדת המלך ג'ורג' הששי מסקר צבאי בירושלים

1. The street in front of the King David Hotel. Seats for dignitaries (mid, 11).
2. Chief Rabbis Yitzhak Halevi Herzog and Ben Zion Meir Chai Uziel and their wives.
3. Pan of Christian clergy (mid, 17).
4. Officers seated in rows (including a Sikh officer wearing a turban) (pan, long, 23).
5. The High Commissioner arrives in his car. The crowd applauds.
6. The High Commissioner stands on the dais and addresses the crowd (c.u., long, 35).
7. A man in civilian clothing is awarded a medal by an officer. The crowd applauds (long, 46).
8. A woman in uniform is awarded a medal (long, 52).
9. A band plays as armoured vehicles pass before the dais (long, 79).
10. The parade: cavalry, followed by sailors, the High Commissioner salutes, soldiers of various regiments as well as WACS march by, tanks and heavy artillery (mid, 141).
11. Airplanes fly by in formation (long, 149).

□ PART B: TITLE: INAUGURATION OF MACCABI SWIMMING POOL IN REHOVOT (153')     כותרת: חנוכת בריכת-שחיה של מכבי ברחובות
1. Maccabi roll-call and flags (mid, 22).
2. Three speakers (c.u., 35).
3. A woman cuts the ribbon and the crowd applauds. Pan of the pool (long, 48).
4. Swimmers on their marks and the beginning of a race. Another race - close-up of a swimmer. A women's race. Other races. The crowd applauding (c.u., long, 153).

□ PART C: TITLE: ROWING COMPETITION ON THE RIVER YARKON (119')
כותרת: תחרות שייט על הירקון
1. The sailing cub, decorated with flags. Boats on the river. Various shots of races. Spectators (c.u., long).
2. The judges award prizes. One of the judges speaks. The oarsmen lined up. The winning captain is awarded a prize (c.u., long, 119).

□ PART D: TITLE: THE 10TH ANNIVERSARY OF SHA'AR HA'AMAKIM SETTLEMENT (281')     כותרת: עשור לשער העמקים
1. Pan of Sha'ar Ha'amakim and vicinity. Small houses (mid, long, 28).
2. Residents gather in an open area (long, 36).
3. A wagon pulled by oxen (mid, 45).
4. Schoolchildren walking together in a procession (long, 75).
5. A band plays while riding on a wagon. Kibbutz members follow the wagon, some in costume - embroidered robes and sashes (mid, long, 115).
6. A handwritten page in English and Hebrew from Judges 4:1 - referring to Deborah the Prophetess (long, 128).
7. Tilt from the hilltop to the celebrations below (long, 152).
8. People in biblical dress. The band plays. A shepherdess in Biblical dress appears with a flock of sheep. The conductor, choir, violins and other instruments (long, 177).
9. Young women in biblical dress dance among the crowd. The band plays to the rhythm of the dance (long, 210).
10. A group of young men, in Arab dress, dance holding daggers. The crowd - including a number of Arabs (mid, 236).
11. Another group of dancers, carrying drums and tambourines, joins the young men in Arab costume (mid, long, 276).
12. An equestrian competition (long, 281).

■ **CARMEL NEWSREEL I-235** · September 1945
Children enjoying free time. The Nitzanim group reviving the barren land. The Jeshurun Synagogue gets a new Torah. Hanoar Ha'oved Youth camp in the heart of the Carmel.

□ PART A: TITLE IN HEBREW: OUR CHILDREN DURING FREE TIME (153')

כותרת: ילדינו בימות הפנאי

1   Children under an awning (long, 20).
2   Children running to the water and playing in the water (long, 37).
3   Collective shower under the spray of a hose (mid, 49).
4   Many children dance in circles on a field (long, 69).
5   Various games in a forest. Children dance *London Bridge*, dance and chat amongst the trees. Crafts (long, 107).
6   Eating at long tables (mid, 121).
7   The children line up and get vitamins put into their mouths (mid, 130).
8   Children sleeping on beds. Close-ups of faces (mid, 153).

□ PART B: TITLE IN HEBREW: REVIVING THE BARREN LAND. THE NITZANIM GROUP ON ITS LAND (134')

כותרת: להחיות את השממה. קבוצת ניצנים על אדמתה.

1   The place where the settlers had previously lived. View from afar of barren land (long, 18).
2   The planting of the young fruit trees (mid, 27).
3   Members of the group talking amongst themselves. Pan of the children and babies (mid, 55).
4   Tent camp (long, 62).
5   Looking at a map of the kibbutz. Tilt up towards a model of the future kibbutz (mid, 74).
6   Arrive at a place where there is a gate with a sign in Hebrew: "I gather you from all the lands and have settled you on this place".

שלט: "אני מקבצכם מכל הארצות והושבתיכם במקום הזה"

7   The crowd gathers. Someone reads from a declaration which is then signed. Laying the cornerstone. The declaration is inserted into a bottle (mid, long, 134).

□ PART C: TITLE IN HEBREW: ...AND THIS IS THE TORAH... A NEW TORAH SCROLL FOR THE JESHURUN SYNAGOGUE (107')

כותרת: "וזאת התורה...ספר תורה חדש לבית הכנסת 'ישורון'"

1   Going into the synagogue. Rabbi Herzog is carrying the Torah. Following him are other men carrying Torah scrolls.
2   The Torah is put into the ark (mid, long, 59).
3   On the podium, the Torah is opened and read from.
4   At the end of the reading, the Torah is lifted for display to all.
5   Pan of the interior of the synagogue during prayer (mid, 107).

□ PART D: TITLE IN HEBREW: FOR WORK, FOR DEFENCE AND FOR PEACE. HANOAR HAOVED WORKING YOUTH CAMP IN THE HEART OF THE CARMEL (359')

כותרת: לעבודה, להגנה ולשלום - מחנה הנוער העובד בלב הכרמל

1   The gate of the camp with a sign in Hebrew: "We will go up to Israel". A line of children walking arm-in-arm enters the camp (mid, long, 23).

כותרת: נעלה ונעפיל.

2   Dissolve to a view of the camp. On the ground, written with stones: "For our bleeding people are building a home".

כתוב באבנים:"לעמינו השותת דם אנו בונים בית"

3   Tilt up to close-up of the tents. The camp. Working in the camp. The camera pans from tent to tent (mid, long, 55).
4   A choir of children singing near a microphone. A technician near the microphone. The choir sings and it is broadcast across the whole camp. Close-up of the microphone (mid, 82).
5   Close-up of a tent. People sitting around as David HaCohen speaks (mid, 122).
6   The children's crafts; posters and models (mid, 142).
7   Walking in a long line (long, 161).
8   Calisthenics (mid, long, 186).
9   The children walk with their plates to get food. They eat outside (mid, 218).
10  Sunset over the ocean. The campers chat in the tents. Playing music and dancing (mid, long, 254).
11  A game recreating illegal immigration: at night children are talking. Suddenly one of them points. Everyone looks. They see a model boat that they built earlier which says on it "The Illegal Immigrant". כתוב: המעפיל
12  The children run, announce what they saw. Blowing the horn. Everyone climbs out of tents and waves. They pretend to be getting off boats, climbing down ladders. Dancing near the model boat. The model on the sand (mid, long, 359).

■ **CARMEL NEWSREEL I-236** · October 1945
A demonstration in Tel Aviv calling for free immigration to Palestine. Laying a cornerstone for a housing project in Haifa for refugees. A Keren Hayesod youth rally in Kfar Vitkin. A Hebrew writers' conference in Ma'aleh Hahamisha. A boat race from Haifa to Tel Aviv.

□ PART A: DEMONSTRATION FOR FREE IMMIGRATION IN TEL AVIV (112')
כותרת: תל-אביב מפגינה לעליית אחים, לתקומה לבנין

1   Demonstrators with placards - hands tearing the White Paper with a map of Palestine in the background and a slogan in Hebrew: "We Will Tear the White Paper"; another slogan in Hebrew: "Free Immigration - A Jewish State".
2   A crowd - including soldiers/police in uniform - carrying placards in Hebrew: "Certificates Now to Save Camp Prisoners"; "Doors and Gates Will Not Close" (The Book of Isaiah, 45:1).
3   Placards in Hebrew: "Workers of England - Stand With our Tormented and Oppressed People"; "Honour and Support for Those Fighting for Immigration and Those Guarding the Frontier in the Northern Galilee" (mid, long, 44).

ססמאות ע"ג פלקטים: סרטיפיקטים מיד להצלת עצורי המחנות; דלתיים ושערים לא יסגרו (ישעיה, מ"ה); פועלי אנגליה עמדו לימין עמנו המעונה והמדוכא; כבוד ועדוד ללוחמי העליה ושומרי הגבולות בגליל העליון.

4   A large demonstration (at a site later to become the Israel Defence Forces and Defence Ministry Headquarters) (long, 55).
5   A crowd carrying flags and placards (long, 62).
6   Mayor Israel Rokah addresses the crowd from the dais. Pan of those on the dais - including a British officer, Moshe Shertok (Sharett) and Chief Rabbi Ben Zion Meir Chai Uziel. The crowd applauding (mid, 85).
7   Levy Eshkol speaks. The crowd applauds (long, mid, 95).
8   The crowd takes an oath - raising right hands (long, 112).

□ PART B: TITLE: FOUNDATION STONE FOR REFUGEE HOUSING BY "MAON" HAIFA (91') כותרת: בתי שכון לפליטים בהדר הכרמל
1   Tilt from Mount Carmel to the building site. A speaker. Guests, including Mr Yosef Almogi (later to become Mayor of Haifa), are seated at a table. Journalists.

2 Another speaker and the guests (mid, long, 44).
3 Laying the cornerstone, depositing a trowel of cement in the foundation.
4 General view of the ceremony and pan of the scenery on Mount Carmel (long, 91).

□ PART C: TITLE: KEREN HAYESOD YOUTH RALLY IN KFAR VITKIN (113')

כותרת: הנער לקרן-היסוד

1 A building and a banner.
2 A tractor pulling a platform full of children to a clearing. The children at roll-call (long, 47).
3 Raising the flag. A speaker. A girl reads something aloud. The children take an oath (mid, 80).
4 A group of religious youth praying (mid, 87).
5 The gathering. A speaker. Tilt up to Kfar Vitkin (long, 113).

□ PART D: TITLE: HEBREW WRITERS CONFERENCE IN MAALEH HAHAMISHA SETTLEMENT (111')        כותרת: כנס הסופרים במעלה החמשה

1 General view of Ma'aleh Hahamisha (long, 26).
2 Writers getting off a bus, walking along a path to the conference area. Writers conversing - Barasch among them (mid, long, 60).
3 A large succah (traditional temporary structure). Inside the succah, pan of the conference. Conversing in the succah.
4 Two speakers addressing the gathering. Journalists. Another speaker (mid, 107).
5 General view of Ma'aleh Hahamisha (long, 111).

□ PART E: HAIFA-TEL AVIV BOAT RACE (51')
1 Sailing boats leaving Haifa Port. Various shots of the boats at sea (mid, 34).
2 Passengers aboard and inboard motor boat. Sailing boats en route to Tel Aviv (mid, 51).

■ **CARMEL NEWSREEL I-237** · November 1945
A nautical training camp for youth at Caesarea. Laying a cornerstone for the Shenkar Trade School in Tel Aviv. Members of the Mizrahi movement go on pilgrimage to Jerusalem on the holiday of succot. Swimming marathon across the Sea of Galilee.

□ PART A: TITLE: JEWISH NATIONAL LEADERS VISIT YOUTH MARITIME TRAINING CAMPS IN CAESAREA (40')

כותרת: פני הנוער לים מחנות הכשרה ימית בקיסריה

1 The camp decorated with nautical flags. Pan of tents.
2 Campers and a speaker. The sailors standing at attention (long, mid, 40).

□ PART B: TITLE: FOUNDATION STONE FOR SHENKAR TRADE SCHOOL (60')

כותרת: מפעל חנוכי חדש בארץ. בית-ספר מקצועי תעשייתי ע"ש א. שנקר

1 General view of the school grounds. Close-up of a sign in Hebrew: Shenkar Industrial Trade School (long, c.u., 26).
2 Jewish and British flags on the school gate. Seated guests watch the ceremony. Three speakers and the crowd applauding (long, 60).

□ PART C: TITLE: "MIZRAHI" PILGRIMAGE TO JERUSALEM (87')

כותרת: עולי-רגל לירושלים

1 The Jerusalem hills seen from a bus (long, 11).
2 Praying inside the bus. On the bus, a man holding a citron (a succot holiday ritual fruit) (mid, long, 28).

3  General view of Jerusalem from Mount Scopus (long, 35).
4  Large crowds of pilgrims gathering (long, 50).
5  A crowd inside a hall - including Rabbis Herzog and Uziel.
6  A procession starts out for the Old City.
7  A large succah. People entering the succah and shaking hands (mid, long, 87).

◻ PART D: TITLE: SWIMMING THE KINNERET (HAPOEL COMPETITION) (178')

כותרת: צליחת הכנרת אורגנה ע"י "הפועל".

1  TITLE IN HEBREW: ACCOMPANIED BY THE HAPOEL ORCHESTRA, CONDUCTED BY A. ZATZ (17)

דיסולב לכותרת שניה: לווי ע"י תזמורת "הפועל" בניצוח של א. זץ.

2  Boats filled with people. Swimmers in the water.
3  Swimmers greasing their bodies for the race. Crowd of spectators (long, 33).
4  Pan of swimmers setting out, accompanied by boats (long, 45).
5  A crowd awaits the swimmers. The winner comes ashore (mid, 55).
6  The winner approaches the dais and receives a cup (mid, 89).
7  Swimmers during the race. Boats filled with people. A woman swimming (mid).
8  The judges' boat (mid, long, 166).
9  A crowd awaits the winners on the shore (long, 160).
10 The second and third place swimmers come ashore (mid, 178).

■ **CARMEL NEWSREEL I-238** · January 1946
Building Michmoret, a new village for ex-servicemen. Celebrating 25 years at Kibbutz Deganya Bet. Meeting of the delegates for immigration and rebuilding in Israel. A third religious settlement is established in the Beit Shean valley. Tu B'shvat in Ramat Gan.

◻ PART A: TITLE: MICHMORET-NEW EX-SERVICEMEN'S VILLAGE ON THE SEA SHORE (171')   כותרת: "מכמורת" ישוב חיילים משוחררים על שפת הים התיכון

1  Overview of the land in the area (long, 18).
2  The residents of Michmoret and their guests gather for a ceremony. A speaker (long, 34).
3  A member of the audience gives his address. Pan across the applauding audience (mid, long, 47).
4  Large rocks near the seashore (long, 49).
5  Arriving at the site by horse and cart. People and equipment arrive (mid, long, 68).
6  Young men and women arrive at the beach front and begin to clear the area (mid, 97).
7  Unloading the equipment. Laying tiles in the huts. Passing the tiles in a line from one to another (long, 119).
8  Young men and women set up a barbed wire fence. Sawing wood. Building the dwellings (mid, long, 162).
9  Pan across the site, up to the ocean (long, 171).

◻ PART B: TITLE: BIRTHDAY OF A COMMUNAL SETTLEMENT DEGANYA B IS 25 YEARS OLD (115')   כותרת: דגניה ב' בת עשרים וחמש

1  Overview of the settlement. Shot from above of the houses and fields of the kibbutz (long, 50).
2  Agricultural vehicles going out to the field (mid, 73).
3  Views of various parts of the kibbutz. A large building with a banner in Hebrew: "And in their death eternal life was granted to us".

שלט:"ובמותם ציוו לנו את החיים עד עולם".

4  Close-up of the water in a canal. The fish pools (long, 115).

## 194  Carmel Newsreels: Series 1

□ PART C: THE GATHERING OF THE DELEGATES FOR IMMIGRATION AND REVIVAL IN ISRAEL (40')
1  Seated in the front row of a large hall are Rabbi Herzog, Rabbi Uziel and Yosef Sprinzak.
2  A man addresses the audience. Following him, Sprinzak speaks. In the audience Zalman Aranne is seated (mid, 24).
3  Ben Gurion speaking. Long shot of the audience. Close-up of Ben Gurion speaking (40).

□ PART D: TITLE: NEW RELIGIOUS SETTLEMENT IN BEIT SAN [sic] VALLEY, SETTLERS OF EMUNIM START WORK (169')

כותרת: ישוב דתי נוסף בעמק בית-שאן קבוצת אמונים עולה על אדמתה

1  General view of the area before settlement (long, 16).
2  Trucks with equipment arrive by night. People start taking the equipment off the trucks (long, 37).
3  Men wrapped in prayer shawls stand outdoors and pray together (mid, 53).
4  Lifting up the open Torah scroll (long, 58).
5  Pan across the area of the huts (long, 86).
6  A welcoming gate with a sign in Hebrew saying: "The third point of settlement by the Religious Kibbutz movement in the Beit Shean valley".

שלט: העליה לנקודה השלישית של הקבוץ הדתי בעמק בית-שאן

7  Moshe Sharett and his son arrive (mid, 100).
8  General gathering. Pan of the area (long, 125).
9  Walking with the Torah scroll under a canopy and putting it into a wooden structure as a large audience crowds around (mid, long, 169).

□ PART E: TU B'SHVAT IN RAMAT GAN (165')
1  Shot from above the city and its parks (long, 6).
2  A large audience watches the stage where some girls are performing.
3  A Tu B'shvat play is performed by girls. The band plays as the audience listens (long, 33).
4  Handing out saplings to the children (mid, 50).
5  Children march to the planting site and begin to plant the saplings which they were given (mid, long, 88).
6  Close-ups of two little girls planting.
7  A table set up with food. Children walking towards the camera.
8  Older children and youth walk on paths through the forest, carrying hoes, singing (165).

■ CARMEL NEWSREEL I-239 · February 1946
Planting a memorial forest in Ma'aleh Hahamisha. The Anglo-American Committee of Inquiry meets at the YMCA. Memorial to the fallen parachutist Enzo Sireni (who was executed in Europe by the Nazis). The High Commissioner F M Lord Gort visits Netanya. Members of Maccabi gather in Tel Aviv.

□ PART A: TITLE: PLANTING THE JEWISH SOLDIERS' FOREST IN MAALE HACHAMISHA (168')     כותרת: יער החייל העברי במעלה החמישה
1  Pan up towards the planting and ceremonial site where a large audience is gathered (long, 28).
2  The audience and the officials. An officer speaks, Rabbi Uziel and others.
3  A female soldier reads the list of the fallen. Signposts in the ground with the names of the fallen. Children seated on the ground. The bereaved families.
4  A cantor says a prayer.
5  A soldier plays "taps" on the horn (mid, long, 117).
6  Members of the audience planting trees with soldiers (mid, long, 168).

□ PART B: TITLE: THE ANGLO-AMERICAN COMMITTEE OF INQUIRY IN PALESTINE (85')     כותרת: ועדת החקירה האנגלית-אמריקאית בארץ ישראל
1  Inquiry members gather at the entrance to the YMCA in Jerusalem. David Ben Gurion, Abba Eban, Chaim Weizmann arrive by car (mid, long).
2  Interior of meeting room. The delegates enter and take their seats near the table. Rabbi Herzog addresses the delegation (mid).
3  Shot of the YMCA building (long).
4  The delegates gathered at the entrance to the YMCA.
5  Weizmann arrives and gets out of his car (85').

□ PART C: TITLE: MEMORIAL TO THE FALLEN PARACHUTIST ENZO SIRENI (145')     כותרת: יד ושם לשלוח הצנחן-אנזו סירני
1  Fade-in to general view of Kibbutz Givat Brenner (long, 37).
2  Interior of the dining hall where a choir is singing. The audience rises and applauds as Chaim Weizmann enters (long, 54).
3  The dedication scroll is put into a bottle and the bottle is covered in cement. Everyone stands at attention as the national anthem is sung (mid, 145).

□ PART D: TITLE: THE VISIT OF THE HIGH COMMISSIONER IN NETANYA (217')     כותרת: הנציב העליון בנתניה
1  Lord Gort, the High Commissioner, arrives in a car. He is received by Mayor Ovad Ben-Ami and other officials. They shake hands (mid, 62).
2  The group walks on the street to visit a factory (long, 74).
3  The interior of a diamond factory. The High Commissioner is shown the various machines and he shows great interest (mid, 131).
4  Members of the scouts line the steps at the entrance to the municipal building and greet the High Commissioner. He stops briefly to chat with one of the female scouts.
5  Interior of the municipality. Pan of the meeting-room.
6  A man addresses the audience.
7  The High Commissoner speaks (mid, 217).

□ PART E: TITLE IN HEBREW: GATHERING OF MEMBERS OF MACCABI IN TEL AVIV (79')     כותרת: כינוס המכבי בתל-אביב
1  Pan across the stadium where groups are assembled behind banners and flags with a large audience watching. A speaker. The arrangement of the field. Another speaker (long, 36).
2  The first few lines of a sign in Hebrew are visible. A military representative speaks (long, 43).
3  Young women march with flags, followed by boys (mid, 79).

■ **CARMEL NEWSREEL I-240** · 1946
Refugees from Specia arrive in Haifa port. Kfar Monash, a new settlement for ex-servicemen is celebrated. The convention of the General Zionists. Hebrew maritime day in Palestine.

□ PART A: TITLE: SPECIA REFUGEES ARRIVING AT HAIFA (215')     כותרת: עולי ספציה בחוף מבטחים
1  Shot of the ship the *ELIYAHU GOLUMB* and on it waving refugees.
2  The ship arrives in the port of Haifa. The refugees wave as they near the dock (long, 57).
3  The refugees disembark with the help of their Israeli escorts (long, 64).
4  Golda Meir and David Remez greet the new immigrants as they continue to disembark (long, 105).
5  The immigrants board buses which start to leave the port area.

6  A group marches by with a flag.
7  Pan of the faces of the new immigrants in a camp in Atlit (mid, 186).
8  Immigrants walking off the ship and onto the dock (long, 215).

□ PART B: TITLE: KFAR MONASH NEW SETTLEMENT OF EX-SERVICEMEN (192')

כותרת: "וכתתו חרבותם לאיתים": כפר מונאש. מושב חדש של חיילים משוחררים

1  General view of the area. Tents and families with children. The equipment is taken off trucks and the building of huts begins (mid, long, 53).
2  A gate with a welcoming sign next to it. People walk through the gate and arrive by horse and carriage.
3  The soldiers stand around and talk. A club house is decorated with photographs and a banner in Hebrew saying: "And they shall beat their swords into plough shares".
4  A long table is set up and guests are seated at it. Pan of the audience. Yosef Sprinzak addresses the audience which applauds (long).
5  Pan of the people and the tents in the background (long, 192).

□ PART C: TITLE: CONVENTION OF GENERAL ZIONISTS (57')

כותרת: אסיפת האחוד של הציונים הכלליים

1  A large hall is decorated with a welcoming sign and a portrait of Herzl.
2  Men seated at a long table where Peretz Bernstein is speaking. The audience listens. Two more men address those gathered (mid, long, 53).
3  Dr Moshe Sneh speaking. The audience applauds (mid, 57).

□ PART D: TITLE: HEBREW MARITIME DAY IN PALESTINE (274')

כותרת: יום הים העברי במולדת

1  People marching in the street with flags. Soldiers and members of youth groups march (long, 62).
2  All the groups march onto the ceremonial field.
3  Members of the naval school march towards the podium.
4  Pan across the yard of the old Technion in Haifa where the ceremony is taking place. A sign in Hebrew above the podium reads: "Jewish ships for Jewish ports". A mural of desperate-looking people reaching out towards the ocean.

שלט: אניות עבריות-לנמל עברי

5  The ceremony begins. The Director of Hasneh in Haifa speaks. A flag display on the field (long, 202).
6  TITLE IN HEBREW: TEL AVIV.
7  Members of youth movements march through the streets (long, 274).
8  Shot from above the ceremony (long).
9  Raising the flag (long).
10 Shot of the sun setting over the ocean taken from the site of the ceremony (274).

■ CARMEL NEWSREEL I-241 · September 1946
Laying the cornerstone for the Weizmann Institute in Rehovot. Hadassah inaugurates a new playground in Haifa. The sea scouts get a new home. Lighting memorial candles in memory of the fallen Jews of Europe. A new swimming pool opens in Hadera. Celebrating 25 years of the women workers' council.

□ PART A: TITLE: LAYING OF CORNERSTONE OF WEIZMANN INSTITUTE IN REHOVOT (189')   כותרת: אבן הפינה למכון ויצמן ברחובות

1  Close-up of a book on Weizmann in English (c.u., 28).
2  Laying the cornerstone. A man puts cement into the corner post.
3  Weizmann arrives escorted by his wife Vera. Audience applauds as they arrive.

## Carmel Newsreels: Series 1      197

4   Journalists seated at the press table. Leaders of the community are seated on the dais and Weizmann joins them (mid, 117).
5   Various people address the seated audience. The audience applauds (long, 158).
6   Weizmann pounds on the cornerpost with a hammer.
7   Rabbi Uziel speaks (mid).
8   The audience and the dais (long, 189).

☐ PART B: TITLE: HADASSAH INAUGURATES NEW PLAYING GROUNDS FOR CHILDREN IN HAIFA (89')

כותרת: פתיחת מגרשי משחקים לילדים ע"י "הדסה" בחיפה

1   Men, followed by Hadassah women, enter through decorated gate (mid).
2   Children run out of crowd and to the swings as the ribbon is cut.
3   More ribbons are cut and more children start swinging.
4   Audience of adults smiles approvingly.
5   Pan across the playground with swinging children (89).

☐ PART C: TITLE: NEW HOUSE FOR SEA SCOUTS OF HAPOEL (78')

כותרת: אבן הפינה לבית צופי ים של הפועל

1   Members of the sea scouts march in procession (mid, 32).
2   Flags atop a flagpole. Someone addresses the audience.
3   Pan across the audience.
4   Laying the cornerstone (mid, 59).
5   Boats sailing on the Yarkon River (long, 78).

☐ PART D: TITLE: CHIEF RABBI HERZOG LIGHTING ETERNAL LIGHT AT RACHEL'S TOMB IN MEMORY OF THE FALLEN JEWS IN EUROPE (27')

כותרת: הדלקת נר תמיד לחללי הגולה בקבר-רחל

1   Exterior of the tomb in Bethlehem with a large crowd.
2   Interior. Lowering the eternal light (c.u.).
3   The people outside the tomb (long).
4   Rabbi Herzog praying inside as his words are broadcast to the outside crowd.
5   Men praying (mid).
6   Rabbi Herzog and other men inside light the memorial candles.
7   Exterior. Large group of men praying. Crowd of men and women.
8   The eternal flame.
9   Pan across the area. Rabbi Herzog leaves the tomb (long, 27).

☐ PART E: TITLE: INAUGURATION OF SWIMMING POOL IN HEDERA (94')

כותרת: פתיחת בריכת שחיה בחדרה

1   Pan from above of the large audience seated around the pool (long).
2   Table with honorary guests. One man at microphone addresses the audience.
3   Cut between the audience and various VIP speakers.
4   The band plays the national anthem. Everyone stands up and sings.
5   The ribbon is cut and children dive into the pool.
6   Swimming (mid).
7   Sprinklers go off in the middle of the pool with the audience in the background (long, 94).

☐ PART F: TITLE: 25TH ANNIVERSARY OF THE WOMEN WORKERS' COUNCIL CELEBRATED IN AYANOTH (184')

כותרת: מחצית היובל למועצת הפועלות בעינות

1   General view of Ayanot. A welcoming gate with a banner in Hebrew: "25 years of the Women's Worker Council". שלט: כ"ה שנה למועצת הפועלות
2   Youths carrying flags enter the kibbutz marching. They arrange themselves on

the ceremonial field (mid, long, 95).
3   Pan across the field. The secretary of Ayanot speaking. Close-ups of the children as they listen to her (long, 127).
4   Mass calisthenics demonstration (mid, long, 184).

■ **CARMEL NEWSREEL I-242** · 1946
The establishment of the new settlement of Kfar Kish. Eleven new settlements in the Negev. Manufacturing steam boilers at the Hamlachim factory. A look at the development of Kiryat Avodah as it celebrates its 10th birthday.

☐ PART A: BUILDING KFAR KISH (222')
1   General view of the area. Vehicles prepare the land, digging to prepare the building foundations. Bricks are laid (mid, 39).
2   Putting up the huts (long, 74).
3   Pan across the area from the already set up huts all the way to a large tent where many people are seated, including local Arabs (long, 118).
4   Dr Avraham Granot speaking (mid, 123).
5   Avraham Herzfeld speaking (long, 136).
6   A representative of Keren Hayesod addresses the attentive audience (mid, 149).
7   The muktar of the neighbouring Arab village speaks as the audience of Arabs and Jews listens (mid, long, 177).
8   The seated audience (long, 196).
9   A tractor passes by the huts as it ploughs (c.u., 222).

☐ PART B: TITLE: ELEVEN NEW SETTLEMENTS IN THE NEGEV (171')
1   A map of the Negev with the eleven points marked on it.
2   View of the Negev Desert (long, 20).
3   A map with an arrow pointing at Hatzerim.
4   A group of women and one man washing clothes in outdoor basins (mid, 52).
5   A Bedouin arrives on a horse. Settlers and Bedouin men greet each other near the entrance to the settlement (c.u., 63).
6   A map with an arrow pointing at Kfar Darom.
7   The settlers make the blessings over the palm branch and citron in the succah. They sit and have a meal in the succah (long, 98).
8   A map with the arrow pointing to Nevatim.
9   The sun rises over the settlement in the desert. General view of the kibbutz and the members chatting on their way to work (long, 135).
10  Bedouin speaking to members of the kibbutz (mid, 151).
11  The members of the kibbutz put up a fence. General view of the Negev (long, 171).

☐ PART C: TITLE: STEAM BOILERS PRODUCTION AT THE HAMLACHIM FACTORY (105')   כותרת: תעשיית דודי קיטור ע"י בי'חר המלחים
1   Moving large boilers inside the factory (long, 33).
2   General view of types of work in the factory (long, 65).
3   Soldering the metal. A machine that rounds out the metal into large boilers (c.u., 103).
4   A large boiler is rolled out of the factory (long, 105).

☐ PART D: TITLE: TEN YEARS KIRYAT AVODA (300')
כותרת: קרית-עבודה בת עשר
1   Footage from 1935 showing the sand dunes before the settlement was there. A tractor appears over the dunes and begins to level the land as a group of men watches (long, 45).
2   Overview of the ceremony and the audience. Mr Kaufman speaks as a

representative of the Housing Authority (mid, long, 77).
3   Yitzhak Gruenbaum speaking. Pan of the audience (mid, long, 77).
4   Tour of the settlement in its present condition (shot from a moving car).
5   Walking with flags in honour of the festivities (long, 151).
6   Golda Meir speaking (c.u., 155).
7   A bottle is placed in the cornerstone of the school (long, 163).
8   Students with flags arrange themselves on the field (long, 195).
9   Planting trees (long, 201).
10  Pan across the beautiful parks and gardens of today where children are playing (long, 236).
11  A swimming pool (long, 249).
12  Shot from above of the houses and street of Kiryat Avodah (long, 268).
13  A group of men stands on sand dunes, surveys the area with a map in their hands as a tractor drives by levelling the land (mid, 300).

■ **CARMEL NEWSREEL I-243** · Autumn 1946
Relocation of Kibbutz Bitania. Loading and unloading of goods at Tel Aviv Port. Building a hospital for tuberculosis patients. The Gavish Glass Factory in Rishon Lezion. 25th anniversary of settlement in the Jezreel Valley.

□ PART A: TITLE IN HEBREW: BITANIYA IN ITS YOUTH, ALUMOT GROUP INAUGURATES ITS NEW HOMES (213')

כותרת: כיתניה בהתנערותה. קבוצת "אלומות" חונכת בתיה

1   Edge of the mountain, near the Sea of Galilee, kibbutz members marching (long, 31).
2   Near the ruins, new housing going up (long, 51).
3   View of the Sea of Galilee and Degania from the mountain (long, 59).
4   View of the edge of the Sea of Galilee and a line of kibbutz members climbing up the mountain (long, 80).
5   General view of the new houses. Pan of the new location (long, 96).
6   Gate decorated with greenery and a sign saying welcome. Members arriving in a children's truck and being received by local members, enter through the gate (mid, 136).
7   Near the door, Shimon Peres in the crowd. Camera cuts, door opens and the crowd goes in (long, 169).
8   Shimon Peres speaks (mid, 182).
9   Example of the farm in the future. The crowd listens while standing (mid, 198).
10  Overview of Degania (long, 213).

□ PART B: TITLE: LOADING OF ORANGES AND DISCHARGING OF GOODS AT TEL AVIV PORT (115')     כותרת: טעינה ופריקה בנמל תל-אביב
1   Boats in the port, pan of the bay (long, 17).
2   Crates arrive in trucks (mid, 27).
3   Crates lowered into boats (mid, 45).
4   Boats leave the bay and head out to the ships at sea (long, 55).
5   From the ships, boats return to the port laden with cars. Cranes lift the cars to the dock (mid, 81).
6   Unloading sacks from the boats to the dock (mid, 102).
7   General view from docks to boats (long, 115).

□ PART C: NEW HOSPITAL FOR TUBERCULOSIS PATIENTS (95')
1   Banner over construction site "League for the Fight Against Tuberculosis".

שלט: ליגה למלחמה בשחפת

2   Connecting the accessories in the building. Members of the League, including Mr Sadeh. Watching the progress of the building (long, 41).

3   Crowd around the scaffolding (long, 95).

□ PART D: TITLE: GLASS INDUSTRY IN PALESTINE. THE "GAVISH" FACTORY
(238')                                              כותרת: בית"ר גביש (8)
1   Workers wearing masks mix sand and other materials in a mixer. Mixing the ingredients (long, 41).
2   Room full of workers blowing glass (mid, long, 88).
3   Blowing glass in a machine (c.u.). Next step is finished jar. Another machine with finished plate (c.u., mid, 133).
4   Blowing glass in a machine. The worker fashions an artistic pitcher (long, 178).
5   In another department, different kinds of bottles made in the factory are on display (mid, 224).
6   In packing department, women pack glass for transportation (long, 238).

□ PART E: 25TH ANNIVERSARY OF THE JEZREEL VALLEY (131')
1   General view of the Jezreel Valley from Mount Gilboa. In background, Kibbutz Ein Harod (long, 39).
2   Avraham Herzfeld makes a speech to a crowd near the springs of Ein Harod.
3   Pan of crowd sitting and clapping (long, 63).
4   Two more people give speeches (long, 71).
5   Hanna Rovina gives a speech and the crowd listens (poor framing - her head is cut off) (mid, long, 81).
6   View of the Jezreel Valley. Soldiers from the Jewish Settlement Police (ghaffirs) marching with flags (long, 110).
7   Schenkin House (from afar). Procession marching towards Schenkin House (long, 131).

■ **CARMEL NEWSREEL I-244** · December 1946-1947
Planting of the Jewish National Fund's Mother's Forest on the Ephraim Hills. A soccer match between Hungary and Maccabi. The manufacturing of citrus products at an Assis Factory in Tel Aviv. Ceremony celebrating the opening of new houses in Nahalat Jabotinsky. Exhibition of steel products and electrical appliances manufactured in Palestine. Refugees from camps in Cyprus arriving and being processed in the camp at Kiryat Shmuel. Scenes of martial law in enforcement in Tel Aviv as British attempt to control terrorism.

□ PART A: TITLE: PLANTATION OF "MOTHER'S FOREST" ON THE MOUNTS OF EPHRAIM (204')                        כותרת: נטיעת "יער האם" בהרי אפרים (8).
1   Pan of general view of Ephraim Hills.
2   Women collecting and distributing flags. Written on flags in Hebrew: "Mother Forest, A Wizo project for the Jewish National Fund in Israel".

כתוב בדגל: יער האם. מפעל ויצו למען הקרן הקימת לישראל.
3   Many women pass quickly through the area. They stop (long, 64).
4   Women standing and one woman giving a speech (long, 95).
5   Abraham Kamini, head of the Jewish National Fund in Israel, makes a speech. Women take saplings in their hands. Receiving a sapling (mid, 133).
6   Planting trees on top of mountain. General view of planting and signs in Hebrew dedicating the forest: "Garden in the name of Tova Katznelson, of blessed memory" and "Garden in the name of Mrs Herzl, of blessed memory" (mid, long, 204).

בשלטים: גן ע"ש טובה כצנלסון ז"ל וגן ע"ש גב' הרצל ז"ל.

□ PART B: TITLE: FOOTBALL-MATCH M.T.K.-MACCABI (106')
כותרת: התחרות כדורגל מ.ט.ק.- "מכבי"
1   Pan of MTK (Hungary) football team (mid, 17).

2  Maccabi football team. Team rushes to the field. MTK team (mid, long, 24).
3  Football game. The crowd watches the game. Crowd claps and cheers. Pan back and forth between game and crowd (long, 106).

□ PART C: TITLE: MANUFACTURE OF CITRUS PRODUCTS BY "ASSIS" FACTORY (185')     כותרת: תוצרת פרי הדר ע"י ביח"ר "עסיס"
1  Factory and building (long, 20).
2  Oranges roll from trucks to the factory. Oranges go up on elevated rollers into the factory. Classification and packaging citrus fruit (mid).
3  Rows of girls at tables squeezing oranges (mid, 119).
4  Dissolve to boiling and sterilizing the juice. Cans rolling in ice water (c.u., 185).

□ PART D: TITLE: INAUGURATION OF HOUSES AT NAHALAT JABOTINSKY (56') כותרת: חנוכת הבתים בנחלת ז'בוטינסקי
1  Row of houses. Someone hoeing in front (long, 15).
2  Crowd passes under banner in Hebrew: "Nahalat Jabotinsky, Welcome".
בשער כתוב: נחלת ז'בוטינסקי. ברוכים הבאים.
3  Child recites. Planting trees (mid, 56).

□ PART E: TITLE: EXHIBITION OF STEEL PRODUCTS AND ELECTRICAL APPLIANCES OF PALESTINIAN MAKE FOR BUILDING-PURPOSES, ARRANGED BY MANUFACTURER'S ASSOCIATION PALESTINE (108')
כותרת: תערוכת תוצרת מתכת וחשמל מתוצרת הארץ, לשימוש כבניה מטעם התאחדות בעלי התעשיה בא"י (11).
1  Exhibition room. People coming to look at different exhibitions.
2  Exhibitions: hot water heaters, bath-tubs, different appliances, taps, building materials and electrical items (mid, 108).

□ PART F: TITLE: LIBERATION OF REFUGEES FROM CYPRUS. THE CAMP OF KIRYAT SHMUEL (189')
כותרת: פליטינו מקפריסין משתחררים במחנה קרית שמואל (9).
1  Raft in the water. Refugees alighting (long, 22).
2  Youths leaving the camp, travelling on the bus and being welcomed at Kiryat Shmuel (long, 36).
3  Belongings on the bus. Travelling to Kiryat Shmuel. General view of Kiryat Shmuel, pan. People near the camp (long, 102).
4  Refugees line up to register. Sign in Hebrew: Baby House. Nurses taking care of the babies. Mothers playing with their babies. General view of registering youths. Leaving the camp (long, 189).

□ PART G: HEADLINES IN NEWSPAPERS *DAVAR* AND *PALESTINE POST*: TEL AVIV OUTLAWED. MARTIAL LAW OVER HALF YISHUV. PARALYSIS TILL TERROR IS ENDED (70').
כותרת: עתונים "דבר" ו"פלסטין פוסט" "רבע מליון יהודים במשטר צבאי בת"א ובירושלים"(10).
1  General view of people walking on street. No traffic (long, 17).
2  Near barrier, barbed wire fence (long, 19).
3  At bus station, under British control, standing in line for identification check (long, 23).
4  Empty Central Bus Station, passing an armoured British car. Empty buses lined up (long, 31).
5  Boy cycling with girl on the bike (car). Old woman sits in tricycle (taxi). Wagons with a lot of people riding (bus). People in the streets of Tel Aviv (long, 70).

## CARMEL NEWSREEL I-245 · 1947

South African visitors at Max Fein Vocational School. Inauguration ceremony for Wizo Childcare Center at Ahuza on Mount Carmel. Shipment of Passover wine by the Joint Distribution Committee to Displaced Persons (DP) camps in Germany. Laying the foundation stone of the Aryeh Shenkar Industrial Center in Bnei Brak.

☐ PART A: TITLE: VISITORS FROM SOUTH AFRICA AT VOCATIONAL SCHOOL MAX FEIN (182')

כותרת: האורחים מאפריקה הדרומית בכיה"ס המקצועי מאקס פיין (7).

1 School building (long, 15).
2 Visitors get out of their cars and enter the building. Among them Israel Marminsky of the Histadrut (mid, 26).
3 Workshops. Marminsky goes first and the guests follow. Students sawing iron (mid, 53).
4 Working with the bellows. Iron is white-hot. People watching (mid, 72).
5 Working on lathes. Marminsky points out the work to the visitors (mid, 127).
6 Electrical department. Working on electrical devices and motors. Marminsky shows off students' work (mid, 182).

☐ PART B: TITLE: INAUGURATION OF THE NEW BUILDING AT THE AUSTRALIAN... (149')

1 TITLE IN HEBREW: INAUGURATION OF THE NEW MOUNT CARMEL WIZO CHILDCARE CENTER

כותרת: חנוכת בנין חדש ב"אחוזת ילדים" של ויצ"ו על הר הכרמל (12).

2 General view of the building. Various corners of the building (long, 57).
3 Women busy next to the building. Two children reciting. Women planting saplings (mid, long, 90).
4 One of the Wizo delegates cuts the ribbon to inaugurate the building. The women enter the building (mid, 113).
5 Hall full of people and students. Around the table sit the leaders of Wizo (long, 134).
6 Someone gives a speech. Children clap (long, 149).

☐ PART C: TITLE: SHIPMENT OF 1/4 MILLION OF BOTTLES OF WINE BY "JOINT" AS GIFTS TO CAMPS IN EUROPE (92')

כותרת: משלוח יינות לשרידי הגולה ע"י הג'וינט לחג הפסח תש"ז (9).

1 Label on bottles: American Jewish Joint Distribution Committee.

תווית על הבקבוק: שי לשרידי הגולה לחג הפסח תש"ז. מאת הועד היהודי האמריקאי המאוחד לסיוע.

2 Rabbi makes a blessing and people tasting the wine. Close-up of labels on the crates.
3 On first crate: "A.J.D.C. Genoa Transit Germany". On second crate: "Grands Caves. Rishon LeZion Palestine". On third crate: "Kosher for Passover". Loading the trucks. Truck driving to the port (c.u., mid, 92).

☐ PART D: TITLE: LAYING OF FOUNDATION-STONE OF THE INDUSTRIAL CENTER BNEI BRAK (124')

כותרת: ירית אבן-הפינה למרכז התעשיה בבני-ברק (9).

1 Welcome written on stones leading to gate decorated with sign in Hebrew: "Industrial Center in the name of Shenkar, Bnei Brak".

כתוב בשער: מרכז התעשיה ע"ש שינקר בבני ברק

2 Pathway below, seated on the stage are the city leaders and heads of businesses. Crowd listens (long, 41).
3 One of the businessmen speaks. Crowd from afar. Mayor of Bnei Brak speaks.

Another speech, the crowd claps (mid, 88).
4   Pouring cement on the foundation stone (long, 107).
5   Tractor working and levelling the ground. Fade-out (long, 124).

■ **CARMEL NEWSREEL I-246** · May 1947
Histadrut May Day parade in Tel Aviv including many groups with banners. A fire at the Shell Refinery in Haifa port. Illegal immigrants being taken off the Haganah ship *THEODOR HERZL* by British soldiers. Exhibition of hygiene and work safety. 25th anniversary of the Neve She'anan neighbourhood in Haifa, including views of Haifa and celebrations. Laying of foundation stone for a Wizo sponsored children's day care centre in Rehovot.

□ PART A: TITLE: MAY DAY AT TEL AVIV (299')

כותרת: ה-1 במאי 1947 בת"א (6).

1   Procession in the streets of Tel Aviv. At its head, a motorcycle and after it, a band. After the band, in line, Mr Levi Eshkol, head of the Histadrut. Then parade of red flags, youth marching.
2   Banner in English: "May 1st 1947 for the Redemption of Israel, Brotherhood of Nations, Unity of Workers, Solidarity with Arab Workers in Palestine".
3   Banner in Hebrew: "Free Immigration, Mass settlement, A Jewish state".

כרזה: "עליה חופשית, התישבות המונית, מדינה יהודית".

4   Parade of Haganah members. Carrying a mock-up of a ship upon which is written in Hebrew: "The Remnant". Delegates from kibbutzim and factories carry flags and placards (long, mid, 97).  כתובת על אוניה: "שאר ישוב".
5   On various placards written in Hebrew: "The Builders Will Build", with picture of man planting; "You shall burst forth Westward, Eastward, North and South" (mid, 123).  נושאי כתובות: "הבונים יבנו", ופרצת ימה, קדמה, צפונה ונגבה".
6   Written on banner in Hebrew: "The Defenders will Defend" with a symbol of a worker. Vehicles decorated. Folk-dancers dancing. Platforms with tractors. Truck with sign in Hebrew: "For work, for defence, for peace. Noar Oved" (long, 17).  כתוב כמשאית: "לעבודה להגנה ולשלום נוער עובד".
7   In the stadium. Participants entering. People sitting on the stage (long, 221).
8   Levi Eshkol gives a speech (mid, 227).
9   The delegations continue to arrive. Procession makes a circle, mass slogans (long, 284).
10  People in the circle form themselves into words (long, 299).

□ PART B: 1ST OF MAY (29')    כותרת: אחד במאי 1947.
1   Placards announcing the 1st of May. Many different posters about the 1st of May. Picture of a ship. Poster in Hebrew: "Life and Creation" (29).

כתוב על אוניה: העפלה. כפלקט: חיים ויצירה.

□ PART C: CLOUD OF SMOKE RISING FROM SHELL REFINERY IN THE BAY OF HAIFA 1947 (21')    כותרת: דליקה ב"של" בחיפה 1947
1   Clouds of smoke rise from Haifa Port. Smoke and fire from the refineries (mid, long, 21).

□ PART D: ILLEGAL IMMIGRANTS ON THE SHIP *THEODOR HERZL* IN HAIFA PORT (20')    כותרת: מעפילי תאודור הרצל בנמל חיפה
1   Close-up of the deck of the Haganah ship *THEODOR HERZL*. Banners on the ship.
2   Illegal immigrants being taken off the ship by British soldiers (mid, 20).

☐ PART E: TITLE: EXHIBITION OF "WATCH AND REMEMBER", PROFESSIONAL HYGIENE ORGANIZED BY THE GENERAL FEDERATION OF LABOUR AND MANUFACTURERS' ASSOCIATION (68')

כותרת: תערוכת "שמור וזכור" להגיינה מקצועית

1   Posters and banners on the wall about hygiene and safety. Different examples (mid, 48).
2   Jacob Zerubabel explains to workers meaning of work safety (mid, 68).

☐ PART F: TITLE: 25 YEARS OF EXISTENCE OF NAVEH SHAANAN [sic] QUARTER HAIFA (262')        כותרת: כ"ה שנה ל"נוה שאנן" בחיפה (7).
1   General view of Mount Carmel. Neve She'anan quarter. From above, pan on the houses and gardens. Traffic on the road (long, 98).
2   Child care centre. Close-up of mother with concentration camp number on her arm (c.u., mid, 109).
3   Car travelling on road next to the view of Carmel. School or synagogue. Pan on various buildings (long, 169).
4   Buildings. Workers building being built (mid, 175).
5   Banner written in Hebrew: "25 Years Neve She'anan". Celebrations in the streets. Crowd gathers. Youth with banners. Schools assist (long, 205).
6   Close-up of children doing exercises on the beach (mid, long, 217).
7   At night, institutions decorated with lights (mid, 220).
8   Gathering on the beach, pan on the crowd (long, 236).
9   Speech by a council man. Crowd claps. Dancing around the fire (mid, 262).

☐ PART G: TITLE: LAYING OF FOUNDATION-STONE OF WIZO CHILDREN-HOUSE AT REHOVOT (50')

כותרת: הנחת אבן הפינה למעון יום של ויצ"ו ברחובות (10).

1   Pan from above on the streets of Rehovot (long, 18).
2   Crowd listens to delegates speeches. Crowd claps. More speeches. Crowd claps (long, mid, 43).
3   Pouring cement into hole for foundation stone (mid, 50).

■ CARMEL NEWSREEL I-247 · 1947
Dr Abba Hillel Silver receives honorary citizenship of Ramat Gan. Opening Histadrut School for members of the General Federation of Labour. Production of silver and silver-plated products at the Machsef Factory. Yishuv delegation departs to celebrate Passover with the refugees in camps in Cyprus. Sea Day celebrations in Haifa.

☐ PART A: TITLE: DR ABBA HILEL SILVER IS PRESENTED WITH HONOURABLE CITIZENSHIP OF RAMAT GAN (260')

כותרת: ד"ר אבא הלל סילבר מקבל אזרחות כבוד ברמת-גן (10).

1   Scouts stand outside. Abba Hillel Silver and Mayor Avraham Krinitzi walk between the scout honour guard. Enter the municipal building (long, 33).
2   Silver and Krinitzi pass through the garden between the scout honour guard (long, 44).
3   Interior. Guests sit on stage. Krinitzi gives speech (mid, long, 60).
4   Silver gives speech in hall. Crowd (long, 65).
5   Silver walks the streets of Ramat Gan. Crowd receives him (long, 72).
6   Silver giving speech (repeat shot) (mid, long, 93).
7   Krinitzi continues speaking (mid, 115).
8   Crowd in the hall (in background Krinitzi speaking) (long, 121).
9   Krinitzi hands Silver certificate of honorary citizenship with a book. Silver rises to speak (mid, 260).

☐ PART B: TITLE: OPENING OF A SCHOOL FOR THE WORKERS OF THE GENERAL FEDERATION OF LABOUR (42')

כותרת: פתיחת בי"ס לפעילי ההסתדרות העובדים (8).

1 Pan of general view of building (long, 14).
2 Members of the General Federation of Labour (Histadrut) enter building (long, 42).

☐ PART C: TITLE: MAKING OF SILVERWARE (278')

כותרת: תעשית מוצרי כסף וצפוי בביח"ר מכסף (10).

1 Silver powder in someone's hands. Dissolve to melting pot. Pouring the liquid into moulds. Workers near the moulds. Manufacturing utensils. General view of hall with barrows. Preparation of a silver cup (long, 195).
2 Silver-plating department: Cleaning the utensils and dipping them into the acid (mid, long, 248).
3 Preparing the parcels to be sent (mid, 262).
4 Exhibition of finished products (long, 278).

☐ PART D: TITLE: DELEGATION OF YISHUV TO THE REFUGEE CAMPS AT CYPRUS (42')    כותרת: משלחת ישובים לגולי קפריסין

1 Avraham Herzfeld, Yitzhak Ben Zvi and Rahel Yanait Ben Zvi. Approaching the plane (mid, 27).
2 Benyamin Yitzhak Michaeli takes his leave of them and they enter the plane (mid, 42).

☐ PART E: TITLE: SEA DAY IN HAIFA (184')    כותרת: יום הים בחיפה (7).

1 Parade of sailors in Haifa streets, sea scouts, Hapoel Yam. Nautical school. Crowd watches "Naval Strip" ensignia (long, 114).
2 In the area near the Technion, which is arranged in the likeness of a ship, Golda Meir sits on the podium. Head of 'HaSneh' in Haifa gives speech (mid, 143).
3 Golda Meir gives speech. Crowd claps (c.u., long, 157).
4 Parade of flags near podium. General parade (mid, long, 184).

■ CARMEL NEWSREEL I-248 · 1947
Members of the United Nation's Special Commission on Palestine tour Tel Aviv and Jerusalem, including a speech by Dr Judah Magnes at the Hebrew University. Launching of a training boat at the Zebulun Sports Club in Ramat Gan. Shavuot first fruit celebration with the children in a Wizo Day Care Centre in Tel Aviv.

☐ PART A: TITLE: UNITED NATIONS' ORGANIZATION SPECIAL COMMISSION ON PALESTINE IN THE COUNTRY (285')    כותרת: ועדת החקירה של או"ם בארץ

1 Members of the commission get out of car. Greeted by crowd clapping (long, mid, 23).
2 Tel Aviv Mayor Israel Rokah speaks. Outside city hall, the crowd. Commission members descend city hall steps and enter cars. Crowd surrounds them (mid, 54).
3 Boats on the Yarkon River. Pan on a restaurant boat (long, 63).
4 Commission members arrive and go on board (long, 78).
5 Next to city hall, big crowd, cars arrive. View of Bialik Street from city hall. Commission members enter (long, 91).
6 The YMCA building in Jerusalem. Commission members entering. David Ben Gurion and Abba Eban entering together.
7 (Boats from Yarkon River reappear out of sequence) (mid, 109).
8 On Mount Scopus. Members of the commission walk in the area (mid, 114).
9 After the walk on the Yarkon River, the commission members enter a

restaurant boat. They talk to each other across the tables (out of context) (mid, 148).
10  Members of the commission get out of their cars and enter the Hebrew University, Mount Scopus (mid, 175).
11  Dr Judah Magnes speaks at the University (long, 182).
12  People leaving University buildings, going to the amphitheatre (mid, 246).
13  Close-up of members of the commission and their wives listening. Pan of Jericho (mid, 269).
14  Members of the commission enter the YMCA (mid, 285).

□ PART B: DR MAGNES ADDRESSING ROYAL COMMISSION AT THE HEBREW UNIVERSITY (301')

כותרת: ד"ר מגנס באוניברסיטה העברית נועם לפני הוועדה המלכותית.

1  Dr Magnes addressing members of the Commission at the Hebrew University (mid, long, 226).
2  UN representative speaks. Dr Magnes rises and shakes his hand (mid, 301).

□ PART C: TITLE: INAUGURATION OF A TRAINING BOAT AT RAMAT GAN (100')     כותרת: חנוכת סירה ראשונה לזבולון בר"ג.

1  Mayor Avraham Krinitzi arrives with Zebulun sports club members. Zebulun members on parade. Krinitzi speaks. Close-up of Zebulun members (mid, long, 32).
2  More speeches (long, 37).
3  Handing out certificates to the sailors (mid, 51).
4  General view of the area (long, 54).
5  Everyone lifts the boat. A woman speaks and breaks a bottle on the boat. People rowing the boat (mid, 74).
6  Sacks (owner of the Meshi-Sacks factory) looks at the boat. On the boat, written in English: 'Meshi-Sacks' (mid, 86).
7  Close-up of boys rowing. Anchorage from afar (mid, 100).

□ PART D: TITLE: FIRST FRUIT FESTIVAL FOR THE CHILDREN OF WIZO DAY CRECHES (97')     כותרת: חג הבכורים לילדי מעונות ויצ"ו כת"א (8).

1  Children file down to stage. From afar, lines of children in the woods, bringing the first fruits (mid, long, 47).
2  Gathering of boys and girls. They mime gathering and serving the first fruits. Skit. Dancing (mid, 97).

□ PART E: BREEDING OF CARP (see **CARMEL NEWSREEL I-136**)

■ **CARMEL NEWSREEL I-249** · 1947
Dr Chaim Weizmann and Dr Judah Magnes receiving honorary degrees at the Hebrew University in Jerusalem. Laying of foundation stone for the new Olamit factory for cement and asbestos in Petah Tikva. Cornerstone-laying ceremony for new building of Wizo vocational girls school in Haifa. The Alumim Bnei Akiva group founding a new kibbutz in the Negev. The ship *EXODUS* arriving at the Haifa Port.

□ PART A: TITLE: H WEIZMANN AND DR I L MAGNES PRESENTED WITH HONORARY DEGREE IN PHILOSOPHY BY THE HEBREW UNIVERSITY (252')

כותרת: תואר כבוד מטעם אוניברסיטה העברית לד"ר חיים וייצמן ולד"ר י. ל. מגנס (11).

1  Weizmann entering the auditorium. Crowd surrounding him (long, 34).
2  Dignitary reading from honorary scroll. Dr Magnes standing. Weizmann sitting, wearing sunglasses and graduation hat.

3  The speaker shakes the hand of Magnes and gives him the honorary scroll.
4  Dr Magnes speaking (pan of clapping crowd, 252).

☐ PART B: TITLE: LAYING OF FOUNDATION STONE AT OLAMIT FACTORY FOR CEMENT AND ASBESTOS AT PETAH TIQUA [sic] (122')

כותרת: אבן הפינה לביח"ר עולמית (8).

1  Gate with welcome banner in Hebrew.
2  Buses arriving, crowd gathering, sitting on benches (long, 26).
3  Ephron speaking to crowd (mid, 29).
4  The founder of the factory standing by the clapping crowd. Close-up of signing of the founding scroll (long, 60).
5  General view of the construction site of the factory (long, 71).
6  Guests gathering around the site of the laying of the foundation stone.
7  Placing the scroll in the foundation. People pouring cement (long, 104).
8  Pan of Olamit's products, including pipes and corrugated roofing (mid, 122).

☐ PART C: TITLE: CORNERSTONE LAYING CEREMONY FOR NEW BUILDING OF WIZO TRADE SCHOOL HAIFA (117')

כותרת: הנחת אבן הפינה למשכן לביה"ס המקצועי של ויצ"ו בחיפה (8).

1  Sign in Hebrew on the gate: "Site of the New Vocational School for Girls, Wizo Haifa".

שלט על שער: פה יבנה הבניין החדש בית הספר המקצוע לנערות ע"ש הנריאטה אירוול "ויצו" חיפה.

2  Guests entering the area.
3  Girls' choir.
4  Pan of guests with scenery of Mount Carmel in the background (mid, long, 49).
5  Woman speaking. Crowd clapping. Man speaking (mid, 66).
6  General view of the area and the guests. Woman speaking (mid, long, 89).
7  Woman laying the foundation stone. Pouring cement into the hole (mid, 106).
8  Scenic shot of Mount Carmel (long, 117).

☐ PART D: TITLE: THE ALUMIM GROUP FOUNDING A NEW VILLAGE IN THE NEGEV (350')

כותרת: קבוצת "עלומים" - בני-עקיבא - עולים לנגב (10).

1  General view of the empty sand before the settlement (long, 33).
2  Preparing the area. Laying water pipe as Bedouin look on (mid, 64).
3  Pan of the Negev (long, 80).
4  Sunset, evening views (long, 92).
5  The new settlers stay up all night marking the event. Kibbutz members sitting around table listening to one man speaking, choir singing (long, 119).
6  Sunrise, pan of the convoy laden with construction materials. Members, including women, unload the trucks (long, 162).
7  Sun rising (long, 168).
8  Morning prayers. Men with prayer shawls and phylacteries. Rabbi Neria in the centre (long, 185).
9  Women building barbed wire fence. Men raising wall of building. Various construction activities (mid, 241).
10 Bedouin on camels approaching. Continued construction (mid, 258).
11 Flag-raising (long, 272).
12 Sign on gate in Hebrew: "Alumim" B'nei Akiva Group. First Akiva (long, 278).

על השער: "עלומים" - קבוצת בני עקיבא - עקיבא הראשונה.

13 Carrying a Torah scroll under a wedding canopy. Dancing hora. Reading from the Torah scroll (mid, 332).
14 General view of settlement (long, 350).

## Carmel Newsreels: Series 1

☐ PART E: THE HAGANAH SHIP *EXODUS* ARRIVING IN ISRAEL (45')
1. The ship.
2. Immigrants looking at the shore.
3. People on stretchers are brought ashore (45).

### ■ CARMEL NEWSREEL I-250 · 1947

A Kol Adama rally of Jewish National Fund settlements in the amphitheatre of the Hebrew University on Mount Scopus. Parents Day is celebrated. Work at the Palalum Aluminium and Enamel factory. A new season opens at the Tel Aviv Art Museum. School health clubs gather in the Tel Aviv stadium for impressive gymnastics demonstration.

☐ PART A: TITLE: KOL ADAMA ("THE VOICE OF THE SOUL") YISHUV'S MEETING OF THE [Jewish National Fund] (189')

כותרת: "קול האדמה" כנוס ישובי ק.ק.ל. על הר הצופים

1. Sign in Hebrew: "Kol Adama".
2. Pan across the large audience seated in bleachers (long, 34).
3. Two men wearing caps escort officials on stage.
4. Youths carrying flags arranged in rows on the stage. Singing the national anthem while the Israeli Orchestra plays (mid, 70).
5. Men seated at long table on stage sing *Hatikva* (mid, 82).
6. Dr Granot speaking as the audience listens. Another speaker (mid, 93).
7. Abraham Kamini lectures while reporters at the press table take notes (mid, 105).
8. A woman in traditional Indian costume speaking into microphone. Golda Myerson (Meir) speaking (mid, 123).
9. Ceremonial display and presentation of the flag of Jerusalem (c.u.). Procession of youths carrying flags on stage (mid, c.u., 189).

☐ PART B: TITLE: OUR PARENTS DAY AT THE EXHIBITION (52')

כותרת: חגיגת "יום להורינו"

1. A large decorated room with parents seated on benches. Members of the Parent Teachers Association seated at table.
2. A man addresses the audience (mid, 35).
3. A boy gives a speech. A little girl recites (c.u.). The parents applaud (long, 52).

☐ PART C: TITLE: THE ALUMINIUM FACTORY "PALALUM" IN PALESTINE (277')

כותרת: תעשיית כלי אלומיניום ואמייל בביח"ר "פלאלום"

1. Various types of work in the factory. Workers near the machines.
2. Flattening sheets of aluminium into bowls and pots (mid-long, 102).
3. Polishing the finished products.
4. Female workers attach handles to the various types of pots.
5. The finished products (mid, long, 102).
6. Coating with enamel.
7. Putting in and taking out the pots and bowls from the oven (mid, 253).
8. Preparing crates for shipment to Istanbul and Cyprus (long, 265).
9. Crowds of workers leave the factory (long, 277).

☐ PART D: TITLE: THE NEW ART SEASON AT THE MUSEUM OF TEL AVIV (133')

כותרת: עם פתיחת העונה במוזיאון תל-אביב

1. Superimposition of images of various galleries and their contents (the museum on Rothschild Boulevard) (long, 58).
2. Portrait of Dr Shatz (c.u., 73).
3. Additional pictures. The camera examines some art works in detail.
4. Dissolve of various sculptures. Statue of Dizengoff (mid, c.u., 133).

□ PART E: TITLE: THE HEALTH GROUPS OF THE SCHOOLS MEET AT THE STADION [sic] (222')

כותרת: כנוס חברי אגודות הבריאות של בתי הספר באיצטדיון תל-אביב

1   TITLE IN HEBREW: CHOIR DIRECTED BY S. HOFFMANN

כותרת: מקהלה בנצוחו: ש. הופמן

2   Girls and boys enter the stadium carrying flags and banners followed by the rest of the school (long, 26).
3   The choir sings. The audience in the front rows listening (mid, 40).
4   Groups of girls begin to dance. They perform gymnastics and jump to the music (long, 73).
5   Overview of the stadium. A speaker addresses the youth (long, 91).
6   Passing the flag from one group to another (mid, 102).
7   First aid exercise and practising transfer of wounded (mid, 125).
8   Gymnastics and athletic exhibition that includes jumping over hurdles by boys (long, 149).
9   More gymnastics and acrobatics (long, 159).
10  Humorous section of acrobatics, shot backwards (long, 170).
11  Costumed children dance in groups and perform types of exercise. The routine ends with the display of a banner in Hebrew: "Health is the source of Life" (long, 222).

דגל: "בריאות מקור החיים"

■ **CARMEL NEWSREEL I-251 · 1947**
Children arriving in Palestine from the camps in Cyprus. The accomplishments of Jewish aviation by the "Aviron" company. Jewish settlers in Palestine support the refugees living on Cyprus. A wedding ceremony in a refugee camp on Cyprus.

□ PART A: TITLE: CHILDREN FROM CYPRUS BACK TO PALESTINE (257')

כותרת: ילדים גולים מקפריסין שבים למולדת

1   Pan of the shore of Cyprus from the sea. The streets of Famagusta (long, 32).
2   Children in a detention camp stand on line and receive documents. Adults stand around them.
3   Getting stamped by officials of the British Army and the Jewish Agency (mid, long, 77).
4   Smiling children leave through a gate. Soldiers check their documents (mid, 99).
5   The sad faces of those staying behind (mid, 107).
6   Kissing goodbye to those staying behind, through the barbed wire fence (mid, 121).
7   Children on trucks are ready to leave. Those left behind wave (mid, 144).
8   The children bid farewell to those who took care of them; nurses and teachers who are left behind the barbed wire fence (mid, long, 159).
9   A convoy of trucks goes on its way (long, 176).
10  The walls of old Famagusta. Many children waiting in the port.
11  Children continue to get off trucks and onto a ship (mid, 221).
12  A ship packed with children leaves the port of Famagusta. The children wave (long, 247).
13  Once in Israel the children leave the ship. Fade-out as they get off ship with flag (long, 257).

□ PART B: TITLE: JEWISH AVIATION (320')

כותרת: תעופה עברית מפעולות אוירון חברה ארצישראלית לתעופה

1   Close-up of sign in Hebrew: "Aviron, Eretz Israel Aviation Company".

שלט: אוירון (חברה א"י לתעופה)

2   The care of airplanes inside a service hangar (long, 82).

3   Repairing an airplane from abroad (mid, 69).
4   Taking the airplanes out of the service hangar (long, 82).
5   Taking off according to the instructions of the instructor.
6   View of the Sharon Valley and Tel Aviv from the air.
7   Pilots on radio transmitters.
8   The plane lands and the pilots get out (long, 153).
9   "Aviron" cars drive up and Nathan Axelrod's children get out on airfield. They join other children as they get into plane (long, 205).
10  Pan of airplanes on a field. An instructor explains the operation of an exterior engine (mid, c.u., 223).
11  Two officials examine the planes while student pilots in pairs stand at attention (long).
12  Two pilots walk towards their airplanes.
13  An airplane taking off (shot from another plane). The plane in the air, then veers off in another direction (long).
14  A group of men looks up at the sky.
15  Footage from 1938 (see **CARMEL NEWSREEL I-159**): Young woman looking through binoculars at the sky. Aerial shot of Tower and Stockade settlement. Pilot wearing goggles throws a parcel from the plane. A parachute opens (long).
16  Propeller planes on the ground.
17  Three airplanes in the air (shot from above, 320).

□ PART C: FROM THE SETTLERS IN PALESTINE TO THOSE IN EXILE (111')
1   Loaded boats sit in the port (shot from above).
2   Group of women (c.u.). Convoy of trucks with crates marked in Hebrew: "The Yishuv supports Cyprus exiles".   כתובת: הישוב למען גולי קפריסין
3   The Secretary for Exiles in Cyprus speaking before an audience of women.
4   Loading the goods onto ships (mid).
5   Shot of ship at sea in the distance.
6   Overview of the dock and the goods on it.
7   Close-up of crates and the stamps on them. Loading the crates onto the ship.
8   The insignia of the Committee for the Sake of the Exiles in Cyprus (111).

□ PART D: A WEDDING IN CYPRUS (54')
1   The groom is escorted to the wedding canopy with the bride and her escorts following.
2   The bride circles her groom while a crowd gathers around the wedding canopy (some of the male guests are wearing vests).
3   The groom says a blessing.
4   A rabbi blesses the couple (c.u.).
5   The groom places a ring on the bride's finger (c.u.).
6   The newly weds kiss and the crowd applauds.
7   Some of the guests perched on a tower in the camp for a good view of the ceremony. Fuzzy shot of people in the camp (54).

■ **CARMEL NEWSREEL I-252 · 1947**
Nursery schoolchildren visit a military base on Purim. Planting trees on Tu B'shvat in Ramat Gan. National blood drive by Magen David Adom.

□ PART A: NURSERY SCHOOLCHILDREN SEND PACKAGES OF GOODIES TO OUR TROOPS (164')
1   Adorable children in Purim costumes parading down street, accompanied by adults, carrying banners. The banner at the head of the procession says in Hebrew: "Despite them we shall celebrate".

שלט: "על אפם וחמתם חג נחוג"

2   Children greeting lined-up soldiers (male and female) and presenting them with cardboard Purim cakes (hamantashen).
3   Soldier on knees speaking to children. Soldiers holding smiling children (mid, c.u.).
4   Woman leading children and uniformed men and women in song.
5   Children and uniformed men and women dancing in circle.
6   The children leave the base singing (long, 164).

□ PART B: TU B'SHVAT IN RAMAT GAN (80')
1   Children marching with hoes.
2   Children holding seedlings while reciting (c.u.).
3   Mayor Avraham Krinitzi and his wife plant a tree (mid, 58).
4   Assorted shots of children and adults planting trees on rock-walled terraces.

□ PART C: NATIONAL BLOOD DRIVE FOR MAGEN DAVID ADOM (97')
1   A city square (Kikar Hamoshavot). Magen David Adom cars (fade-out) (long, 4).
2   Interior of laboratory. Female laboratory technician carrying beaker into a room where several people are involved in laboratory work (mid, c.u.).
3   Man opens refrigerator, puts in two bottles, removes two bottles.
4   Man carefully packing bottles in crate on which he attaches sign in Hebrew: "Caution, Bottles of plasma for the Negev" (97).

# Sample Listings from Additional Carmel Productions

## Sample Listings from Additional Carmel Productions 215

■ **Appendix [001]**: CAMPAIGN FILM FOR HISTADRUT ELECTIONS · 1935
Histadrut campaign film 1935, showing contrast between rich and poor neighbourhoods (386').

1. Pan of city street. Pan of poor neighbourhood, shacks.
2. Back view of woman in bath robe, walking down the street.
3. Fancy, clean street.
4. Shacks, muddy streets.
5. HANDWRITTEN HEBREW TITLE: AFFAIRS OF THE CITY - TO ITS BUILDERS.
כותרת: עניני העיר - לבוניה.

■ **Appendix [002]**: DIZENGOFF FILM
Compiled footage on the life and death of Tel Aviv's first Mayor, Meir Dizengoff, including his funeral.

TITLE ON FILM (with symbol of Carmel Studio): CARMEL SOUND NEWS, DIRECTED BY AXELROD. HEBREW TITLE: MEIR DIZENGOFF, OF BLESSED MEMORY. כותרת: יומן קולני כרמל, בהנהלת אקסלרוד. ר' מאיר דיזנגוף ז"ל.

□ PART A (600')
1. HEBREW TITLE: ENTERPRISES OF THE GREAT: THE LEVANT FAIR, PRESS CONFERENCE. כותרת: ממפעלי הכברים: יריד המזרח, במסיבת עתונאים.
2. Dizengoff speaking to reporters, sitting around tables, in Café Galina, Tel Aviv (from **CARMEL NEWSREEL I-032**, October 1935).
3. HEBREW TITLE: RECEPTION FOR ROMANIAN PILOTS.
כותרת: קבלת טייסים מרומניה.
4. Young men leaving cars, being greeted, entering municipal building. Dizengoff greets them.
5. HEBREW TITLE: PRESENT FROM THE KING OF ENGLAND TO THE "PRESIDENT" OF TEL AVIV; M. DIZENGOFF RECEIVES A MEDAL OF HONOUR FROM THE KING OF ENGLAND.
כותרת: תשורת מלך אנגליה לנשיאה של תל-אביב. מ. דיזנגוף מקבל אות כבוד ממלך אנגליה.
6. Interior. Dizengoff wearing medal of honour (cross). Large crowd outside.
7. HEBREW TITLE: CITIZENS OF TEL AVIV FEAR FOR THE WELFARE OF THEIR LEADER. כותרת: בני תל אביב חרדים לשלום נשיאם.
8. Large crowds in street outside hospital.
9. HEBREW TITLE: THE HONOURABLE HIGH COMMISSIONER COMES TO VISIT THE "PRESIDENT" OF TEL-AVIV.
כותרת: ה. מ. הנציב העליון בא לשאול לשלום נשיאה של ת"א.
10. Men leaving hospital and entering car, surrounded by crowd.
11. Hebrew signs announcing death of Dizengoff. Lines of mourners. Funeral procession through streets. Crowds on roofs. Dignitaries.
12. Massive, slow procession in street. Shot from assorted angles. Men carrying coffin. Wreaths.

□ PART B (670')
1. TITLE IN ENGLISH, HEBREW AND ARABIC: APRIL 30TH 1936. Footage from Levant Fair, 1936 (see **CARMEL NEWSREEL I-050**, April 1936).
2. Photograph of large crowd in a book.
3. Pan of building with "Great Britain" written on sign.
4. Shot of building with "Tel Aviv Municipality" written on it in Hebrew and English.
5. Pan of Tel Aviv rooftops.

6  Group of naked children (four, five years old), showering on beach. Playing in water. Children in communal dining-room (see **CARMEL NEWSREEL I-104**, September 13 1937).
7  Dizengoff talking to reporters, Café Galina (see above).
8  HEBREW TITLE: FROM ABROAD TO THE HOMELAND.
9  Men in fezzes helping Dizengoff in straw hat down ramp from ship.
10 Dizengoff joins two men in suits and two women in hats and gloves in small boat on way to shore.
11 At the establishment of Beit HaMehandess. HEBREW TITLE: DIZENGOFF THE BUILDER WITH TEL AVIV BUILDERS (titles for **CARMEL NEWSREEL I-001**).

כותרת: דיזנגוף הבונה עם מקימי הבניין בת"א כהקמת בנינם הם: בית המהנדס.

12 HEBREW TITLE: THE PRINCE OF TEL AVIV WITH THE PRINCE OF LAND - DIZENGOFF AND USSISHKIN - ON THEIR TRIP ABROAD (titles from **CARMEL NEWSREEL I-017**).

כותרת: נסיך תל-אביב עם נסיך הקרקע, מ. דיזנגוף - מ.מ. אוסישקין בנסיעתם לחוץ לארץ.

13 Unclear footage of a group of men on boat, getting into a car.
14 HEBREW TITLE: BENEFACTOR OF THE ARTS AT A CELEBRATION OF THE HABIMAH. CORNERSTONE LAYING FOR HABIMAH THEATRE (titles from **CARMEL NEWSREEL I-016**).

כותרת: נדיב האומנות בשמחת אמני הבימה: אבן פינה לבית הבימה.

15 Group shot, posing for stills. Dizengoff looking at plans, signing document, cutting cake.
16 HEBREW TITLE: CULTURAL CONNECTIONS BETWEEN THE PEOPLE OF THE BOOK AND THE PEOPLE OF FREEDOM, OPENING OF THE ERETZ ISRAEL-FRANCE LIBRARY.

כותרת: קשרי תרבות בין עם הספר לעם החופש. פתיחת הספריה א"י - צרפת.

17 Dizengoff speaking (mid).
18 HEBREW TITLE: TEL AVIV, CENTER OF MEDICAL AND HEALTH INSTITUTIONS, M DIZENGOFF AT THE OPENING OF ASSUTA.

כותרת: תל-אביב, מרכז למוסדות רפואה ובריאות. מ. דיזנגוף בפתיחת "אסותא".

19 Dizengoff in crowded room.

■ **Appendix [003]**: THE REMAINS OF RAMBAM BEING BROUGHT TO TIBERIAS
Dramatisation of the transfer of Maimonides' remains to Tiberias. Old man tells the inspirational story which is re-enacted. Young boy watches builders and imagines himself a worker (approx. 883').

1  An old man telling a story to a crowd. Focus on the face of one attentive boy.
2  Group of men in turbans leading camel, carrying the coffin through the hills.
3  Marauders attack, causing Jews to flee.
4  Unable to open the coffin, the marauders fall to their knees and call the Jews to return.
5  Open copy of THE GUIDE TO THE PERPLEXED (in Hebrew). Assorted archival documents.
6  HEBREW TITLES: "FROM MOSES UNTIL MOSES, THERE WAS NONE LIKE MOSES. A MAN AND NOT A MAN, AND IF A MAN, THEN YOUR MOTHER WAS IMPREGNATED BY AN ANGEL. HERE LIES MOSES BEN MAIMON (MAIMONIDES)".

כותרת: ממשה ועד משה לא קם כמשה. אדם ולא אדם ואם אדם היית ממלאכי רום אמך הרתה. פה טמון משה בן מיימון.

7   Men building, laying bricks; lots of double exposure and artistic framing. Split-screen showing modern buildings "rising" from ruins. Pan of ancient ruins.
8   The old man talks to the young boy. Boy sees a vision of himself as a worker hammering.
9   Interspersed scenes of an ancient building in Tiberias and the old man talking to the boy.

■ **Appendix [004]: THE SEA OF GALILEE AND SURROUNDINGS**
Footage of the Sea of Galilee and surrounding settlements. Including agriculture, construction and Middle Eastern urban scenery (800').

1   Chickens outside.
2   Field with sprinklers.
3   Assorted agricultural scenes. Men and women weeding, hoeing, planting. Cow and calf. Sheep. Men and women picking vegetables.
4   Machine digging on banks of the Sea of Galilee. Pan of hills.
5   Young girl singing.
6   TITLE IN HEBREW: SEA OF GALILEE.
7   Woman in biblical dress, playing harp on bank.
8   Map focussing on Kinneret.
9   Pan of lake, hills.
10  Rowing boat with four rowers and girl singing.
11  Busy street (long).
12  Brickmaking factory. Putting clay in moulds, bricks drying. Construction worker laying bricks.
13  Rowing boat. Lake and hills (long).
14  Mosque by the water.
15  Two small Arab boys playing children's game of stones.
16  Shot of alley from boat moving on lake.
17  Map with pointer. Sign in Hebrew and English: TIBERIAS.
18  Map with pointer. Sign in Hebrew and English: DEGANYA.
19  Map with pointer. Sign in Hebrew and English: KINNERET.
20  Map with pointer. Sign in Hebrew and English: MIGDAL.
21  Pan of settlement by water's edge. Empty rowing boat by shore. Young men and women push out the rowing boat and jump in.
22  Construction site. Cement mixer.
23  Construction of a three-storey apartment building, through time-lapse photography.
24  Street (long). Bus. Horse and wagons.
25  Arabs sweeping street in alley in crowded market area. Clothes hanging from awnings.
26  Arabs in keffiyehs. Man in business suit. Man in fez. Woman with bundle on her head. Little girl holding baby on hip, buying from butcher. Donkey in alley.
27  Street scene. Knife sharpener. Lots of ethnic types. Modern-looking women and men. Men in fez. Religious Jew.
28  Pan of port. Large ships (this is apparently a port on the Mediterranean).
29  Flooded streets. Men in raincoats in water up to knees, carrying man on shoulder.

■ **Appendix [005]: THE ESTABLISHMENT OF THE STATE OF ISRAEL**
Footage assembled as work material for a film about the War of Independence and the early days of statehood. Includes dramatised war footage, siege of Jerusalem, first elections, Chaim Weizmann, David Ben Gurion, Moshe Sharett, immigration, transit camps, Youth Aliyah and military parades.

## Sample Listings from Additional Carmel Productions

◻ **PART A (1751')**
1. Assorted landscapes including the Sea of Galilee.
2. Dramatised military scenes, including: War of Independence, Arab soldiers on horseback attacking, infantry fighting, soldiers in gas masks run quickly by, man carrying wounded man on his shoulders.
3. Tanks. Armoured car. Lookout in keffiya driving through the Old City. Field with explosions. Military manoeuvres. Foot soldiers. Soldier talking on field phone. Throwing hand grenades.
4. Training camp. Men wrestling. Obstacle course. Young men in bathing suits by pool. Put on hats and backpacks. Carry wounded out on stretcher.
5. Surrender of Acre and Jaffa. Watchtower in Jaffa. Arched courtyard. Monk in black robes pointing out scenery from rooftop.
6. Soldiers enlisting.
7. Battle for Jerusalem. Arab soldiers with keffiyot running, on horseback.
8. Siege of Jerusalem. Woman and children receiving water from a man at a tap. Carrying it in containers. Lookouts on Old City Walls. Pan of Jerusalem.
9. Preparations. Jewish soldiers on horseback. Man launching glider plane.
10. Dedication of ambulance plane bought with money raised by schoolchildren in Tel Aviv. Children cut ribbon. Loading "wounded" on plane.
11. View of old ruin through binoculars.
12. Nazareth: street scenes. Jewish soldiers. Jeeps driving through. Two soldiers walking down street. Soldiers guarding.
13. Entourage passes by honour guard. Interior shots of Weizmann becoming provisional president. Ben Gurion seated in front as Weizmann speaks to group.
14. Elections for first Knesset: election posters. Weizmann voting. Ben Gurion voting. Sign on ballot box in Hebrew: The State of Israel Elections.

שלט : מדינת ישראל בכחירות

15. Installation of first Knesset: crowds in the street. Dignitaries, including religious leaders, passing honour guard on steps. Weizmann installed as president. Hand vote.
16. Desert scenery with palm trees.
17. Kibbutz Degania: fixing war-damaged buildings. Children returning after war, running across lawn, playing in trenches. Man feeding chickens.
18. Wedding: crowd consisting mainly of uniformed men and women under bridal canopy. Bride and others walk around groom. Veiled bride and groom in uniform. Dancing hora with man in centre playing accordion. Cutting cake.
19. Establishing Kibbutz Yasur: truck with sign in Hebrew, "YASUR". Trucks full of young men and women. Group marching up hill with tools in their hands. Young men on horses next to tank. Unloading pre-fab houses.
20. Men and women clearing ground, digging holes, putting up fence, tents, wooden pre-fab houses. Breaking stones to make road.
21. Negev: bulldozer. Digging trenches. Laying large water pipes. Ploughing. Water flowing into field. Wheat growing. Harvesting wheat. Preparing bales. Loading wagon with bales of wheat.
22. Beersheva: renovating and repairing buildings. Construction work.
23. Immigration: immigrants disembarking from ship. Sign on ship in Hebrew and English: HAIM ARLOZOROFF. Ship with sign: HAGANAH SHIP EXODUS 1947. Refugees disembarking, looking tired and dirty. British soldiers lined up and guarding the refugees. Prosperous-looking people on ship, brought to shore on smaller boat.
24. Close-ups of assorted faces representative of different national origins. Occasional glimpses of transit camps in background. Tents.
25. Yemenite Jews arriving, leaving plane. Woman with baby.
26. Faces, ethnic types.

## Sample Listings from Additional Carmel Productions 219

☐ PART B (960')
1. Immigrants disembarking from a ship. Men carrying stretcher down gangplank.
2. Old people sitting on benches. Close-ups of faces.
3. Immigrants arriving via truck to transit camp. Residents greet them. Piles of luggage.
4. Inoculations. Doctor and mother holding baby (mid). Close-up of the baby. Men receiving chest X-rays.
5. Mother and child lying on bed in tent. Mother holding baby outdoors. Children playing.
6. Rows of shacks in transit camp. Laundry hanging on lines, as residents walk by. Additional domestic scenes in transit camp, such as man fixing bicycle, man cooking, mothers and children.
7. Officer of ship carries a baby down the gangplank. Immigrants coming down gangplank.
8. Assorted close-up of boys in Youth Aliyah village. Pan of village. Tracking shot through kitchen where food is prepared. Dining-room. Children in youth village sitting on ground. Discussion led by older men. Youth leader sitting with children (mid, c.u.).
9. Children working in vegetable patch. Children playing (mid, c.u.).
10. Working on the land: moving boulders by crane. Herd of sheep and goats. Picking grapes. Picking oranges.
11. Industry: fishermen letting out nets. Shovelling into a furnace. Work on an assembly line in a glass factory. Pan of looms in textile factory.
12. Unloading crates in port, shot from crane. Pan of port. Large ships at dock.
13. Shots of assorted homes - old stone houses, new pre-fabs. Woman drawing water from a well. Close-up of oriental women.
14. Assorted views of the land, including the Jezreel Valley, a kibbutz, Haifa.
15. Immigration: smokestack of large ship (c.u.). Fade to mass of immigrants waving from boat. Large group walking up from quay. Fade to (staged) group of immigrants carrying suitcases, old men and women as well as children, trudging along through fields. The group is singing.
16. Israeli flag flying (c.u.). Honour guard of children holding flags. Youth parade with float: "To Torah, To Work, To Study, and To the Community". Masses of youth marching by with flags.
17. Military parade marches past reviewing stand, with dignitaries including Prime Minister David Ben Gurion (in distance). Marching in commercial district. Soldiers on horseback, in jeeps and by foot. Large crowds line the streets along the parade route. Military parade marching past President Chaim Weizmann, Abba Eban, among others. Parade of male and female sailors marching past ships.
18. Interior of General Assembly of the United Nations. Moshe Sharett speaking. Montage of newspapers announcing Israel's acceptance as a member. Including: *Ha'aretz*, *Davar*, *Al Hamishmar* and *The Palestine Post*. Exterior of the United Nations with international flags. Interior of General Assembly hall. Sharett is congratulated as he and Abba Eban leave the hall.
19. Close-up of hopeful young faces.

■ **Appendix [006]:** SPRINKLER ADVERTISEMENT
Advertisement for LEGO sprinklers (250').

1. Man hoeing in irrigation ditch in orchard.
2. Woman hoeing.
3. Water sprinkler spinning. Dusty plant.
4. Sprinklers dissolve into pile of fruit.
5. TITLE: LEGO.   כותרת: לגו
6. Pan of newly planted field with sprinklers.

7 Time lapsed photographs of growing field.
8 Man in suit and woman in dress walk through orchard.

■ **Appendix [007]: OFEK**
Rushes or screen tests from a 1930s drama starring Alexander Penn, entitled *AVIVA* or *CHALUTZ*, which was never completed (1540').

1 TITLE IN HEBREW AND FRENCH: THIS SMALL FILM WILL TELL ABOUT A CREATIVE ERETZ ISRAEL ENDEAVOUR.
כותרת: הסרט הקטן הזה יספר לכם על מפעל ארץ - ישראלי שכולו רצון ויצירה
2 Two men meet in a café. The older man takes the younger one home to a village.
3 Men working in construction, taking lunch break.
4 Scene of man and woman on rooftop. Man appears to be explaining vision, overcoming depression.
5 Scene repeated with different men, apparently try-outs for part.
6 Several takes of man waving goodbye.
7 Several takes of woman in car waving goodbye.

Subject and Personality Index

# Subject and Personality Index 223

This index is intended as a guide to specific topics, locations and personalities. It includes: HEADINGS, *see* and *see also* references and the numbers of the relevant entries.

The entries are indicated by three different types of number:
- M.001-M.139 refer to the Moledet Productions in the first part of the catalogue.
- C.I-001-C.I-252 refer to the Carmel Newsreels in the second part of the catalogue.
- A.001-A.007 refer to the Carmel Productions in the appendix.

The index has been compiled on an alphabetical word-by-word basis. All entries are arranged in running order within each section of the catalogue.

**AARONOWITZ, YOSEF**
C.I-080

**AARONSOHN, SARAH**
C.I-034, C.I-103, C.I-227.

**ACCIDENTS**
C.I-047, C.I-082, C.I-108, C.I-204.

**ACRE**
A.005, C.I-154.

**ADLOYADA** see JEWISH HOLIDAYS - PURIM

**ADVERTISEMENTS**
A.006, C.I-079, M.004, M.008, M.009, M.010, M.011, M.060, M.061, M.067, M.068, M.071, M.093, M.096, M.101, M.111.

**AERIAL PHOTOGRAPHY**
C.I-036, C.I-099, C.I-106, C.I-159, C.I-168, C.I-188, C.I-251.

**AFFORESTATION**
C.I-041, C.I-088, C.I-122, C.I-128, C.I-170, C.I-207, C.I-224, C.I-226, C.I-239, C.I-244, M.003.

**AFIKIM AIRPORT**
C.I-159, C.I-188 · *see also* AIRPORTS

**AFULA**
C.I-031, C.I-219.

**AGADATI, BARUCH**
M.047, M.098.

**AGRICULTURAL SCHOOLS**
C.I-200 · *see also* KADOURI AGRICULTURAL SCHOOL, MIKVEH ISRAEL

AGRICULTURAL SCHOOL, MIZRAHI AGRICULTURAL SCHOOL, SCHOOLS

**AGRICULTURE**
A.006, C.I-149, C.I-154, C.I-161, C.I-162, C.I-175, C.I-191, C.I-203, C.I-206, M.004, M.026, M.029, M.039, M.063, M.064, M.065, M.066, M.069, M.100, M.123 · *see also* ANIMAL HUSBANDRY, APICULTURE, BANANA TREES, CITRUS FRUIT, HARVEST, INDUSTRY, ORCHARDS, TNUVA, VINEYARDS

**AHAD HA'AM**
C.I-010, C.I-046, C.I-070.

**AHAD HA'AM SCHOOL FOR BOYS**
C.I-138 · *see also* SCHOOLS

**AHARONSON, RABBI SHLOMO**
C.I-004 · *see also* RABBIS

**AIRPORTS**
C.I-155, C.I-159, C.I-168 · *see also* AFIKIM AIRPORT, HAIFA AIRPORT, LOD AIRPORT, SDEH DOV AIRPORT

**ALEXANDER RIVER**
C.I-110

**ALMOGI, YOSEF**
C.I-160, C.I-236.

**ALONIM**
C.I-149 · *see also* KIBBUTZIM

**ALROY**
C.I-163

**ALUF, Y**
M.017

**ALUMIM**
C.I-249 · *see also* KIBBUTZIM

**AMIEL, RABBI MOSHE AVIGDOR**
C.I-045, C.I-082, C.I-085, C.I-102, C.I-104, C.I-117, C.I-179 · *see also* RABBIS

**AMIKAM, YISRAEL**
C.I-002

**ANDREWS, LEWIS Y**
C.I-115, C.I-127.

**ANDREWS HOSPITAL** *see* NETANYA, ANDREWS HOSPITAL

**ANGLO-AMERICAN COMMISSION**
C.I-239

**ANIMAL HUSBANDRY**
C.I-149, C.I-209, C.I-213, C.I-239 · *see also* AGRICULTURE, INDUSTRY

**ANIMATION**
M.004, M.011.

**ANOCHI, Z**
C.I-077

**ANZAC** *see* AUSTRALIA NEW ZEALAND ARMED CORPS

**APICULTURE**
C.I-174, M.069 · *see also* AGRICULTURE

## Subject and Personality Index

**ARAB CHILDREN**
M.116

**ARAB RIOTS**
C.I-104, M.078.

**ARAB TERRORISM**
C.I-108

**ARAB VILLAGES**
C.I-018

**ARAB WOMEN**
M.135

**ARABS**
C.I-012, C.I-182, C.I-214, M.012, M.068, M.116.

**ARANNE, ZALMAN**
C.I-168, C.I-177, C.I-189, C.I-238.

**ARCHAEOLOGY**
C.I-045, C.I-128, C.I-169, C.I-183.

**ARLOZOROFF, CHAIM**
M.058-059

**ASSIS**
C.I-244, M.030, M.040.

**ATHLETICS**
C.I-027, C.I-048, C.I-081, C.I-086, C.I-090, C.I-096, C.I-098, C.I-133, C.I-135, C.I-143, C.I-178, C.I-232 · see also SPORTS

**ATLIT**
C.I-189, C.I-227.

**AUSTRALIA NEW ZEALAND ARMED CORPS**
C.I-210, C.I-217.

**AUXILIARY MILITARY PIONEER CORPS**
C.I-216 · see also JEWISH BRIGADE

**AVIATION**
A.005, C.I-081, C.I-094, C.I-099, C.I-159, C.I-179, C.I-188, C.I-251, M.096, M.107 · see also GLIDERS, PALESTINE AIRWAYS LTD

**AVIHAIL**
C.I-029

*AVIVA*
A.007 · see also FILM-MAKING

**AXELROD, MOSHE**
C.I-139

**AXELROD, NATHAN**
C.I-060, C.I-089, C.I-094, M.103, M.136.

**AYANOT**
C.I-241 · see also KIBBUTZIM

**AYELET HASHACHAR**
C.I-110 · see also KIBBUTZIM

**AZAR** see RABINOWITZ, ALEXANDER ZISSKIND

**BALFOURIA BUILDING** see TEL AVIV, BALFOURIA BUILDING

**BANANA TREES**
M.026, M.065 · see also AGRICULTURE

**BAR ADON, PESSACH**
C.I-169

**BAR ILAN (BERLIN), RABBI MEIR**
C.I-021, C.I-041 · see also RABBIS

**BASKETBALL**
C.I-173 · see also SPORTS

**BEACHES**
M.037 · see also TEL AVIV BEACH, NETANYA BEACH

**BEAUTY QUEENS**
M.025, M.087, M.113.

**BEDOUIN**
C.I-062, C.I-151, C.I-182, C.I-242.

**BEERSHEVA**
A.005

**BEILINSON, MOSES**
C.I-061, C.I-062, C.I-111.

**BEILINSON HOSPITAL**
C.I-013, C.I-046, C.I-061 · see also HOSPITALS

**BEIT HINUCH**
C.I-092 see also SCHOOLS

**BEIT SHEAN VALLEY**
C.I-094, C.I-238.

**BEIT SHEARIM**
C.I-149, C.I-169 · see also KIBBUTZIM

**BEIT YOSEF**
C.I-082

**BEN-AMI, OVAD**
C.I-002, C.I-016, C.I-086, C.I-127, C.I-231, C.I-239.

**BEN GURION, DAVID**
A.005, C.I-024, C.I-044, C.I-134, C.I-176, C.I-227, C.I-229, C.I-238, C.I-239, C.I-248.

**BEN GURION, PAULA**
C.I-176

**BEN SHEMEN**
C.I-022, C.I-027, C.I-164.

**BEN TZVI, YITZHAK**
C.I-072, C.I-102, C.I-146, C.I-227, C.I-228, C.I-232, C.I-233, C.I-247.

**BEN YA'AKOV, YITZHAK**
C.I-188

**BEN YEHUDA, ELIEZER**
C.I-167

**BERGER, YA'AKOV**
C.I-008

**BERLIN, RABBI MEIR** see BAR ILAN (BERLIN), RABBI MEIR

**BERLINSKY, ZE'EV**
C.I-108

**BETAR**
C.I-034, C.I-099, C.I-220, M.072 · see also YOUNG BETAR

**BETHLEHEM**
C.I-241

**BIALIK, CHAIM NACHMAN**
C.I-010, C.I-021, C.I-093, C.I-188.

**BIALIK AWARDS**
C.I-044

**BILU** see GEDERA

**BITANIA**
C.I-243

**BITZARON AID SOCIETY**
C.I-042

**BLIND CHILDREN**
C.I-089

**BLOCH, AARON**
C.I-060

**BLOCH, YEHUDIT**
C.I-060

## Subject and Personality Index    225

**BLOOD DONATIONS**
C.I-252

**BNEI AKIVA**
C.I-194, C.I-231, C.I-249 ·
see also YOUTH
MOVEMENTS

**BNEI BINYAMIN**
C.I-036

**BNEI BRAK**
C.I-082, C.I-095, C.I-194,
C.I-245.

**BOATING**
C.I-095, C.I-102, C.I-134,
M.070, M.126 · see also
SPORTS, WATER SPORTS

**BOXING MATCHES**
C.I-046 · see also SPORTS

**BRANDEIS, JUDGE LOUIS**
see LOUIS BRANDEIS
SCHOOL

**BRASS BAND**
C.I-121 · see also MUSIC

**BRENNER, YOSEPH CHAIM**
C.I-025

**BRIDGES**
C.I-066, C.I-100.

**BRITISH ARMY**
C.I-086, C.I-114, C.I-158,
C.I-216 · see also
MILITARY, SARAFEND

**BRITISH MANDATE**
C.I-005, C.I-010, C.I-061,
C.I-062, C.I-065, C.I-068,
C.I-083, C.I-086, C.I-114,
C.I-231, C.I-234, C.I-236,
C.I-239, C.I-244, C.I-248,
M.015, M.035, M.044,
M.050, M.052, M.106,
M.109 · see also WHITE
PAPER

**BRITISH MANDATE, CENSORSHIP**
C.I-141

**BROD, MAX**
C.I-174

**BUILDING INDUSTRY**
A.003, A.004, A.005,
C.I-019, C.I-026, C.I-074,
C.I-111, C.I-114, C.I-117,
C.I-139, C.I-207, C.I-232,
M.027, M.028

**CAESAREA**
C.I-237

**CALISTHENICS**
C.I-134, M.128, M.134,
M.139 · see also
GYMNASTICS, SPORTS

**CAR RACING**
C.I-104 · see also SPORTS

**CARL GUSTAV, PRINCE OF SWEDEN**
C.I-002

**CARMEL FILM**
C.I-060, C.I-089 · see also
FILM-MAKING

**CARMEL MIZRACHI**
M.010, M.011, M.060,
M.061.

**CARNIVALS** see JEWISH
HOLIDAYS - PURIM

**CEMETERIES**
C.I-037, C.I-061, M.050,
M.078 · see also
FUNERALS

**CHANCELLOR, SIR JOHN**
M.017, M.044.

**CHANUKAH** see JEWISH
HOLIDAYS - CHANUKAH

**CHARITY ORGANISATIONS** see
BITZARON AID SOCIETY,
JOINT DISTRIBUTION
COMMITTEE, KOFER
HAYISHUV.

**CHESS COMPETITIONS**
C.I-017 · see also SPORTS

**CHILDCARE**
C.I-012, C.I-135, C.I-142,
C.I-143, C.I-156, C.I-174,
C.I-198, C.I-226, C.I-229,
C.I-245, C.I-246, C.I-248,
M.094 · see also FAMILY
LIFE, TEL AVIV, MOTHER
AND CHILD CENTRE,
WIZO.

**CHILDREN**
C.I-022, C.I-023, C.I-042,
C.I-045, C.I-073, C.I-092,
C.I-098, C.I-104, C.I-114,
C.I-118, C.I-121, C.I-129,
C.I-140, C.I-150, C.I-172,
C.I-181, C.I-187, C.I-192,
C.I-193, C.I-200, C.I-223,
C.I-226, C.I-235, C.I-248,
M.007, M.016, M.026,
M.030, M.032, M.043,
M.051, M.064, M.079,
M.085, M.094, M.101,
M.108, M.116, M.119,
M.121, M.130 · see also
FAMILY LIFE

**CINEMAS** see CULTURAL
LIFE, TEL AVIV, ESTHER
CINEMA, TEL AVIV,
MIGDALOR CINEMA, TEL
AVIV, MUGRABI CINEMA,
TEL AVIV, OPHIR
CINEMA, TEL AVIV,
RIMON CINEMA.

**CITRUS FRUIT**
C.I-039, C.I-067, C.I-068,
C.I-070, C.I-100, C.I-106,
C.I-109, C.I-153, C.I-198,
C.I-215, C.I-244, M.004,
M.063, M.064, M.101 ·
see also AGRICULTURE

**CIVIL DEFENCE**
C.I-194, C.I-196, C.I-197,
C.I-206, C.I-209, C.I-222,
C.I-225, C.I-228.

**COHEN, AHARON**
C.I-043

**COHEN, ROSA**
C.I-112

**COMMERCE**
C.I-092, C.I-176, M.008,
M.096 · see also
INDUSTRY

**COMMISSIONS** see
ANGLO-AMERICAN
COMMISSION, PEEL
COMMISSION, SHAW
COMMISSION, UN
SPECIAL COMMISSION

**CO-OPERATIVE COUNCIL**
C.I-048

**COSMETICS**
M.009

**CRETE**
C.I-030

**CROSBIE, ROBERT EDWARD HAROLD**
C.I-150

**CULTURAL LIFE** see
CINEMAS, DANCING,
FOLK DANCING,
MUSEUMS, MUSIC,
SONGS, THEATRE.

**CYPRUS**
C.I-244, C.I-247, C.I-251.

**CZECH ARMY**
C.I-201

## 226  Subject and Personality Index

**DAFNA**
C.I-182, C.I-230 · see also KIBBUTZIM

**DAIRY INDUSTRY**
C.I-211, M.093 · see also INDUSTRY

**DAN**
C.I-182 · see also KIBBUTZIM

**DANCING**
C.I-071, C.I-105, C.I-107, C.I-109, C.I-112, C.I-117, C.I-120, C.I-145, C.I-172, M.030, M.039 · see also CULTURAL LIFE, FOLK DANCING

**DAVAR**
C.I-013 · see also NEWSPAPERS

**DAY CARE CENTRES** see CHILDCARE

**DEAD SEA**
C.I-028

**DEGANYA**
A.005, C.I-049, C.I-243 · see also KIBBUTZIM

**DEGANYA BET**
C.I-238 · see also KIBBUTZIM

**DEGEL ZION MOVEMENT**
C.I-188

**DELLA PERGOLA, EDITH**
C.I-187

**DIASPORA RELATIONS**
C.I-160, C.I-162.

**DIZENGOFF, MEIR**
A.002, C.I-001, C.I-010, C.I-016, C.I-017, C.I-030, C.I-044, C.I-050, C.I-060, C.I-075, C.I-104, C.I-157, M.001, M.015, M.021, M.025, M.077, M.087, M.109.

**DIZENGOFF, TSINA**
M.001, M.021.

**DRAMATIC FOOTAGE**
A.003, A.005, A.007, M.003, M.007, M.024, M.062.

**DUBEK**
C.I-095

**DVIR - BIALIK PUBLISHING HOUSE**
C.I-044

**EBAN, ABBA**
A.005, C.I-239, C.I-247, C.I-248.

**EDRI, YEHOSHUA**
C.I-060

**EGGED**
C.I-171, C.I-218.

**EILON**
C.I-175 · see also KIBBUTZIM

**EIN GEV**
C.I-136, C.I-227 · see also KIBBUTZIM

**EIN HAKOREH**
C.I-079 · see also KIBBUTZIM

**EIN HAMIFRATZ**
C.I-152, C.I-165 · see also KIBBUTZIM

**EIN HAROD**
C.I-243 · see also KIBBUTZIM

**EIN IRON**
C.I-035

**EL YASHIV**
C.I-223 · see also KIBBUTZIM

**ELDERLY**
M.030 · see also OLD AGE HOMES

**ELECTIONS**
A.005, C.I-021, C.I-024, C.I-025, C.I-041, C.I-062, C.I-094, C.I-124.

**EMEK HEFER** see HEFER VALLEY

**EMEK YIZREEL** see JEZREEL VALLEY

**EMEK ZEVULUN** see ZEBULUN VALLEY

**EPSTEIN, ELIAHU**
C.I-001, C.I-010, C.I-011.

**ESHKOL, LEVY**
C.I-163, C.I-236, C.I-246.

**EVEN YEHUDA**
C.I-142, C.I-229.

**EXHIBITIONS**
C.I-031, C.I-045, C.I-066, C.I-130, C.I-131, C.I-145, C.I-162, C.I-180, C.I-218, C.I-226, M.002, M.021, M.052, M.055, M.076 · see also FLOWER EXHIBITION, NEW YORK EXHIBITION, TEL AVIV, LEVANT FAIR.

**"EXODUS"**
A.005, C.I-249.

**FACTORIES** see ASSIS, CARMEL MIZRACHI, DUBEK, GALAM FACTORY, GAVISH GLASS FACTORY, HAMLACHIM FACTORY, HILLEL PHARMACEUTICAL COMPANY, INDUSTRY, IZHAR, JAFFA IRON WORKS, KREMENER (VULCAN), MICHSAF FACTORY, OKAVA FACTORY, PALALUM ALUMINIUM FACTORY, PRI MAZON, PRI-PERI, YAHALOM, YAKHIN.

**FAIRS** see EXHIBITIONS

**FAISAL, CROWN PRINCE**
C.I-024

**FAMILY LIFE**
M.099, M.114 · see also CHILDCARE, CHILDREN

**FASHION**
C.I-043

**FILM-MAKING**
C.I-060, M.007, M.014, M.019, M.022, M.103 · see also AVIVA, CARMEL FILM, ODED THE WANDERER, OFEK, ONCE UPON A TIME

**FIRE-FIGHTING**
C.I-002, C.I-029, C.I-155, C.I-214.

**FIRES**
C.I-017, C.I-023, C.I-038, C.I-066, C.I-079, C.I-083, C.I-099, C.I-129.

**FISHING INDUSTRY**
C.I-136, C.I-189, C.I-208 · see also INDUSTRY

**FISHMAN, RABBI YEHUDA** see MAIMON, RABBI YEHUDA (FISHMAN)

**FLOODS**
C.I-001, C.I-161, C.I-162,
C.I-209, C.I-063, C.I-040,
C.I-068, C.I-110, C.I-125.

**FLORA**
C.I-079, C.I-120, C.I-145.

**FLOWER EXHIBITION**
C.I-140

**FOLK DANCING**
C.I-062, C.I-223, C.I-249,
M.047, M.084, M.095,
M.098 · see also
CULTURAL LIFE,
DANCING

**FOOD INDUSTRY**
C.I-123, C.I-173, C.I-244,
M.105 · see also
INDUSTRY

**FOREIGN RELATIONS**
A.002, C.I-002, C.I-036.

**FRIEDLAND, URIEL**
C.I-160, C.I-217.

**FRIEDMAN, RABBI MORDECHAI**
C.I-173

**FUNERALS**
A.002, C.I-004, C.I-011,
C.I-016, C.I-027, C.I-032,
C.I-035, C.I-062, C.I-080,
C.I-099, C.I-104, C.I-112,
C.I-148, C.I-203, C.I-230,
M.001, M.012,
M.058-059 · see also
CEMETERIES, MEMORIAL
SERVICES

**GABAI, YEHUDA**
C.I-124

**GALAM FACTORY**
C.I-231

**GALILEE**
C.I-018, C.I-040, C.I-110,
C.I-231.

**GARDENS** see PARKS
AND GARDENS

**GAVISH GLASS FACTORY**
C.I-243

**GEDERA**
C.I-001, C.I-221, C.I-222.

**GENERAL ZIONIST ASSOCIATION**
C.I-123

**GENSIN, MENACHEM**
C.I-141

**GERMAN JEWS**
C.I-049, C.I-073, C.I-103,
C.I-178, C.I-245.

**GHAFFIRS** see JEWISH
SETTLEMENT POLICE

**GIVAT BRENNER**
C.I-138, C.I-215, C.I-239 ·
see also KIBBUTZIM

**GIVAT HASHLOSHA**
C.I-032 · see also
KIBBUTZIM

**GIVAT ZAYIT**
C.I-169

**GIVAT ZEID**
C.I-232

**GIVATAYIM**
C.I-042

**GIVATAYIM, BOROCHOV CENTRE**
C.I-114

**GLICKSON, MOSHE**
C.I-222

**GLIDERS**
C.I-064, C.I-096 · see also
AVIATION

**GOLAND, SARAH**
C.I-130

**GOLAND, YOSEF**
C.I-062, C.I-066, C.I-130.

**GOLDBERG, YITZHAK LEIB**
C.I-031

**GOLDMAN, NAHUM**
C.I-101

**GORDON, ELIYAHU**
C.I-217

**GORDONIA MAAPILIM GROUP**
C.I-189

**GORT, F M LORD**
C.I-231, C.I-239.

**GOTTLIEB, SUE**
M.025, M.087, M.113.

**GOVERNING COUNCIL OF THE YISHUV** see VA'AD LEUMI

**GRADINGER, KALMAN**
C.I-093

**GRANOT, AVRAHAM**
C.I-044, C.I-242, C.I-250.

**GREECE**
C.I-103

**GRINBAUM, OSCAR**
C.I-158

**GRONEMAN, SAMMY**
C.I-044, C.I-099.

**GROSSMAN, MEIR**
C.I-024

**GRUENBAUM, YITZHAK**
C.I-024, C.I-119, C.I-188,
C.I-190, C.I-222, C.I-227,
C.I-242.

**GUREVITZ, DOV**
C.I-019

**GYMNASIA HERZLIYAH**
M.022, M.051, M.129,
M.136 · see also
SCHOOLS

**GYMNASTICS**
C.I-002, C.I-099, M.022 ·
see also CALISTHENICS,
SPORTS

*HA'ARETZ*
C.I-043, C.I-071, C.I-142 ·
see also NEWSPAPERS

**HABIMAH THEATRE**
A.002, C.I-016, C.I-076,
C.I-120, C.I-141 · see also
THEATRE

*HACARMEL*
C.I-161 · see also
NEWSPAPERS

**HACOHEN, DAVID**
C.I-227, C.I-235.

**HADASSAH UNIVERSITY HOSPITAL** see
JERUSALEM, HADASSAH
UNIVERSITY HOSPITAL

**HADERA**
C.I-044, C.I-087, C.I-092,
C.I-127, C.I-171.

**HAGANAH**
C.I-141, C.I-207.

**HAIFA**
C.I-002, C.I-005, C.I-081,
C.I-086, C.I-099, C.I-107,
C.I-111, C.I-117, C.I-118,

## Subject and Personality Index

C.I-121, C.I-128, C.I-130,
C.I-131, C.I-133, C.I-135,
C.I-139, C.I-155, C.I-156,
C.I-157, C.I-158, C.I-161,
C.I-168, C.I-170, C.I-176,
C.I-202, C.I-217, C.I-221,
C.I-241, C.I-245, C.I-247,
M.028.

**HAIFA, AHUZA**
C.I-130

**HAIFA AIRPORT**
C.I-099

**HAIFA, ALLENBY PARK**
C.I-131

**HAIFA GOVERNMENT HOSPITAL**
C.I-118, C.I-168 · see also HOSPITALS

**HAIFA, KIRYAT AMAL**
C.I-104

**HAIFA, MOUNT CARMEL**
see MOUNT CARMEL

**HAIFA NAVAL HIGH SCHOOL**
C.I-189, C.I-240 · see also SCHOOLS

**HAIFA, NEVE SHE'ANAN**
C.I-246

**HAIFA PORT**
C.I-002, C.I-005, C.I-070,
C.I-192, C.I-227, C.I-236,
C.I-246.

**HAIFA-TEL AVIV HIGHWAY** see TEL AVIV-HAIFA HIGHWAY

**HALEVY, MOSHE**
C.I-099

**HAMEIRI, AVIGDOR**
C.I-116

**HAMLACHIM FACTORY**
C.I-242

**HANDICAPPED**
C.I-118

**HANDICRAFTS**
C.I-096, C.I-113, C.I-151,
C.I-163, C.I-167.

**HANITA**
C.I-146, C.I-175 · see also KIBBUTZIM

**HANKIN, YEHOSHUA**
C.I-042

**HANOAR HA'OVED**
C.I-023, C.I-076, C.I-095,
C.I-149, C.I-164, C.I-180,
C.I-196, C.I-235 · see also YOUTH MOVEMENTS

**HAOHEL THEATRE**
C.I-075, C.I-124 · see also THEATRE

**HAPOEL**
C.I-004, C.I-008, C.I-018,
C.I-027, C.I-028, C.I-034,
C.I-037, C.I-046, C.I-047,
C.I-070, C.I-085, C.I-090,
C.I-095, C.I-099, C.I-102,
C.I-107, C.I-115, C.I-134,
C.I-135, C.I-177, C.I-204,
C.I-232, C.I-237, C.I-241 ·
see also SPORTS

**HAPOEL HAMIZRACHI**
C.I-082, C.I-141 · see also SPORTS

**HAPOEL TEL AVIV**
C.I-168 · see also SPORTS

**HARVEST**
C.I-083, C.I-093, C.I-191,
C.I-223 · see also AGRICULTURE

**HASHOMER**
C.I-105, C.I-133.

**HASSIDIM**
C.I-028, C.I-045, C.I-173.

**HATZERIM**
C.I-242 · see also KIBBUTZIM

**HEBREW LANGUAGE**
C.I-002, C.I-106.

**HEBREW UNIVERSITY**
C.I-007, C.I-037, C.I-228,
C.I-248, C.I-249, C.I-250.

**HEBREW WRITERS**
C.I-236 · see also individual writers

**HEFER VALLEY**
C.I-207, C.I-029, C.I-110,
C.I-135, M.081.

**HEFTZIBAH**
C.I-207

**HERZFELD, AVRAHAM**
C.I-082, C.I-099, C.I-146,
C.I-147, C.I-152, C.I-228,
C.I-243, C.I-247.

**HERZL MEMORIAL**
C.I-116

**HERZLIYAH GYMNASIUM**
see GYMNASIA
HERZLIYAH · see also SCHOOLS

**HERZOG, RABBI YITZHAK HALEVI**
C.I-011, C.I-070, C.I-072,
C.I-135, C.I-142, C.I-227,
C.I-230, C.I-234, C.I-237,
C.I-239, C.I-241 · see also RABBIS

**HILLEL PHARMACEUTICAL COMPANY**
C.I-081

**HISTADRUT**
A.001, C.I-025, C.I-110,
C.I-115, C.I-176, C.I-247 ·
see also LABOUR UNIONS, KUPAT CHOLIM

**HOLIDAY CAMPS**
C.I-021, C.I-022, C.I-027,
C.I-033, C.I-150, C.I-186.

**HOLOCAUST**
C.I-229, C.I-241, C.I-246.

**HOLON, KIRYAT AVODAH**
C.I-074

**HORSE RACING**
C.I-107, C.I-217, C.I-219,
M.080 · see also SPORTS

**HOSPITALS** see
BEILINSON HOSPITAL,
HAIFA GOVERNMENT
HOSPITAL, JERUSALEM:
HADASSAH UNIVERSITY
HOSPITAL, NETANYA:
ANDREWS HOSPITAL, TEL
AVIV: ASSUTA
HOSPITAL.

**HOZ, DOV**
C.I-133, C.I-177, C.I-188,
C.I-225.

**HULA VALLEY**
C.I-110, C.I-136, C.I-151 ·
see also SWAMPS

**HULATA**
C.I-136 · see also KIBBUTZIM

**HULDAH**
C.I-092, C.I-102 · see also KIBBUTZIM

**HURVA SYNAGOGUE** see
JERUSALEM, HURVA
SYNAGOGUE

## Subject and Personality Index    229

**HUSSEINI, MUSA KAZEM AL**
M.012

**ILLEGAL IMMIGRATION**
C.I-189, C.I-246 · *see also* IMMIGRATION

**IMAS, CLARA**
C.I-187

**IMMIGRATION**
A.005, C.I-005, C.I-028, C.I-030, C.I-049, C.I-073, C.I-103, C.I-113, C.I-118, C.I-132, C.I-157, C.I-178, C.I-196, C.I-200, C.I-204, C.I-223, C.I-231, C.I-240, C.I-249 · *see also* ILLEGAL IMMIGRATION, REFUGEES

**INDUSTRY**
A.004, C.I-045, C.I-048, C.I-065, C.I-095, C.I-116, C.I-123, C.I-133, C.I-139, C.I-154, C.I-156, C.I-165, C.I-183, C.I-205, C.I-225, C.I-231, C.I-239, C.I-242, C.I-243, C.I-244, C.I-245, C.I-247, C.I-249, C.I-250, M.048, M.060, M.061, M.064, M.067, M.068, M.105, M.108 · *see also* AGRICULTURE, ANIMAL HUSBANDRY, BUILDING INDUSTRY, COMMERCE, DAIRY INDUSTRY, FACTORIES, FISHING INDUSTRY, FOOD INDUSTRY, LEATHER INDUSTRY, OIL REFINERIES, WINERIES

**IRRIGATION**
A.006, C.I-116, C.I-152, C.I-154, M.065, M.066, M.124, M.137.

**ISRAEL DEFENCE FORCES**
A.005

**IZHAR**
C.I-070, C.I-116.

**JAFFA**
A.005, C.I-002, C.I-019, C.I-023, C.I-030, C.I-104, M.070.

**JAFFA IRON WORKS**
M.002

**JAFFA PORT**
C.I-039, C.I-049.

**JAFFE, LEIB**
C.I-182

**JAMM, HELA**
C.I-163

**JERICHO**
C.I-248

**JERUSALEM**
A.005, C.I-026, C.I-033, C.I-039, C.I-047, C.I-085, C.I-086, C.I-089, C.I-118, C.I-124, C.I-128, C.I-161, C.I-176, C.I-185, C.I-201, C.I-219, C.I-232, C.I-237, M.005, M.012, M.044, M.049, M.050.

**JERUSALEM, BAYIT VEGAN**
C.I-049

**JERUSALEM, CENTRAL POST OFFICE**
C.I-142

**JERUSALEM COMMUNITY COUNCIL**
C.I-124

**JERUSALEM, GOVERNMENT HOUSE**
C.I-047

**JERUSALEM, HADASSAH HOUSE**
C.I-074

**JERUSALEM, HADASSAH UNIVERSITY HOSPITAL**
C.I-101, C.I-180, C.I-228, C.I-230 · *see also* HOSPITALS

**JERUSALEM, HEBREW UNIVERSITY** *see* HEBREW UNIVERSITY

**JERUSALEM, HURVA SYNAGOGUE**
C.I-230 · *see also* SYNAGOGUES

**JERUSALEM, JAFFA GATE**
C.I-096

**JERUSALEM, JESHURUN SYNAGOGUE**
C.I-026, C.I-235 · *see also* SYNAGOGUES

**JERUSALEM, JEWISH AGENCY BUILDING**
C.I-021, C.I-026, C.I-232 · *see also* JEWISH AGENCY

**JERUSALEM, KING DAVID HOTEL**
C.I-024, C.I-026, C.I-234, M.044.

**JERUSALEM, MOSQUE OF OMAR**
M.012

**JERUSALEM, MOUNT OF OLIVES**
C.I-027

**JERUSALEM, MOUNT SCOPUS**
C.I-007, C.I-037, C.I-061, C.I-101, C.I-180, C.I-227, C.I-228, C.I-248, C.I-249, C.I-250, M.050.

**JERUSALEM, OLD CITY**
C.I-027, M.012.

**JERUSALEM, RAILWAY STATION**
C.I-024

**JERUSALEM, ROCKEFELLER MUSEUM**
C.I-128

**JERUSALEM-TEL AVIV ROAD**
M.005

**JERUSALEM, TOWER OF DAVID**
C.I-096

**JERUSALEM, YMCA BUILDING**
C.I-026, C.I-239, C.I-248.

**JEWISH AGENCY**
C.I-119 · *see also* JERUSALEM, JEWISH AGENCY BUILDING

**JEWISH BRIGADE**
C.I-216, C.I-228 · *see also* AUXILIARY MILITARY PIONEER CORPS, MILITARY

**JEWISH HOLIDAYS** *see also* RELIGIOUS LIFE

**JEWISH HOLIDAYS - CHANUKAH**
C.I-042, C.I-114, C.I-115, C.I-166, C.I-228.

**JEWISH HOLIDAYS - LAG BA'OMER**
C.I-012, C.I-084, C.I-085, C.I-086, C.I-180, C.I-221.

**JEWISH HOLIDAYS - PURIM**
C.I-002, C.I-075, C.I-099, C.I-130, C.I-252, M.006, M.023, M.036, M.040, M.042, M.046, M.084,

M.092, M.094, M.095,
M.097, M.121, M.125.

**JEWISH HOLIDAYS -
SHAVUOT**
C.I-015, C.I-087, C.I-088,
C.I-093, C.I-139, C.I-140,
C.I-181, C.I-248, M.030,
M.032, M.079, M.085,
M.120, M.130.

**JEWISH HOLIDAYS -
SIMCHAT BEIT
HASHOEVA**
C.I-035

**JEWISH HOLIDAYS -
SUCCOT**
C.I-100, C.I-237, C.I-242.

**JEWISH HOLIDAYS - TU
B'SHVAT**
C.I-048, C.I-049, C.I-073,
C.I-074, C.I-121, C.I-170,
C.I-207, C.I-238, C.I-252.

**JEWISH HUNTERS
ASSOCIATION**
C.I-128, C.I-141, C.I-143,
C.I-158 · see also SPORTS

**JEWISH LEGION**
C.I-037, C.I-061, C.I-080,
C.I-086, C.I-197, M.049,
M.050 · see also MILITARY

**JEWISH NATIONAL FUND**
C.I-033, C.I-036, C.I-069,
C.I-070, C.I-127, C.I-160,
C.I-170, C.I-244, C.I-250,
M.042, M.046.

**JEWISH SETTLEMENT
POLICE**
C.I-102, C.I-133, C.I-146,
C.I-149, C.I-152, C.I-155,
C.I-156, C.I-191, C.I-201,
C.I-214, C.I-219, C.I-231,
C.I-243 · see also POLICE

**JEZREEL VALLEY**
C.I-093, C.I-096, C.I-116,
C.I-159, C.I-163, C.I-191,
C.I-213, C.I-243.

**JOINT DISTRIBUTION
COMMITTEE**
C.I-245

**JORDAN RIVER**
C.I-230, C.I-231.

**JORDAN VALLEY**
C.I-018, C.I-028, C.I-151,
C.I-159.

**JOURNALISTS**
C.I-098, C.I-233.

**JUDEAN HILLS**
M.005, M.049.

**KADOURI AGRICULTURAL
SCHOOL**
C.I-012 · see also
AGRICULTURAL
SCHOOLS, SCHOOLS

**KALYA**
C.I-028

**KAMINI, ABRAHAM**
C.I-069, C.I-244, C.I-250.

**KAMZON, YA'AKOV D**
C.I-002

**KAPLAN, ELIEZER**
C.I-046, C.I-119, C.I-190,
C.I-228.

**KARIT**
C.I-203 · see also
KIBBUTZIM

**KARKUR**
C.I-231

**KARLEBACH, DR EZRIEL**
C.I-233

**KATZ, MANEH**
C.I-031

**KATZ, YITZHAK**
M.021

**KATZNELSON, BERL**
C.I-013, C.I-069.

**KATZNELSON, TOVA**
C.I-244

**KEITH-ROACH, SIR
EDWARD**
C.I-002, C.I-070, C.I-081,
C.I-086, C.I-099, C.I-105,
C.I-106, C.I-131, C.I-155.

**KEREN HAYESOD**
C.I-119, C.I-236, M.043.

**KFAR CHAIM**
C.I-207

**KFAR DAROM**
C.I-242 · see also
KIBBUTZIM

**KFAR GEULIM**
C.I-201 · see also
KIBBUTZIM

**KFAR GIL'ADI**
C.I-110 · see also
KIBBUTZIM

**KFAR HAROEH**
C.I-231 · see also
KIBBUTZIM

**KFAR HASSIDIM**
C.I-204

**KFAR HAYOVEL**
C.I-036

**KFAR KISH**
C.I-242

**KFAR MACCABI**
C.I-009

**KFAR MALAL**
C.I-097 · see also
KIBBUTZIM

**KFAR MALAL, JOSEPH
AARONOVITCH SCHOOL**
C.I-097 · see also
SCHOOLS

**KFAR MASARYK**
C.I-214 · see also
KIBBUTZIM

**KFAR MENACHEM**
C.I-097, C.I-203 · see also
KIBBUTZIM

**KFAR NETTA**
C.I-195 · see also
KIBBUTZIM

**KFAR SABA**
C.I-210

**KFAR SHMARYAHU**
C.I-088

**KFAR SUMMETS**
C.I-011

**KFAR VITKIN**
C.I-236 · see also
KIBBUTZIM

**KHOUSHY, ABBA**
C.I-091

**KIBBUTZIM**
C.I-213, C.I-242 · see also
ALONIM, ALUMIM,
AYANOT, AYELET
HASHACHAR, BEIT
SHEARIM, DAFNA, DAN,
DEGANYA, DEGANYA
BET, EILON, EIN GEV, EIN
HAKOREH, EIN
HAMIFRATZ, EIN HAROD,
EL YASHIV, GIVAT
BRENNER, GIVAT
HASHLOSHA, HANITA,
HATZERIM, HULATA,
HULDAH, KARIT, KFAR

*Subject and Personality Index* 231

GEULIM, KFAR DAROM, KFAR GIL'ADI, KFAR HAROEH, KFAR MALAL, KFAR MASARYK, KFAR MENACHEM, KFAR NETTA, KFAR VITKIN, KIRYAT ANAVIM, MA'ABAROT, MA'ALEH HAHAMISHA, MENARA, MERHAVIA, MISHMAR HA'EMEK, MISHMAR-ZEBULUN, MIZRAH, NA'AN, NEVATIM, NIR DAVID, NITZANIM, RAMAT HAKOVESH, RAMAT YOHANAN, TIRAT TZVI, TZOFIT, YAGUR.

**KING DAVID HOTEL** *see* JERUSALEM, KING DAVID HOTEL

**KING GEORGE V**
C.I-010, C.I-047.

**KING GEORGE VI**
C.I-086, C.I-234.

**KIRYAT AMAL**
C.I-104, C.I-156, C.I-232.

**KIRYAT ANAVIM**
C.I-122 · *see also* KIBBUTZIM

**KIRYAT ARYEH**
C.I-178, C.I-220.

**KIRYAT AVODAH**
C.I-170, C.I-242.

**KIRYAT BIALIK**
C.I-154, C.I-200.

**KIRYAT HAIM**
C.I-154, C.I-181.

**KIRYAT MOTZKIN, MACCABI HOUSE**
C.I-119

**KIRYAT ONO**
C.I-210

**KIRYAT SHMUEL**
C.I-244

**KIRYAT YAM**
C.I-139, C.I-152.

**KLAUSNER, YOSEF**
C.I-044, C.I-106, C.I-229.

**KLAUZNER, MARGOT**
C.I-016

**KLINOV, YISHAYAHU**
C.I-043, C.I-227.

**KNESSET**
A.005

**KOFER HAYISHUV**
C.I-160, C.I-166.

**KOOK, RABBI AVRAHAM**
C.I-004, C.I-027, C.I-099, C.I-142 · *see also* RABBIS

**KRAUS, ELIAHU**
C.I-045

**KRAUS, GERTRUDE**
C.I-084

**KREMENER (VULCAN)**
C.I-133

**KRINITZI, AVRAHAM**
C.I-170, C.I-181, C.I-188, C.I-206, C.I-214, C.I-229, C.I-247, C.I-248, C.I-252.

**KUPAT CHOLIM**
C.I-013, C.I-046 · *see also* HISTADRUT

**KURDISH JEWS**
C.I-163

**KUTAI, ARI**
C.I-141

**LABOUR RELATIONS**
C.I-246

**LABOUR UNIONS**
C.I-156, C.I-176 · *see also* HISTADRUT

**LABOUR YOUTH**
C.I-034, C.I-121 · *see also* YOUTH MOVEMENTS

**LAG BA'OMER** *see* JEWISH HOLIDAYS - LAG BA'OMER

**LAND DEVELOPMENT**
A.005, C.I-155, C.I-172, M.013.

**LEATHER INDUSTRY**
C.I-232 · *see also* INDUSTRY

**LEIBOWITZ, DOV ARIEL**
C.I-221

**LEIVIK, H**
C.I-106

**LETTONIA INDEPENDENCE DAY**
C.I-125

**LEVANT FAIR** *see* TEL AVIV, LEVANT FAIR

**LEVIN, SHMARYAHU**
C.I-016, C.I-088.

**LEVINE, DANYA**
C.I-071, C.I-089, C.I-120.

**LEVINSTEIN, DR MORDECHAI**
C.I-178

**LEVIUSH, ZALMAN**
C.I-137

**LEVONTIN, Z D**
C.I-037

**LIBRARIES**
A.002, C.I-037.

**LIEBERMAN, ZVI**
C.I-030

**LIEF, NAOMI**
C.I-062, C.I-066.

**LIFELONG EDUCATION**
C.I-247

**LITHUANIA**
C.I-125

**LOCUSTS**
C.I-233

**LOD**
C.I-107

**LOD AIRPORT**
C.I-061, C.I-065, C.I-067, C.I-081, C.I-101, C.I-168, C.I-179 · *see also* AIRPORTS

**LOLA FLIEDERBAUM STUDIO**
C.I-145

**LONDON, BEZALEL**
C.I-079

**LOUIS BRANDEIS SCHOOL**
C.I-138 · *see also* SCHOOLS

**LUBRANI, ELIEZER**
C.I-227

**LUNAR ECLIPSE**
C.I-044

## Subject and Personality Index

**MA'ABAROT**
C.I-110 · *see also* KIBBUTZIM

**MA'ALEH HAHAMISHA**
C.I-147, C.I-226, C.I-236, C.I-239 · *see also* KIBBUTZIM

**MACCABI**
C.I-002, C.I-004, C.I-014, C.I-017, C.I-018, C.I-020, C.I-037, C.I-046, C.I-047, C.I-048, C.I-064, C.I-093, C.I-096, C.I-107, C.I-124, C.I-133, C.I-134, C.I-180, C.I-188, C.I-193, C.I-234, C.I-239, C.I-244, M.017, M.022, M.038, M.075, M.082, M.083, M.085 · *see also* SPORTS

**MACCABI HAIFA**
C.I-103 · *see also* SPORTS

**MACCABI HATZAIR**
C.I-009, C.I-024, C.I-033, C.I-197, C.I-220 · *see also* YOUTH MOVEMENTS

**MACCABI TEL AVIV**
C.I-043, C.I-173 · *see also* SPORTS, TEL AVIV, MACCABI STADIUM

**MACCABIA, 2ND**
C.I-001, C.I-006, C.I-099 · *see also* SPORTS

**MACCABIA, 3RD**
C.I-109 · *see also* SPORTS

**MACMICHAEL, SIR HAROLD**
C.I-128, C.I-133, C.I-142, C.I-158, C.I-168, C.I-179, C.I-211, C.I-228.

**MAGEN DAVID ADOM**
C.I-135, C.I-198, C.I-227, C.I-252.

**MAGNES, JUDAH**
C.I-007, C.I-228, C.I-248, C.I-249.

**MAIERZAK, HANNA** *see* MERON, HANNA

**MAIMON, RABBI YEHUDA (FISHMAN)**
C.I-142 · *see also* RABBIS

**MAIMONIDES**
A.003, C.I-009.

**MALARIA RESEARCH**
C.I-110, C.I-151.

**MAPAI**
C.I-137

**MARGALIT, MEIR**
C.I-124

**MARITIME LEAGUE** *see* PALESTINE MARITIME LEAGUE

**MARKETS**
C.I-217

**MARMINSKY, ISRAEL**
C.I-020, C.I-061, C.I-245.

**MARTIAL LAW**
C.I-244

**MASSADA**
C.I-233

**MATATEH THEATRE**
C.I-065, C.I-075, C.I-079, C.I-137 · *see also* THEATRE

**MATMAN-COHEN, YEHUDA L**
C.I-214

**MAX FEIN VOCATIONAL SCHOOL** *see* TEL AVIV, MAX FEIN VOCATIONAL SCHOOL

**MAY DAY**
C.I-085, C.I-246.

**MAZAR, BENJAMIN**
C.I-169

**MEDITERRANEAN SEA**
C.I-020, C.I-049, C.I-068, M.037, M.110.

**MEGIDO, ARYEH**
C.I-144

**MEIR, GOLDA**
C.I-030, C.I-227, C.I-240, C.I-242, C.I-247, C.I-250.

**MEIRON** *see* MOUNT MEIRON

**MEISLER, BENJAMIN** *see* MAZAR, BENJAMIN

**MEKOROT**
C.I-116, C.I-163 · *see also* WATER SUPPLY

**MELCHETT, VISCOUNT LUDWIG**
C.I-006, C.I-008, C.I-099.

**MEMORIAL SERVICES**
C.I-010, C.I-021, C.I-034, C.I-037, C.I-046, C.I-061, C.I-070, C.I-082, C.I-088, C.I-093, C.I-104, C.I-111, C.I-115, C.I-156, C.I-167, C.I-180, C.I-188, C.I-222, C.I-227, M.078 · *see also* FUNERALS

**MENARA**
C.I-232 · *see also* KIBBUTZIM

**MERHAVIA**
C.I-191 · *see also* KIBBUTZIM

**MERON, HANNA**
C.I-123

**MESKIN, AARON**
C.I-152

**METZUDAT USSISHKIN**
C.I-182

**MICHMORET**
C.I-238

**MICHSAF FACTORY**
C.I-247

**MIGDAL TZEDEK**
C.I-081

**MIKVEH ISRAEL AGRICULTURAL SCHOOL**
C.I-012, C.I-018, C.I-045, C.I-145, C.I-209, C.I-232, M.040 · *see also* AGRICULTURAL SCHOOLS, SCHOOLS

**MILITARY**
A.005, C.I-201, C.I-226, M.050 · *see also* BRITISH ARMY, JEWISH BRIGADE, JEWISH LEGION, SARAFEND, WAR OF INDEPENDENCE, WORLD WAR II

**MINDLIN, A**
C.I-147

**MISHMAR HA'EMEK**
C.I-147 · *see also* KIBBUTZIM

**MISHMAR-ZEBULUN**
C.I-165 · *see also* KIBBUTZIM

**MIZRACHI**
C.I-237

**MIZRAH**
C.I-093 · see also
KIBBUTZIM

**MIZRAHI AGRICULTURAL SCHOOL**
C.I-135 · see also
AGRICULTURAL
SCHOOLS, SCHOOLS

**MOJICA, JOSE**
M.016

**MONTEFIORE SCHOOL**
C.I-094

**MOREVSKY, ABRAHAM**
C.I-135

**MOSES, DR WALTER**
C.I-128

**MOSHAVIM**
C.I-223

**MOSQUE OF OMAR** see
JERUSALEM, MOSQUE OF
OMAR

**MOSSAD HARAV KOOK**
C.I-142

**MOTHER AND CHILD HOUSE** see WIZO

**MOTORCYCLING**
C.I-018, C.I-028, C.I-034 ·
see also SPORTS

**MOTZAH**
C.I-047, M.005.

**MOUNT CARMEL**
C.I-235, C.I-236, C.I-246,
C.I-249.

**MOUNT HERMON**
C.I-213, C.I-231.

**MOUNT MEIRON**
C.I-012, C.I-085, C.I-221.

**MOUNT OF OLIVES** see
JERUSALEM, MOUNT OF
OLIVES

**MOUNT SCOPUS** see
JERUSALEM, MOUNT
SCOPUS

**MOUNT TABOR**
C.I-018

**MUKION THEATRE**
C.I-157 · see also
THEATRE

**MUNICIPAL ELECTIONS**
C.I-041

**MUSEUMS** see
JERUSALEM,
ROCKEFELLER MUSEUM,
TEL AVIV MUSEUM

**MUSIC**
C.I-064, C.I-088, C.I-110,
C.I-163, C.I-166, C.I-172,
M.024 · see also OPERA,
PALESTINE
PHILHARMONIC
ORCHESTRA, PALESTINE
SYMPHONY ORCHESTRA,
SONGS

**MYERSON, GOLDA** see
MEIR, GOLDA

**NA'AN**
C.I-023, C.I-164 · see also
KIBBUTZIM

**NADIVI, YEHUDA**
C.I-001, C.I-060, C.I-087.

**NAHAL ARNON**
C.I-028

**NAHAL YABUK**
C.I-028

**NAHAL ZARKON**
C.I-028

**NAHALAL**
C.I-159, C.I-186, C.I-228.

**NAHALAT JABOTINSKY**
C.I-244

**NAHALAT YEHUDA**
C.I-095, C.I-162.

**NAHALAT YITZHAK**
C.I-023, C.I-063.

**NAHARIYA**
C.I-174

**NAMIR, MORDECHAI**
C.I-168

**NATIONAL ASSEMBLY, FOURTH**
C.I-227 · see also VA'AD
LEUMI

**NATURALISATION**
C.I-072

**NAZARETH**
A.005, C.I-115.

**NECAS, F**
C.I-214

**NEGEV**
A.005, C.I-242, C.I-249,
C.I-252.

**NERDI, NAHUM**
C.I-060

**NETANYA**
C.I-002, C.I-086, C.I-087,
C.I-092, C.I-105, C.I-127,
C.I-143, C.I-231.

**NETANYA, ANDREWS HOSPITAL**
C.I-127 · see also
HOSPITALS

**NETANYA BEACH**
C.I-200, M.110 · see also
BEACHES

**NEVATIM**
C.I-242 · see also
KIBBUTZIM

**NEVEH HAIM**
C.I-092

**NEW YORK EXHIBITION**
C.I-162 · see also
EXHIBITIONS

**NEWSPAPERS**
C.I-013, C.I-071, C.I-142,
C.I-144, C.I-161 · see also
DAVAR, HA'ARETZ,
HACARMEL

**NIKOVA, RINA**
C.I-107, C.I-109.

**NIR DAVID**
C.I-136, C.I-208 · see also
KIBBUTZIM

**NITZANIM**
C.I-235 · see also
KIBBUTZIM

**NORDAU, MAX**
C.I-010, C.I-103.

*ODED THE WANDERER*
C.I-060 · see also FILM-
MAKING

*OFEK*
A.007 · see also FILM-
MAKING

**OIL REFINERIES**
C.I-246, M.028 · see also
INDUSTRY

**OKAVA FACTORY**
C.I-105

## Subject and Personality Index

**OLD AGE HOMES**
C.I-024, C.I-078 · *see also* ELDERLY

***ONCE UPON A TIME***
C.I-060 · *see also* FILM-MAKING

**OPERA**
C.I-122 · *see also* MUSIC

**ORCHARDS**
M.026, M.063, M.064, M.065, M.066, M.137 · *see also* AGRICULTURE

**OXENBERG, YOSEF**
C.I-137

**PALALUM ALUMINIUM FACTORY**
C.I-250

**PALESTINE AIRWAYS LTD**
C.I-099 · *see also* AVIATION

**PALESTINE MARITIME LEAGUE**
C.I-091, C.I-160, C.I-171, C.I-189.

**PALESTINE PHILHARMONIC ORCHESTRA**
C.I-062 · *see also* MUSIC

**PALESTINE SYMPHONY ORCHESTRA**
C.I-125 · *see also* MUSIC

**PAPYRUS REEDS**
C.I-151

**PARADES**
C.I-002, C.I-075, C.I-084, C.I-085, C.I-107, C.I-167, C.I-191, C.I-201, C.I-202, C.I-204, C.I-246, M.023, M.040, M.044, M.046, M.082, M.084, M.085, M.095.

**PARDES HANNA**
C.I-127, C.I-129.

**PARDESS KATZ**
C.I-020

**PARKS AND GARDENS**
C.I-014, C.I-120, C.I-124, C.I-131, C.I-134, C.I-214, C.I-225, C.I-228, M.033, M.039.

**PATTERSON, COLONEL JOHN HENRY**
C.I-080

**PAVSNER, ZALMAN**
C.I-144

**PEEL COMMISSION**
C.I-061, C.I-062, C.I-065.

**PENN, ALEXANDER**
M.103, A.007.

**PERES, SHIMON**
C.I-243

**PERLSON, ELIEZER**
C.I-233

**PERSITZ, SHOSHANA**
M.106

**PETAH TIKVA**
C.I-035, C.I-082, C.I-084, C.I-106, C.I-131, C.I-181, C.I-211, C.I-219, C.I-249.

**PETS**
C.I-004, C.I-139.

**PINCAS, DAVID ZVI**
C.I-098, C.I-228.

**PINES, DAN**
C.I-013

**PIONEER WOMEN**
C.I-096

**PIONEERING**
C.I-001, C.I-049, C.I-083, C.I-172, C.I-175, C.I-191, C.I-223, C.I-232, M.063, M.064, M.066.

**POLICE**
C.I-033, C.I-231 · *see also* JEWISH SETTLEMENT POLICE

**POVERTY**
A.001, C.I-085.

**PRI MAZON**
M.105

**PRI-PERI**
C.I-123

**PRISONERS OF WAR**
C.I-233

**PUBLISHERS** *see* DVIR-BIALIK PUBLISHING HOUSE, MOSSAD HARAV KOOK, NEWSPAPERS.

**PUPPET THEATRE**
C.I-157 · *see also* THEATRE

**PURIM** *see* JEWISH HOLIDAYS - PURIM

**QUARRIES**
C.I-081

**RABBI OF GUR**
C.I-028

**RABBIS**
C.I-173 · *see also* AHARONSON, RABBI SHLOMO; AMIEL, RABBI MOSHE AVIGDOR; BAR ILAN, RABBI MEIR (BERLIN); HERZOG, RABBI YITZHAK HALEVI; KOOK, RABBI AVRAHAM; MAIMON, RABBI YEHUDA (FISHMAN); RABBI OF GUR; ROBINSON, RABBI YEKHEZKIEL; UZIEL, RABBI BEN ZION MEIR CHAI

**RABINOWITZ, ALEXANDER ZISSKIND**
C.I-004, C.I-010, C.I-021, C.I-025, C.I-029, C.I-072, C.I-088, C.I-111, C.I-122, C.I-177.

**RACHEL'S TOMB**
C.I-241

**RADIO STATIONS**
C.I-038

**RAILWAYS** *see* TRAINS

**RAIN** *see* FLOODS

**RAMAT GAN**
C.I-014, C.I-134, C.I-170, C.I-181, C.I-183, C.I-198, C.I-206, C.I-207, C.I-214, C.I-217, C.I-229, C.I-247, C.I-248, C.I-252.

**RAMAT HAKOVESH**
C.I-148 · *see also* KIBBUTZIM

**RAMAT YOHANAN**
C.I-231 · *see also* KIBBUTZIM

**RAMLEH**
C.I-111

**RAS-EL-EIN (ROSH HA'AYIN)**
C.I-108

**RAV KOOK INSTITUTE** *see* MOSSAD HARAV KOOK

**RAVITZ CHOIR**
C.I-071

**RECREATION**
C.I-002, C.I-021, C.I-183, C.I-198, C.I-200, C.I-225, C.I-230, C.I-235, M.114, M.126 · see also SPORTS

**RECYCLING**
C.I-127

**REFUGEES**
C.I-104, C.I-240, C.I-244, C.I-245, C.I-247, C.I-251 · see also IMMIGRATION

**REHOVOT**
C.I-002, C.I-039, C.I-065, C.I-076, C.I-081, C.I-123, C.I-124, C.I-129, C.I-197, C.I-198, C.I-215, C.I-246.

**REHOVOT, WEIZMANN INSTITUTE** see WEIZMANN INSTITUTE

**RELIGIOUS LIFE**
A.003, C.I-009, C.I-019, C.I-027, C.I-135, C.I-184, C.I-185, C.I-194, C.I-204, C.I-221, C.I-223, C.I-228, C.I-230, C.I-231, C.I-235, C.I-249 · see also HASSIDIM, JEWISH HOLIDAYS, TORAH SCROLLS

**RELIGIOUS SCOUTS**
C.I-019, C.I-034 · see also YOUTH MOVEMENTS

**REMEZ, DAVID**
C.I-062, C.I-085, C.I-091, C.I-101, C.I-227, C.I-240.

**RIMALT, ELIMELECH SHIMON**
C.I-170

**RISHON LEZION**
C.I-033, C.I-062, C.I-105, C.I-130, C.I-150.

**ROAD ACCIDENTS** see ACCIDENTS

**ROAD CONSTRUCTION**
C.I-076, C.I-081, C.I-100, C.I-105, C.I-106, C.I-176, C.I-210.

**ROBINSON, RABBI YEKHEZKIEL**
C.I-035 · see also RABBIS

**ROCKEFELLER MUSEUM**
see JERUSALEM, ROCKEFELLER MUSEUM

**RODANSKY, SHMUEL**
C.I-065, C.I-079.

**ROKAH, ISRAEL**
C.I-021, C.I-064, C.I-067, C.I-086, C.I-098, C.I-099, C.I-103, C.I-104, C.I-113, C.I-117, C.I-128, C.I-130, C.I-132, C.I-133, C.I-155, C.I-162, C.I-176, C.I-197, C.I-210, C.I-217, C.I-228, C.I-236, C.I-248, M.001, M.106.

**ROSE, ALAN EDWARD PERCIVAL**
C.I-214

**ROSENBAUM, S**
C.I-002

**ROSH HA'AYIN**
C.I-032, C.I-039, C.I-108.

**ROSH PINA**
C.I-110

**ROTARY CLUB**
C.I-005

**ROTHSCHILD, BARON BENJAMIN DE**
C.I-038

**ROVINA, HANNA**
C.I-016, C.I-141, C.I-243.

**ROWING**
C.I-166, C.I-168, C.I-234 · see also SPORTS, WATER SPORTS

**RUBEN, REUVEN**
C.I-141

**RUDI SHIMON**
C.I-119

**RUPPIN, ARTHUR**
C.I-001, C.I-042, C.I-044, C.I-067.

**SACHNEH RIVER**
C.I-136

**SADEH, YITZHAK**
C.I-178, C.I-243.

**SAFED**
C.I-077

**ST JOHN OF ACRE** see ACRE

**SALOMON, CARL**
C.I-007

**SAMMET, SHIMON**
C.I-060

**SAMUEL, HERBERT**
C.I-210

**SANDBERG, LILLI**
C.I-105

**SAPIR, PINCHAS**
C.I-210

**SARAFEND**
C.I-200, C.I-201, C.I-216 · see also BRITISH ARMY, MILITARY

**SCENIC LANDSCAPE**
C.I-018, C.I-020, C.I-028, C.I-063, C.I-122, C.I-136, C.I-147, C.I-151, C.I-159, C.I-163, C.I-224, C.I-227, C.I-231, C.I-238, C.I-243, C.I-244, C.I-249, C.I-251.

**SCHACK, ADA**
C.I-143

**SCHIFF, POLICE CHIEF MAJOR**
C.I-114

**SCHOOLS**
C.I-023, C.I-031, C.I-033, C.I-098, C.I-119, C.I-135, C.I-249, M.051, M.134 · see also AGRICULTURAL SCHOOLS, AHAD HA'AM SCHOOL FOR BOYS, BEIT HINUCH, GYMNASIA HERZLIYAH, HAIFA NAVAL HIGH SCHOOL, KADOURI AGRICULTURAL SCHOOL, KFAR MALAL: JOSEPH AARONOVITCH SCHOOL, LOUIS BRANDEIS SCHOOL, MIKVEH ISRAEL AGRICULTURAL SCHOOL, MIZRAHI AGRICULTURAL SCHOOL, TEL AVIV: BILU SCHOOL, TEL AVIV: AMAL VOCATIONAL SCHOOL, TEL AVIV: BOROCHOV SCHOOL, TEL AVIV: MAX FEIN VOCATIONAL SCHOOL, TEL AVIV: MONTEFIORE SCHOOL, TEL AVIV: SAFRA SCHOOL, TEL AVIV: SHENKAR TRADE SCHOOL, TEL LITWINSKY-ZIV SCHOOL, VOCATIONAL SCHOOLS, ZEBULUN NAVAL HIGH SCHOOL.

## Subject and Personality Index

**SCHWARTZ, MAURICE**
C.I-089, C.I-094, C.I-148.

**SCOUTS**
C.I-022, C.I-083, C.I-084, C.I-106, C.I-150, C.I-202 · see also YOUTH MOVEMENTS

**SDEH DOV AIRPORT**
C.I-155 · see also AIRPORTS

**SEA OF GALILEE**
A.004, C.I-136, C.I-159, C.I-188, C.I-227, C.I-237, C.I-243.

**SEGAL, YERUSHALAYIM**
C.I-225, M.006, M.099.

**SELA (BLUBSTEIN), DR**
C.I-032

**SENATOR, DAVID WERNER**
C.I-072

**SETTLEMENT**
C.I-036, C.I-079, C.I-092, C.I-097, C.I-146, C.I-147, C.I-149, C.I-152, C.I-182, C.I-203, C.I-210, C.I-214, C.I-232, C.I-235, C.I-238, C.I-242, C.I-249.

**SEVEN MILLS WATERFALL**
C.I-033

**SHA'AR HA'AMAKIM**
C.I-234

**SHALVA HIGH SCHOOL**
see TEL AVIV, SHALVA HIGH SCHOOL

**SHAPIRO, A**
C.I-096, C.I-217.

**SHARAF, KATZIN**
C.I-214

**SHARETT, MOSHE**
A.005, C.I-016, C.I-042, C.I-119, C.I-126, C.I-127, C.I-146, C.I-228, C.I-233, C.I-236, C.I-238.

**SHARON VALLEY**
C.I-251

**SHAVLOV, ZALMAN**
C.I-043

**SHAVUOT** see JEWISH HOLIDAYS - SHAVUOT

**SHAW, SIR WALTER**
M.015

**SHAW COMMISSION**
M.015, M.077.

**SHECHORY, ZUSIA**
C.I-207

**SHECTERMAN, ZVI**
C.I-179

**SHERMAN, BEN**
C.I-144

**SHERTOK, MOSHE** see SHARETT, MOSHE

**SHIPS**
A.005, C.I-002, C.I-005, C.I-030, C.I-035, C.I-068, C.I-093, C.I-103, C.I-153, C.I-155, C.I-156, C.I-157, C.I-168, C.I-184, C.I-186, C.I-189, C.I-229, C.I-246, C.I-249, C.I-251 · see also "EXODUS"

**SHLONSKY, AVRAHAM**
C.I-068

**SHOCKEN, YOSEFA**
C.I-078

**SHOOTING COMPETITIONS**
C.I-117, C.I-141, C.I-143, C.I-158 · see also SPORTS

**SHOSHANI, SA'ADIA**
C.I-180

**SHUKRI, MAYOR HASSAN BEY**
C.I-002, C.I-081, C.I-086, C.I-131, C.I-168.

**SHULSINGER, M**
C.I-099

**SILVER, ABBA HILLEL**
C.I-247

**SIRENI, ENZO**
C.I-239

**SIROTA, GERSHON**
C.I-100

**SMILANSKY, MOSHE**
C.I-001, C.I-221.

**SNAKES**
C.I-148

**SNEH, MOSHE**
C.I-240

**SOCCER**
C.I-004, C.I-014, C.I-018, C.I-037, C.I-043, C.I-047, C.I-070, C.I-107, C.I-122, C.I-244, M.092, M.102 · see also SPORTS

**SOCIAL WELFARE**
A.001, C.I-085 · see also CHARITY ORGANISATIONS

**SOKOLOW, NAHUM**
C.I-007, C.I-009, C.I-024, C.I-099.

**SONGS**
C.I-060, C.I-062, C.I-066, C.I-071, C.I-078, C.I-083, C.I-088, C.I-113, C.I-123, C.I-130, C.I-143, C.I-144, C.I-147, C.I-163, C.I-187, C.I-191, C.I-213, C.I-225 · see also MUSIC

**SOUTH AFRICA**
C.I-244, C.I-245.

**SPORTS**
C.I-006, C.I-008, C.I-012, C.I-099, C.I-115, C.I-124, C.I-131, C.I-137, C.I-158, C.I-177, C.I-188, C.I-192, C.I-214, C.I-219, C.I-221, C.I-248, M.017, M.022, M.024, M.037, M.038, M.075, M.080, M.082, M.083 · see also ATHLETICS, BASKETBALL, BOATING, BOXING MATCHES, CALISTHENICS, CAR RACING, CHESS COMPETITIONS, GLIDERS, GYMNASTICS, HAPOEL, HAPOEL HAMIZRACHI, HAPOEL TEL AVIV, HORSE RACING, JEWISH HUNTERS ASSOCIATION, MACCABI, MACCABI HAIFA, MACCABI TEL AVIV, MACCABIA: 2ND, MACCABIA: 3RD, MOTORCYCLING, RECREATION, ROWING, SHOOTING COMPETITIONS, SOCCER, SWIMMING, TEL AVIV YACHT CLUB, WALKING COMPETITIONS, WATER SPORTS, ZEBULUN SPORTS CLUB.

**SPRINZAK, YOSEF**
C.I-035, C.I-227, C.I-229.

## Subject and Personality Index 237

**STAMPFER, SHLOMO**
C.I-082, C.I-084, C.I-096,
C.I-181, C.I-190, C.I-211.

**STEINBERG, WILLIAM**
C.I-062

**STORMS**
C.I-068, C.I-120 · see also
FLOODS

**SUCCOT** see JEWISH
HOLIDAYS - SUCCOT

**SWAMP DRAINAGE**
C.I-154

**SWAMPS**
M.013 · see also HULA
VALLEY

**SWIMMING**
C.I-020, C.I-028, C.I-033,
C.I-087, C.I-098, C.I-103,
C.I-160, C.I-234, C.I-237,
M.114 · see also SPORTS,
WATER SPORTS

**SYNAGOGUES**
C.I-029, C.I-066, C.I-102,
C.I-141, C.I-235, M.088 ·
see also JERUSALEM,
HURVA SYNAGOGUE,
JERUSALEM, JESHURUN
SYNAGOGUE, TEL AVIV,
GREAT SYNAGOGUE, TEL
AVIV, SHIVAT ZION
SYNAGOGUE.

**SZOLD, HENRIETTA**
C.I-047, C.I-226, C.I-228,
C.I-230.

**TABENKIN, YITZHAK**
C.I-229

**TAGER, ZIONA**
M.021

**TAUBE, MICHAEL**
C.I-166

**TAWIL, MOSHE**
C.I-060

**TCHERNICHOVSKY,
SHAUL**
C.I-001, C.I-042, C.I-044,
C.I-071, C.I-106, C.I-128.

**TECHNION**
C.I-121, C.I-157, C.I-189,
C.I-240.

**TEL AVIV**
A.002, C.I-026, C.I-032,
C.I-036, C.I-040, C.I-041,
C.I-075, C.I-084, C.I-085,
C.I-086, C.I-099, C.I-110,
C.I-113, C.I-115, C.I-117,
C.I-119, C.I-120, C.I-123,
C.I-125, C.I-127, C.I-129,
C.I-131, C.I-133, C.I-161,
C.I-162, C.I-164, C.I-167,
C.I-181, C.I-197, C.I-202,
C.I-205, C.I-209, C.I-210,
C.I-219, C.I-221, C.I-225,
C.I-244, C.I-246, C.I-251,
M.001, M.006, M.015,
M.016, M.017, M.022,
M.025, M.031, M.033,
M.042, M.043, M.082,
M.083, M.089, M.091,
M.095, M.096, M.097,
M.104, M.106, M.109,
M.115, M.118, M.135.

**TEL AVIV, ABU HEDRA**
C.I-137

**TEL AVIV, ALIYAH
STREET**
C.I-166

**TEL AVIV, ALLENBY
STREET**
M.034, M.035.

**TEL AVIV, AMAL
VOCATIONAL SCHOOL**
C.I-077 · see also
SCHOOLS, VOCATIONAL
SCHOOLS

**TEL AVIV, ASSUTA
HOSPITAL**
A.002, C.I-041 · see also
HOSPITALS

**TEL AVIV, BALFOURIA
BUILDING**
M.115

**TEL AVIV BEACH**
C.I-017, C.I-021, C.I-022,
C.I-148, C.I-150, C.I-211,
C.I-225 · see also
BEACHES

**TEL AVIV, BEIT
HAMEHANDESS**
A.002, C.I-001, C.I-121.

**TEL AVIV, BEIT HAMOREH**
C.I-094

**TEL AVIV, BEIT ZEIROTH
MIZRACHI**
C.I-184

**TEL AVIV, BETAR CLUB**
C.I-011

**TEL AVIV, BILU SCHOOL**
C.I-098 · see also
SCHOOLS

**TEL AVIV, BOROCHOV
SCHOOL**
C.I-115 · see also
SCHOOLS

**TEL AVIV, BRENNER
HOUSE**
C.I-011, C.I-025, C.I-045.

**TEL AVIV, CAFE GALINA**
C.I-046

**TEL AVIV, CARMEL
MARKET**
C.I-083, C.I-179.

**TEL AVIV, CENTRAL BUS
STATION**
M.002

**TEL AVIV, ESTHER
CINEMA**
C.I-229

**TEL AVIV, EXHIBITION
GROUNDS**
C.I-079, M.002.

**TEL AVIV, GENERAL
ZIONIST CLUB**
C.I-019

**TEL AVIV, GREAT
SYNAGOGUE**
C.I-228, M.025, M.088,
M.089 · see also
SYNAGOGUES

**TEL AVIV, HADAR HOUSE**
C.I-074

**TEL AVIV-HAIFA
HIGHWAY**
C.I-105, C.I-106.

**TEL AVIV, HATIKVAH**
C.I-066

**TEL AVIV, HERBERT
SAMUEL SQUARE**
C.I-075

**TEL AVIV, HERZL STREET**
M.018, M.054, M.074,
M.090.

**TEL AVIV, JEWISH
AGENCY BUILDING**
M.043 · see also JEWISH
AGENCY

**TEL AVIV, KEREM
HATEIMANIM**
C.I-023

**TEL AVIV, KING GEORGE
STREET**
C.I-010

## Subject and Personality Index

TEL AVIV, LEVANT FAIR
A.002, C.I-032, C.I-046,
C.I-050, M.052, M.076.

TEL AVIV, LILIENBLUM
STREET
M.112

TEL AVIV, MACCABI
NEIGHBOURHOOD
C.I-026

TEL AVIV, MACCABI
STADIUM
C.I-048 · see also SPORTS,
MACCABI TEL AVIV

TEL AVIV, MAGEN DAVID
ADOM BUILDING
C.I-043

TEL AVIV, MAGEN DAVID
ADOM SQUARE
C.I-075

TEL AVIV, MAX FEIN
VOCATIONAL SCHOOL
C.I-020, C.I-107, C.I-164,
C.I-244, C.I-245 · see also
SCHOOLS, VOCATIONAL
SCHOOLS

TEL AVIV, METZUDAT
ZE'EV
C.I-080

TEL AVIV, MIGDALOR
CINEMA
C.I-001, C.I-036.

TEL AVIV, MIZRACHI
PIONEER WOMEN'S
BUILDING
C.I-085

TEL AVIV, MONTEFIORE
NEIGHBOURHOOD
C.I-077

TEL AVIV, MONTEFIORE
SCHOOL
C.I-184 · see also
SCHOOLS

TEL AVIV, MOTHER AND
CHILD CENTRE
C.I-174 · see also
CHILDCARE

TEL AVIV, MUGRABI
CINEMA
C.I-075

TEL AVIV, MUNICIPALITY
BUILDING
C.I-064, C.I-143, C.I-248,
M.077, M.106, M.109.

TEL AVIV MUSEUM
C.I-063, C.I-089, C.I-250,
M.055.

TEL AVIV, NAHALAT
YITZHAK
C.I-038

TEL AVIV, NAHLAT
BINYAMIN
C.I-083

TEL AVIV, OPHIR CINEMA
M.073, M.119.

TEL AVIV, PAGODA
HOUSE
M.020

TEL AVIV PORT
C.I-063, C.I-067, C.I-087,
C.I-091, C.I-093, C.I-098,
C.I-104, C.I-109, C.I-112,
C.I-114, C.I-120, C.I-125,
C.I-126, C.I-132, C.I-141,
C.I-153, C.I-155, C.I-157,
C.I-158, C.I-168, C.I-173,
C.I-176, C.I-178, C.I-186,
C.I-243.

TEL AVIV, READING
STATION
C.I-189

TEL AVIV, RIMON
CINEMA
C.I-002, C.I-043.

TEL AVIV, ROTHSCHILD
BOULEVARD
C.I-002, C.I-011, C.I-029,
C.I-098, C.I-225, C.I-250,
M.008, M.009, M.074,
M.084, M.111.

TEL AVIV, SAFRA SCHOOL
C.I-187 · see also
SCHOOLS

TEL AVIV, SAN REMO
CASINO
C.I-078

TEL AVIV, SCHOOL OF
LAW AND ECONOMICS
C.I-198 · see also
UNIVERSITIES AND
COLLEGES

TEL AVIV, SHALVA HIGH
SCHOOL
C.I-086, C.I-087, C.I-140

TEL AVIV, SHENKAR
TRADE SCHOOL
C.I-237 · see also
SCHOOLS, VOCATIONAL
SCHOOLS

TEL AVIV, SHIVAT ZION
SYNAGOGUE
C.I-102 · see also
SYNAGOGUES

TEL AVIV, TSINA
DIZENGOFF SQUARE
C.I-124

TEL AVIV, WOMEN
TEACHERS SEMINARY
C.I-145 · see also
UNIVERSITIES AND
COLLEGES

TEL AVIV, WOMEN
WORKERS HOUSE
C.I-134

TEL AVIV YACHT CLUB
C.I-100, C.I-171 · see also
SPORTS

TEL AVIV, ZEBULUN
NAVAL HIGH SCHOOL see
ZEBULUN NAVAL HIGH
SCHOOL

TEL AVIV, ZEBULUN
SPORTS CLUB see
ZEBULUN SPORTS CLUB

TEL AVIV ZOO
C.I-045, C.I-108, C.I-139,
C.I-144, C.I-148, C.I-167,
C.I-205.

TEL HAI
C.I-068, C.I-076, C.I-110,
C.I-129.

TEL LITWINSKY-ZIV
SCHOOL
C.I-113

TEL SHALOM
C.I-129

THEATRE
C.I-065, C.I-079, C.I-084,
C.I-108, C.I-124, C.I-137 ·
see also HABIMAH
THEATRE, HAOHEL
THEATRE, MATATEH
THEATRE, MUKION
THEATRE, PUPPET
THEATRE

TIBERIAS
A.003, A.004, C.I-009,
C.I-136, C.I-188, C.I-221,
C.I-230.

TIBERIAS HOT SPRINGS
C.I-207, C.I-230.

TIRAT TZVI
C.I-094 · see also
KIBBUTZIM

## Subject and Personality Index

**TIVON**
C.I-104, C.I-149.

**TNUVA**
C.I-083, C.I-211, C.I-225 · see also AGRICULTURE

**TORAH SCROLLS**
C.I-012, C.I-085, C.I-102, C.I-141, C.I-228, C.I-231, C.I-235, C.I-238, C.I-249, M.025, M.088, M.115 · see also RELIGIOUS LIFE

**TOSCANINI, ARTURO**
C.I-067, C.I-079.

**TOWER AND STOCKADE**
C.I-152, C.I-172, C.I-182, C.I-195, C.I-222, C.I-230, C.I-251.

**TOWER OF DAVID** see JERUSALEM, TOWER OF DAVID

**TRADE** see COMMERCE

**TRAINS**
C.I-044, C.I-070, C.I-108, C.I-125, M.041, M.107, M.113 · see also TRANSPORTATION

**TRANSIT CAMPS**
A.005

**TRANSPORTATION**
C.I-026, C.I-218, M.035, M.049, M.054, M.107 · see also TRAINS

**TSUR, MOSHE**
C.I-159, C.I-203.

**TU B'SHVAT** see JEWISH HOLIDAYS - TU B'SHVAT

**TUBERCULOSIS RESEARCH**
C.I-178, C.I-243.

**TUVYA, MORDECHAI**
C.I-117

**TUVYA, ZION**
C.I-117

**TZOFIT**
C.I-171 · see also KIBBUTZIM

**UNITED NATIONS**
C.I-248

**UN SPECIAL COMMISSION**
C.I-248

**UNIVERSITIES AND COLLEGES** see HEBREW UNIVERSITY, TECHNION, TEL AVIV: SCHOOL OF LAW AND ECONOMICS, TEL AVIV: WOMEN TEACHERS SEMINARY, WEIZMANN INSTITUTE.

**USSISHKIN, MENACHEM**
A.002, C.I-001, C.I-007, C.I-009, C.I-017, C.I-033, C.I-041, C.I-042, C.I-044, C.I-060, C.I-101, C.I-126, C.I-142, C.I-154, C.I-182, C.I-203.

**UZIEL, RABBI BEN ZION MEIR CHAI**
C.I-001, C.I-004, C.I-009, C.I-011, C.I-020, C.I-034, C.I-037, C.I-041, C.I-044, C.I-070, C.I-082, C.I-085, C.I-104, C.I-114, C.I-117, C.I-121, C.I-125, C.I-135, C.I-179, C.I-185, C.I-193, C.I-227, C.I-230, C.I-234, C.I-236, C.I-237, C.I-239, C.I-241 · see also RABBIS

**V.D. CELEBRATIONS**
C.I-232

**VA'AD LEUMI**
C.I-194 · see also NATIONAL ASSEMBLY, FOURTH

**VAN VRIESLAND, S**
C.I-203

**VARDIMON, AKIVA**
C.I-060

**VINEYARDS**
M.029, M.100 · see also AGRICULTURE

**VOCATIONAL SCHOOLS**
C.I-077, C.I-094, C.I-107, C.I-237, C.I-245, C.I-249 · see also SCHOOLS, TEL AVIV: AMAL VOCATIONAL SCHOOL, TEL AVIV: MAX FEIN VOCATIONAL SCHOOL, TEL AVIV: SHENKAR TRADE SCHOOL.

**WADI MUSRARA**
C.I-066, C.I-100, C.I-110.

**WADI NA'AMAN**
C.I-152

**WALKING COMPETITIONS**
C.I-129 · see also SPORTS

**WALLIN, MOSHE**
C.I-113

**WAR EFFORT**
C.I-201, C.I-217 · see also MILITARY, WORLD WAR II

**WAR OF INDEPENDENCE**
A.005 · see also MILITARY

**WATER BUFFALO**
C.I-151

**WATER FESTIVAL**
C.I-035

**WATER SPORTS**
C.I-193, C.I-195, C.I-227, C.I-234 · see also BOATING, ROWING, SPORTS, SWIMMING, ZEBULUN SPORTS CLUB

**WATER SUPPLY**
C.I-023, C.I-032, C.I-035, C.I-039, C.I-116, C.I-163 · see also MEKOROT

**WAUCHOPE, SIR ARTHUR**
C.I-001, C.I-016, C.I-018, C.I-020, C.I-038, C.I-045, C.I-050, C.I-061, C.I-067, C.I-070, C.I-082, C.I-086, C.I-088, C.I-097, C.I-098, C.I-114, C.I-115, C.I-121, C.I-123, C.I-127, C.I-132.

**WECHSLER, MOSHE**
C.I-060

**WEDDINGS**
A.005, C.I-223, C.I-251.

**WEISS, ELIYAHU**
C.I-104

**WEITZ, YOSEF**
C.I-170, C.I-224.

**WEIZMANN, CHAIM**
A.005, C.I-002, C.I-007, C.I-024, C.I-041, C.I-050, C.I-063, C.I-123, C.I-176, C.I-228, C.I-239, C.I-249.

**WEIZMANN INSTITUTE**
C.I-215, C.I-241.

**WHITE PAPER**
C.I-236 · see also BRITISH MANDATE

**WINE**
M.010, M.060, M.061.

## Subject and Personality Index

**WINERIES**
C.I-048, C.I-097, C.I-099, C.I-150, M.011 · see also INDUSTRY

**WIZO**
C.I-065, C.I-143, C.I-167, C.I-174, C.I-229, C.I-244, C.I-245, C.I-246, C.I-248, C.I-249 · see also CHILDCARE

**WOLF, ALFRED**
C.I-089

**WOMEN'S INTERNATIONAL ZIONIST ORGANISATION** see WIZO

**WOMEN'S WORKERS COUNCIL**
C.I-162, C.I-241.

**WORK SAFETY**
C.I-246

**WORLD WAR I**
M.050

**WORLD WAR II**
C.I-201, C.I-206, C.I-217, C.I-222, C.I-226, C.I-231, C.I-232, C.I-233 · see also MILITARY, WAR EFFORT

**WORLD ZIONIST CONGRESS, 19TH, LUCERNE 1935**
C.I-021, C.I-024.

**WORLD ZIONIST CONGRESS, 20TH, ZÜRICH 1937**
C.I-094, C.I-099, C.I-101.

**WORLD ZIONIST CONGRESS, 21ST, GENEVA, 1939**
C.I-190

**YAGUR**
C.I-163 · see also KIBBUTZIM

**YAHALOM**
C.I-205

**YAKHIN**
M.026, M.029, M.063, M.064, M.065, M.066, M.123, M.124.

**YANAIT-BEN TZVI, RAHEL**
C.I-247

**YARKON RIVER**
C.I-008, C.I-032, C.I-063, C.I-076, C.I-095, C.I-102, C.I-109, C.I-171, C.I-241, C.I-248, M.114.

**YASUR**
A.005

**YATSIV, YITZHAK**
C.I-013

**YELLIN, DAVID**
C.I-176

**YEMENITE JEWS**
A.005, C.I-023, C.I-028, C.I-066, C.I-108, C.I-179, C.I-186, C.I-223, C.I-231, M.003, M.098.

**YOUNG BETAR**
C.I-098, C.I-099, C.I-178, C.I-179 · see also YOUTH MOVEMENTS, BETAR

**YOUNG JUDEA**
C.I-021 · see also YOUTH MOVEMENTS

**YOUTH**
C.I-103, C.I-186, C.I-220, M.128, M.129, M.139.

**YOUTH ALIYAH**
A.005

**YOUTH LEADERS**
C.I-090

**YOUTH MOVEMENTS**
A.005, C.I-149, C.I-150, C.I-160, C.I-164, C.I-178, C.I-180, C.I-188, C.I-194, C.I-196, C.I-202, C.I-235, M.072 · see also BNEI AKIVA, HANOAR HA'OVED, LABOUR YOUTH, MACCABI HATZAIR, RELIGIOUS SCOUTS, SCOUTS, YOUNG BETAR, YOUNG JUDEA

**ZEBULUN NAVAL HIGH SCHOOL**
C.I-032, C.I-166, C.I-192 · see also SCHOOLS

**ZEBULUN SPORTS CLUB**
C.I-100, C.I-102, C.I-107, C.I-109, C.I-202, C.I-248 · see also SPORTS, WATER SPORTS

**ZEBULUN VALLEY**
C.I-009, C.I-139, C.I-154, M.013, M.107, M.108.

**ZEFIRA, BRACHA**
C.I-060

**ZEID, ALEXANDER**
C.I-149

**ZERUBAVEL, YA'AKOV**
C.I-085, C.I-106, C.I-246.

**ZICHRON YA'AKOV**
C.I-034, C.I-038, C.I-048, C.I-098, C.I-143, C.I-227.

**ZILBERG, YOEL**
C.I-166

**ZIONIST CONFERENCE, 4TH**
C.I-229

**ZIONIST ORGANISATIONS**
see DEGEL ZION MOVEMENT, GENERAL ZIONIST ASSOCIATION, JEWISH AGENCY, JEWISH NATIONAL FUND, KEREN HAYESOD, PIONEER WOMEN, YOUTH ALIYAH

**ZISLING, AHARON**
C.I-101, C.I-227.

**ZOOS** see TEL AVIV ZOO